GLOBAL
MARTIN PARR
WARNING

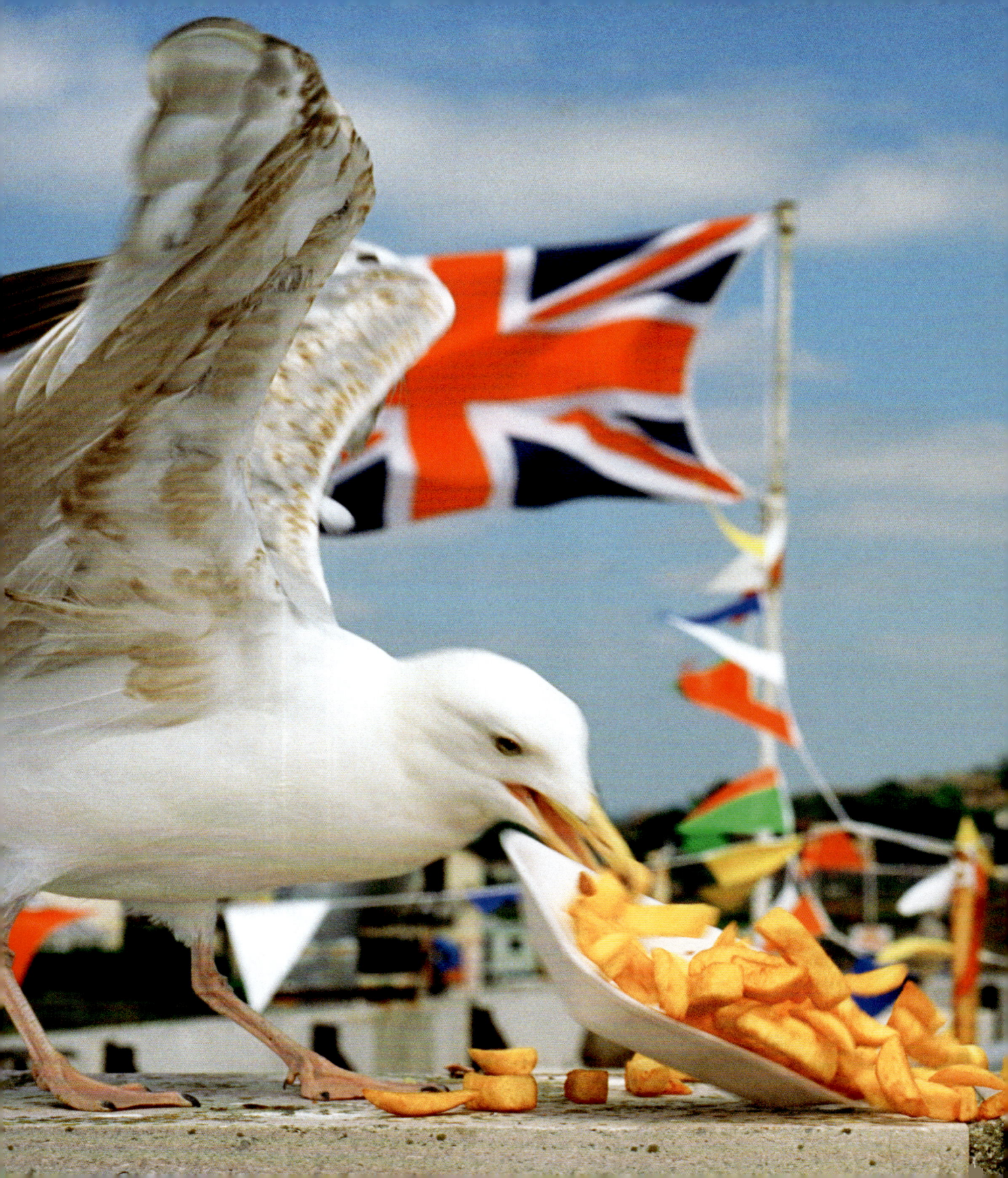

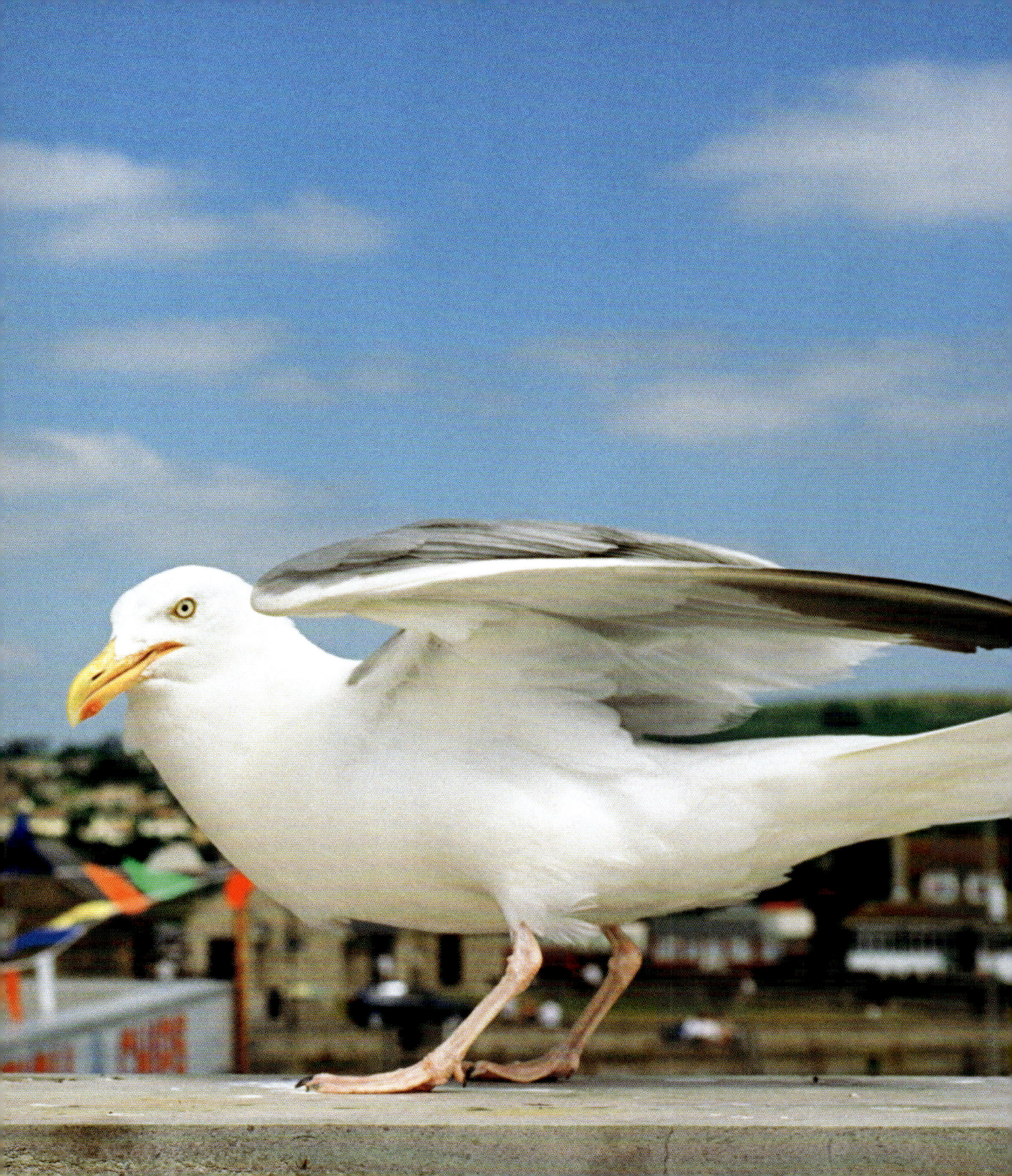

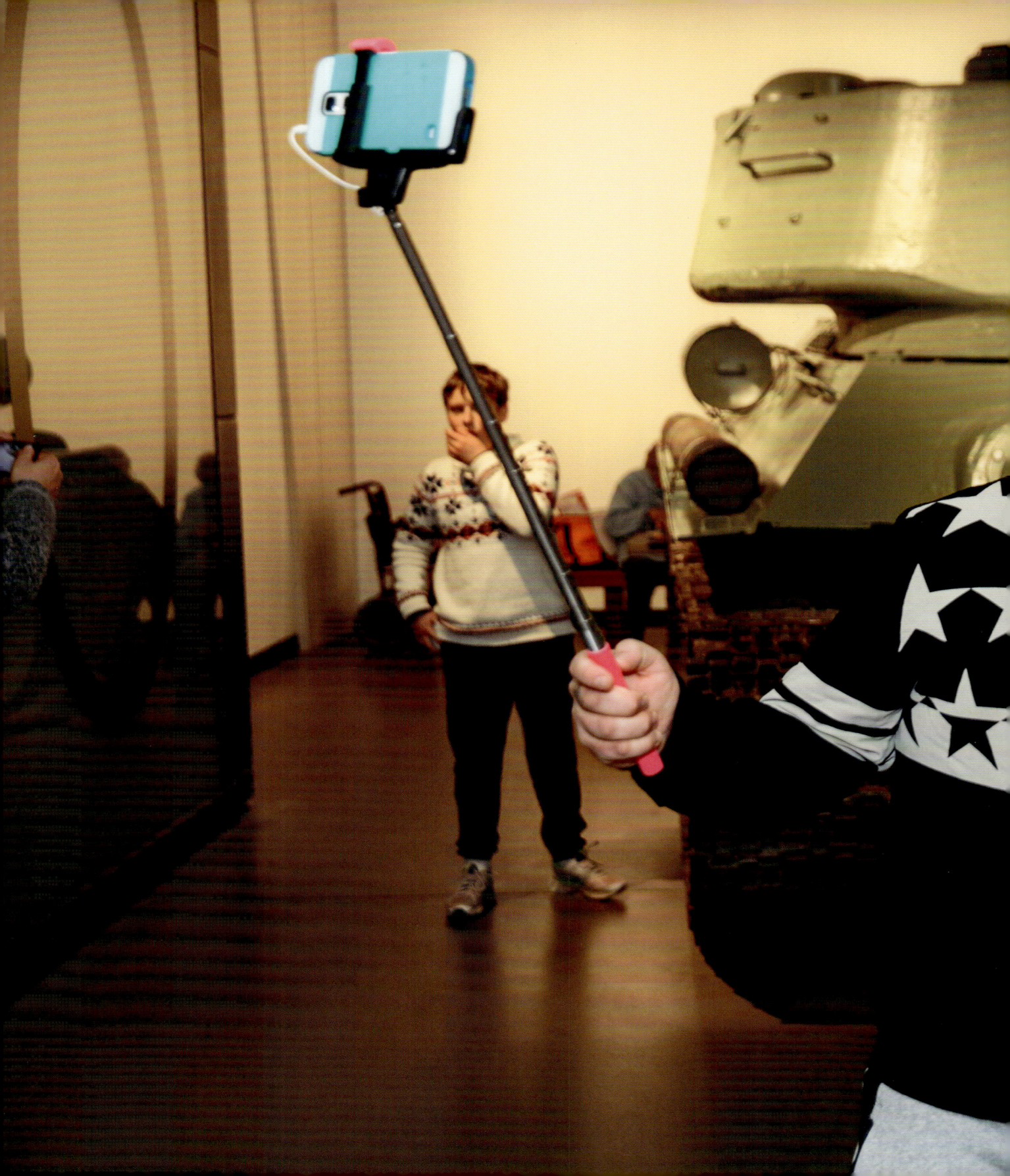

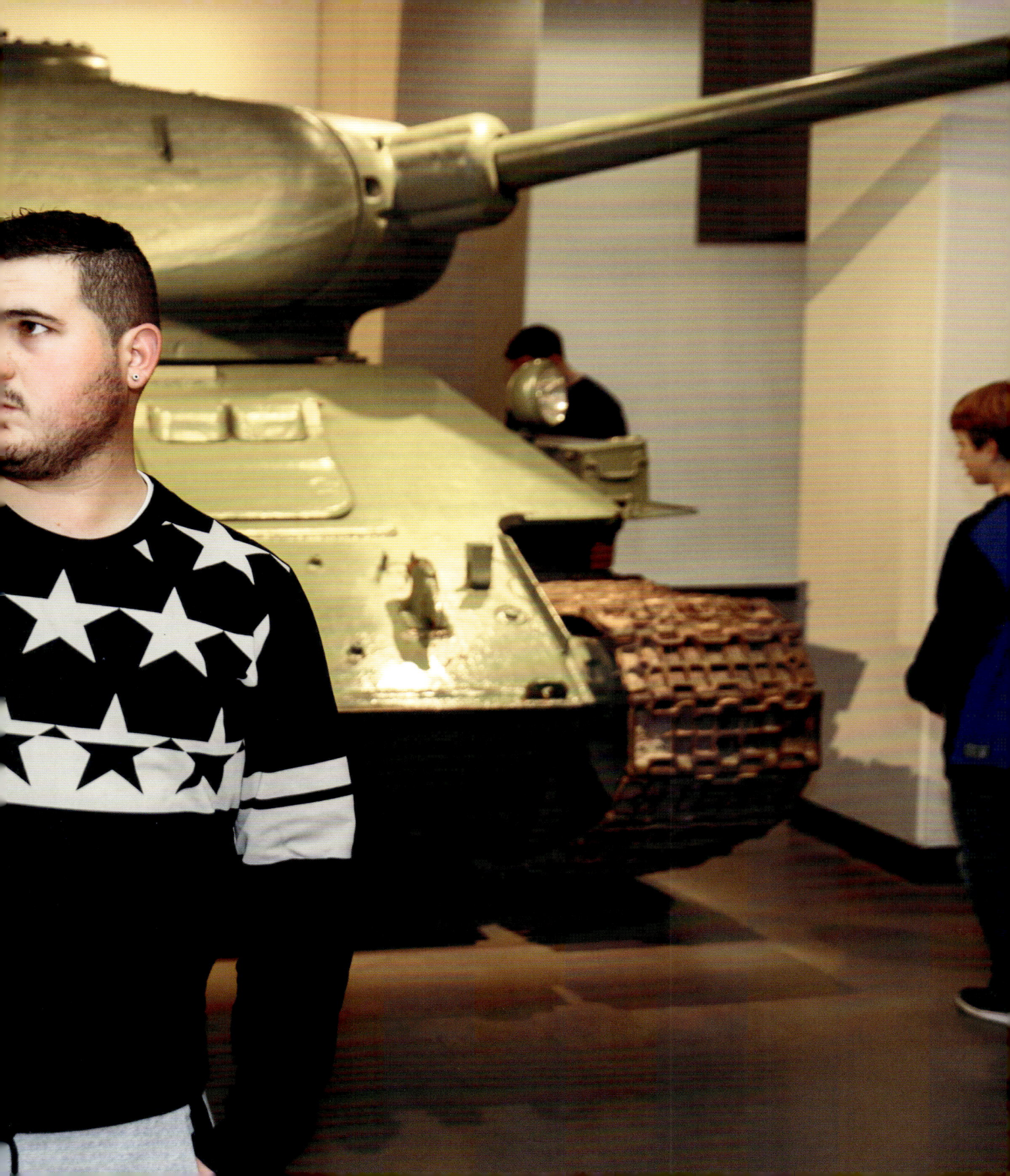

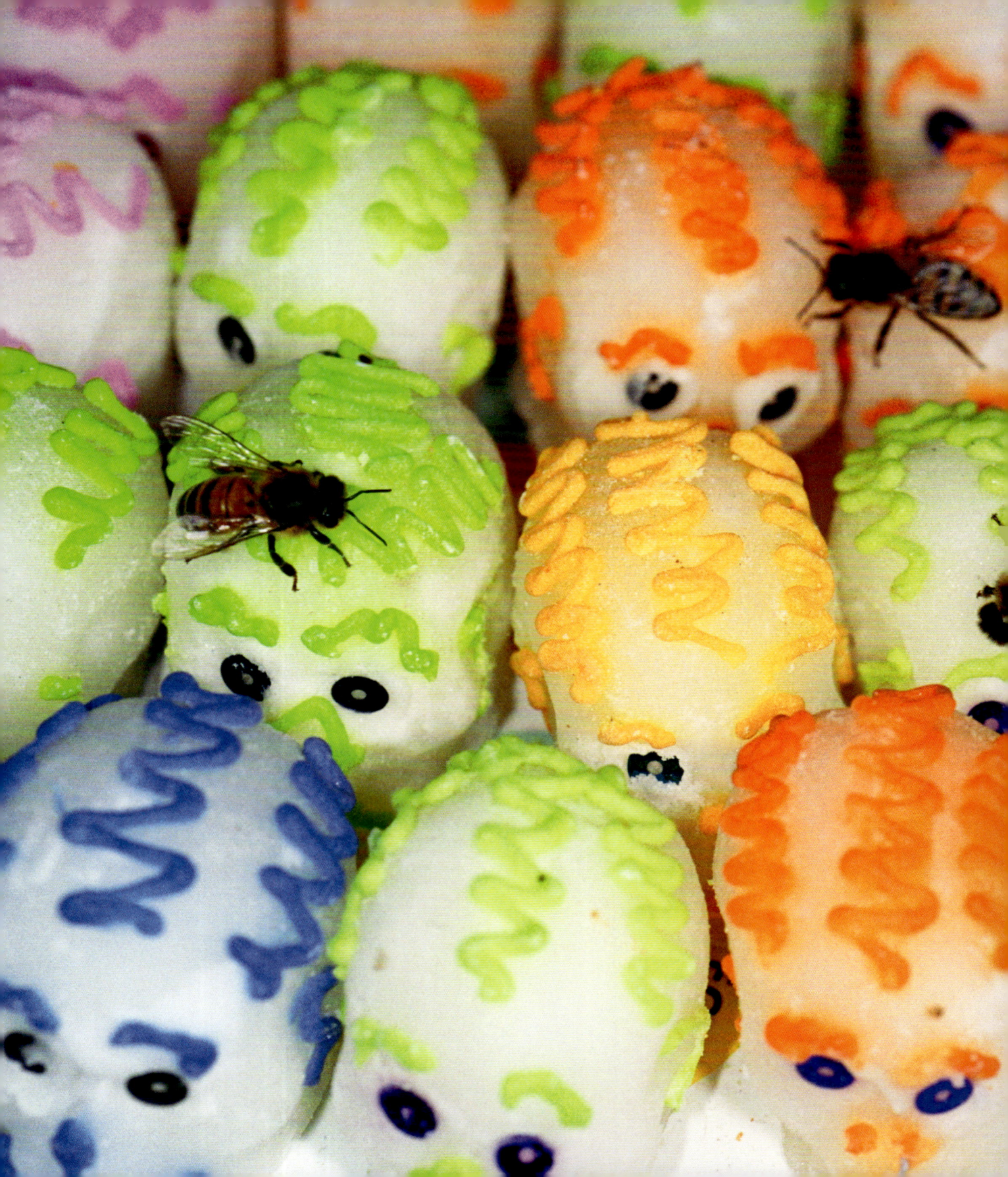

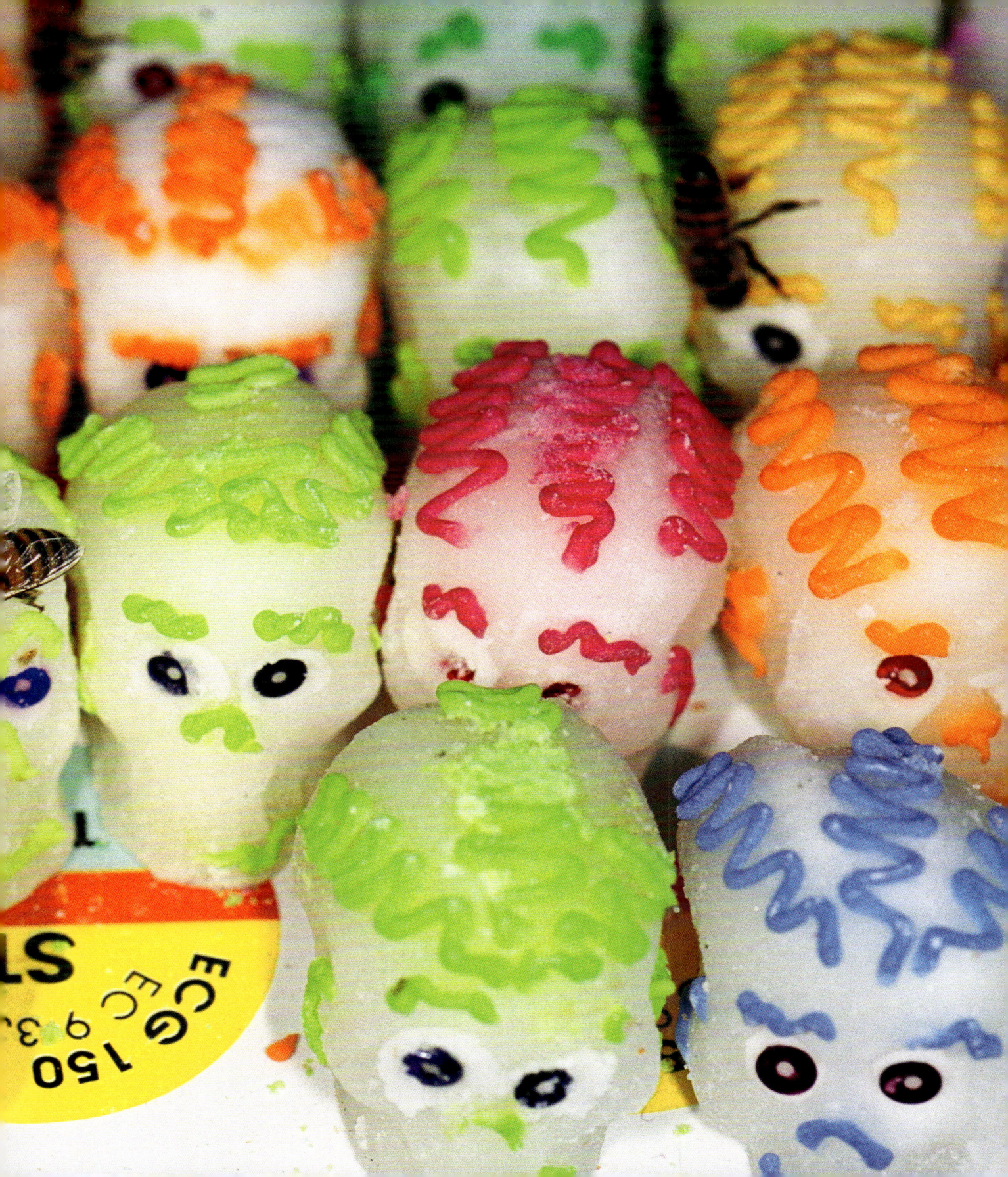

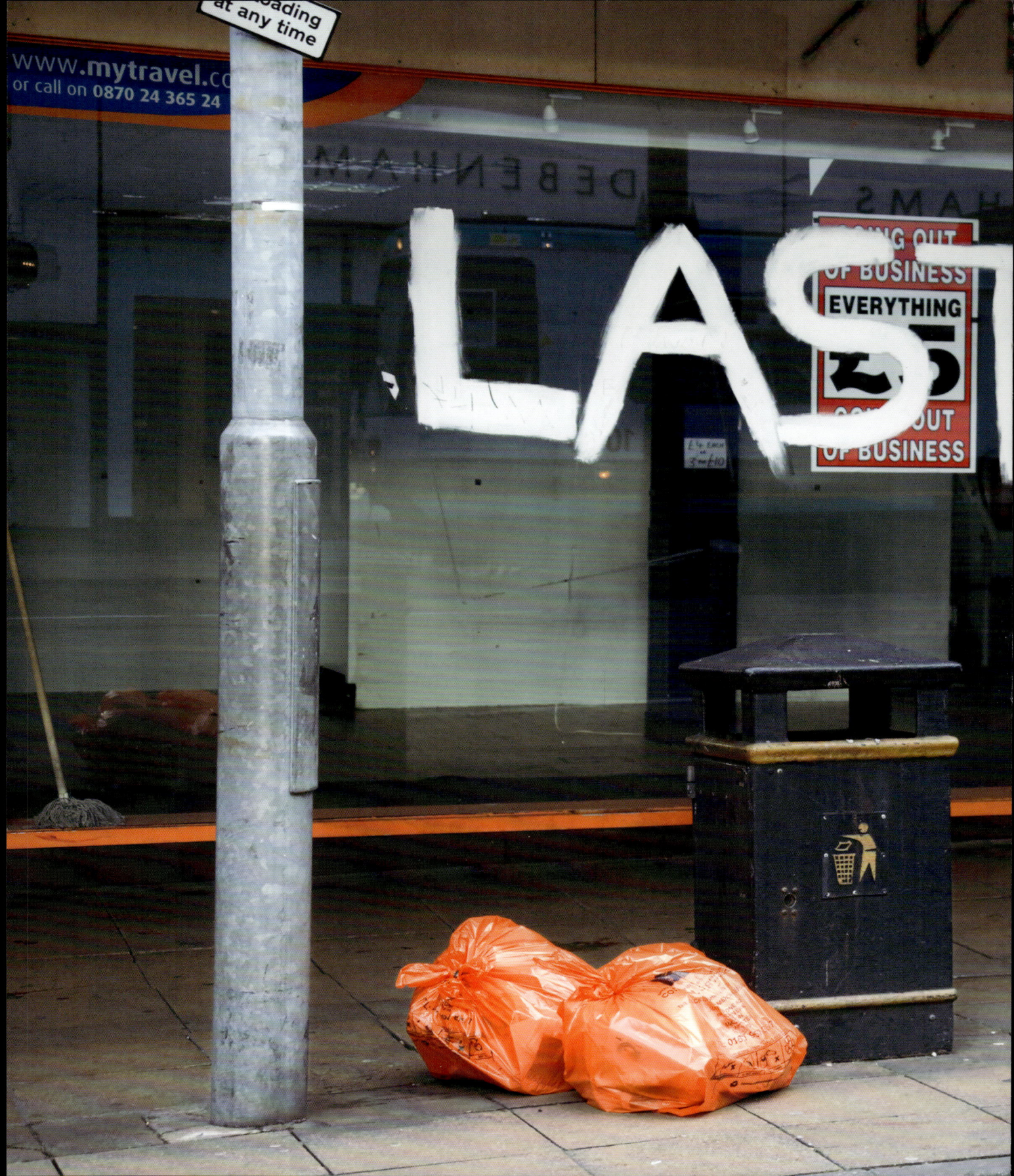

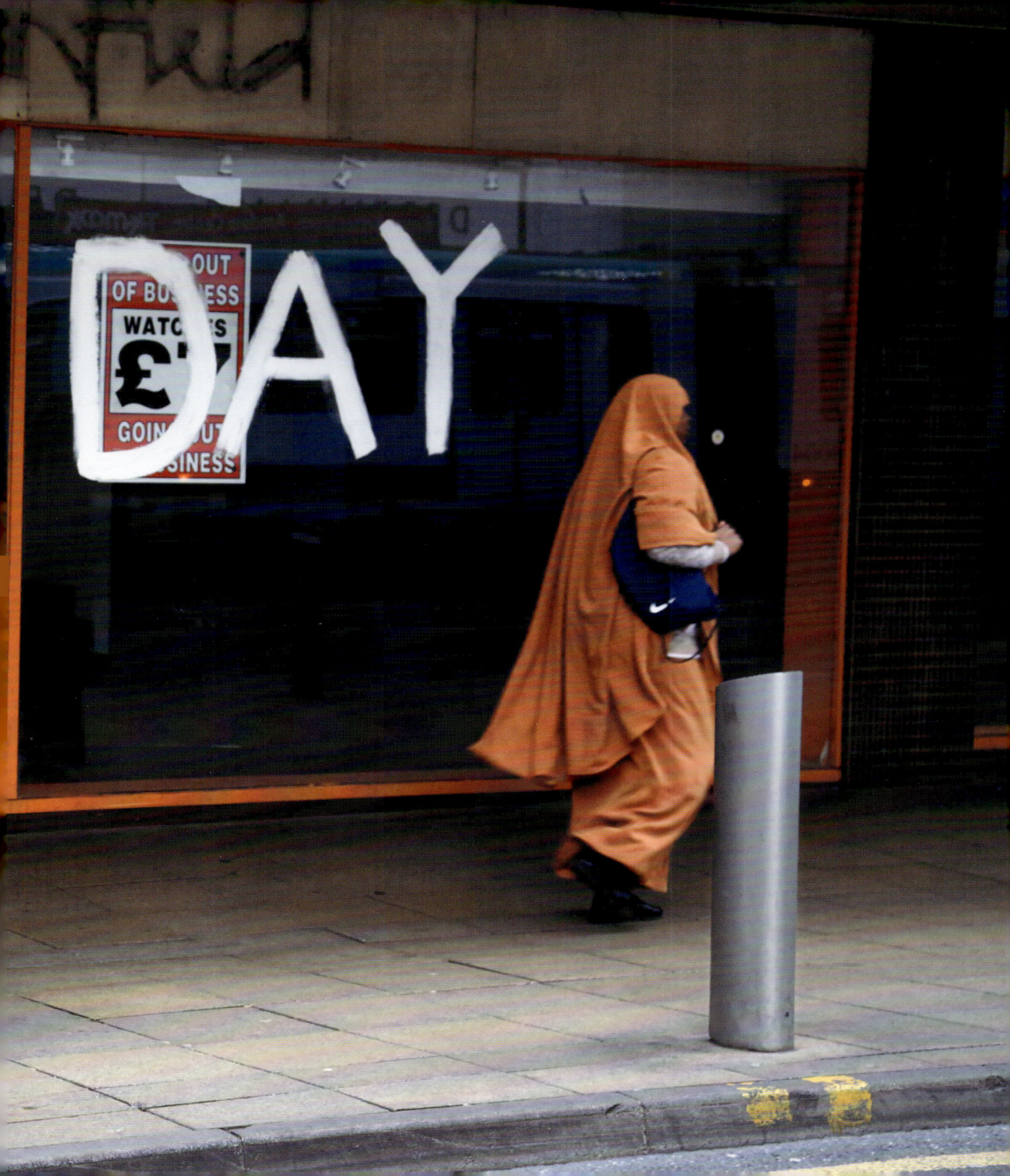

GLOBAL WARNING

MARTIN PARR

INTRODUCTION BY
QUENTIN BAJAC

ESSAYS BY
ADAM GREENFIELD
VIOLETTE POUILLARD
ROBERTA SASSATELLI
AND **JEAN-FRANÇOIS STASZAK**

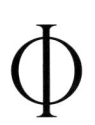

● **JEU DE PAUME**

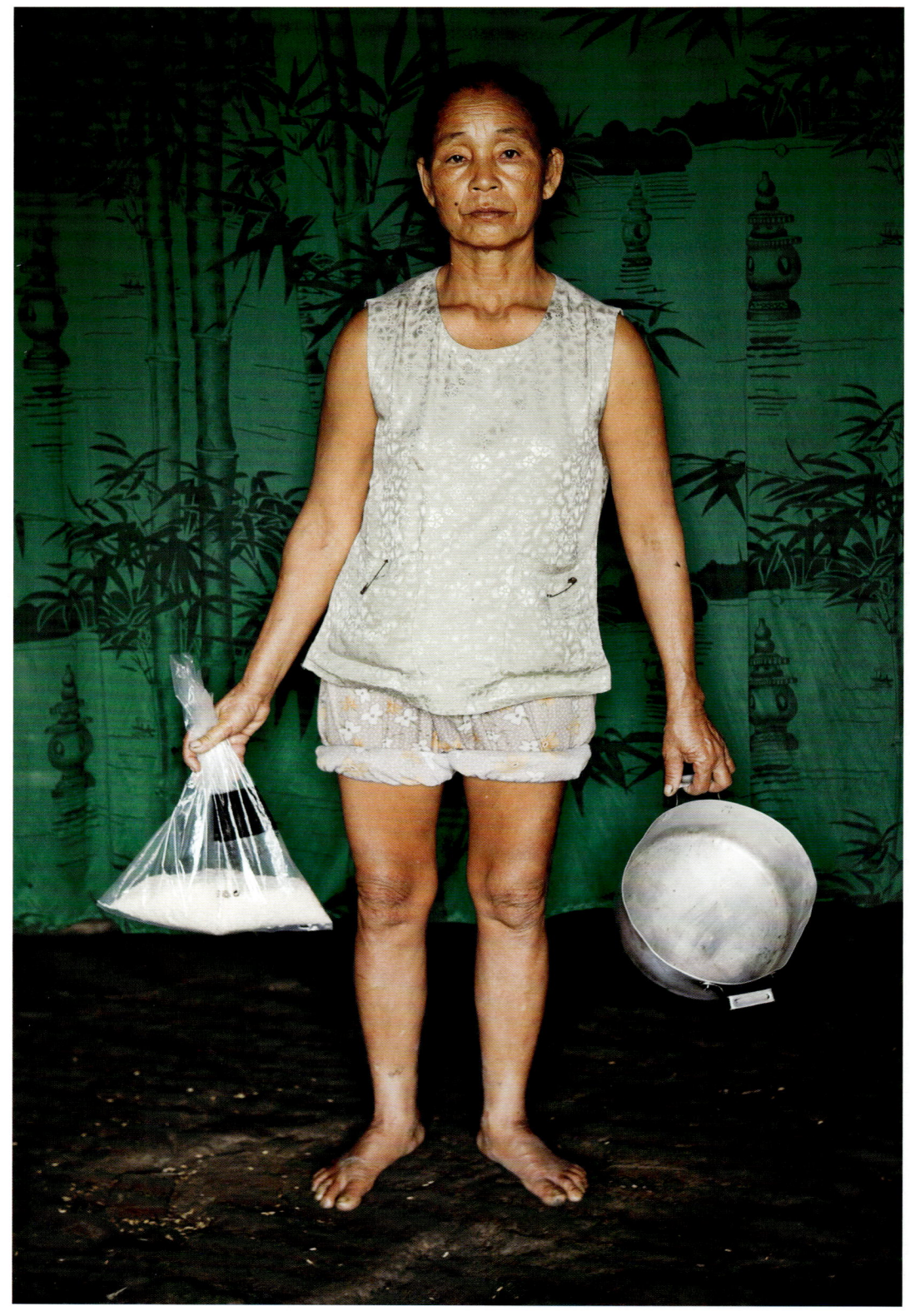

fig. 1 Martin Parr, Quang Tri province, Vietnam, 2009

GLOBAL WARNING

BY

QUENTIN BAJAC

Imagine a generative AI trained exclusively on Martin Parr's work: the images it creates would form the portrait of a world saturated with supermarkets, shopping centres, crowded beaches and leisure parks, its scenery punctuated by a relentless repetition of visual elements in all four corners of the earth. A world filled with seemingly futile objects, fated to rapid obsolescence and their inevitable demise in a trash heap. We would see figures clad in bathing suits and rain ponchos, sporting baseball caps, logo-adorned t-shirts and backpacks, roaming in groups or standing in queues, pushing shopping trolleys or sunbathing with dazed expressions. A world driven by an insatiable appetite – hungry for things, images, experiences, sensations – where interactions take place frenetically and a hodgepodge of goods is consumed with machine-like gluttony. A world populated by a race of mutant humans partially fused with technology – constantly plugged into their phones, eyes riveted to screens, at one with their cars – struggling to co-exist with the planet's other living creatures, between exaggerated anthropomorphism and actual predatoriness.

Such a world is partially our own. For fifty years, Martin Parr has trotted the globe with a sly grin on his face, creating a striking portrait of the imbalances of our planet and the excesses of our lifestyles. In this catalogue, we re-examine Parr's work in light of the general disarray of our times. A platform is given to researchers from the social sciences – a geographer, an anthropologist, a sociologist, a historian of science and life sciences – each of whom sheds light on a certain aspect of Parr's work. Recurring themes emerge throughout his numerous series, which originate in the UK and Ireland and, beginning in the 1990s, extend across six of the world's seven continents: the depravity and devastating effects of mass tourism, the domination of the automobile, dependence on technology, consumer frenzy and our ambivalent relationship with other living things. Through his unique gaze, Parr indirectly tackles several of the major causes of climate change in the Anthropocene: intensive use of transportation, fossil fuels, global overconsumption and environmental degradation. With hindsight, his scathing irony seems to place him within a certain tradition of British satire: Parr's sharp humour and wry derision indirectly offer a critical yet profound take on our world.

In 1981, an Irish network broadcast one of the first news reports to feature Martin Parr.[1] In it, we see the young photographer travelling around the countryside at the wheel of his Morris Minor – an emblematic car of the post-war British middle classes, which ceased production in 1971 – in search of wrecked… Morris Minors. Through Parr's lens, the abandoned vehicles become a novel motif of contemporary ruin (see pp.188-9). They are always framed in their entirety so as to capture their environment, providing a documentary rigour while maintaining freedom of interpretation. Today, the photos in the series can be read in several ways: as modern vanitas symbolizing the inevitable decline of progress, a subtle criticism of pollution linked to the automotive industry, a homage to Irish scenery, or even a somewhat optimistic meditation on the resilience of nature: 'The more weeds and trees that are growing out of them, the better they are', a young Parr states in the report.

The series can also be viewed as a celebration of human ingenuity: some of the abandoned cars have been repurposed to keep chickens or dogs, or to store hay. In a way, the images offer an oblique history not only of pollution, but of adaptation. Forty years later, this same Parr photographs a family in lawn chairs behind a fence, watching a parade of smoke-spewing tractors and farm machinery, the way others gaze at the sea admiring the horizon (see pp.176-7). The scene is the Great Dorset Steam Fair, the largest show of steam-powered vehicles in the world. Depending on the viewer, the seemingly anachronistic activity could trigger either surprise or indignation, but Parr, true to his methods, treats it with the same ironic distance he used with the abandoned Morris Minors. There is humour, yet meaning is never imposed – quite the contrary.

Throughout his work, Parr has continued to display unwavering faith in the critical power of documentary photography, a genre he defends tirelessly, well beyond his own images. This documentary approach has drawn him to photograph the quirks of our era with a blend of apparent neutrality and clinical precision. Incongruity often arises from the contrast between the banality of his subjects and the methodical discipline of his photography – devoid of judgement, empathy or hostility. This does not, however, imply an absence of critical analysis; the analysis is merely carried out insidiously, indirectly, in a disguised or 'hidden' manner. I use that term deliberately because Martin Parr himself, when discussing this exhibition and his critical approach to our post-industrial consumerism and lifestyle over the past fifty years, mentioned a 'hidden agenda'. What he meant was that, although he recognizes this obvious aspect of his work, the theme has developed gradually in a non-linear, unintentional, inexplicit and unpolitical manner. And if his perception is sharper today, it no doubt reflects an evolution in our thinking and our awareness of the issues that are raised in the images. The way we look at the work has changed alongside the work itself.

Across the globe, Martin Parr has shot countless photos of various abuses of the Western capitalistic lifestyle, which is greatly responsible for climate disruption. While he has surveyed the – at times artificial – overabundance in our society, he has never explored poverty, or directly focused on the effects of climate change. That being said, in 2009, Parr was commissioned by Oxfam to visit Quang Tri province in Vietnam to make a series of full-length portraits of farmers who were losing their rice harvests to increasingly heavy floods (fig. 1). The assignment sparked a bit of a breakthrough for him, as he wrote on his blog that same year:

> I can now see how nearly all the images that I have recently taken and produced are indirectly related to climate change. For example, my recent book entitled *Luxury* is an exploration of how the wealthy go about parading themselves at horse racing events, art fairs or fashion shows. I photograph wealth in the same spirit as has traditionally been associated with photographing poverty, an updated version of the 'concerned photographer' but disguised as entertainment. For surely, what is the main indirect cause of our increasing carbon emissions, but the increasing wealth of our planet? Other recent subjects, such as an arms fair in the Middle East (see p.109) or tourism in Machu Picchu (see p.88), all have a link to climate change…

> So from now on I am just interpreting the serious issue of climate change in as many creative and lateral ways [as] possible.[2]

Treating serious subjects as 'entertainment in disguise' is a constant in Martin Parr's work, which he has addressed in early interviews as well as in recent statements. In 2021, he said, 'I'm creating entertainment, which has a serious message if you want to read into it, but I don't expect to change anyone's mind – I'm just showing them what they think they may know already. I'm in the entertainment business!… I don't want confrontation; your idea is as good as mine.'[3]

This stance is anything but activist, and contains an unabashed rejection of dogmatism. In fact, Parr insists that he fully belongs to the world he documents and criticizes. As for the climate and environmental crisis: 'We're headed for disaster, but we're all headed there together. No one would ever dare ban cars or plane travel,' he said in 2022.[4] As a tireless photographer often in between two flights, and a beach lover who can't swim, Parr never seeks to give lessons. He readily acknowledges the impact of his lifestyle – notably his own shocking carbon footprint – and refuses to look down on his subjects, as he states in a broadly negative article on global tourism: 'I'm not saying that tourism is bad – far from it as it brings a livelihood for many people'.[5] This ambivalent position as both actor and critic, observer and observed, is a keystone of his artistic identity. The reflexive posture of the artist both inside and outside the system he explores has become a defining feature of Parr's work.

His series 'Autoportrait' (fig. 2), begun in the 1990s, can be interpreted from this perspective. In it, Parr adopts the standard imagery of tourist photography in the form of the souvenir picture taken in a photo booth or on-site by a local photographer: a kitsch portrait of Mr Everyman – international Western tourist and willing victim of the souvenir-photo business rampant in the world's most visited sites. The only, albeit crucial, distance from the practice lies in the absence of a smile: the unflappable seriousness with which Parr greets the flash underscores an ironic discrepancy. An acknowledgement of partial participation in the very activity he denounces, substituting the heroic figure of the committed photojournalist of yesterday with today's photo-tourist, a modern variation of the archetypal innocent or buffoon. For that matter, Parr's work has often been shown in exhibitions which, in the 2000s, critically questioned the issue of global tourism, a subject many artists apart from Parr were exploring in those years. [6]

With such a calling card, the fact that Martin Parr was able to join the Magnum Photos agency, historically associated with humanistic and hard-hitting photojournalism, seems like a sign of the times, even if he was admitted by the skin

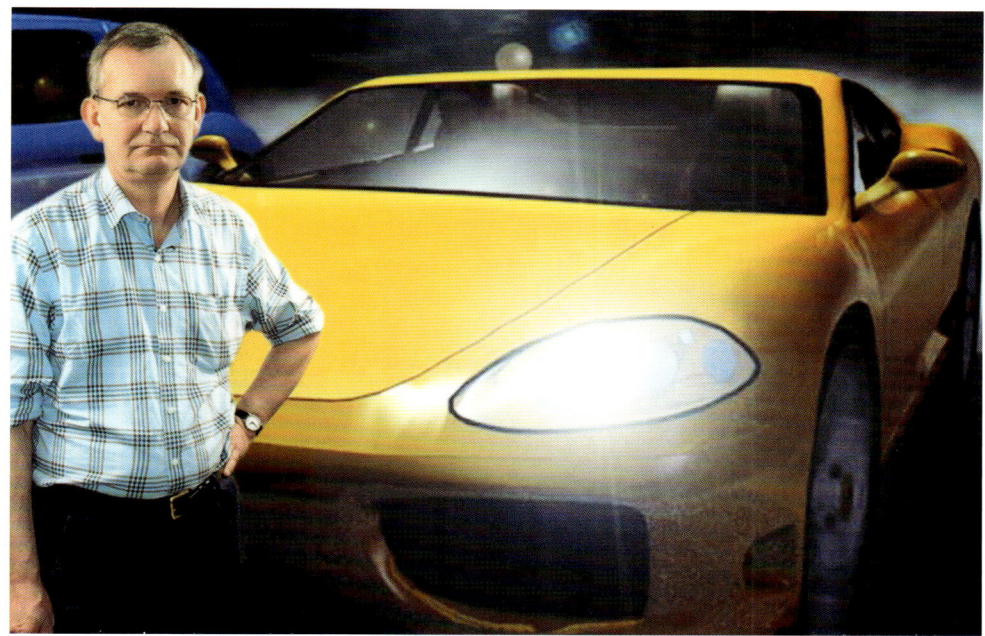

fig. 2 Martin Parr, from the series 'Autoportrait,' Delhi, India, 2009

of his teeth.[7] Even then, in 1994, the staunchly humanist approach of the 'moderns' that distinguished the founding generation of Magnum was not exactly on display in Parr's work, despite its preoccupation with the human element. At the time, French photographer Henri Cartier-Bresson, who opposed Parr's membership, described their approaches as 'two different solar systems', building a wall where the boundary was actually more porous. For Parr, as for Cartier-Bresson, humanity is the focus, and Parr's field of observation is indeed real life – in all its social, cultural, economic and anthropological dimensions. Parr's reply – 'I acknowledge there is a large gap between your celebration of life and my implied criticism of it' – underscores their difference in tone, though fails to acknowledge the critical and mainly anti-consumerist element inherent in much of Cartier-Bresson's postwar work. On the other hand, Parr also seems to minimize the subtle joy that infuses many of his own photos. But while Cartier-Bresson orbits in the realm of the Serious, Parr seeks every means to distance, thwart and spoil it.

Let us suggest that Parr is a postmodern photographer:[8] postmodern in the sense of expressing a certain doubt or perplexity towards the great humanist narratives – including those within Magnum – that had characterized the previous generation, to which his own generation responded with more modest and less overtly political stories; but also postmodern in the sense of being an agency photographer who is relatively integrated into media and cultural industries – advertising, fashion and commissioned corporate work. If we use Italian philosopher Umberto Eco's formula coined

in 1964[9], contrasting 'apocalyptic' artists, opposed to the system, with 'integrated' artists, we can posit that Parr is clearly more integrated than apocalyptic. It would be absurd to label Martin Parr a 'whistle-blower', a term that corresponds to neither his intentions nor his character. More simply put, Parr works within the system, subverting its tools with steadfast humility. He knows that images can no longer change the world, yet nevertheless pursues a sort of unassuming activism, a 'visual guerrilla warfare' able to shatter the dominant representations – from adverts to family photo albums – feeding into an idealized collective imagination that tends to smooth out reality and make it more palatable. For Martin Parr – because 'the tourist does not travel to things, but to images of things'[10] – the tourism industry is a prime target. '[Mass tourism] is a subject full of propaganda', he said in 2019. 'All the travel pages in the newspapers make it look very attractive, but they would never want to show the issues or the problems with over-popularity in places like Barcelona and Venice. It just seemed like a natural thing to do and I've been doing it ever since.'[11]

By the same token, we can claim that much of the series *Common Sense* (see pp.128–30, 132–3, 136–7, 139), with its steady insistence on eating and drinking as primary forms of consumption, subverts the clichés of food photography: the food it shows is anything but appetizing. More broadly, Parr's work on overconsumption – through a blunt, lurid depiction of a wide range of appetites and desires, social classes and cultures – pokes fun at the idealized and carefully staged images of advertising photography. We might even say that Parr's approach rests on the invariable questioning of traditional photography genres. Thus the postcard, with its sleek aesthetics and stereotypes, is mocked in his photos of famous monuments, often shown in a (real or symbolic) lessened state – whether swarming with crowds (see pp.80–1), or through copies and reproductions of 'authentic' monuments (see p.61), if the term even applies anymore. Moreover, he deconstructs the conventions of wildlife photography, based on capturing an animal in its natural habitat. In Parr's images, animals exist only through their inclusion in human society and their relationship to humans (see pp.142–3, 146–9). Whether object of attention or of affection, captive or sacrificed, the animal – like the humans alongside it – is caught in a system of radical otherness, of dependence and domination, which is at times explicit and at others obscured by apparent benevolence: it may be pampered, anthropomorphized, domesticated, protected, encaged, slaughtered, butchered, consumed or even displayed as a trophy.

According to Parr, the fight against visual propaganda can only be fought using the same channels as the propaganda itself: addressing the greatest number of people through the recognized conventions and visual language of the present. This is why, for forty years, Parr has worked in colour, a popular, modern language that is more immediate and forthright than the black and white medium associated with art photography. He uses flash, the frontality of an amateur snapshot, and postcard aesthetics – elements that reinforce visual impact while rooting his images in a mass culture he understands perfectly and knows how to employ. Parr was quick to adopt a motto of one of his major influences, English photographer Tony Ray-Jones (fig. 3), whose work he encountered in the early 1970s: 'Don't take boring photographs'. This accessibility lies at the heart of Parr's strategy: win over in order to subvert, captivate in order to question. Through humour, vivid colours and a degree of apparent frivolity,

Parr captures our attention, then prompts us to perceive seemingly ordinary scenes differently. Instead of an overly didactic tone, he adopts a tradition dating back to Aristotle and Horace: *docere et placere*, to instruct and to please. Because pleasing also implies creating a space in which to doubt, question and raise awareness.

It is often pointed out that humour has always been key in the appeal of Martin Parr's work. As early as 1982, in the introduction to Parr's first book, *Bad Weather*, Peter Turner remarked, 'On first looking, it is easy to guess that these pictures have been made by a humourist'.[12] The switch to colour in 1983 only reinforced the comical tone – an aspect Parr fully embraces, yet refuses to be reduced to. He tells a story of how, when he joined Magnum, French-born American photographer Elliott Erwitt – also recognized for his use of humour – welcomed him as 'another funny guy'.[13] Not quite the artistic recognition he had hoped for. Parr is not a humourist, because a humourist's main and sole objective is to make people laugh. Parr's humour is always coupled with a critical or satirical reflection. He fits into a well-established English tradition rooted in the eighteenth century – with William Hogarth, Jonathan Swift and Thomas Rowlandson – where serious, ironic satire is underpinned by reality and the observation of human behaviour, in both literature and the visual arts.

Without claiming a direct lineage, we could view Martin Parr as a modern-day satirist, much as the artist Grayson Perry does.[14] In his own way, Parr pursues this critical vein without actually adopting a moralizing attitude. Just as satire sought to ridicule the noble genres of painting, Parr uses wry humour and the reversal of clichés to disrupt idealized visual representations – notably those conveyed by the media and cultural industry. We can push the parallel further: Parr's deliberate amateur aesthetic (harsh flash, blurriness, intentional 'mistakes') operates similarly to caricature in satirical prints, asserting a degree of technical ineptitude and lack of artistry to attain a powerfully striking stylization that collides with the sleek, artificial perfection of propaganda images. It is amusing to note that the development of satirical art in England in the late eighteenth century coincided with the rise of the Grand Tour and travel among the British elite – in other words, the start of tourism. Some of the caricatures of this period already targeted the misadventures and ludicrousness of the English abroad (fig. 4), somewhat heralding Parr's subjects two centuries later, notably those in his study of global tourism, *Small World* (1996).

When we talk about humour in Parr's work, it is probably important to be more nuanced. Because he obviously – and fortunately – does not automatically seek to elicit laughter (or perhaps more accurately a smile, as we are unlikely to actually laugh at his images); and because several forms of this 'laughter' – or satire – exist, ranging from irony to the grotesque, from caricature to the blackly comic. The burlesque

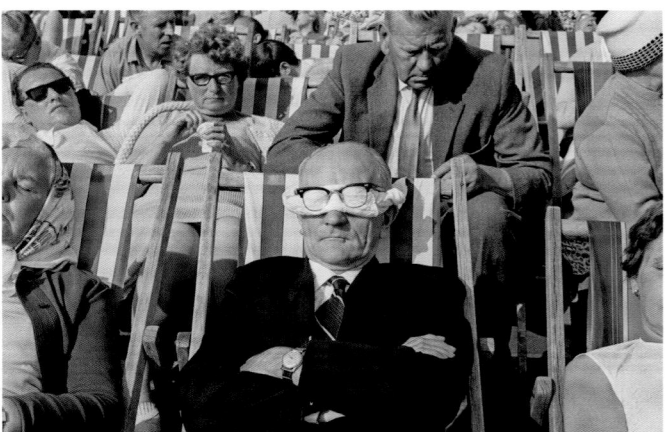

fig. 3 Tony Ray-Jones, *Blackpool*, 1966, National Science and Media Museum, Bradford

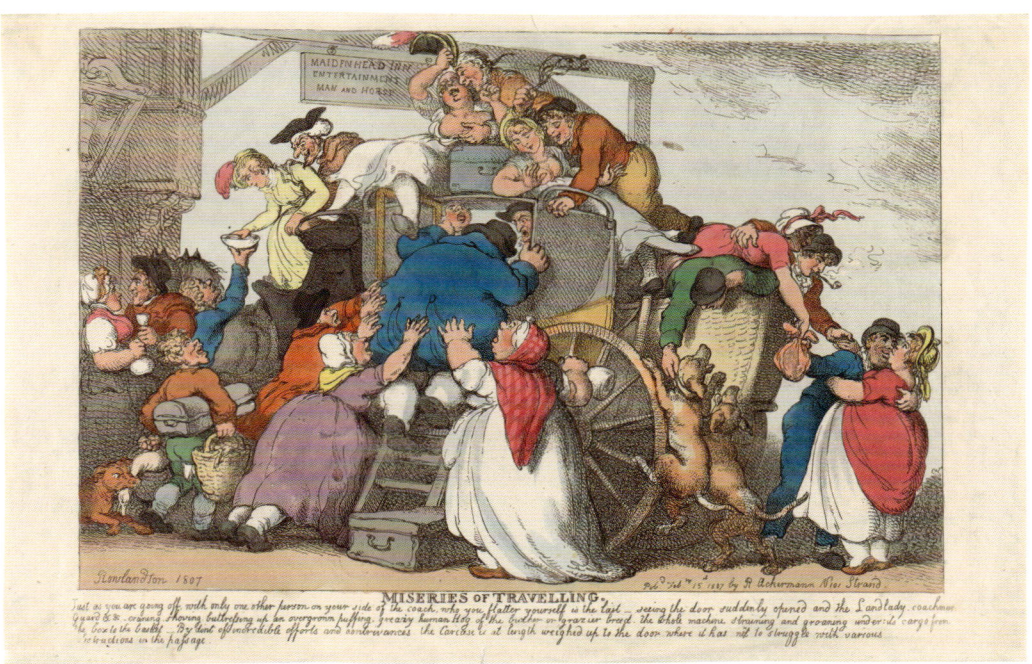

fig. 4 Thomas Rowlandson, *The Overloaded Coach* from the series 'Miseries of Travelling,' 1807, Metropolitan Museum of Art, New York

humour that emerges from a curious arrangement of bodies and postures in the study of people's relationship to their car, now fully integrated into the family circle is clearly different from the darker irony in the depiction of a natural cycle so disrupted by humankind that a pigeon can wind up eating a chicken (see p.146). Once more, this humour differs from the grotesque, kitschy accumulation seen in the images of 'Common Sense', where close-ups, flash lighting and saturated colour contribute to the extreme, standardized ugliness of the consumer world – making the work some of Parr's most political. As a whole, his body of work offers a cutting human comedy, where the attitudes and behaviour of its anonymous protagonists, regardless of social class, reveal a degree of collective absurdity. Let us not forget that the folly of human existence is a major theme of the satiric tradition, and that every social class and all human types are represented: what is this world in which adults behave like children, where tourists resemble prisoners (see p.85), where people are paid to photograph a stranger's funeral (see p.73), where a child is neglected in favour of gambling (see pp.172–3), where a romantic relationship is based on exploitation (see p.91) or one individual's pleasure collides with another's misery?

Among all the strategies that Martin Parr employs to side-step the register of Serious, irony is no doubt the most characteristic. Often this irony is allegorical: many of his images can be interpreted as forms of visual allegory. While Parr gladly asserts the documentary dimension of his work – with an almost tautological insistence on the obvious nature of the image ('what you see is what you see') – it would certainly be more accurate to say: what you see is not limited to what there is to see. His photos often have a double meaning: they show one thing while implying another. For example, the series 'Luxury' (see pp.102, 164) cannot be reduced to a factual observation of the behaviours of a globalized elite. Admittedly, it records the transcontinental repetition of the same outer symbols of wealth – cigars, champagne, luxury brands, typical pastimes, such as horse racing or art fairs – but beyond that, it also probes a kind of conspicuous vacuity where appearance takes precedence over being. In his foreword to the book about 'Luxury', Paul Smith describes it as a series of variations on the theme of 'falseness'.[15] The allegory operates by shifting and concealing meaning. Thus, when Parr photographs a group of tourists impeccably lined up in front of the Parthenon (see p.72), he does more than simply document a moment of tourist conviviality: he challenges conformity, questions the limits of cultural escape and exposes the deep divide separating the myth of a site from the actual experience of it today.

Parr's persistent tracking of these situations reinforces the idea that the use of allegory is intentional. His shots of tourist hotspots around the world – from Barcelona (see p.71) to Venice, his favourite destination (see p.210) – are underpinned by what we might call situational irony: an inversion of values, where the 'noble' subject becomes commonplace. This reversal, specific to satire, brings the image of the sublime back down to the realm of the ordinary. Through Parr's lens, Machu Picchu contains little of the sacred and sublime; it becomes an accessory, a misty backdrop for the shapeless forms of international visitors, displaying incongruous attitudes often at odds with the setting. Similarly, a beach no longer provides a moment of escape and communion with nature, as advertised in tourist brochures. And when it does remain 'natural' – which is by no means a given – it is merely a sandy extension of urban life, with the same social comportments and population density: we queue up to buy food (see pp.36–7), surf in a sea as dense with bodies as a subway platform (see pp.42–3) and swim in water as congested as a public pool (see pp.44–5). For Parr, the beach is not a site of exotic escape, but a place of alienation.

In a 2025 interview, Parr summed up his current attitude:

I feel pretty upbeat, but when I think about the planet and the world and our country, I can't help but get depressed. Net-zero, climate change – impossible. Since Covid, tourism has gone completely mad. More and more people are traveling. There's no slowdown in places like America or China, who are the big polluters. It's an impossible mission, really, and every day you see the evidence. Look at L.A., you had the fires and you had the floods. It's a total disaster, as you know.[16]

Over time, Parr's work has taken on a degree of gravity that he may now be more willing to admit. The implied double meaning of 'Last Day', painted on the window of an out-of-business shop in Bradford, West Yorkshire, becomes even more sinister when interpreted as a sort of modern, profane and everyday version of the Last Judgement (see p. 127). The title of one of his recent books, *Acropolis Now*[17] (fig. 5), also evokes finality through destruction in its obvious allusion to Francis Ford Coppola's film *Apocalypse Now* (1979). The book contains a dozen shots of tourists taken while Parr was visiting the Acropolis in Athens in 1991 (see p.72). Two years later, the prints were damaged by a water leak, resulting in blemishes, marks and discoloration. The images have faded over time, and their forms and figures have grown less visible and more ghostlike, as if seared by a blazing light. However, they have gained a sort of mysterious, unsettling aura: decayed images, damaged pictures, snapshots of a lost world; as if, two thousand years from now, archaeologists had unearthed peaceful, joyous, ordinary photographs of a world *before*.

1   "Morris Minor Obsessed Photographer", RTÉ Archives, 1981 (online: www.rte.ie/archives/2021/0415/1210039-morris-minor-mad-martin-parr/).

2   Martin Parr, "My Climate Change Conversation", 12 November 2009 (online: www.martinparr.com/2009/my-climate-change-conversation/).

3   Ana Bogdan, 'Martin Parr: "I don't Expect to Change Anyone's Mind"', *The Talks*, 2025 (online: www.the-talks.com/interview/martin-parr/).

4   Benjamin Locoge, 'Martin Parr: "Je n'ai jamais été un activiste, juste un photographe lâché dans le parc d'attractions"', *Paris Match*, no 3875, 10 August 2023 (online: www.parismatch.com/culture/art/martin-parr-je-nai-jamais-ete-un-activiste-juste-un-photographe-lache-dans-le-parc-dattractions-228084).

5   Martin Parr, *Global Tourism*, Magnum Photos (online: www.magnumphotos.com/arts-culture/travel/global-tourism-martin-parr/).

6   Notably, 'All Inclusive, A Tourist World', Francfort, Schirn Kunsthalle, 2008 and 'Dreamlands. Des parcs d'attractions aux cités du futur', Paris, Centre Pompidou, 2010.

7   For more on this issue, see Phillip Prodger, 'Who Do You Think You Are?', *in* Phillip Prodger (ed.), *Only Human*, exh. cat., London, Phaidon / National Portrait Gallery, 2019 and Clément Chéroux (ed.), *Henri Cartier-Bresson*, exh. cat., Paris, Centre Pompidou, 2013.

8   I explored this hypothesis in the preface to *Martin Parr, Le Mélange des genres. Entretien avec Quentin Bajac*, Paris, Textuel, 2010.

9   See Umberto Eco, *Apocalittici e integrati: Comunicazioni di massa e teorie della cultura di massa*, Milan, Bompiani, 1964.

10 Olivier Burgelin, 'Le touriste jugé', *Communications*, no 10, 1967, p. 66.

11 'All you see is lazy photography everywhere': Martin Parr in conversation with *It's Nice That*, *It's Nice That*, 9 September 2019 (online: www.itsnicethat.com/features/martin-parr-in-conversation-photography-090919).

12 Peter Turner, Introduction to Martin Parr, *Bad Weather*, Zwemmer, 1982, p. 7.

13 Baudouin Eschapasse, 'Rendez-vous avec Martin Parr: "J'aime ne pas être là où on m'attend"', *Le Point*, 28 April 2024 (online : www.lepoint.fr/culture/rendez-vous-avec-martin-parr-plus-le-sujet-que-je-traite-est-grave-plus-je-tente-d-y-introduire-de-l-humour-28-04-2024-2558883_3.php#11).

14 Grayson Perry, Introduction, in Phillip Prodger (ed.), *Only Human*, *op. cit.*, p. 10.

15 Paul Smith in Martin Parr, *Luxury*, London, Chris Boot, 2009, p. 5.

16 *Interview Magazine*, 28 February 2025: (online: www.interviewmagazine.com/film/photographer-martin-parr-on-trump-tourism-and-the-trials-of-modern-living).

17 Martin Parr, *Acropolis Now*, Richmond, Surrey, Setanta Books, 2022.

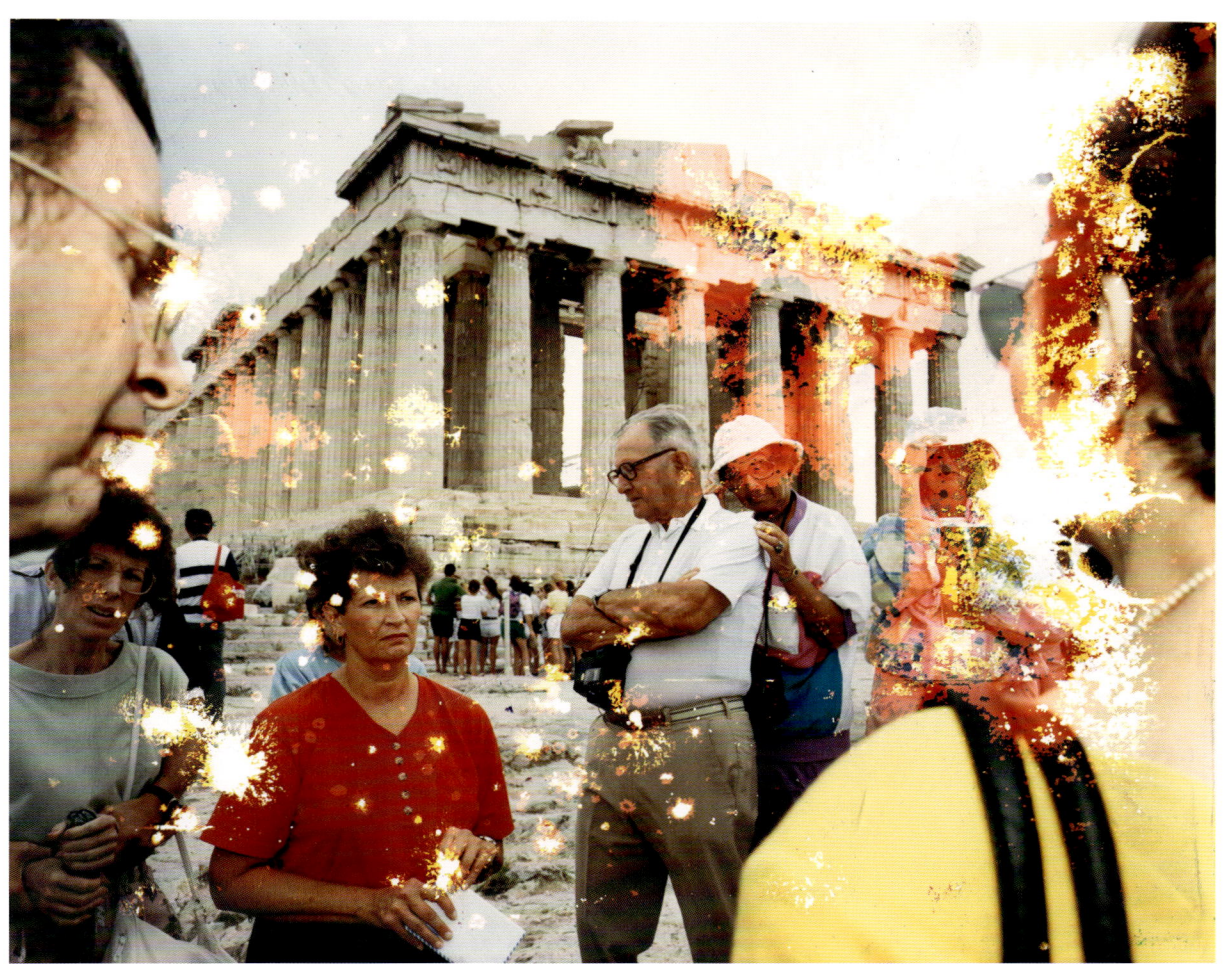

fig. 5 Martin Parr, from the series 'Acropolis Now,' Athens, Greece, 1991

LEISURE
&
WASTELANDS

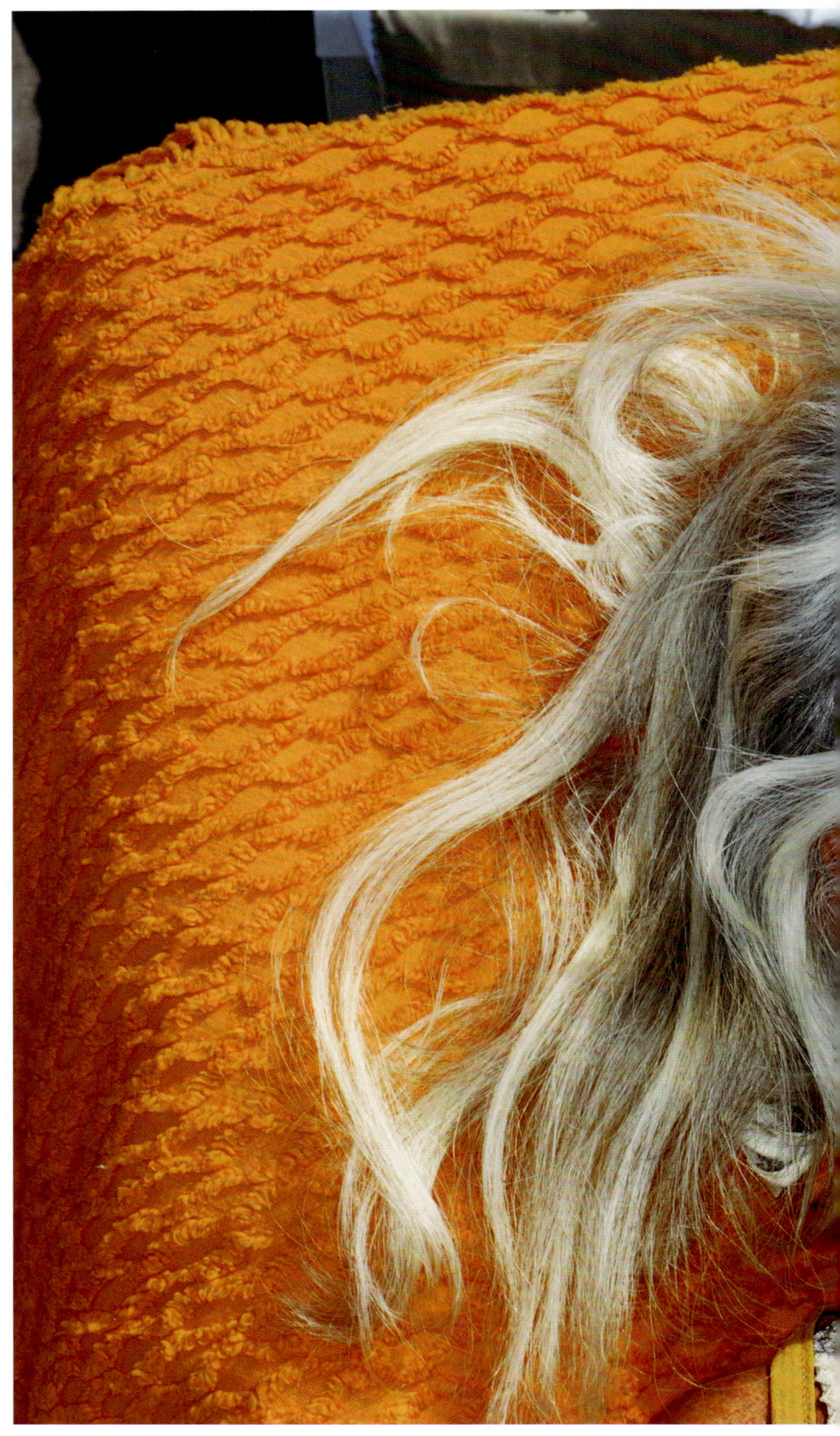

Cannes, France, 2018

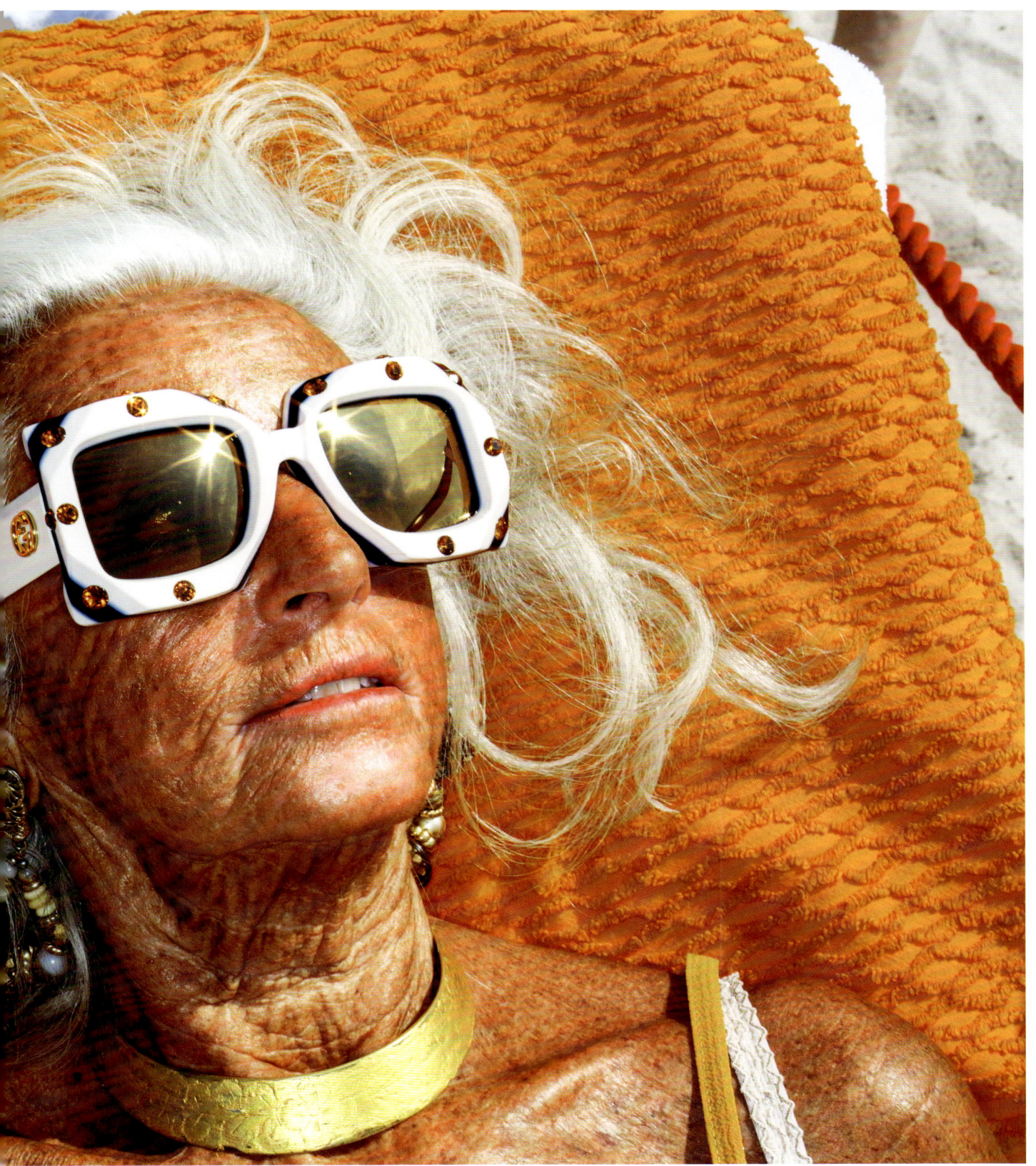

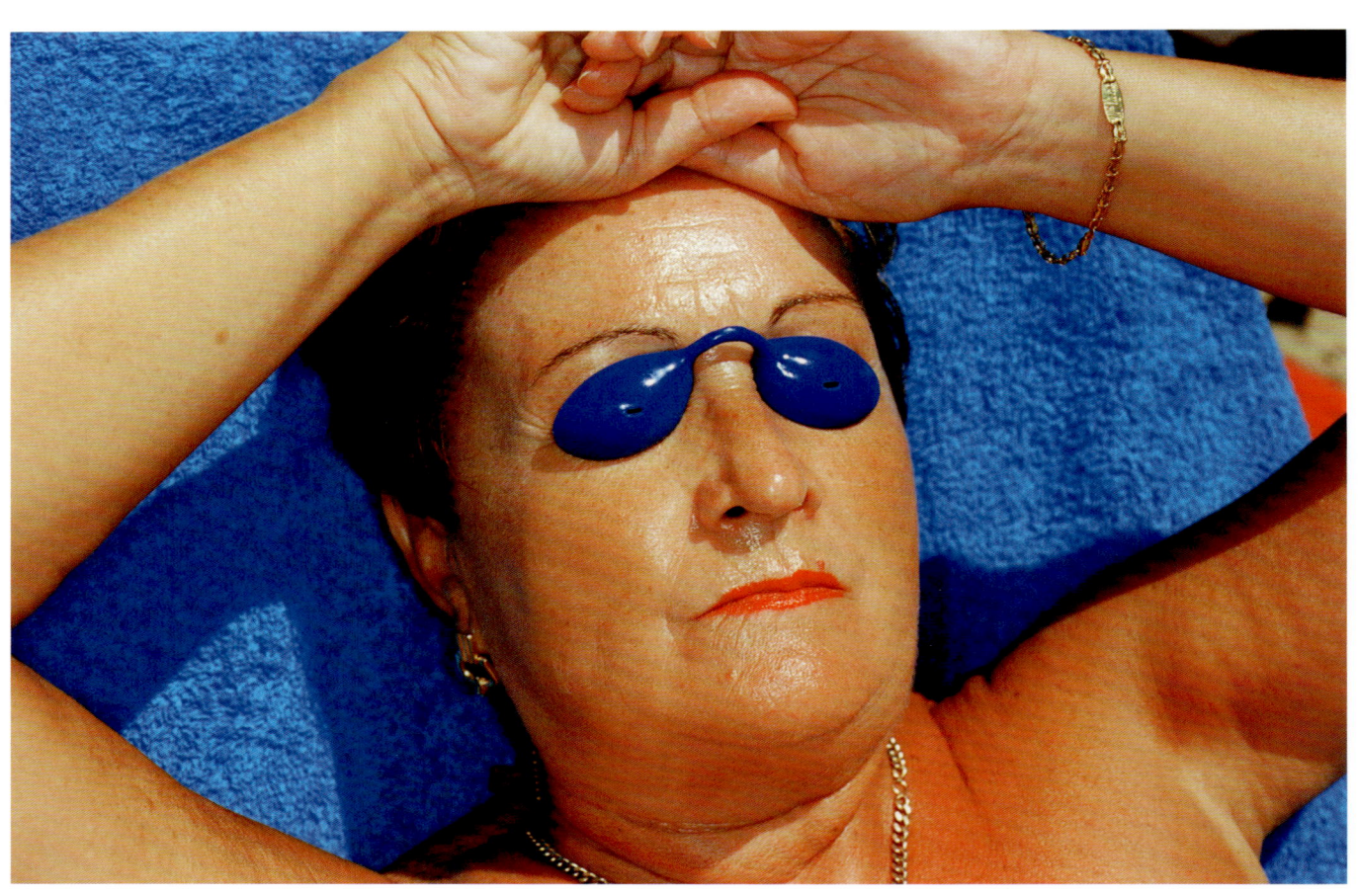

Benidorm, Spain, 1997

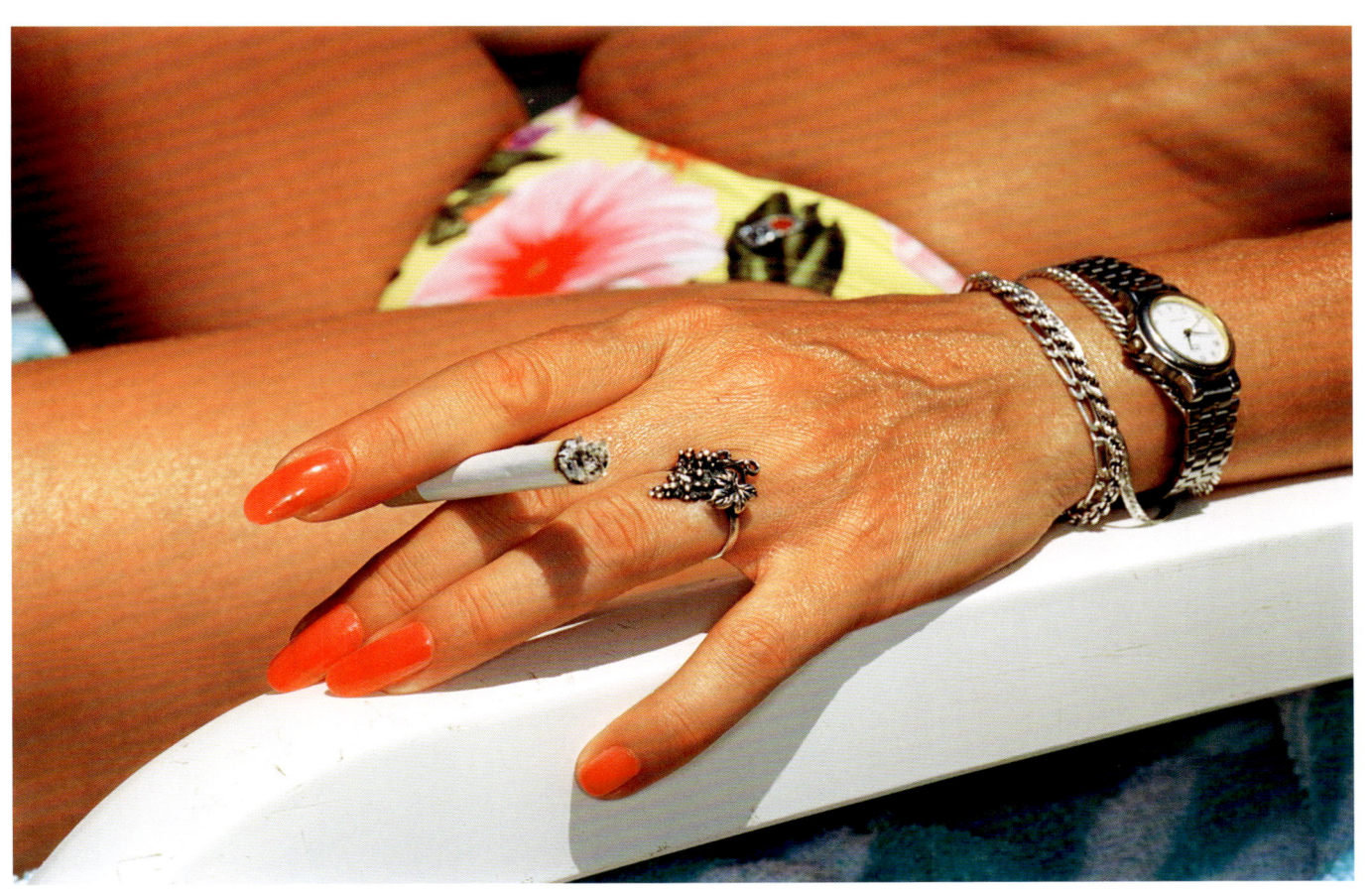

Benidorm, Spain, 1997

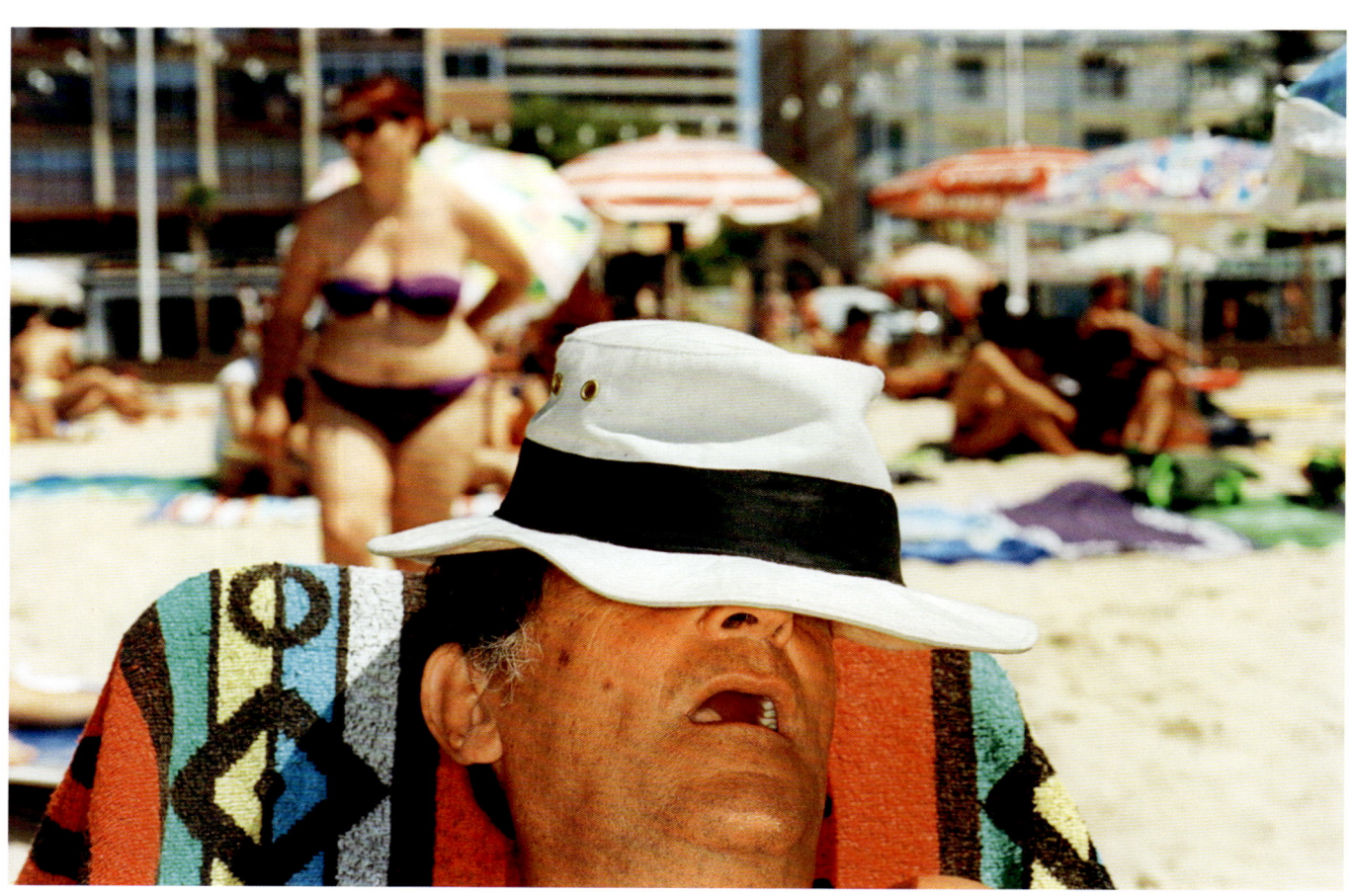

Benidorm, Spain, 1997

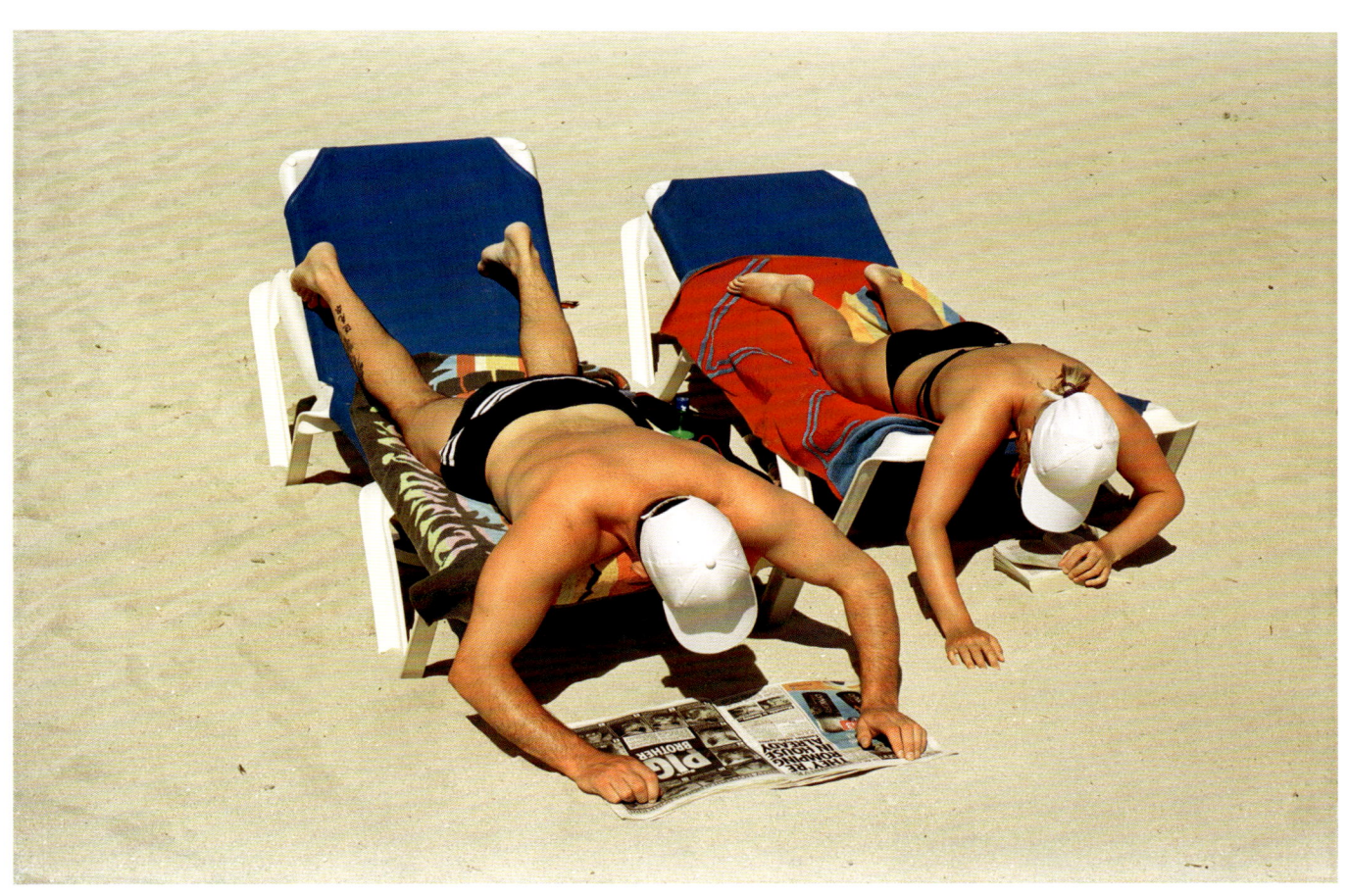

Magaluf, Majorca, Spain, 2003

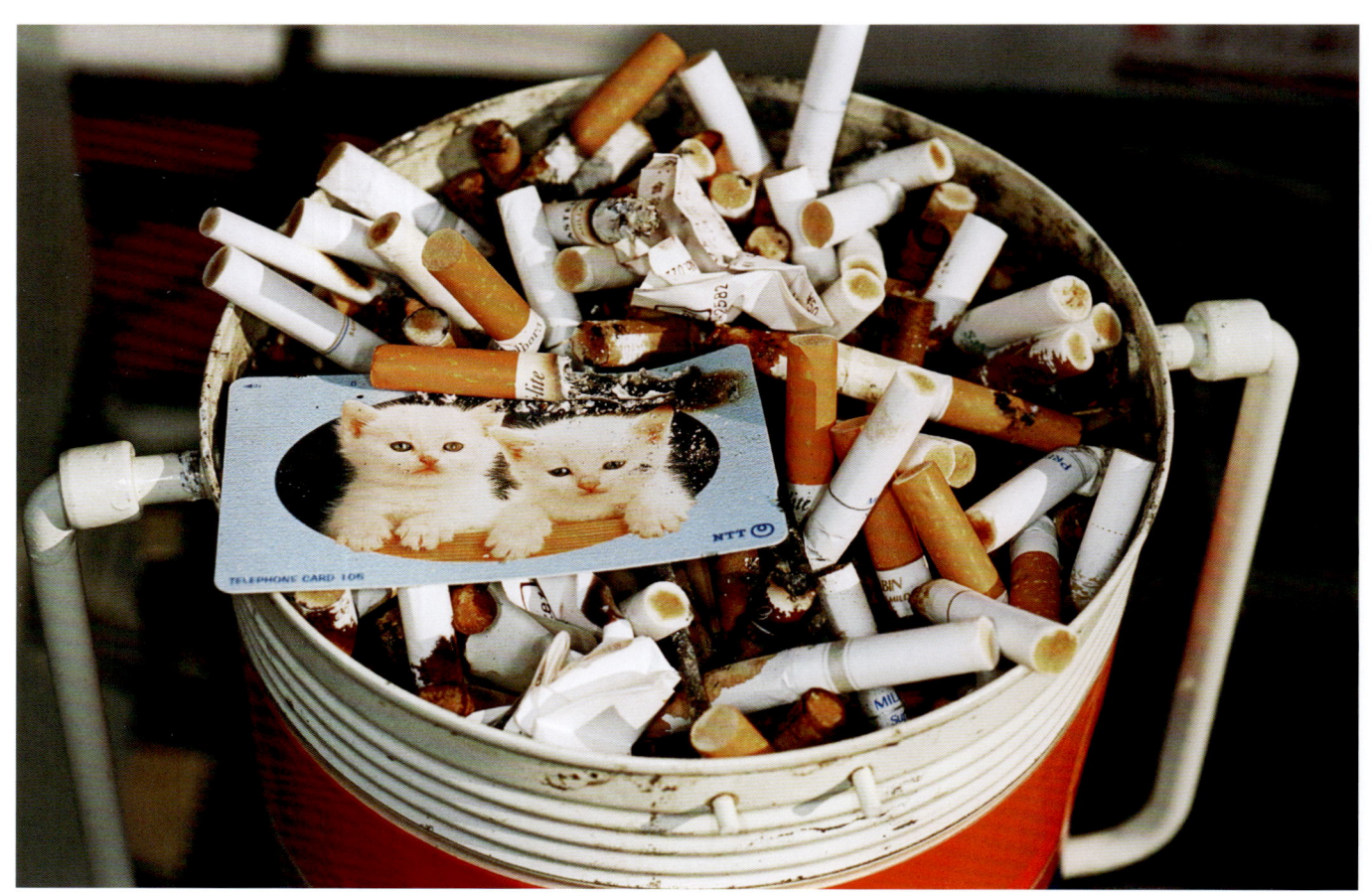

Tokyo, Japan, 2000

Opposite:
Benidorm, Spain, 1997

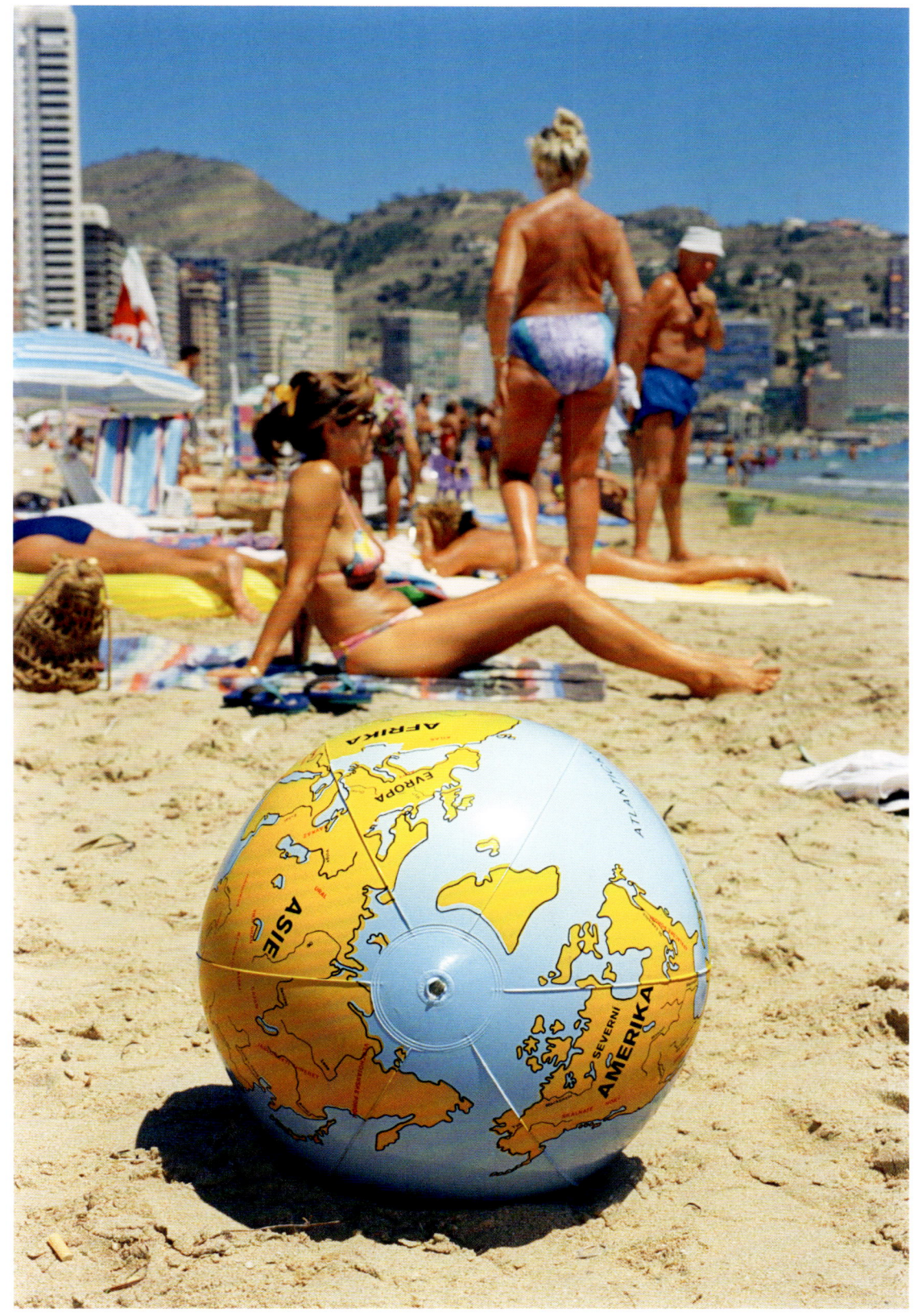

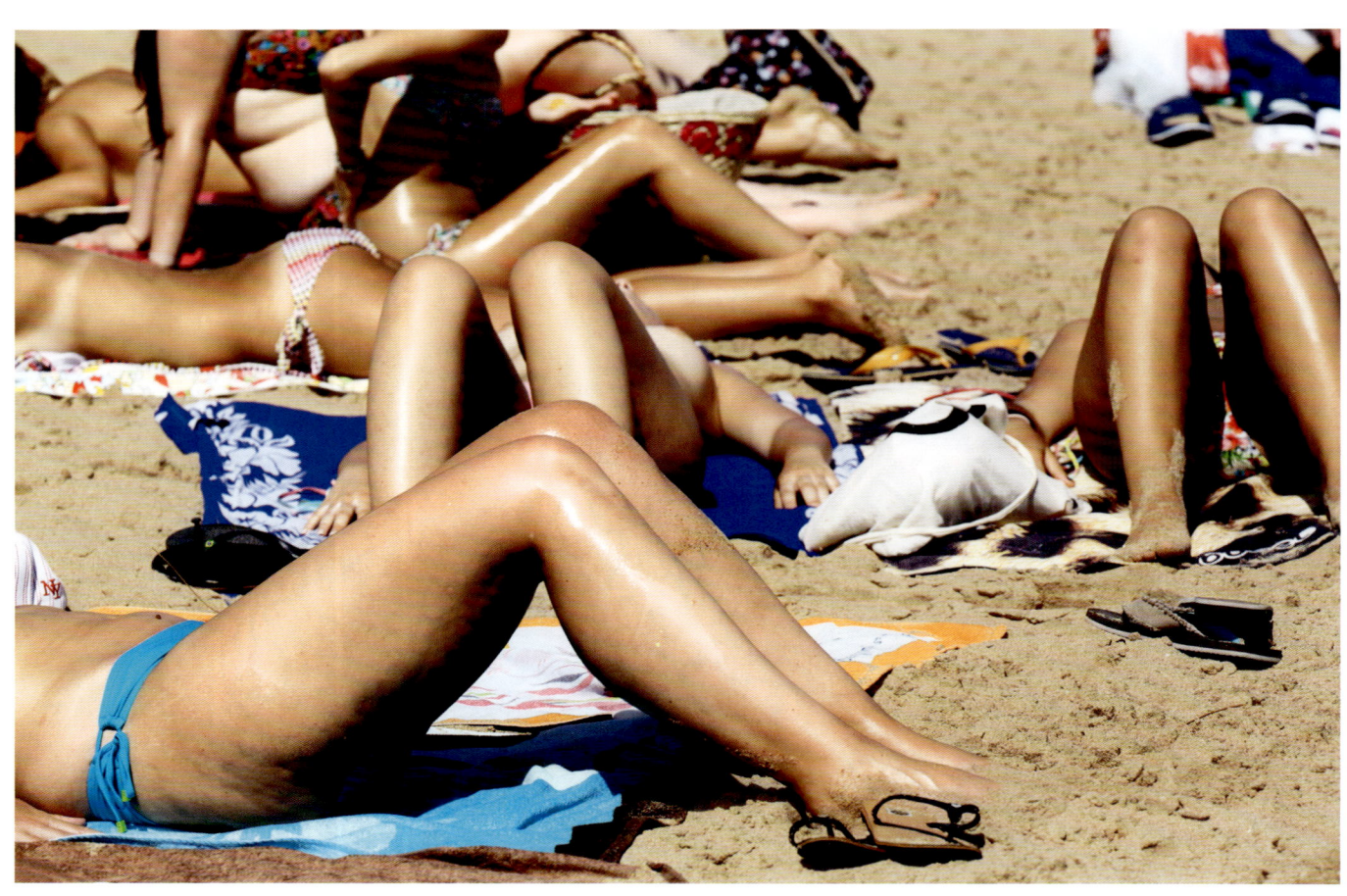

Benidorm, Spain, 2014

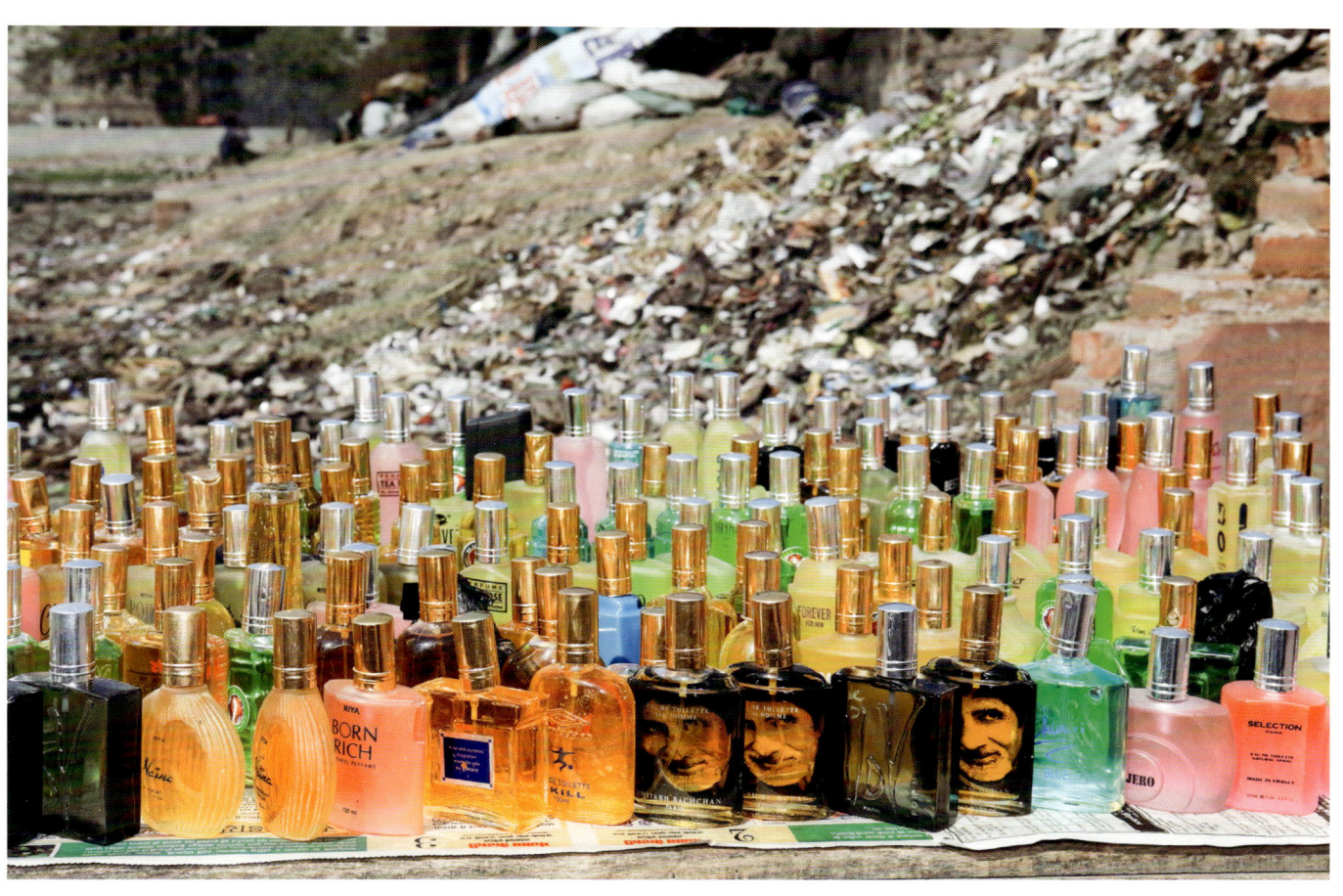

Delhi, India, 2010

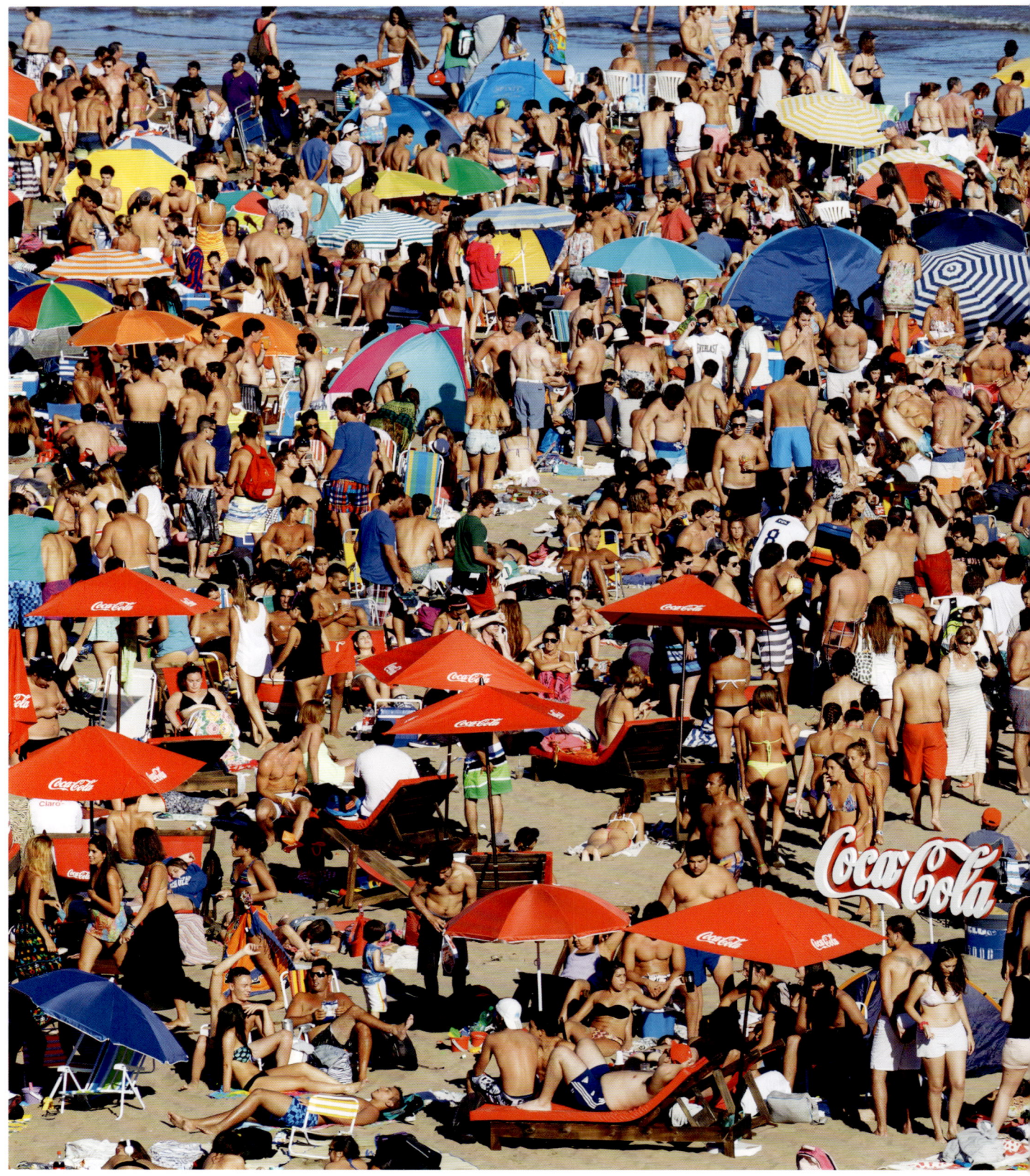

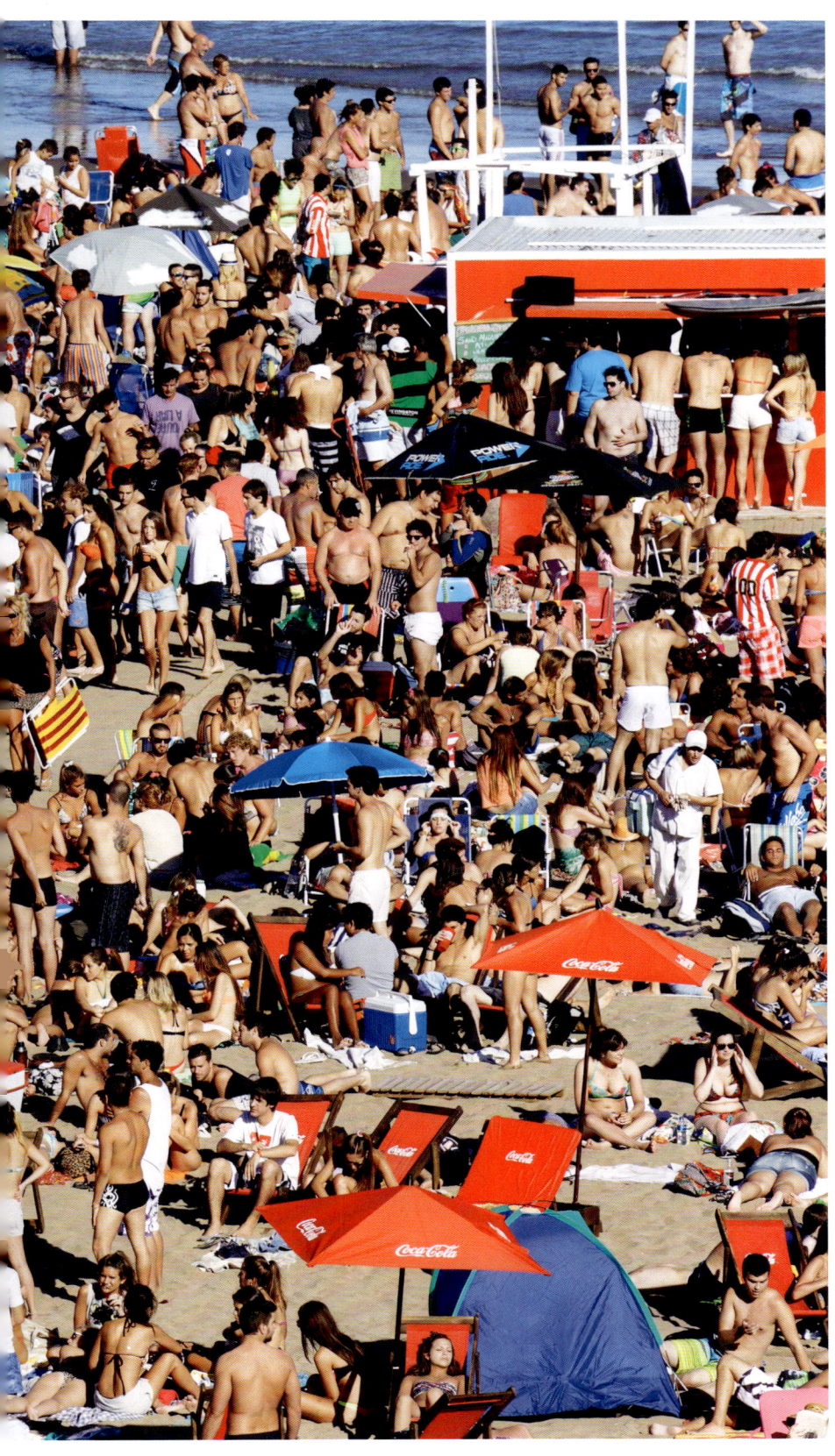

Mar del Plata, Argentina, 2014

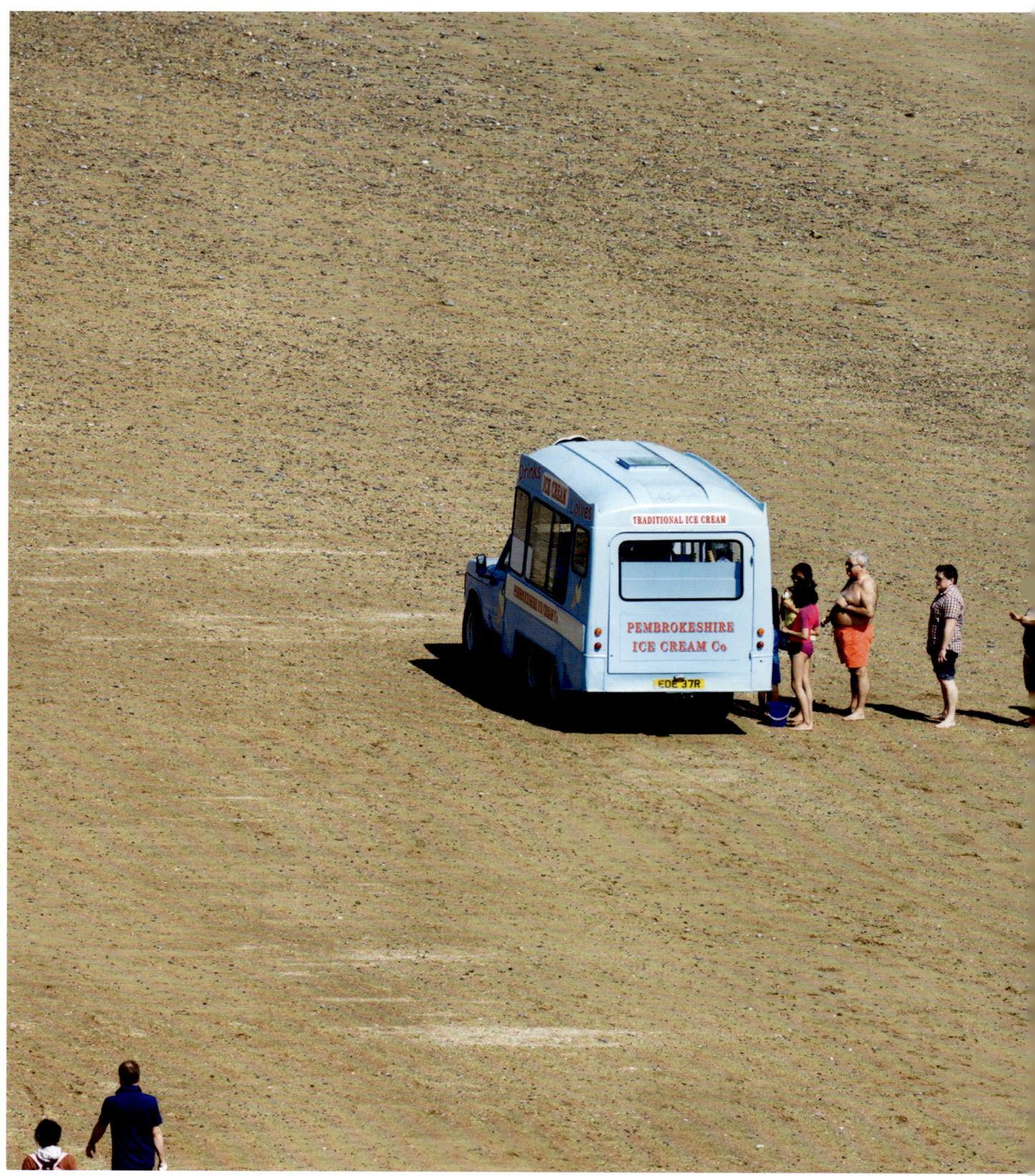

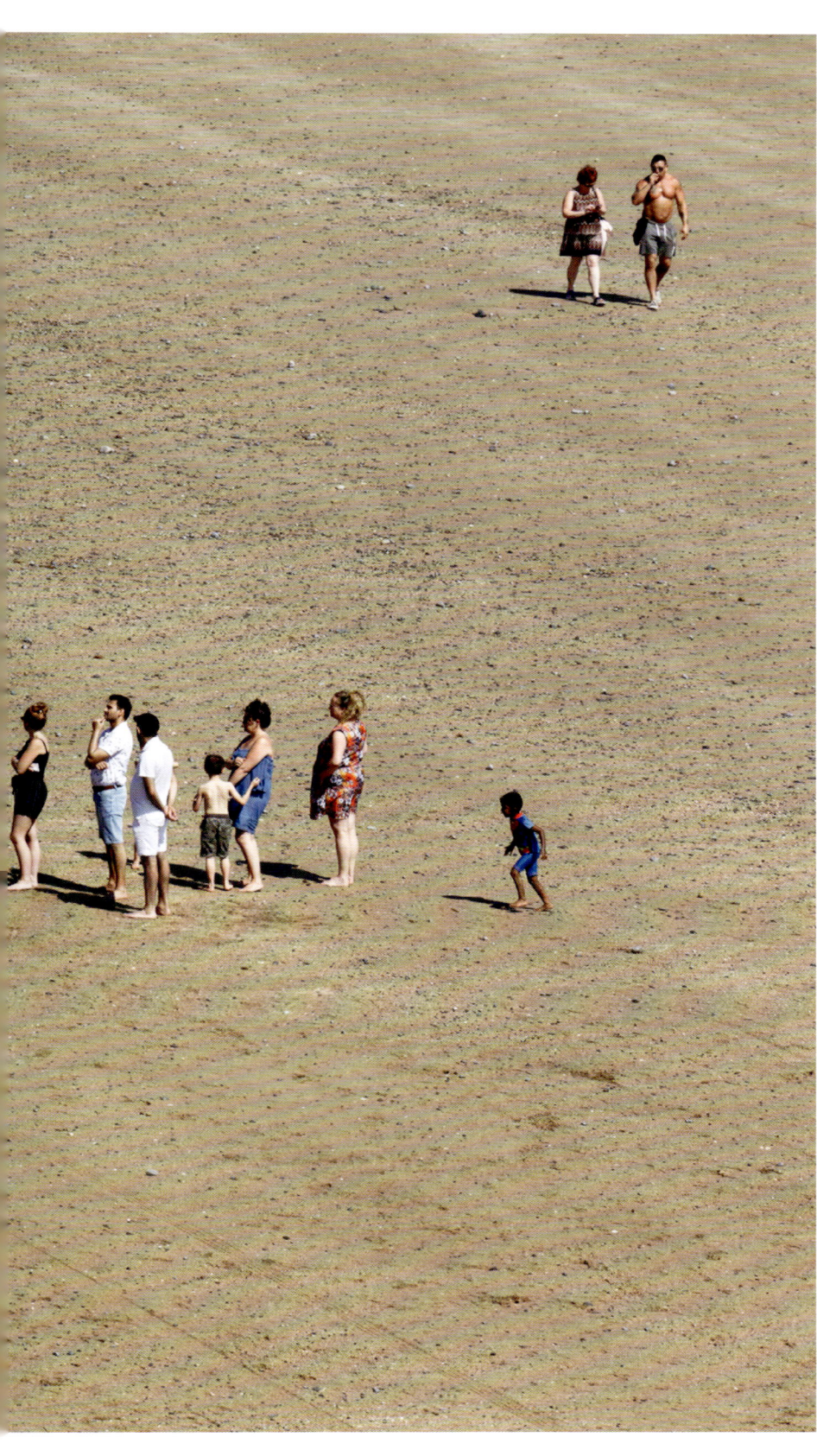

Tenby, Wales, 2018

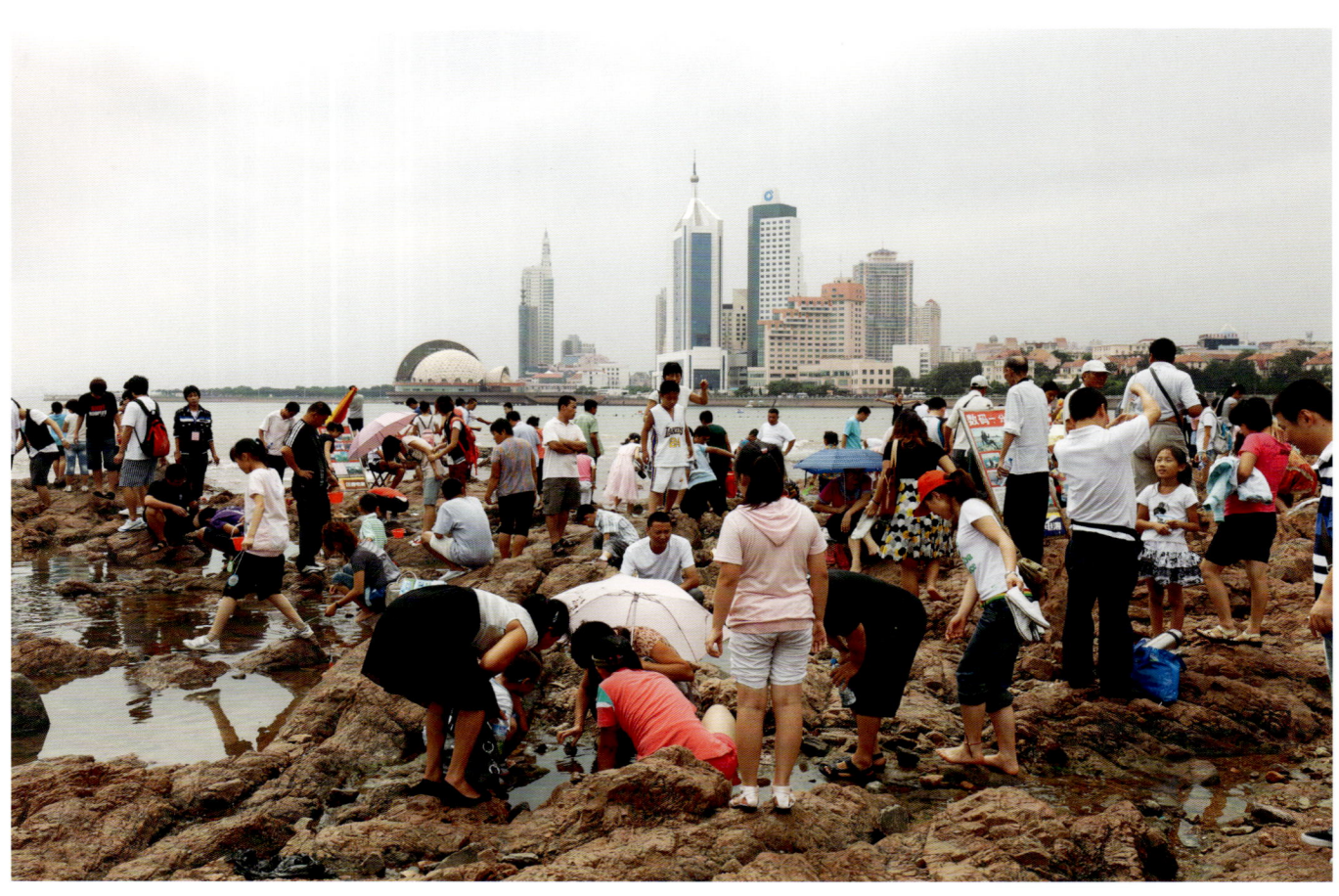

Qingdao, China, 2010

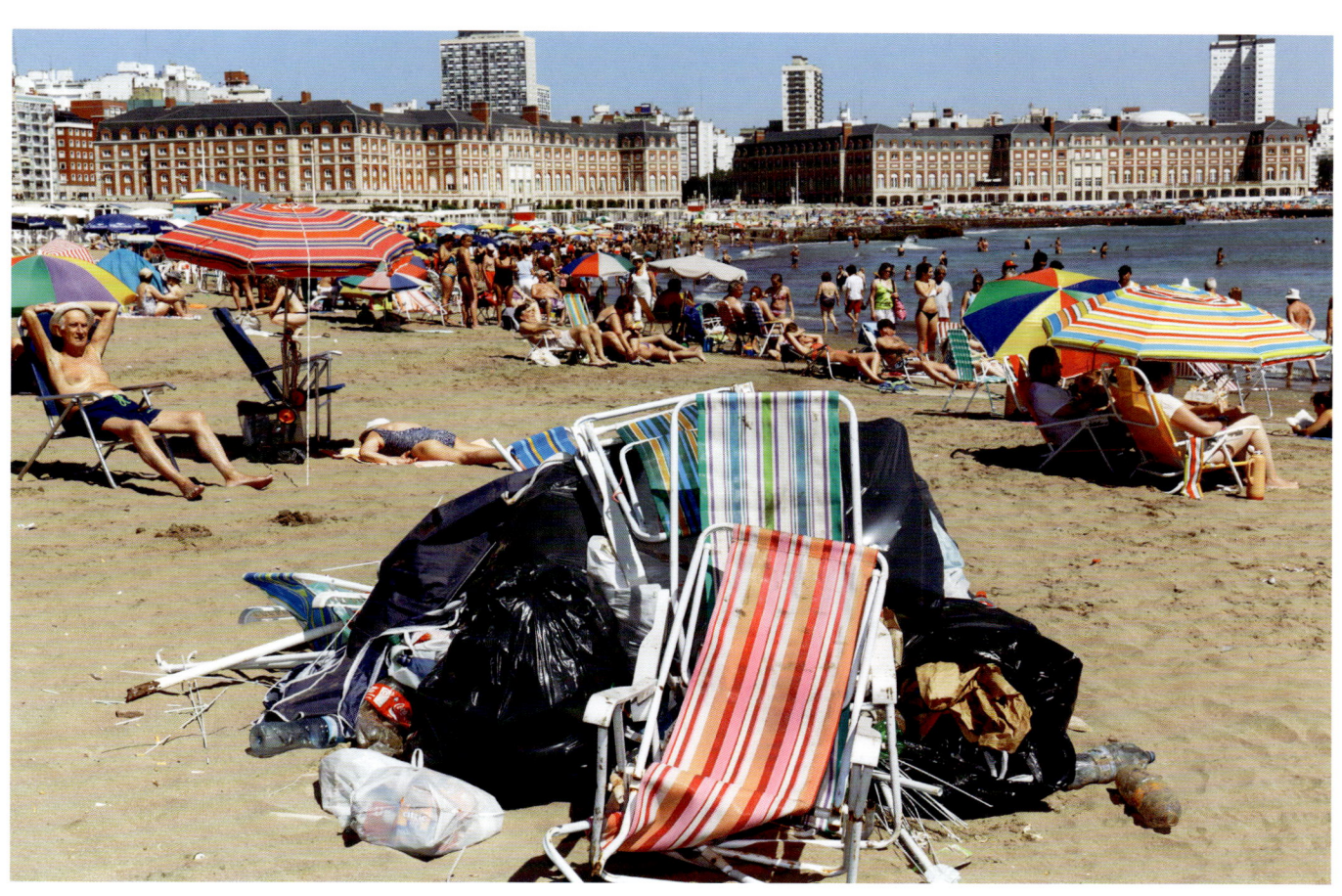

Mar del Plata, Argentina, 2014

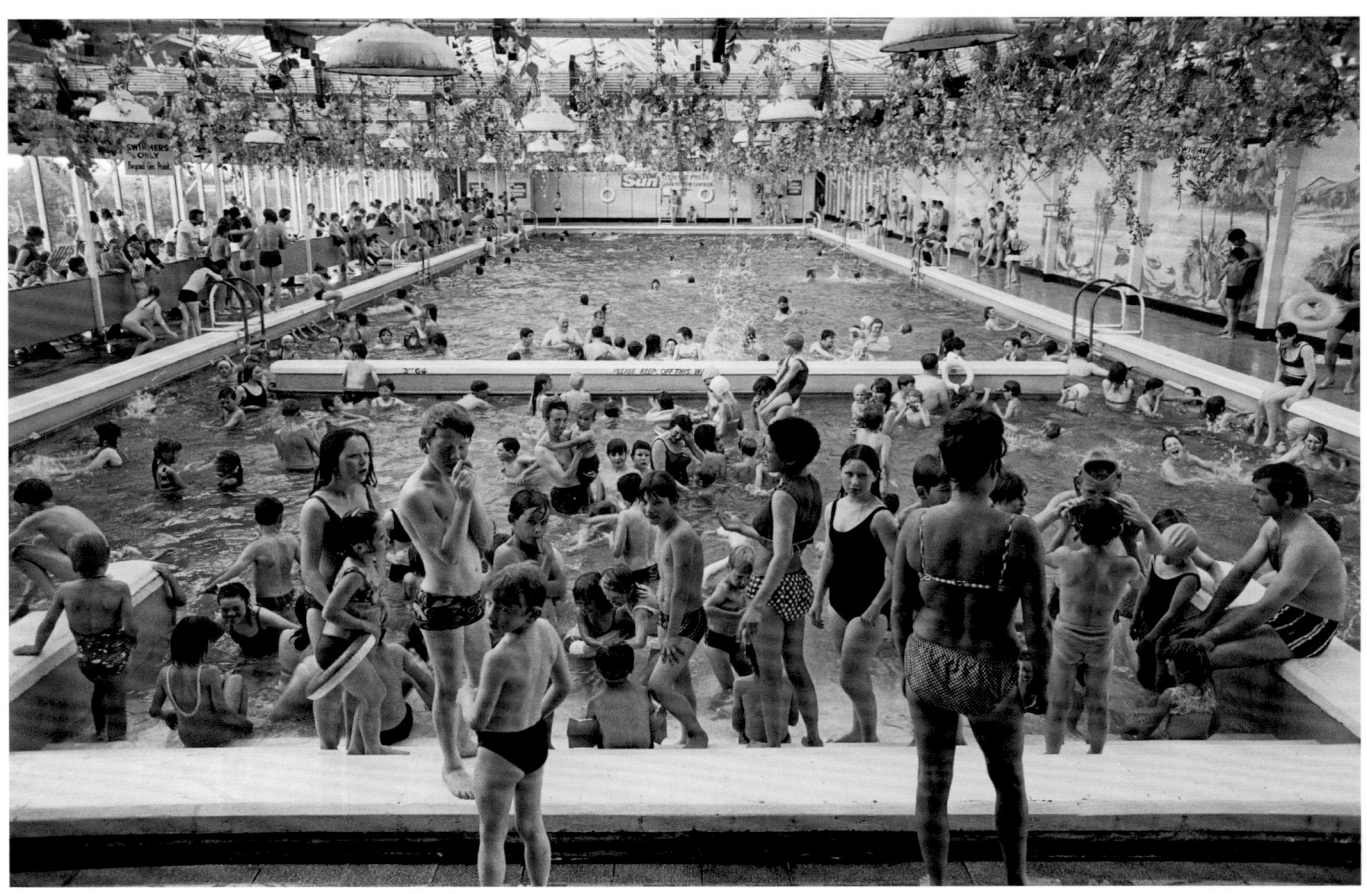

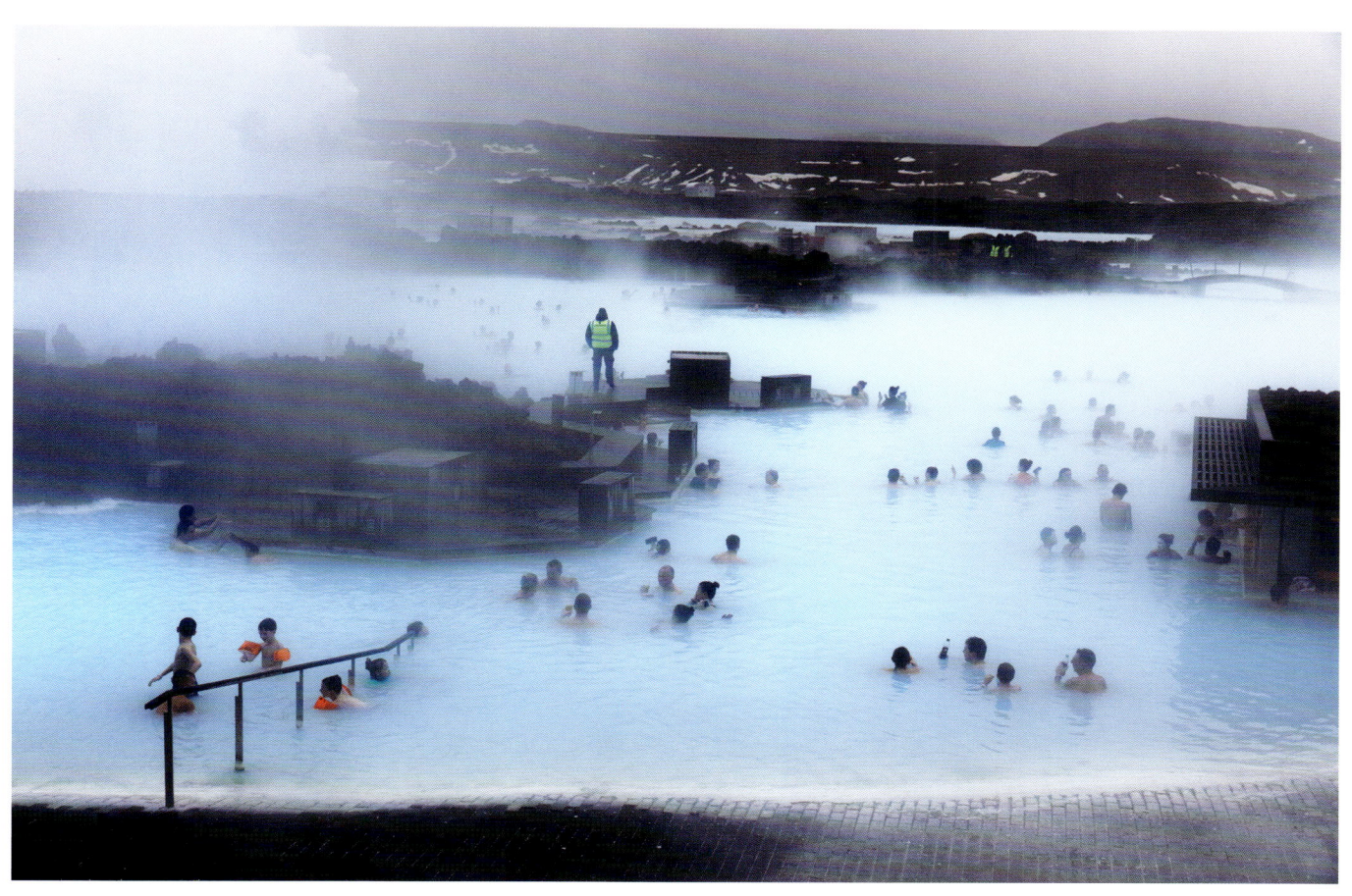

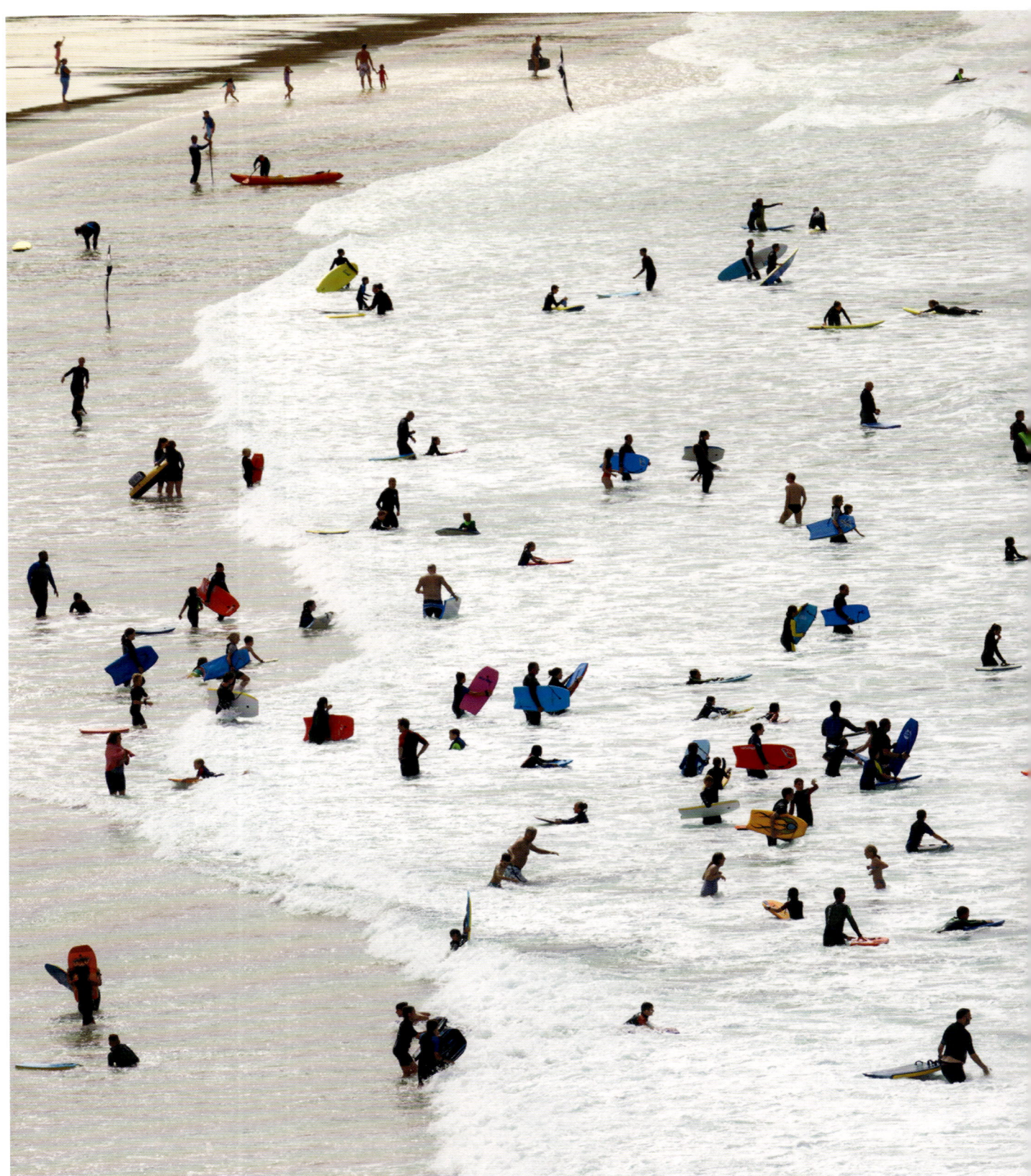

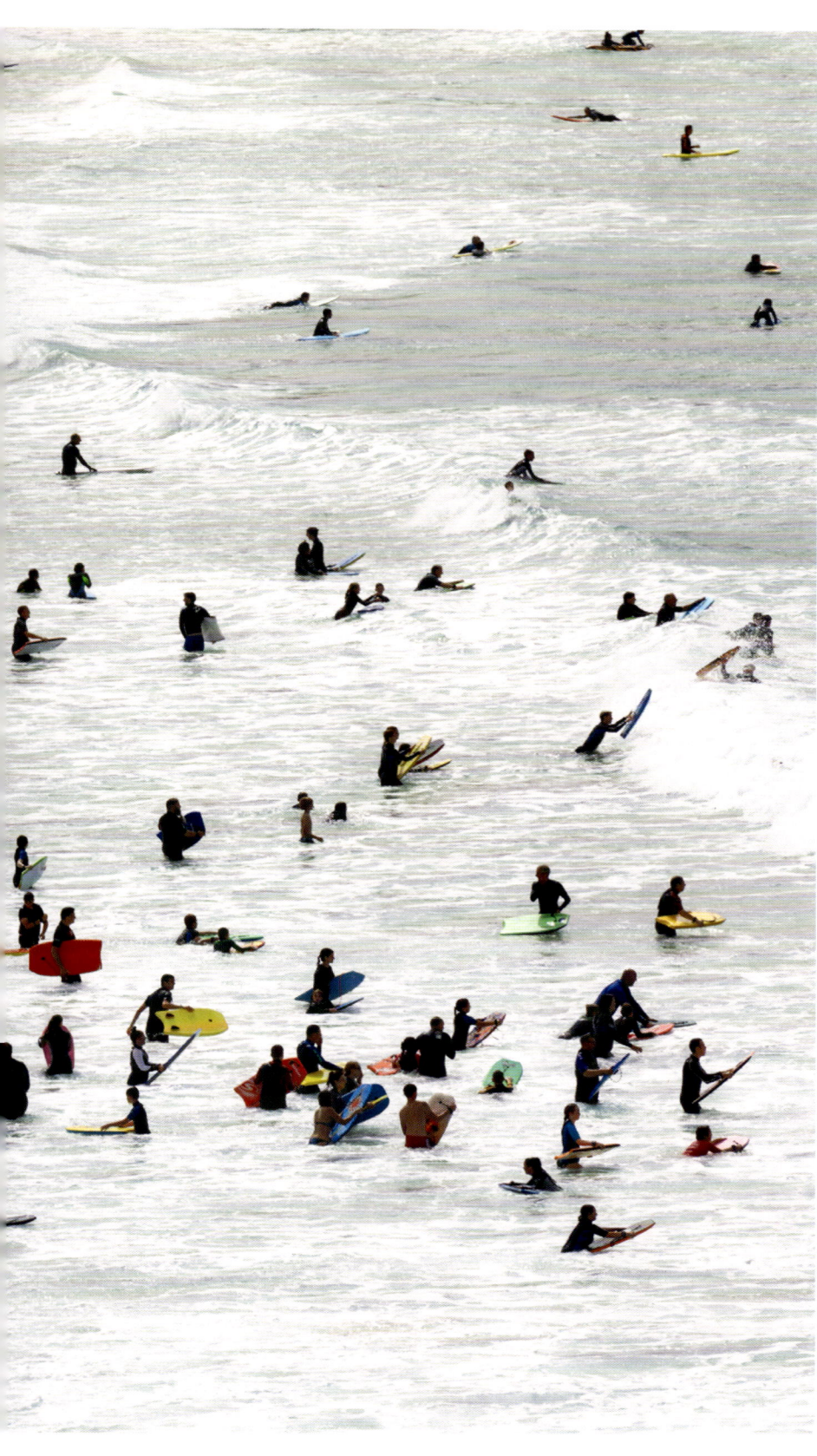

St Ives, England, 2017

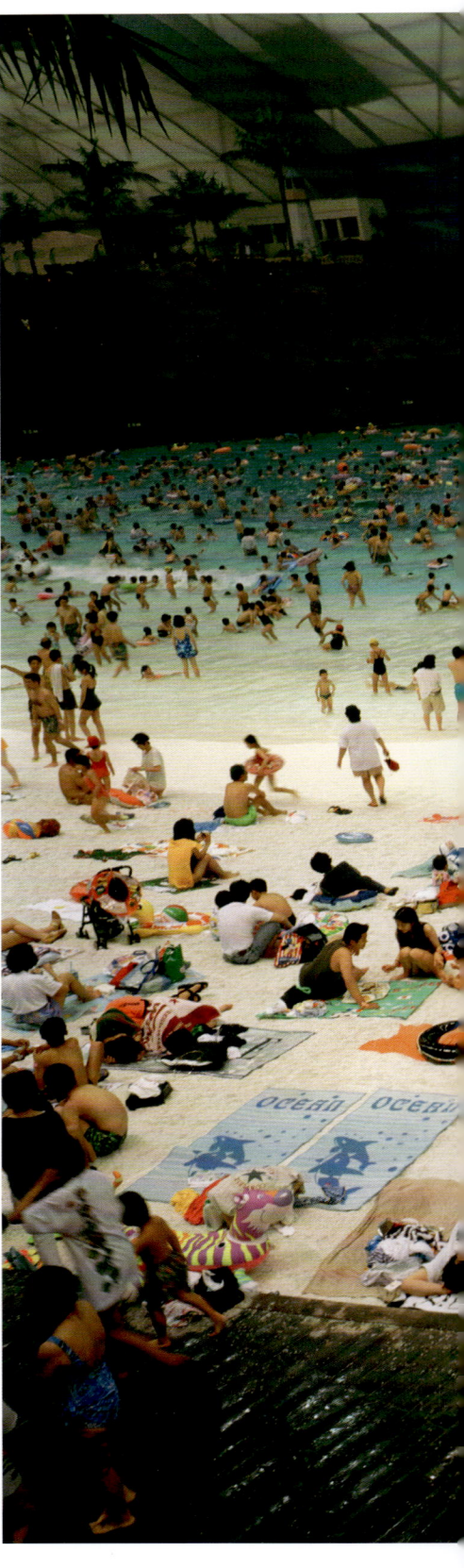

Seagaia Ocean Dome, Miyazaki, Japan, 1996

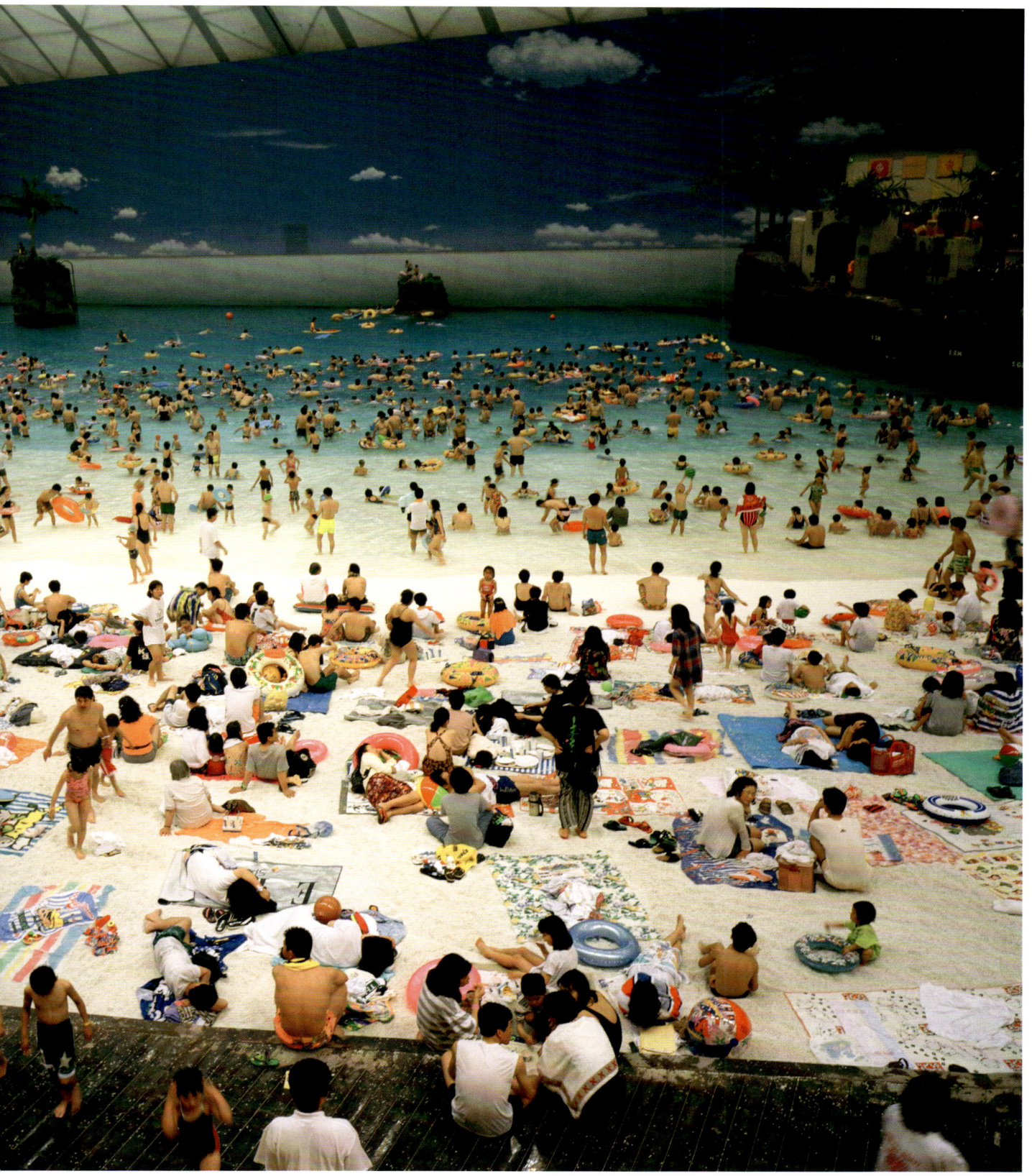

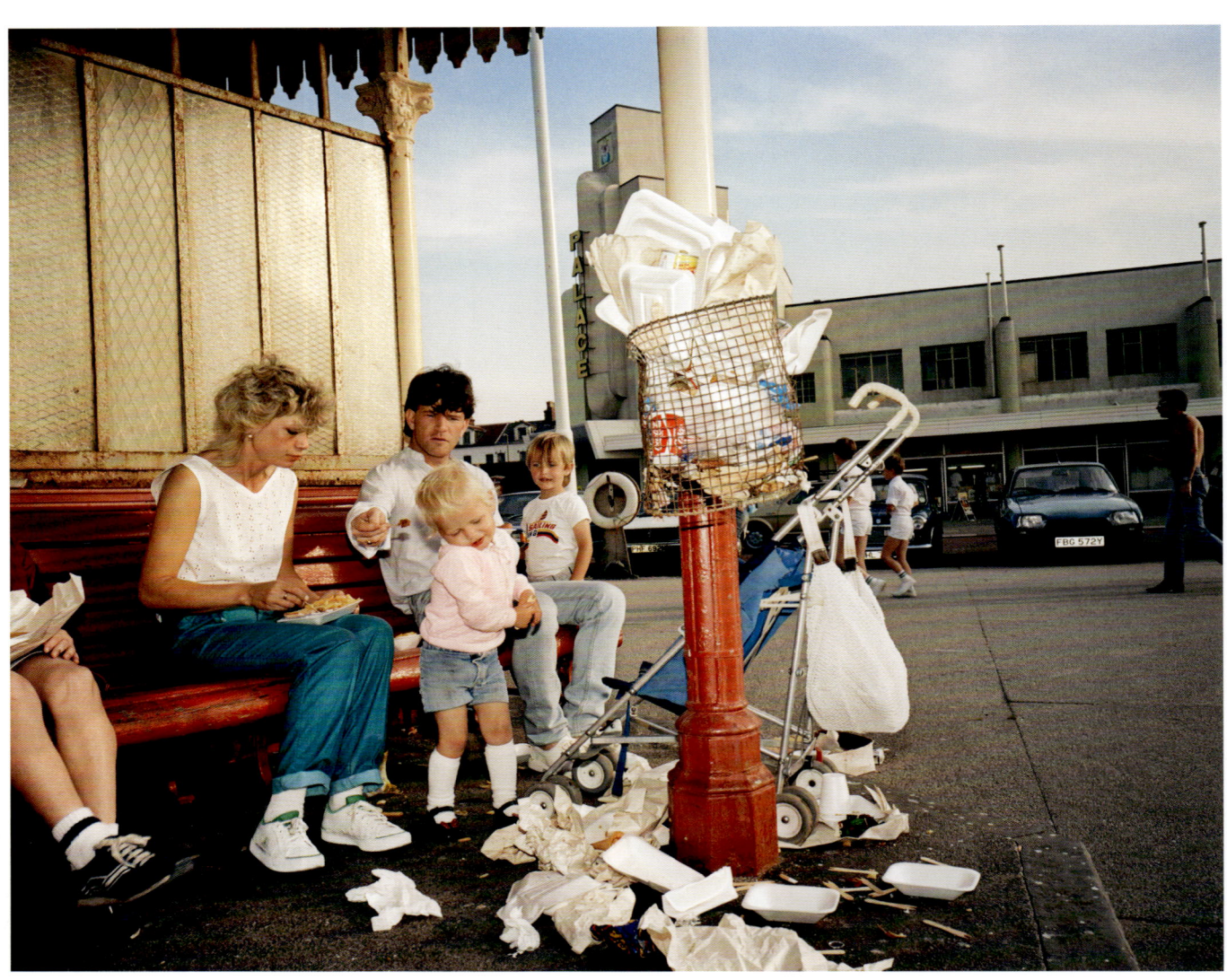

New Brighton, England, 1983–5

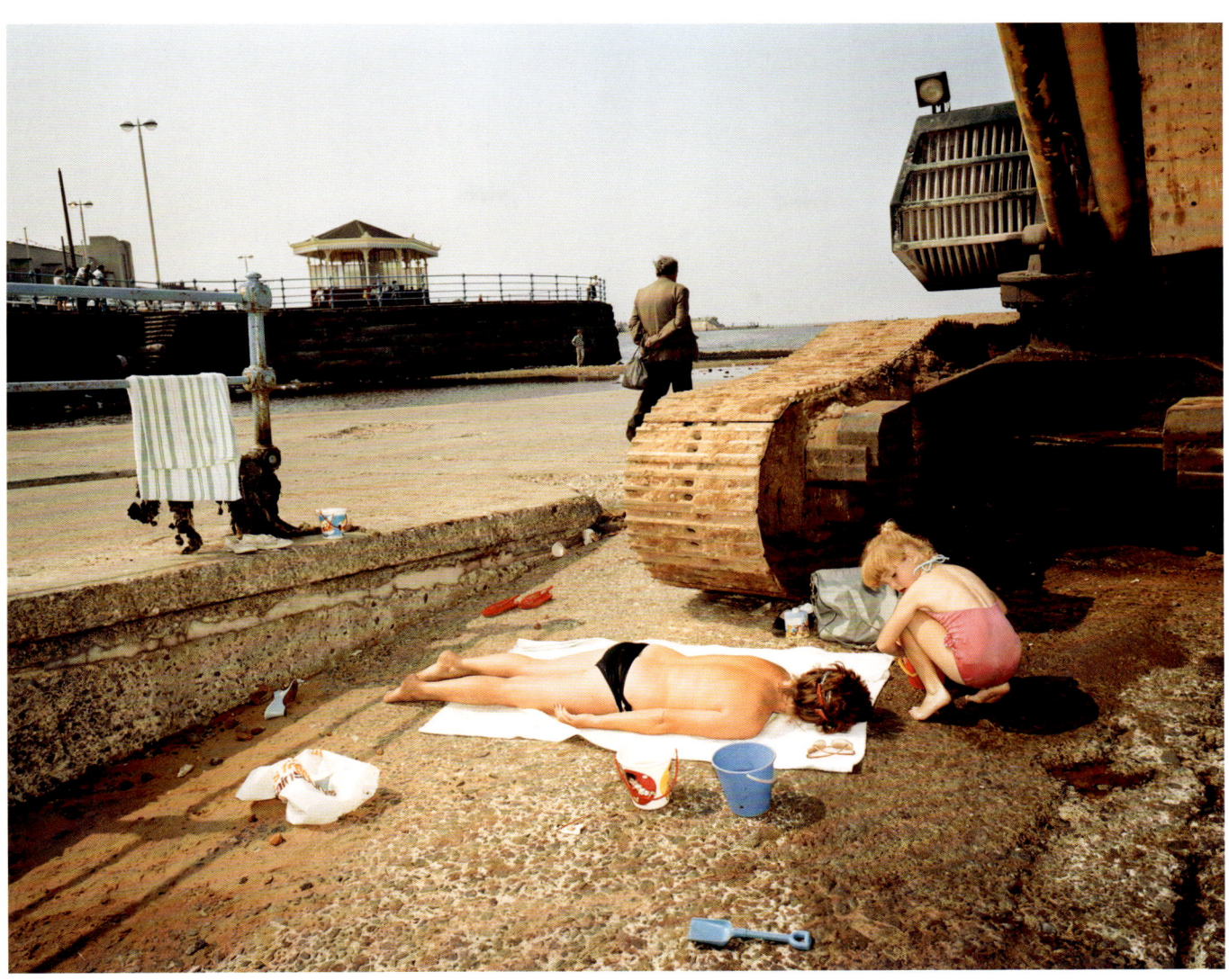

New Brighton, England, 1983–5

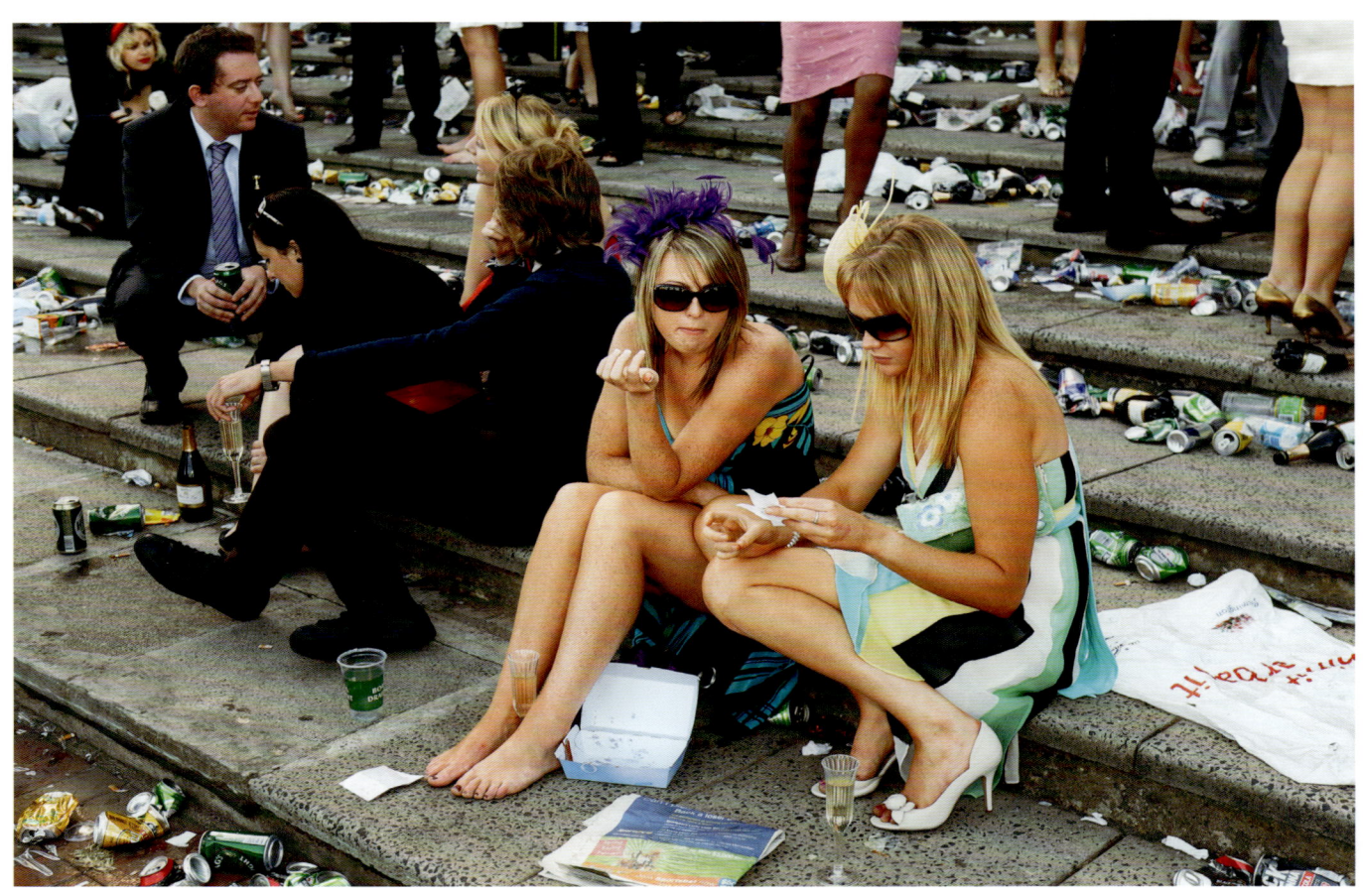

Melbourne, Australia, 2008

MARTIN PARR'S SMALL WORLD AND GLOBETROTTERS

BY

JEAN-FRANÇOIS STASZAK

Martin Parr is the first photographer to pay such close attention to tourism and tourists. Before him, tourists had never been deemed worthy of interest, even by photographers whose work focused on everyday life. This is probably because tourism is thought to lack authenticity, and its democratization since the 1960s is seen as contributing to its vulgarity. Both reasons that capture Parr's attention.

His preoccupation with the subject began as early as 1975, photographing tourists in black and white at famous attractions around the United Kingdom, including Snowdon, Stonehenge, and Lands End, for a project titled Beauty Spots. Parr's first publication of note (*The Last Resort*, 1986) explored the beaches of New Brighton,[1] documenting the seaside practices of England's working class (see pp.46, 47, 96–7, 172–3). Parr was interested not so much in the beach as in what was happening there: a public space in the midst of a major transformation (the country was in crisis and tourists were travelling further afield), where society was on display, if not laid bare. Parr's controversial methods landed him accusations of voyeurism and of spreading an unflattering view of the working class. And it is true that rather than seeking to embellish reality, his documentary manner offers a banal and unbecoming view of everyday life – one we are not used to seeing, and which Parr continues to reveal in what he describes as an ethnographical approach.

Small World, published in 1995, contains some of his best-known pictures. The title evokes the shift of tourist activity to a planetary scale, as well as the global homogenization that makes each place resemble the next, in part due to tourists.

The internationally successful book has been re-published several times with additional photographs; for Parr, too, the planet has become a small world, one that he travels extensively and where his work is celebrated.

Tourists, Their Gaze, Their Photos

Small World seeks out tourists far from the beaches of Great Britain, wherever they are found in France, Spain, Italy, Switzerland, Greece, USA, Mexico, Peru and Thailand. We recognize the Leaning Tower of Pisa (see pp.56–7), the Grand Canyon (see p.58), Versailles (see p.69), Sagrada Família (see p.71), the Parthenon (see p.72), the Pyramids (see p.74), the Matterhorn (see p.76), the Mona Lisa (see p.84) and Notre-Dame de Paris (see p.85). But, relegated to the background, out of focus, out of the frame, or obscured by the tourist horde, these major attractions are not the subject of Parr's photographs.

His subjects most often appear in the foreground, brightly coloured and well lit: the tourists themselves. And it is rare to find them in the spotlight. Tourists do not take pictures of other tourists. When they photograph a monument, they do everything they can to choose the right moment and angle to exclude other visitors. Parr focuses on tourists in their similarity, ordinariness and everydayness to the detriment of the unique, spectacular and extraordinary attractions; he reverses the conventions and values of the tourist photo, and even of tourism itself.

That being said, Martin Parr's photos are not portraits of tourists. Often their faces aren't visible or their backs are turned. The people in the pictures are not valued for their individuality, but for the class or activity they represent. Who they are matters less than what they are doing. Parr photographs tourists going about the business of being tourists. On the beach, they swim and sunbathe (see p.29); in the mountains, they ski or hike (see pp.77–9). But what occupies tourists most – perhaps what defines them – is what they look at. Tourists' consumption of sites is above all visual, concerned with what there is 'to see'. Tourism is a matter of performance, staging, decor, landscape, viewpoint, panorama and the picturesque.

How to portray someone who is looking at something? If we show their eyes, we don't see what they are looking at, and vice versa. Parr does not attempt to solve or circumvent the issue: he emphasizes it and makes it the motive of many of his shots, which show tourists taking pictures of, or pointing their fingers at, something we do not see (see p.85). Conversely, the tourists Parr photographs from behind invite us to turn our gaze in the same direction as theirs, while their own gaze and its meaning remain hidden (see p.61). When his book on selfies was published (*Death by Selfie*, 2019), Parr discussed how the practice was a boon for him because it meant he could photograph both the tourist at work – head-on, with smartphone or selfie stick in hand – and, in the background, the monument or site that was the attraction (see pp.203, 209, 210). But actually, and beginning back in 1996, Martin Parr managed to show both the subject and the object of the gaze, by photographing tourists posing in front of sites for other tourists. Nevertheless, Parr does not photograph the visual face-to-face between the subject and the object of the gaze that is the essence of tourism as an activity – and in this way he questions it.

Notably, Parr shows how the camera diverts the tourist from the attraction. He says it himself: the reason he shoots so many photos of tourists taking pictures is that he has no other choice. Digital cameras and smartphones are everywhere; they've become extensions of tourists' bodies (see p.84). The connection between tourism and photography is both old and fundamental.[2] Photos showcase sites and make them familiar and attractive, they format the tourists' gaze and expectations, and provide a visual record of the trip. Photos are what tourists do. Even when they are not holding a camera. Their quest for the picturesque is photographic. The literal and original definition of picturesque is that which is worthy of being painted – or, today, being photographed. But how can one know if this is the case with any given view? Precisely because it has already been seen in a painting, engraving, or nowadays a postcard or photo. Maybe not this exact view, but one similar to it.

We have a mental repertoire of images that make up the catalogue of the picturesque, and we contribute to this by taking photos of views that resemble those which already exist. Tourism is not about the discovery of new places and pristine landscapes, but rather a return to recognizable sites made familiar through images, places we want to see with our own eyes and photograph for ourselves. This catalogue of imagery contributes to a visual culture that is the driving force of tourism.

The planning and design of tourist sites – to which Martin Parr pays a lot of attention – helps make this clear. Spectacular views are indicated; elevated observation points are made easily accessible; benches are placed before stunning vistas; an artwork is displayed in its own room; perspectives, façades and decors are built. Things are pointed out. Visitors are urged to look at and take pictures of the same views, over and over again. This is how clichés are fabricated, a massive, standardized practice that has only intensified in the age of Instagrammability.

A Criticism of Tourism?

The tourists in Parr's photos seem less than thrilled. They rarely display any positive emotion. They look exhausted, stand in queues, are enclosed behind gates. They shelter as best they can from the rain (see pp.86–7). There are so many of them packed together that actually visiting and enjoying the attractions seems compromised (see pp.80–81). They are anxious: hounded by vendors or pestered by children (see pp.64–5). Their interactions with locals are skewed by issues of power. This lack of authenticity also extends to the attractions that draw them: not the actual Empire State Building, Sacré-Coeur Basilica, Eiffel Tower, Arc de Triomphe or the Great Sphinx of Giza, but replicas of these iconic monuments in theme parks or Las Vegas (see pp.59–63).

Martin Parr's photographs are worlds away from the imagery we encounter in travel brochures. He does not promote destinations or tourism itself. He neither fuels the catalogue of the touristic imagination, nor criticizes it by questioning its commodification and authenticity. Parr admits there is a certain political element to his approach, though is careful not to specify what it is.[3]

It's a Small World is the name of a famous attraction that offers a virtual tourism experience, created by Disney for the 1964 New York World's Fair, then replicated in five of its parks. Visitors board small boats and, in a matter of minutes, sail around the world visiting practically every country, with scenes and landscapes animated by costumed dolls, all to the catchy refrain of 'it's a small world after all'. A world reduced to exotic and picturesque clichés – which, for some, make the attraction emblematic of the soppiness and imperialism of Disney, whose goal was nevertheless to celebrate the brotherhood of mankind.[4] We talk about 'Disneyfication' to describe the transformation of the world into a tourist-friendly theme park.[5] The term fits into a demonization of Disney that is shared by many European intellectuals such as Umberto Eco and Jean Baudrillard, and a negative view of tourism that is as old as tourism itself, yet undergoing a revival with the development of what we call – not without class contempt – 'mass tourism'.

This is not Martin Parr's vision. Certainly, in several of his interviews and essays, he talks about mass tourism and his concerns about overtourism. He feels that taking pictures of, for instance, the Mona Lisa prevents tourists from seeing it. Anticipating the question, he himself has asked, 'Do I think tourism is a good thing? Of course. It provides a much-needed economic boost to countries that are struggling. It educates and enlightens the tourist.'[6] Parr nevertheless photographs tourists unflinchingly; he does not seek to redeem them or to restore their long-lost dignity or beauty. Parr does not attempt to sugar-coat. He shows tourists as they are; he documents, as he did with the beaches in *The Last Resort*. The controversy surrounding the alleged voyeurism and classicism of his 1986 book has no reason to re-emerge in his 1995 work. Parr staunchly refuses the label of cynic, which is sometimes attributed to him. If we see contempt in his pictures, it stems from our own class prejudices, not his. That doesn't mean that his photos aren't critical – on the contrary. What interest him are the contradictions and flaws in what tourists do.

In Parr's photos, something often arouses our curiosity or seems off: tourists turning their backs to the attraction (see p.68); a postcard display in the site depicted on the postcards themselves (see p.79); a cowboy in Egypt (see p.60); a traffic jam of boats (see pp.82–3); visitors trapped in a cage, flanked by gargoyles (see p.85); tourists lying on the floor as if they'd been massacred (see pp.92–3); fleeting gazes.

The problem often arises from 'Armstrong syndrome',[7] which affects many tourists who, like the famous astronaut, want to be the first to set foot in the places they visit. The presence of other visitors prevents them from enjoying distinction: Parr's photographs show the highly standardized nature of a tourist experience that is intended to be unique. Worse yet, the crowd of tourists affects the site itself. 'Tourism can often destroy the very thing that people came to visit in the first place,' Parr warns.[8] Tourists have come to see somewhere different and typical of the local setting and society: something authentic. Yet this authenticity is compromised by the presence of tourists. On the one hand, they have a direct social and environmental impact on the site they frequent and contribute to transforming. On the other hand, the 'touristification'[9] which aims to make a site more in keeping with visitors' expectations tends to turn it into a stage on which locals perform for tourists. The authenticity comes from the performance.[10] The paradox for tourists is that they want to go where there are no tourists. To put it another way: they turn the places they go into places they don't want to go to.

It would be naive to think tourists do not understand this. The tourist attraction can be prized not for its authenticity but for the quality of the performance. In a theme park, the aim is not to be fooled by the mock attractions on offer, but to appreciate them for what they are. No one confuses the original with the copy. It's not the authenticity of the site that matters but the experience. The monument itself is not the attraction; what counts is what you do with it. The Tower of Pisa is undoubtedly an authentic masterpiece of Romanesque architecture, but the fact that it leans is also a playful appeal to tourists' choreographic and photographic talents.[11] We speak of 'post-tourists'[12] to refer to those who escape the tourist paradox, scoff at the authenticity of sites, and ironically embrace the world as a theme park.

A Tourist Among Tourists
Some of Martin Parr's pictures document these post-tourists in Pisa or Las Vegas. Does travelling the world to see the best-known attractions – only to turn his camera away from them to humorously capture tourists' paradoxical behaviour – make Parr a professional post-tourist?[13]

In 1995, in reference to a futile distinction that has long fed tourismophobia, Parr acknowledged,[14] 'Inevitably, I am a tourist too. We all want to kid ourselves that we are travellers and the others are tourists. But in the end, you are just one more bum on a seat or bed in a hotel. Last summer we went on a family holiday to Turkey. Although I had no intention of working, it ended up being so exciting that I had to take some pictures. One of them has ended up in the book.'[15]

In *Small World*, as in *The Last Resort*, Parr photographs the community he belongs to. In 2012, he admitted, 'If anyone has a shocking carbon footprint it is me. What am I doing at these sites? Doing exactly what I am now questioning: i.e. taking photographs.'[16] In his introduction to *Death by Selfie*, as well as in several interviews, he tells how, in India, where most of the photos in that book were taken, strangers would often ask to get a selfie with him simply because he was European, and he gladly obliged. Not only did Parr assert his place among the tourists he took photos of, but he delighted in the fact they returned the favour. It is within this proximity that the tenderness he lays claim to flourishes[17] – a tenderness that gives his work its strength and worth.

Martin Parr's interaction with tourists also takes place on an aesthetic register – that of kitsch. The word is often used more or less good-naturedly to describe the style of his photos which, with their irony and bright, saturated colours, pay little mind to the conventions of 'art photography'. The kitschiness extends to his subject matter: the working classes with their culture and habits. Parr's interest in these things is clear from his impressive collection of postcards and tourist souvenirs – items that are kitsch *par excellence* and that occasionally appear in his pictures. 'Kitsch' is often also used rather condescendingly to describe the world of tourism, especially the mainstream variety characterized by artificiality, consumerism, stereotypes, ease, the spectacular... or even poor taste, which are seen to run rampant in Las Vegas or Disneyland.[18] This lack of taste is something that Parr shares and is drawn to. In 2024, he told *Vogue*, 'Calling me kitsch is a great compliment',[19] positioning himself firmly in the camp of the tourists he loves and enjoys photographing. Parr's pictures prompt us to reflect critically not only on tourism, but on photography itself, as well as on what distinguishes an art photo from a vulgar tourist snapshot.

Tourism fascinates Martin Parr as an ordinary activity of ordinary people. Its spectacular international development since the 1970s is symptomatic of the way societies have converged into what now forms a 'small world'. As a keen observer of tourist behaviour, Parr documents – with no moral judgement – the incoherencies that are less those of travellers than of the concept of tourism itself, at least when it aims for an authentic experience of sites. Many of Parr's photos show tourists pursuing this dream; the absurdity of their situation may be amusing, but there is also something pathetic about their inevitable failure. Ultimately, those who enjoy the most successful or even the most authentic experience are post-tourists who, like Parr, adapt to – or even embrace – the artificiality of these situations. Kitsch is not the problem, it is the answer.

1   Cf. Silvia Pireddu, 'Ad Limine: Martin Parr's Humans on the Beach. Re-empowering the English Seaside Resorts as Pop Culture', Imaginaires, no. 24, 2022, pp.110–30; Cammie Tipton-Amini, 'Martin Parr and the Legacy of British Colonial Photography', Third Text, vol. 37, no. 3, May 2023, pp.309–28.

2   Cf. John Urry and Jonas Larsen, The Tourist Gaze 3.0, Los Angeles, Sage, 2011.

3   Cf. Lee Shulman, I Am Martin Parr, documentary, United Kingdom, 2025, 52 min.

4   Cf. Laudan Nooshin, 'Circumnavigation with a Difference? Music, Representation and the Disney Experience: "It's a Small, Small World"', Ethnomusicology Forum, vol. 13, no. 2, November 2004, pp.236–51; Katherine Baber and James Vernon Spickard, 'Crafting Culture: "Tradition", Art, and Music in Disney's "It's A Small World"', The Journal of Popular Culture, vol. 48, no. 2, 2015.

5   Sylvie Brunel, La Planète disneylandisée. Chroniques d'un tour du monde, Auxerre, Éditions Sciences humaines, 2006.

6   Martin Parr, 'Too Much Photography', April 2012 (online: www.martinparr. com/2012/too-much-photography/).

7   Jean-Didier Urbain, L'idiot du voyage. Histoires de touristes, Paris, Payot & Rivages, 2002.

8   Martin Parr, 'Global Tourism', no date, (online: www.magnumphotos.com/arts-culture/travel/global-tourism-martin-parr/).

9   See the work of geographer Rémy Knafou and his team at MIT (Mobilités, Itinéraires, Tourismes) beginning in the late 1990s.

10 Dean MacCannell, The Tourist: A New Theory of the Leisure Class, New York, Schocken Books, 1976.

11 Jean-François Staszak, 'La tour de Pise et le smartphone du post-touriste', Via. Tourism Review, no 10, 2016 (online: www.journals.openedition.org/viatourism/1516).

12 Erik Cohen, 'Alternative Tourism – A Critique', Tourism Recreation Research, 1987, vol. 12, no 2, p. 13-18.

13 Theopisti Stylianou-Lambert and Elena Stylianou, 'Martin Parr: A Traveller-Critic and a Professional Post-Tourist in a Small World', in Tijana Rakić and Jo-Anne Lester (dir.), Travel, Tourism and Art, London and New York, Routledge, 2013, p. 161-173.

14 Cf. Jean-Christophe Gay, Tourismophobie. Du 'tourisme de masse' au 'surtourisme', ISTE, 2024.

15 Cited in Peter Hamilton, 'All-Out World: The Photographs of Martin Parr', Art on Paper, vol. 5, no. 3, January-February 2001, p. 44-51.

16 Martin Parr, 'Too Much Photography',

17 Paola Genone, 'Martin Parr: "Prendre la bonne photo, c'est comme partir à la pêche, la plupart du temps, on rentre les mains vides"', Madame Figaro, 9 February 2025 (online: www.madame.lefigaro.fr/celebrites/culture/martin-parr-j-adore-le-mauvais-gout-20250209).

18 Valérie Arrault, L'Empire du kitsch, Paris, Éditions Klincksieck, 2010.

19 Lolita Mang, interview with Martin Parr: 'Dire de moi que je suis kitsch, c'est le plus beau des compliments', Vogue France, 26 March 2024 (online: www.vogue.fr/article/martin-parr-livre-fashion-faux-interview).

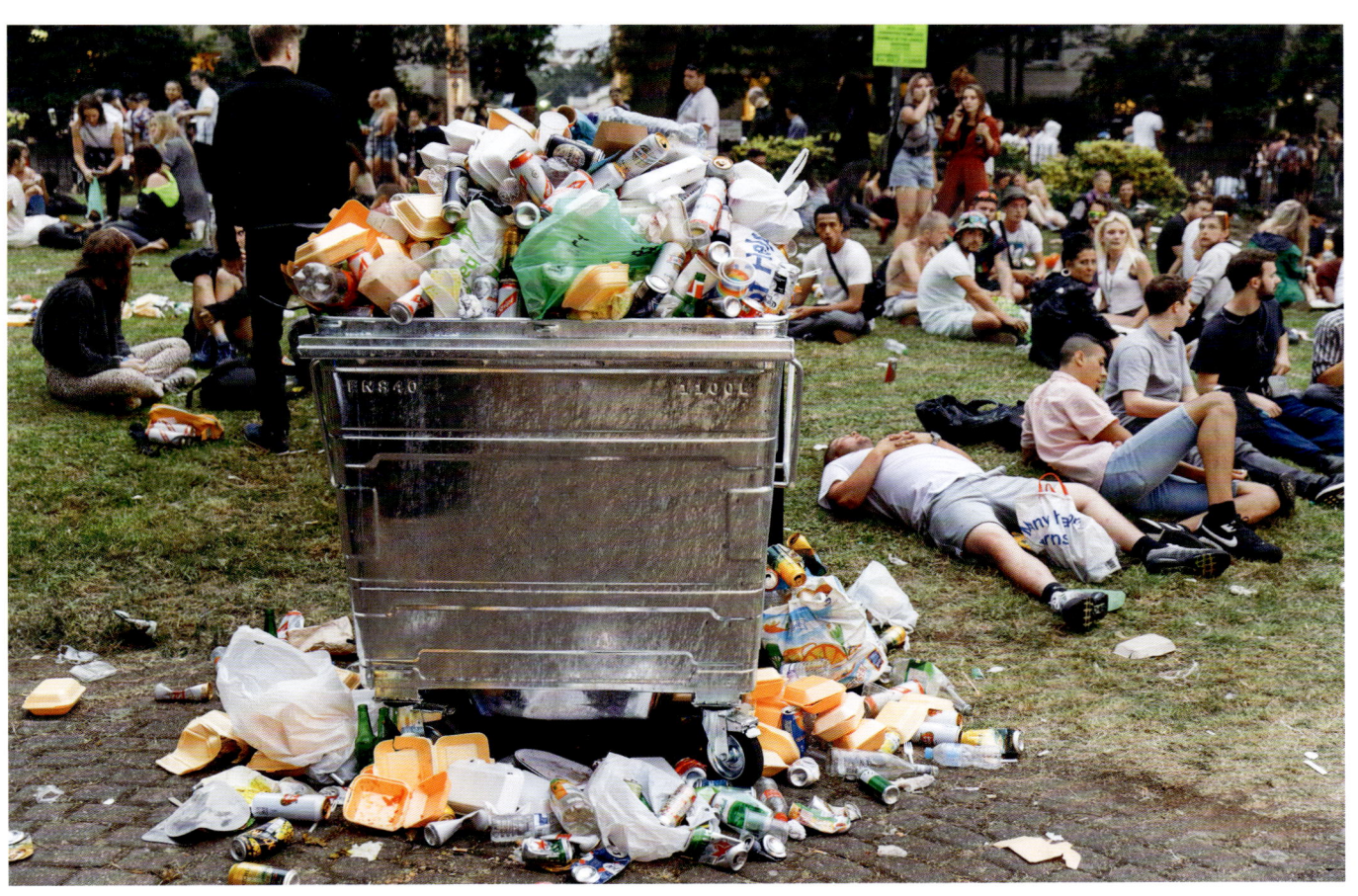

Bristol, England, 2019

SMALL WORLD

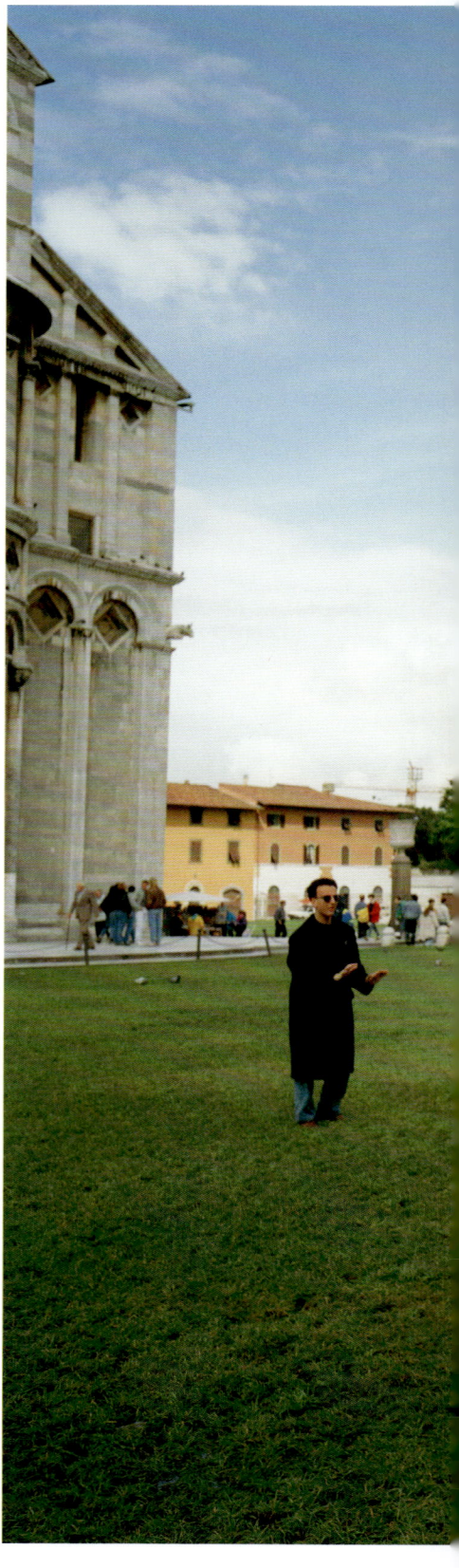

Leaning Tower of Pisa, Italy, 1990

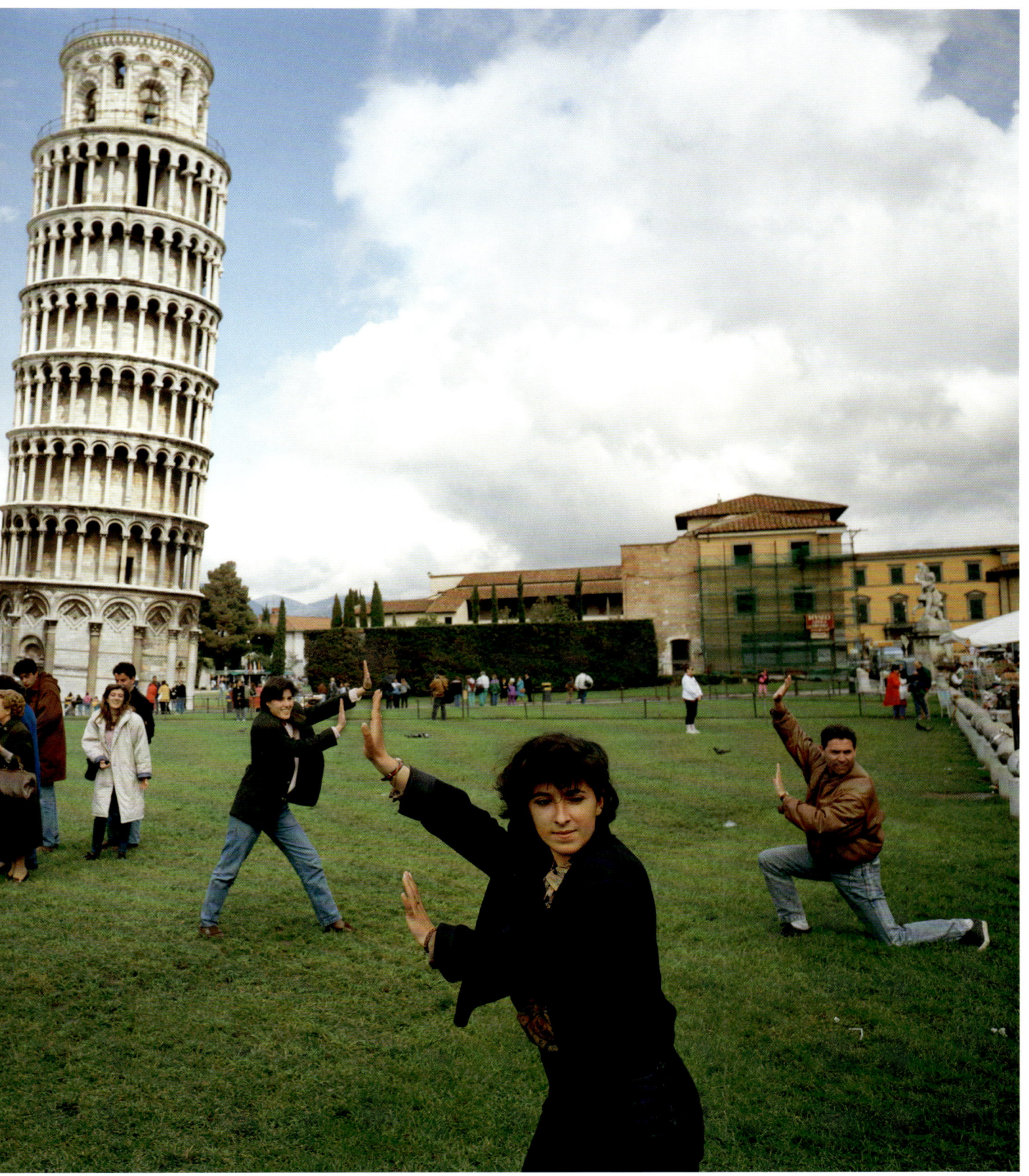

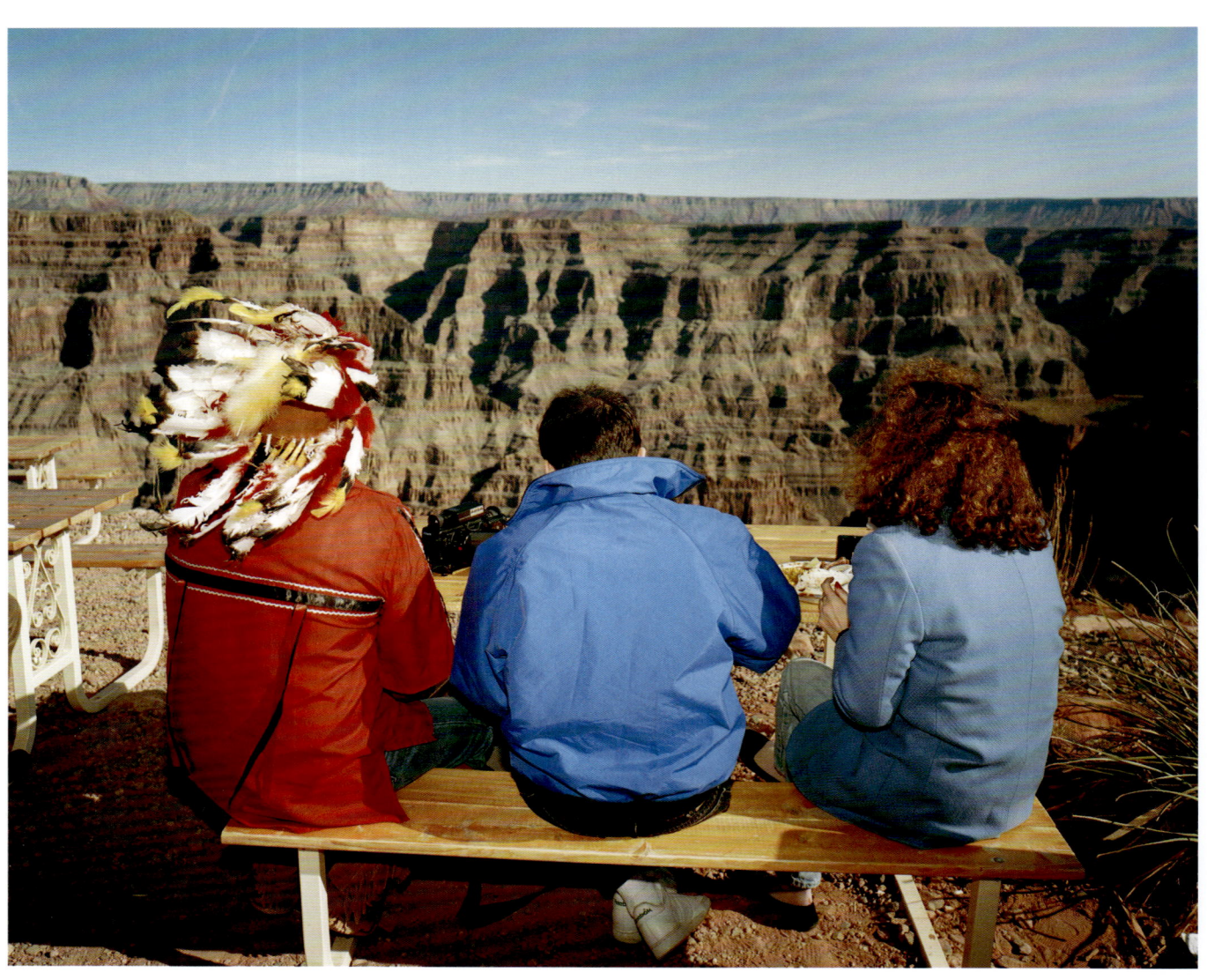

Grand Canyon, Arizona, USA, 1994

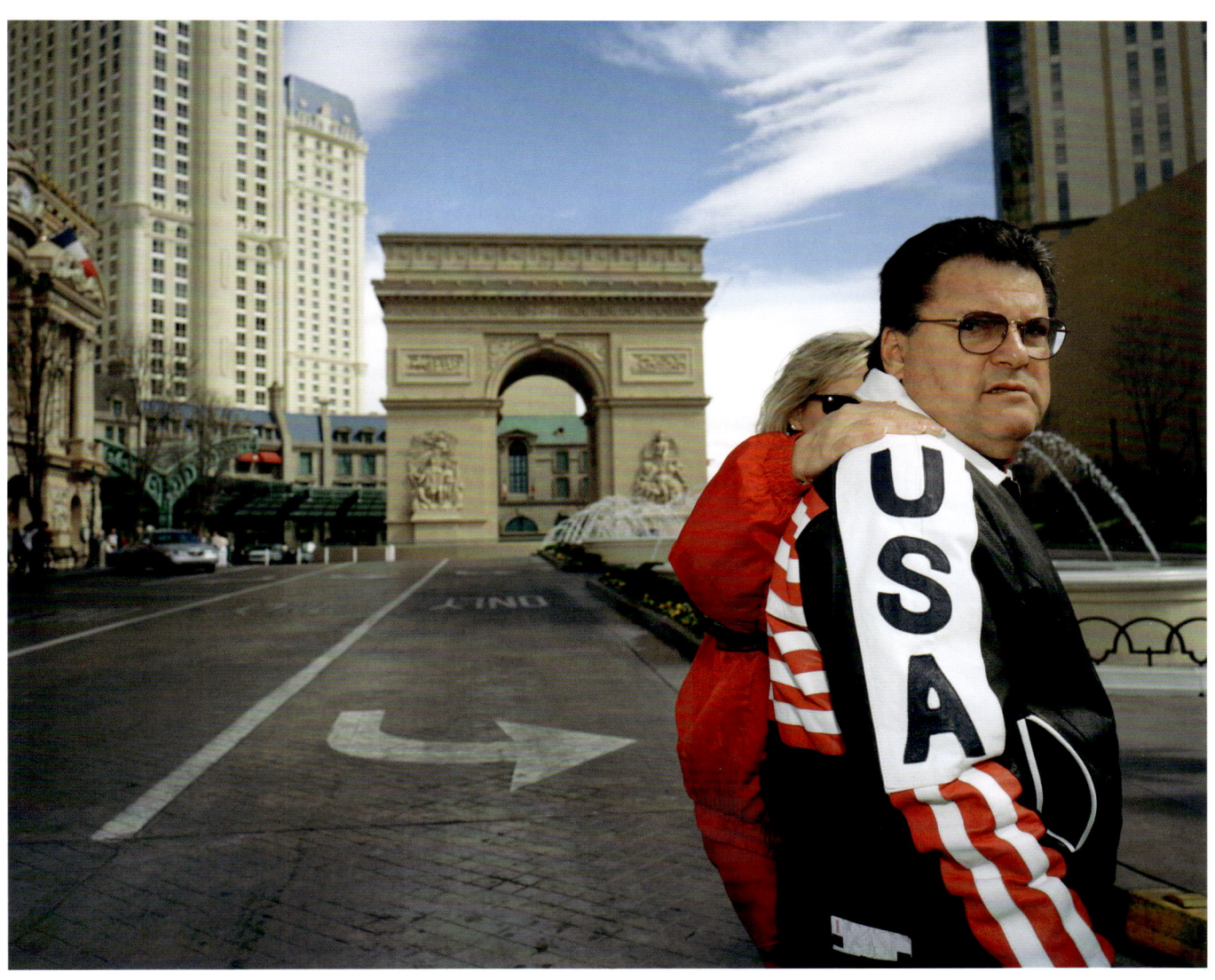

Las Vegas, Nevada, USA, 2000

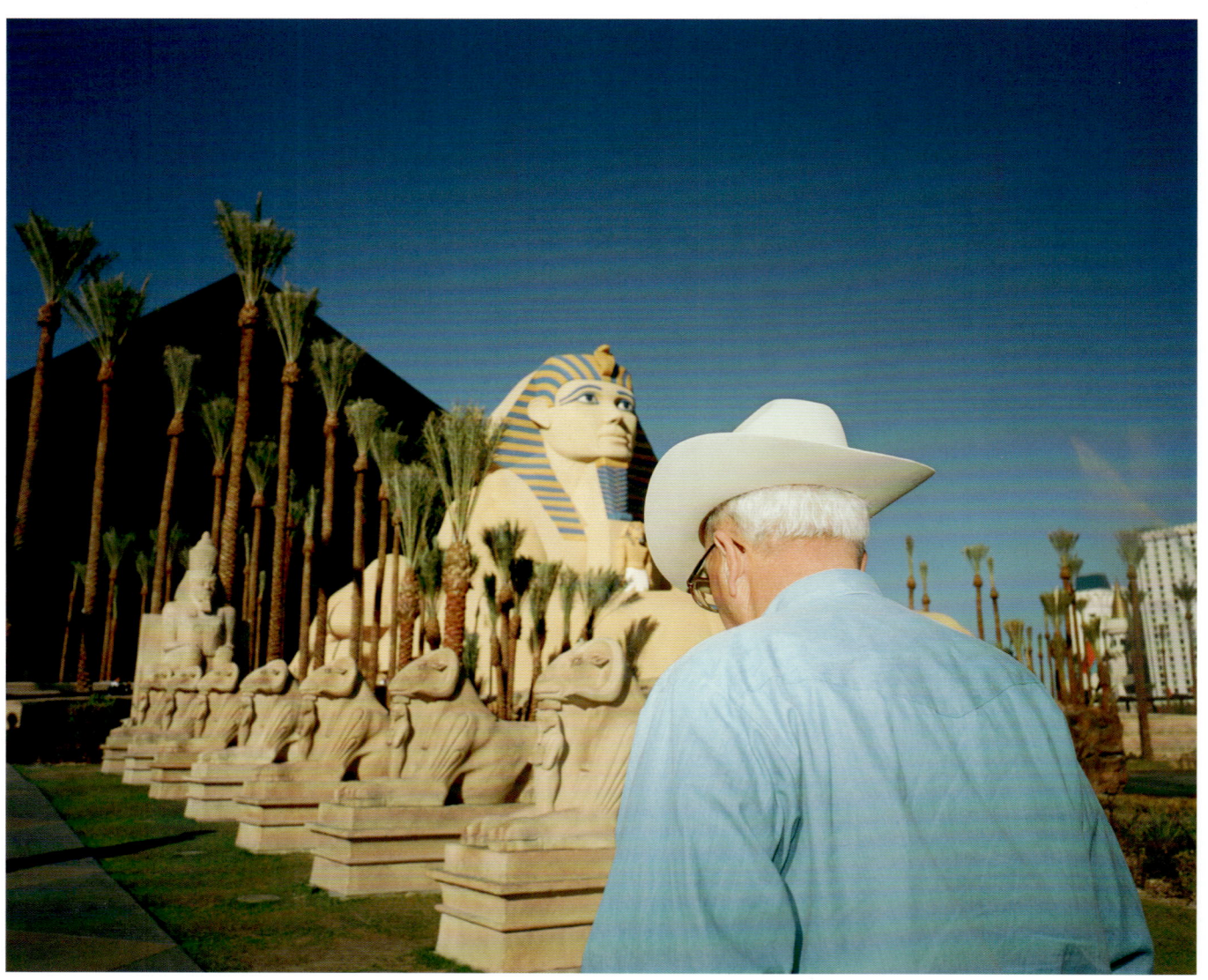

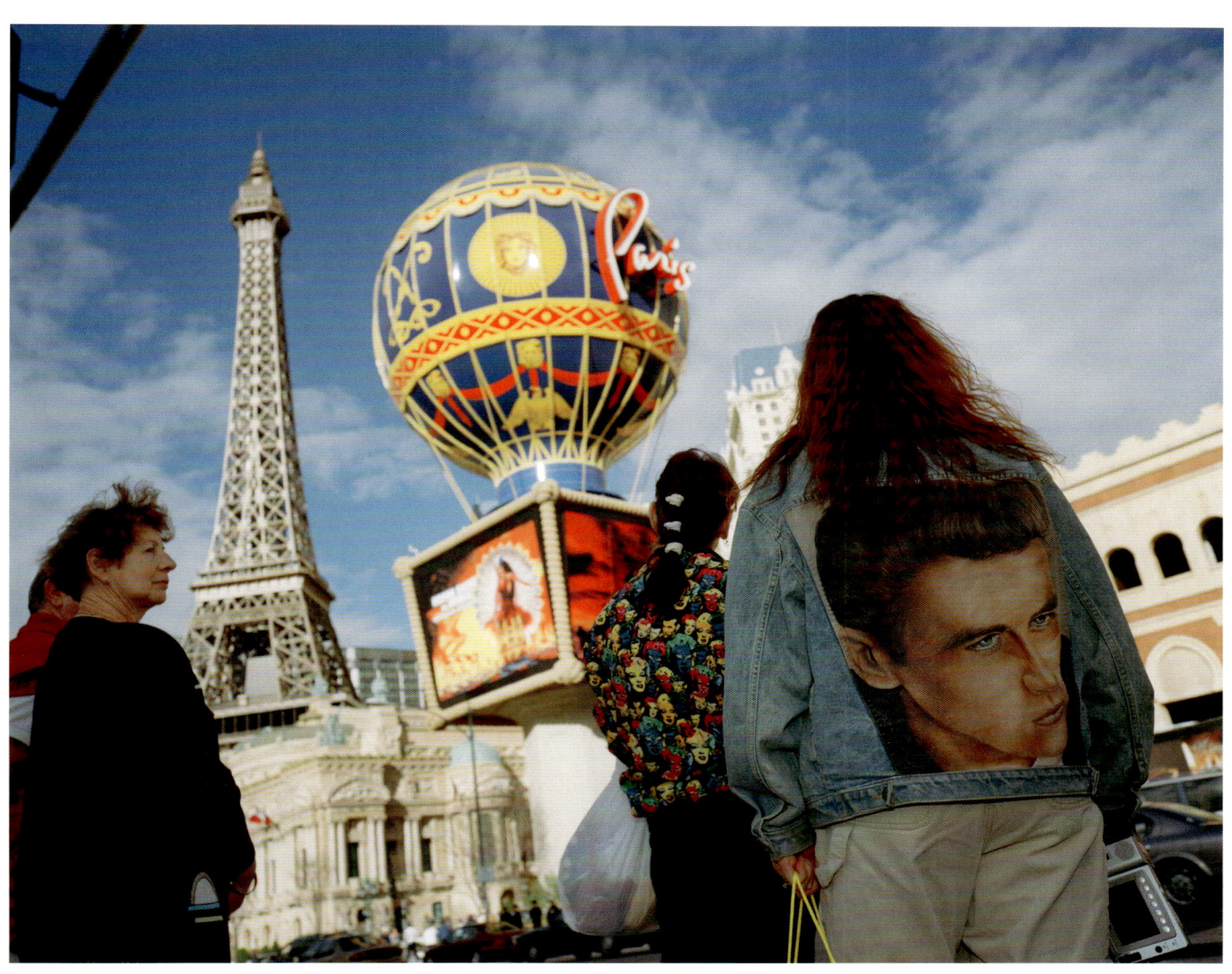

Opposite:
Las Vegas, Nevada, USA, 1994   Las Vegas, Nevada, USA, 2000

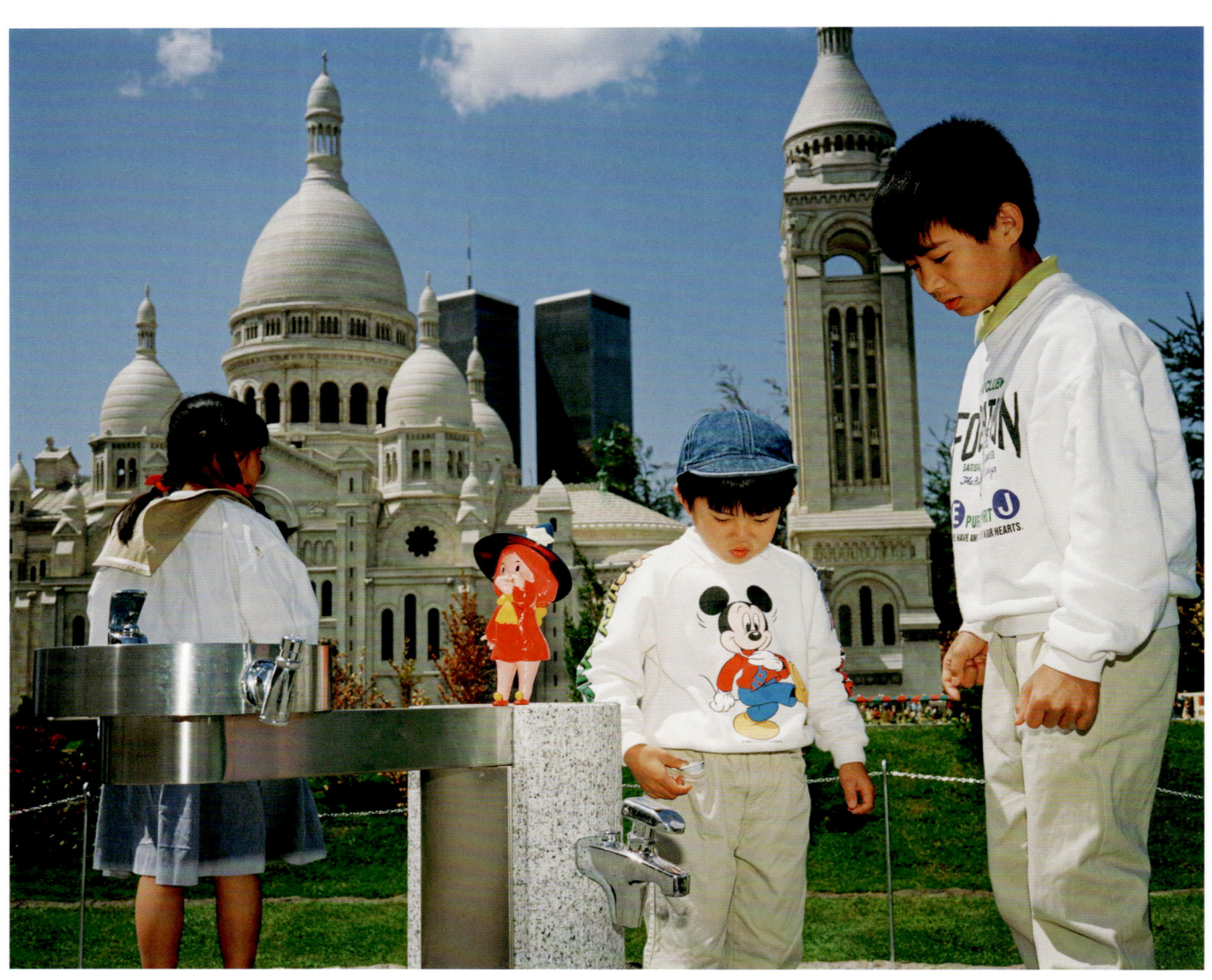

Tobu World Square, Nikkō, Japan, 1993

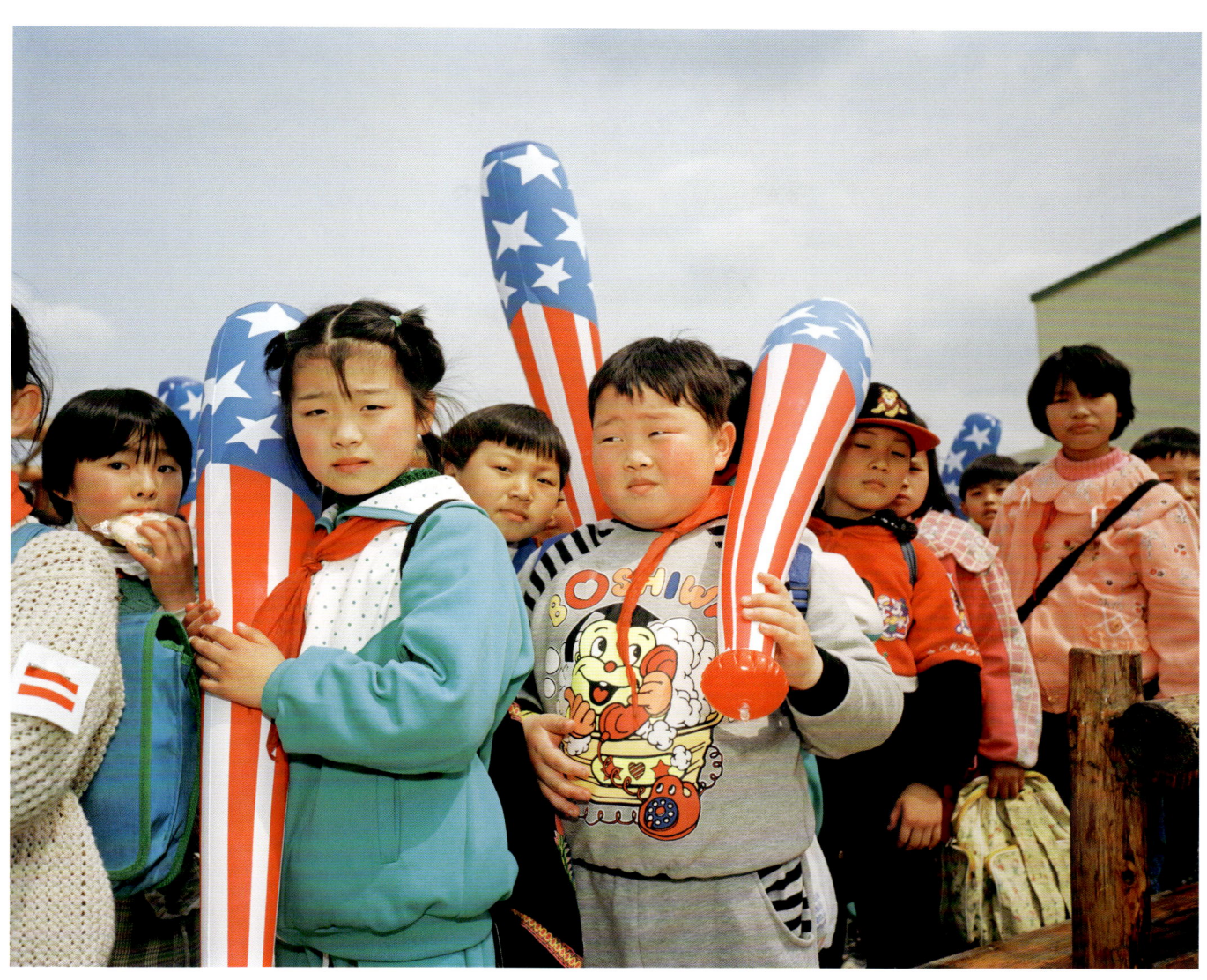

American Dream Park, Shanghai, China, 1997

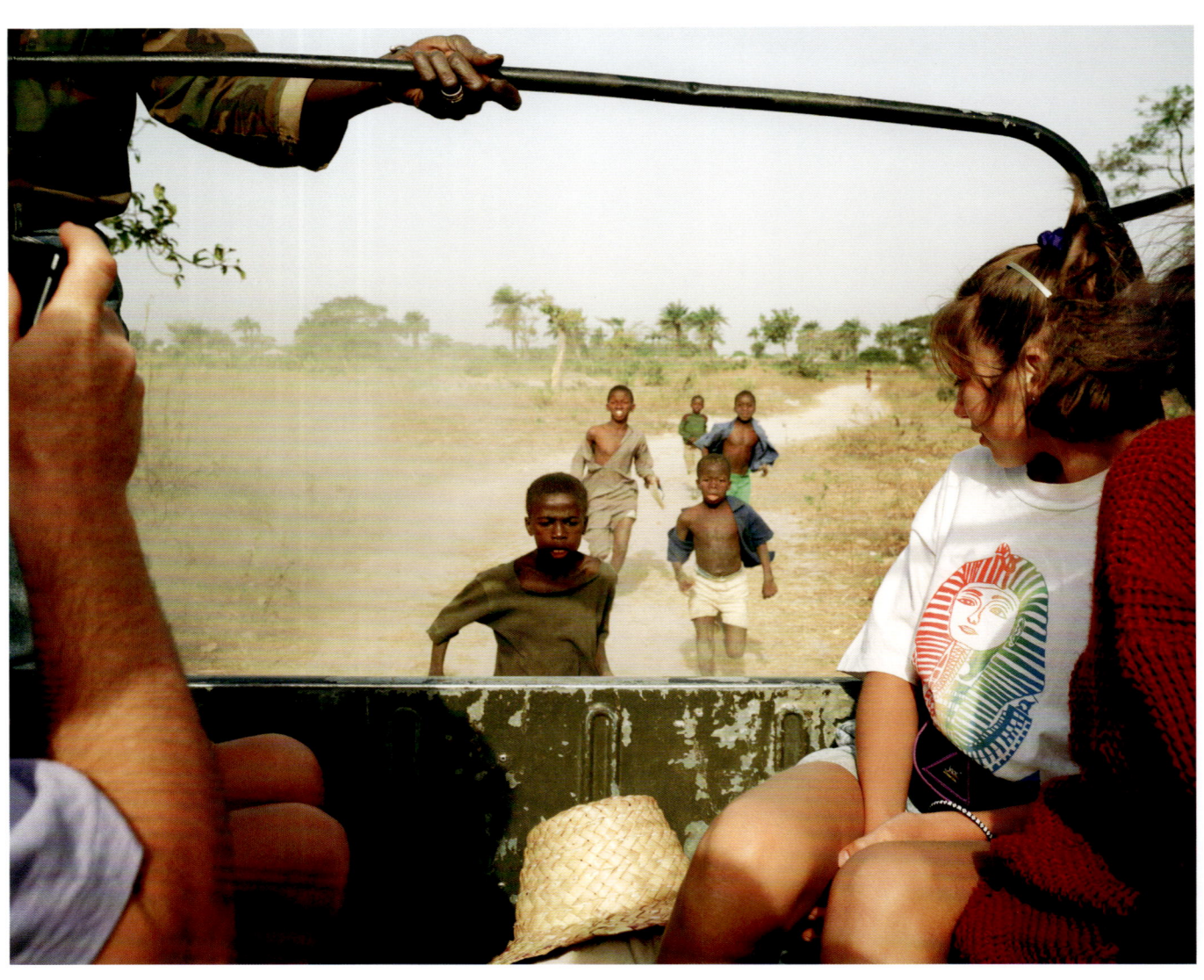

Above and opposite:
Jufureh, The Gambia, 1991

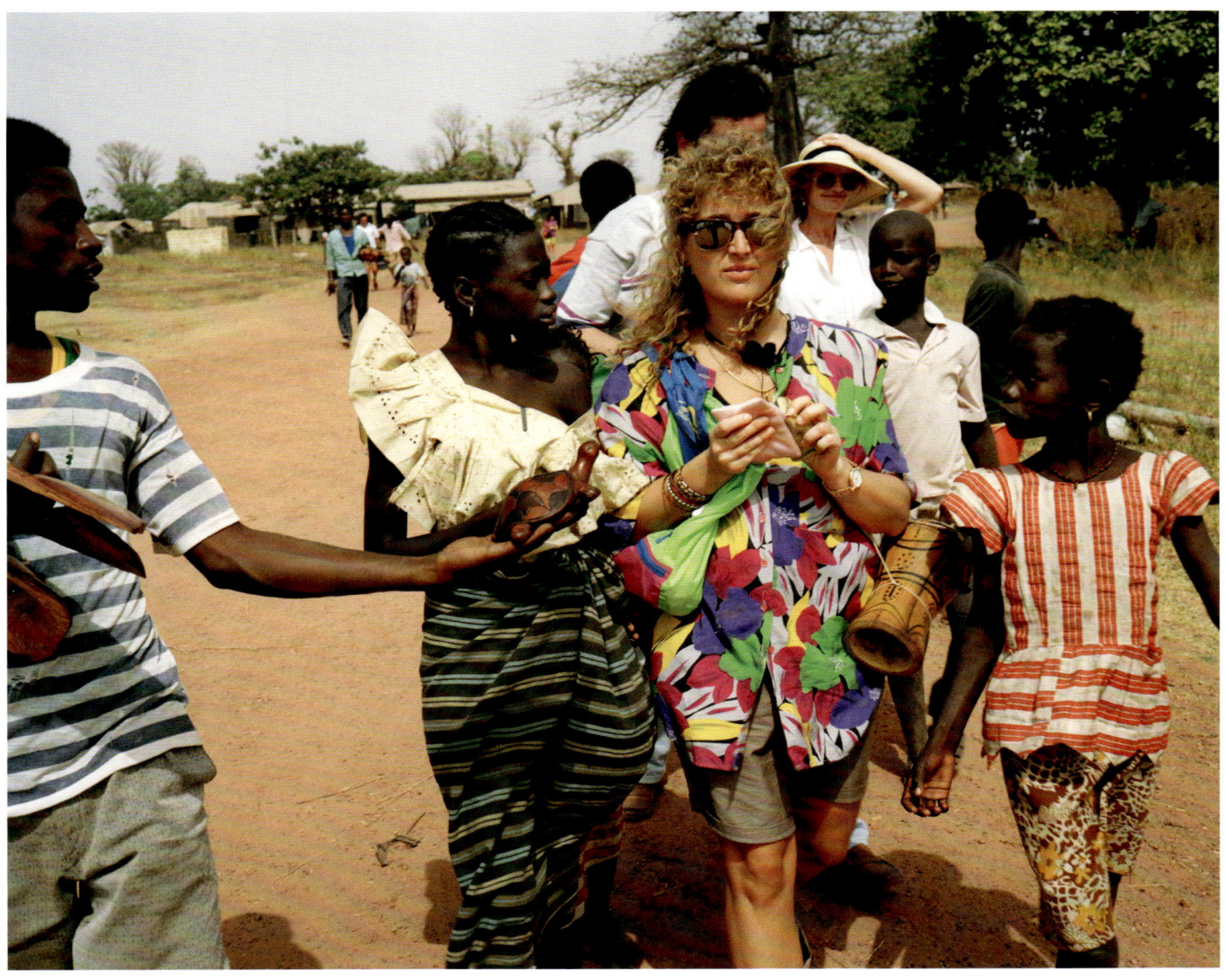

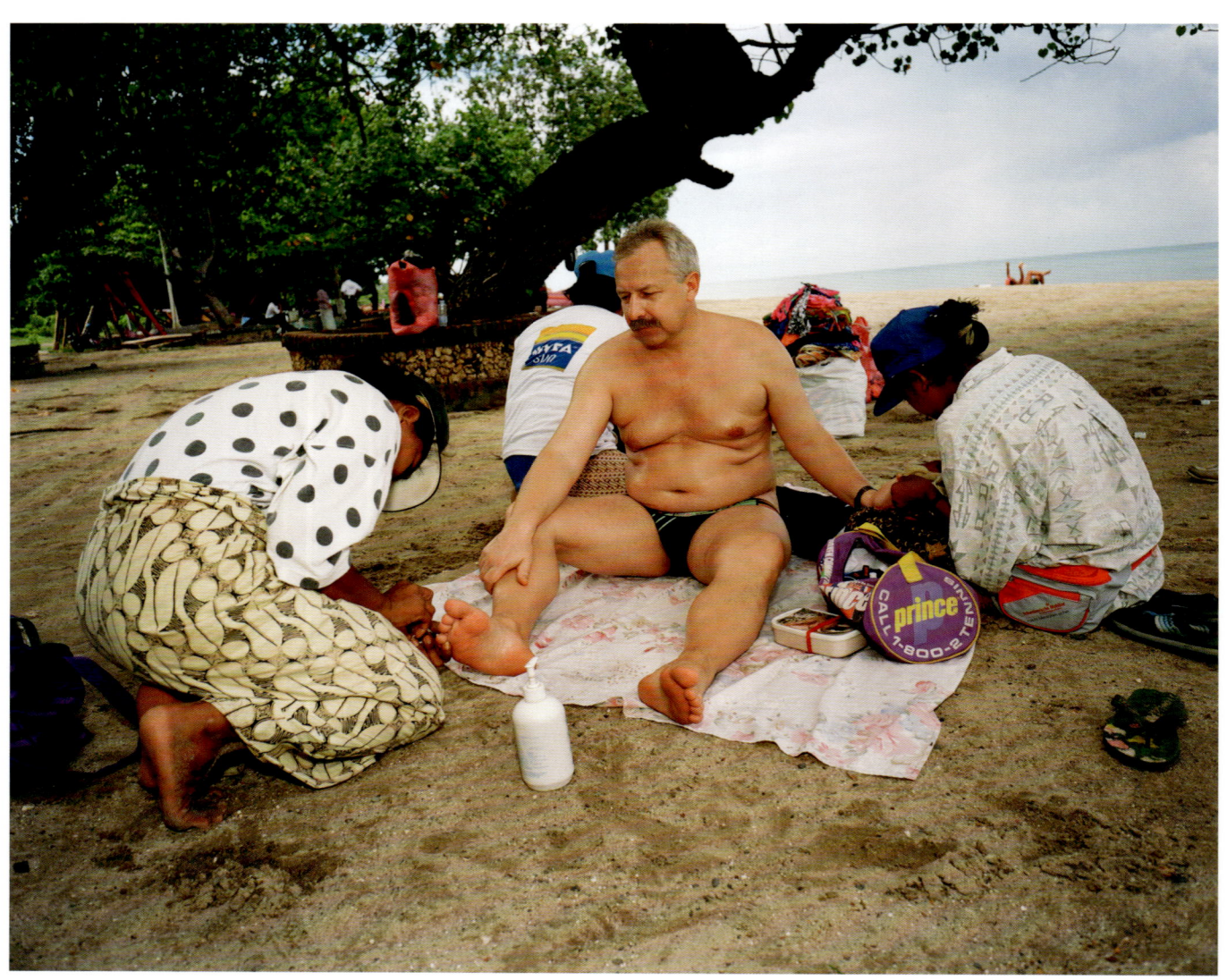

Kuta, Bali, Indonesia, 1993

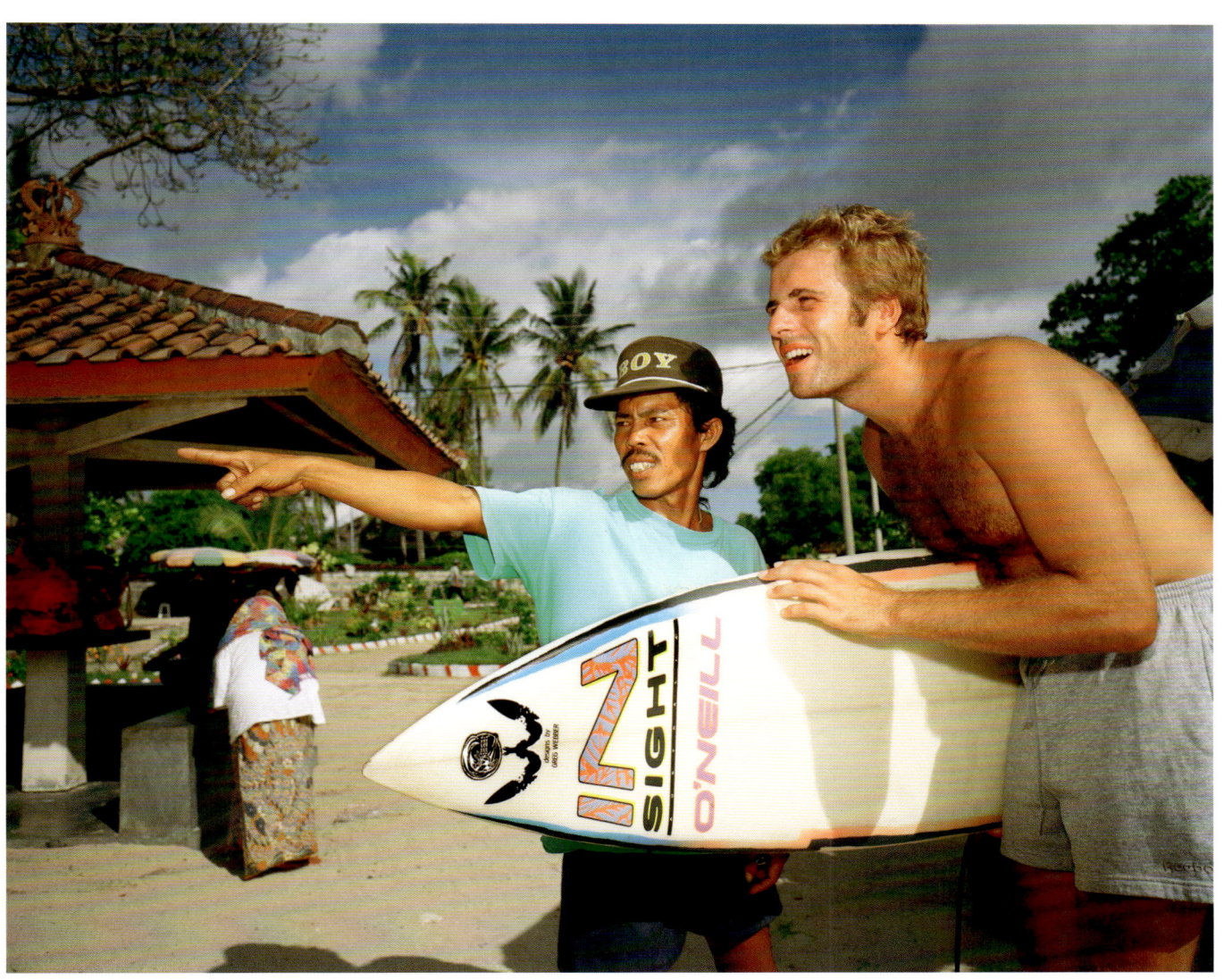

Kuta, Bali, Indonesia, 1993

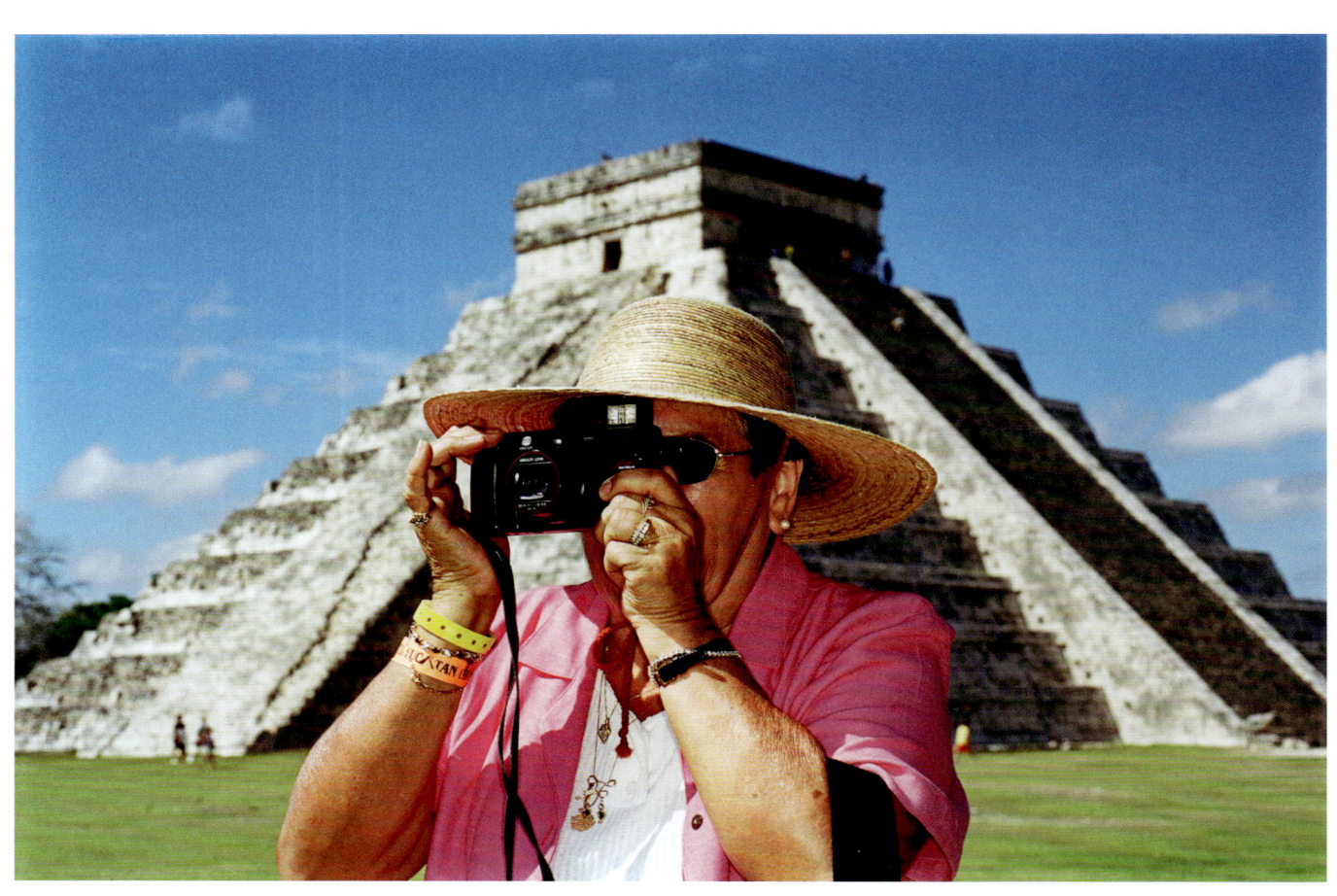

Chichén Itzá, Mexico, 2002

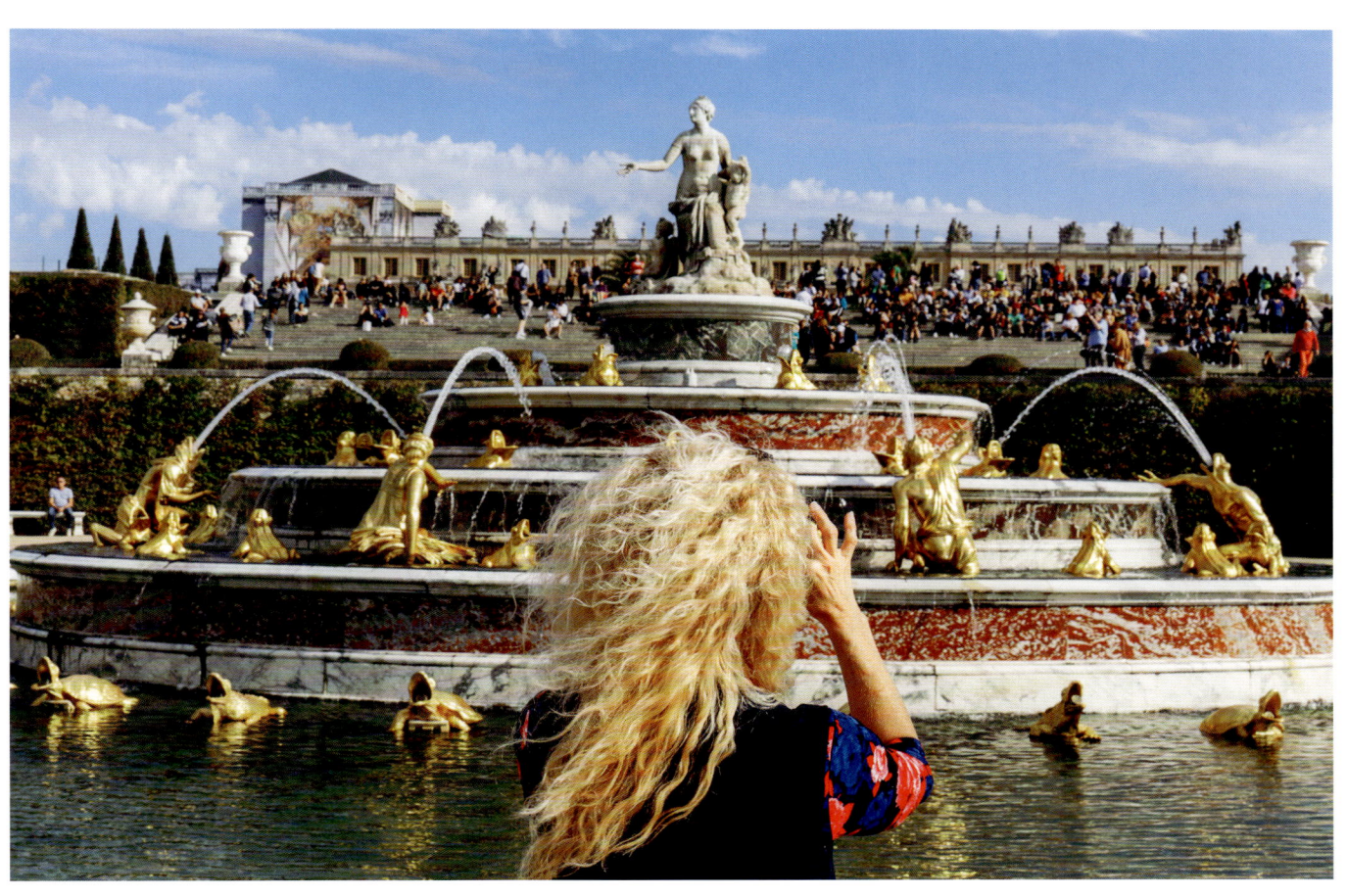

Château de Versailles, France, 2018

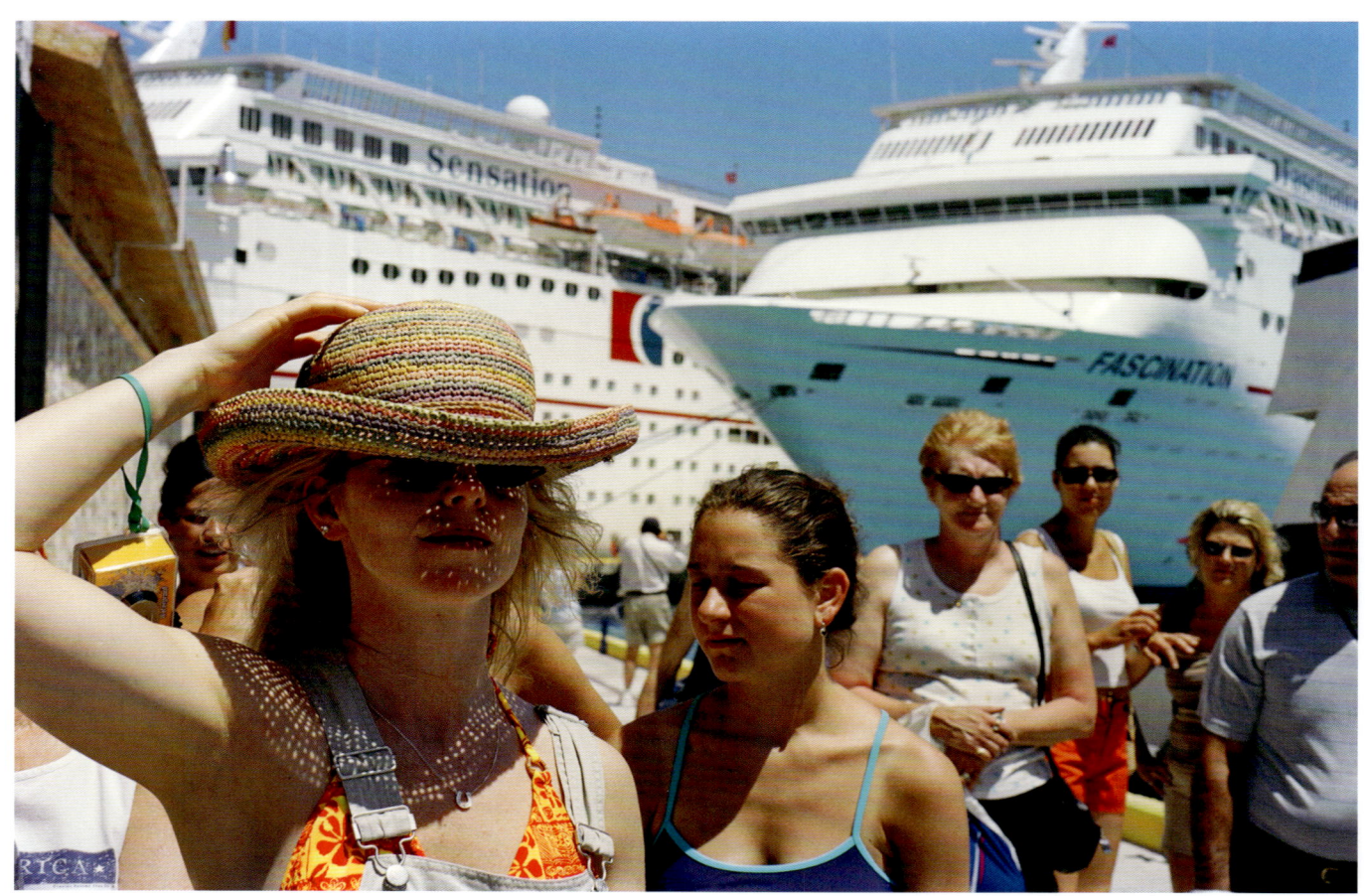

Cozumel, Mexico, 2002

Opposite:
Sagrada Família, Barcelona, Spain, 1993

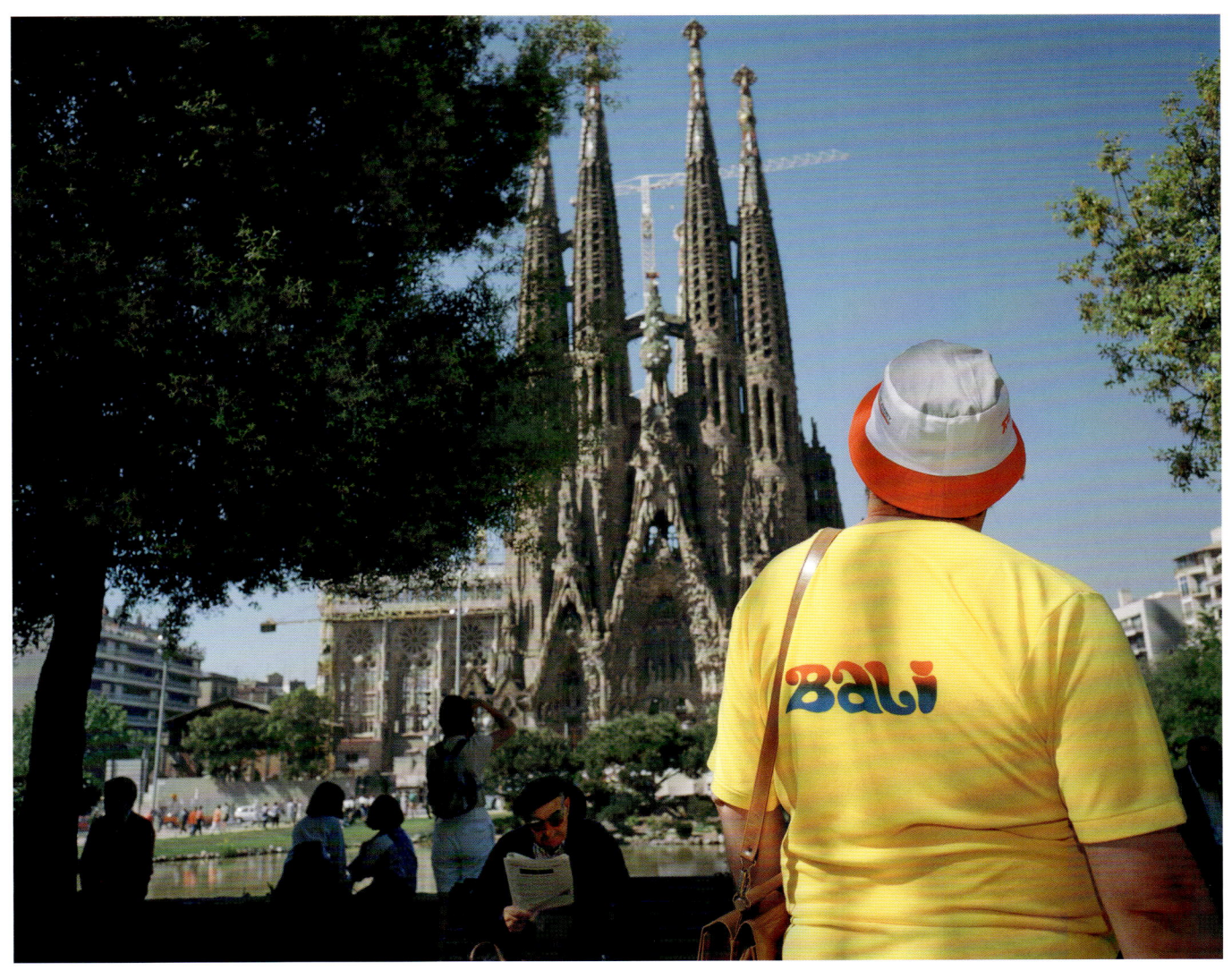

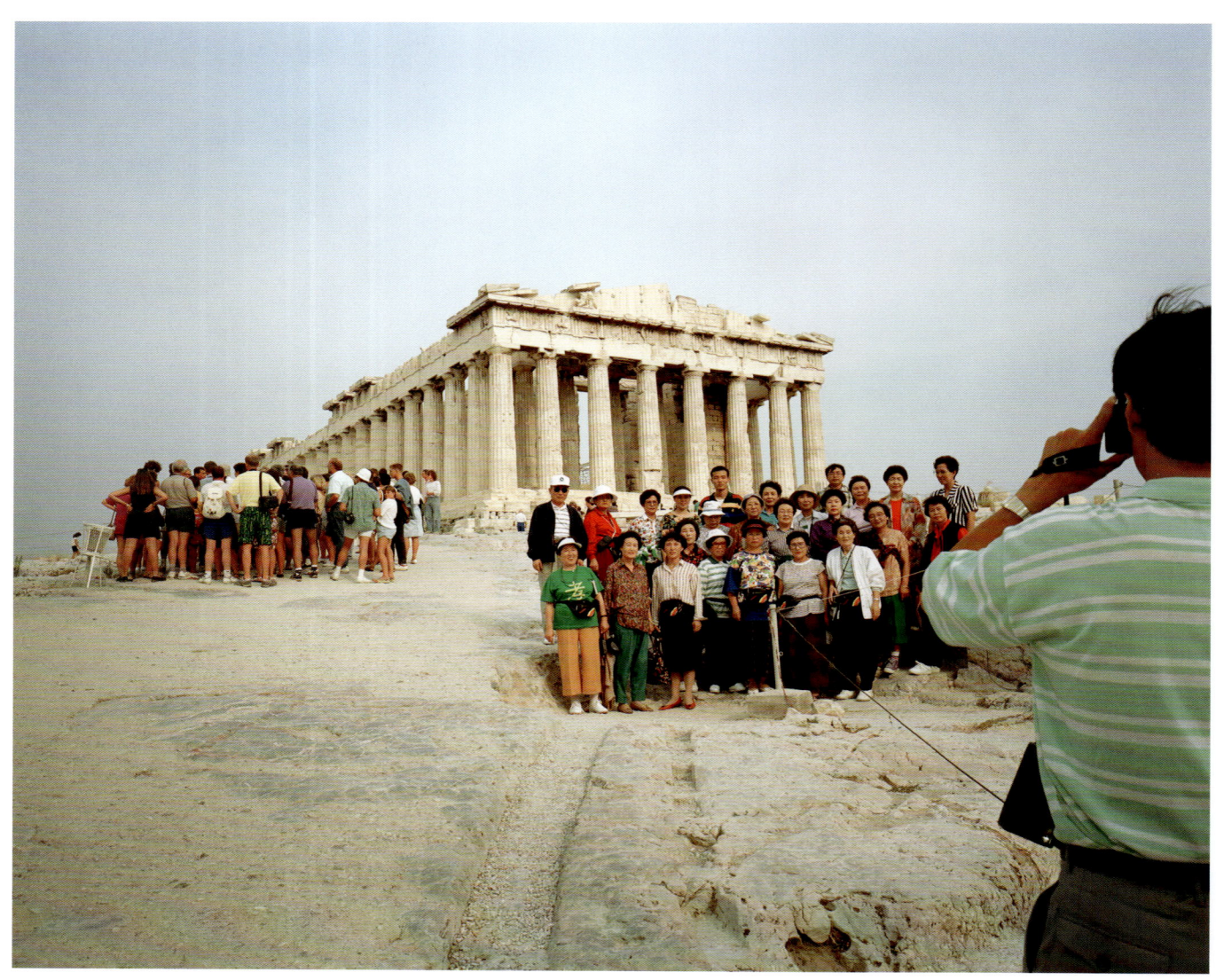

Acropolis, Athens, Greece, 1991

Opposite:
Bali, Indonesia, 1993

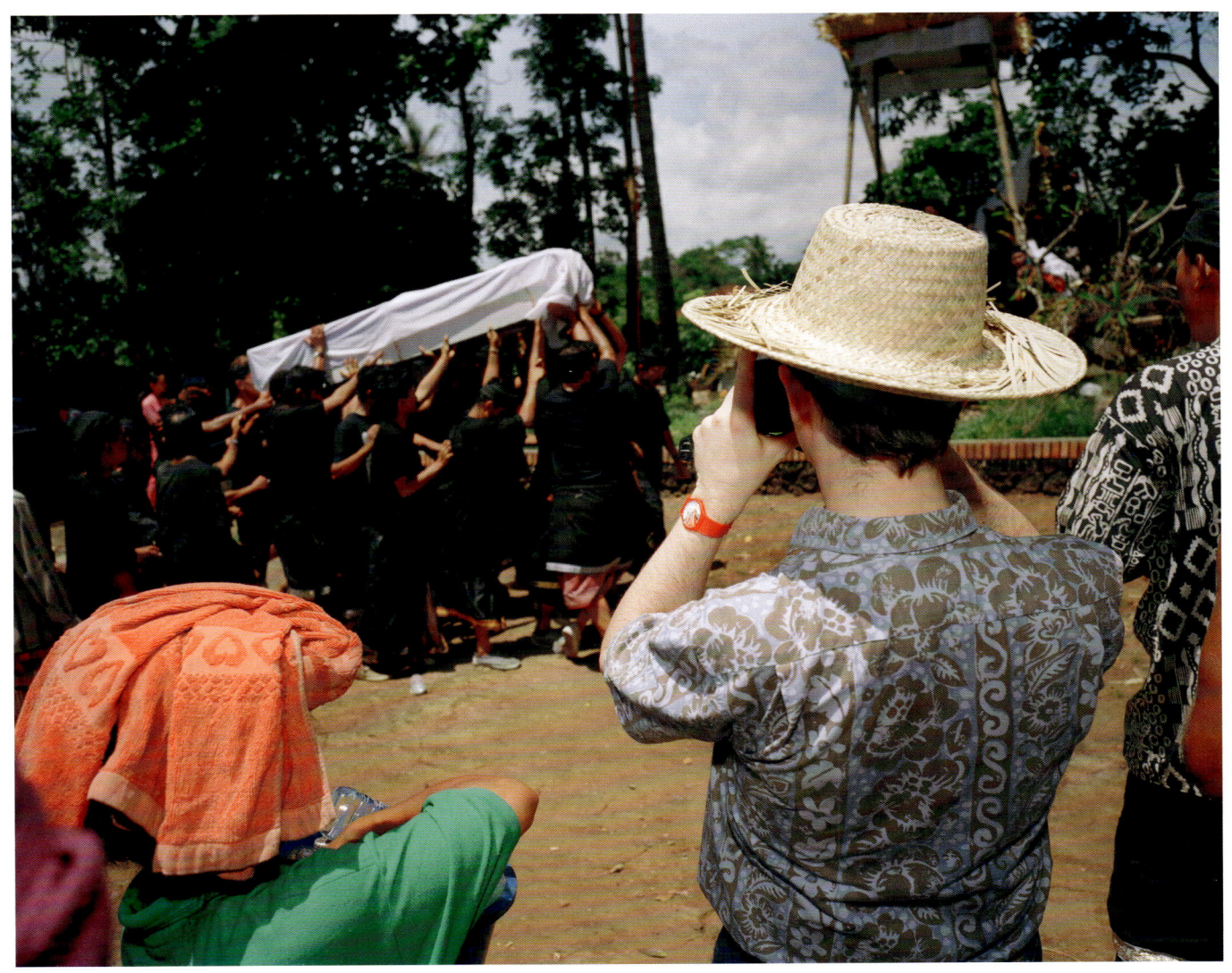

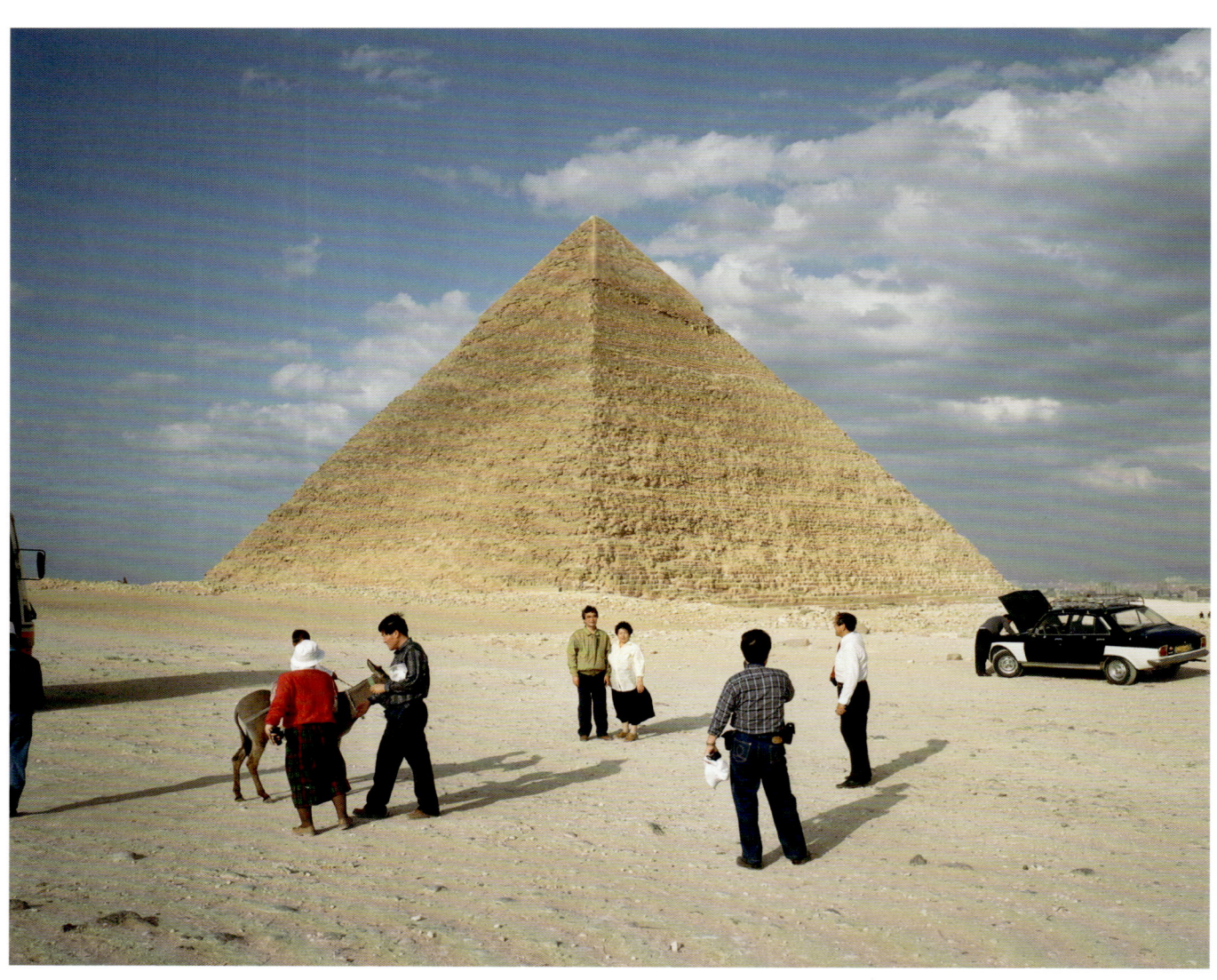

Pyramids of Giza, Egypt, 1992

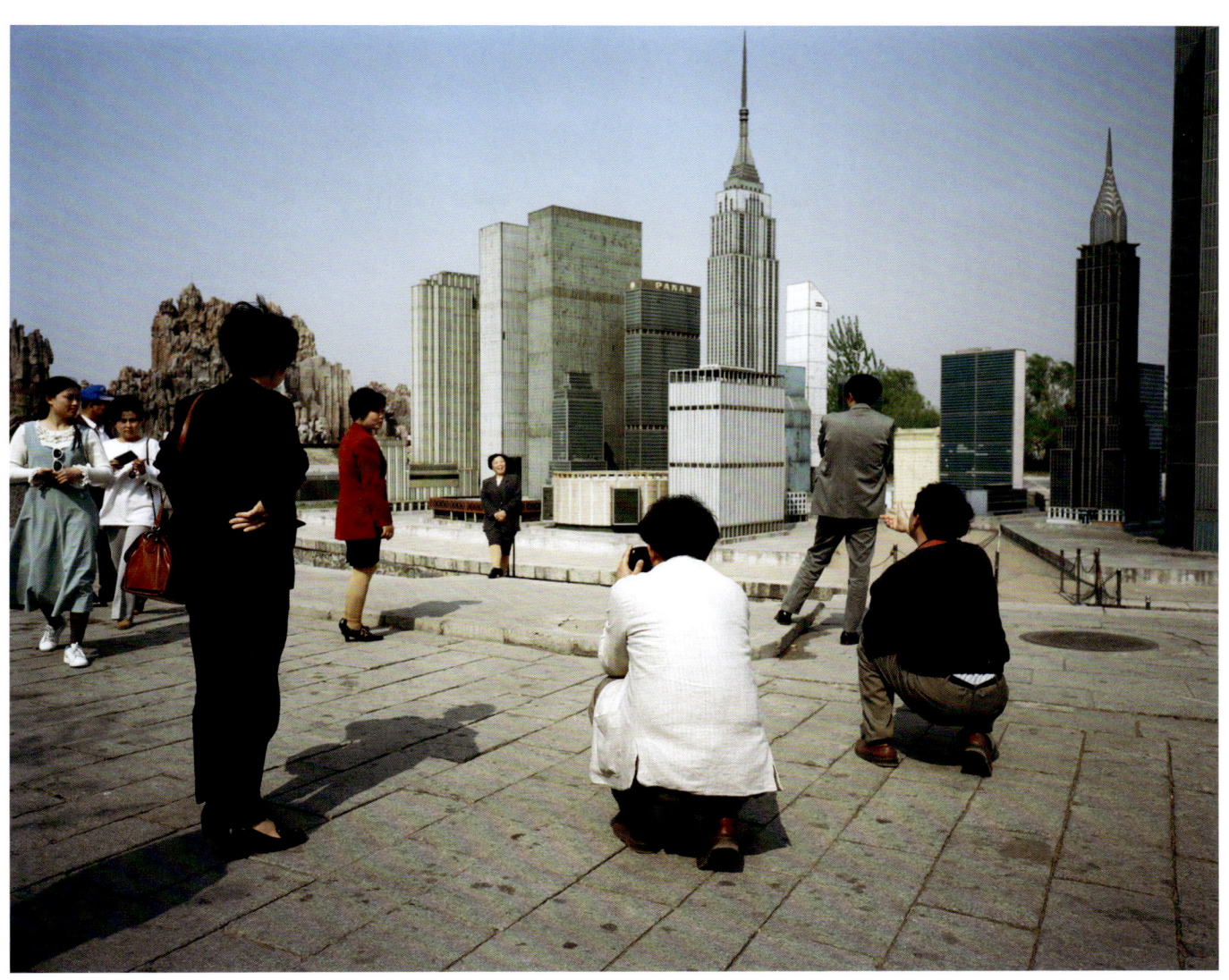

American Dream Park, Shanghai, China, 1997

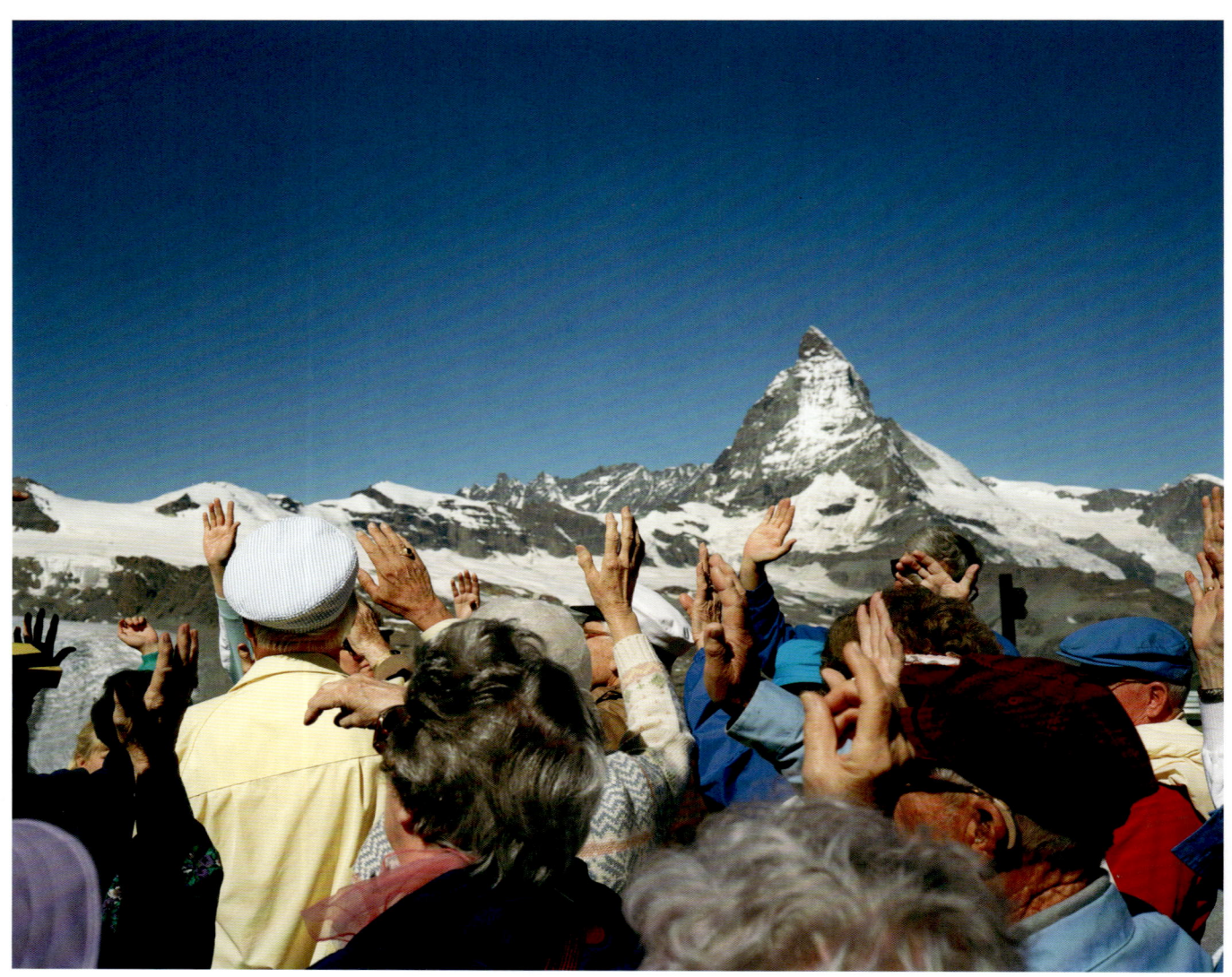

The Alps, Switzerland, 1990

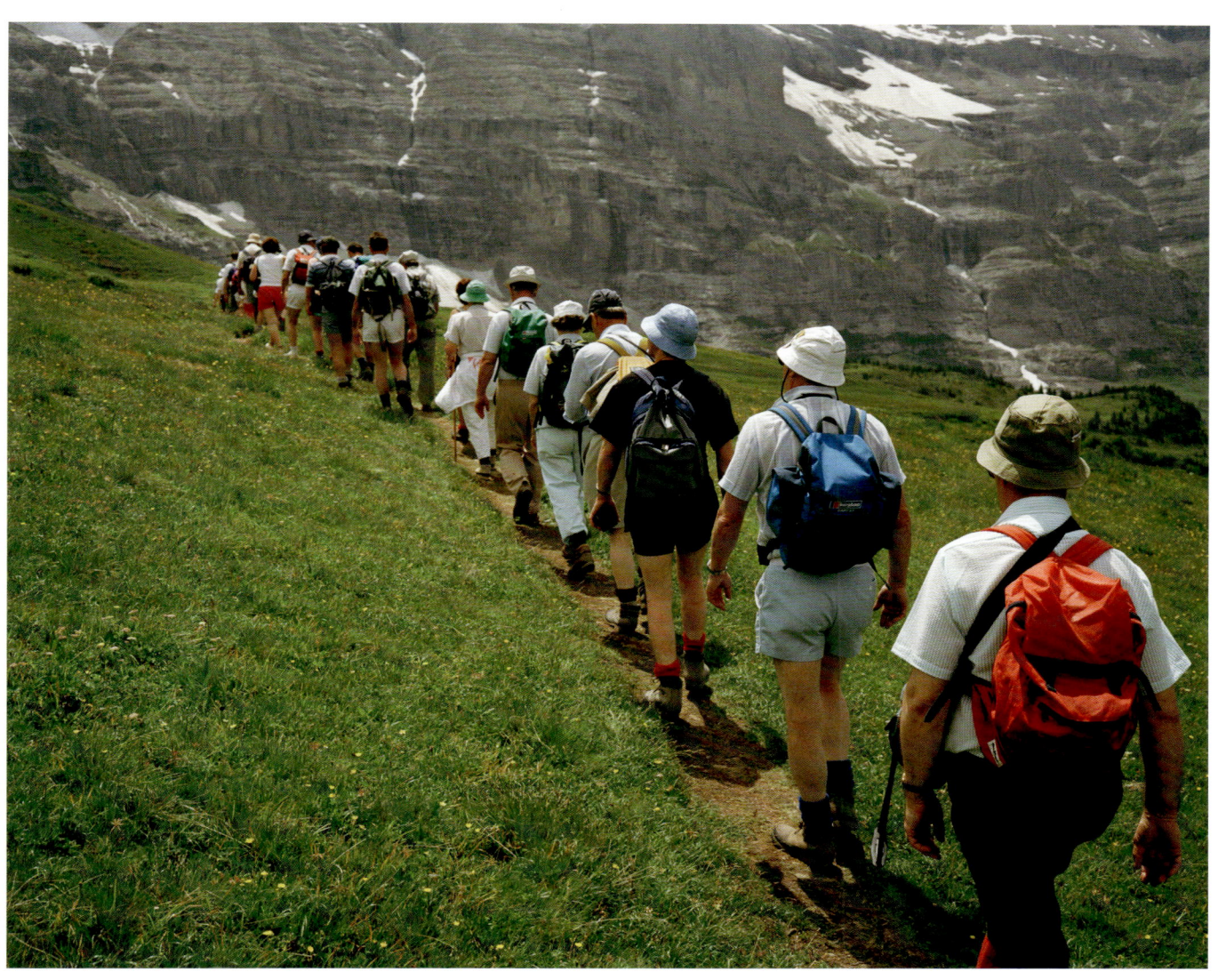

Kleine Scheidegg, Switzerland, 1990

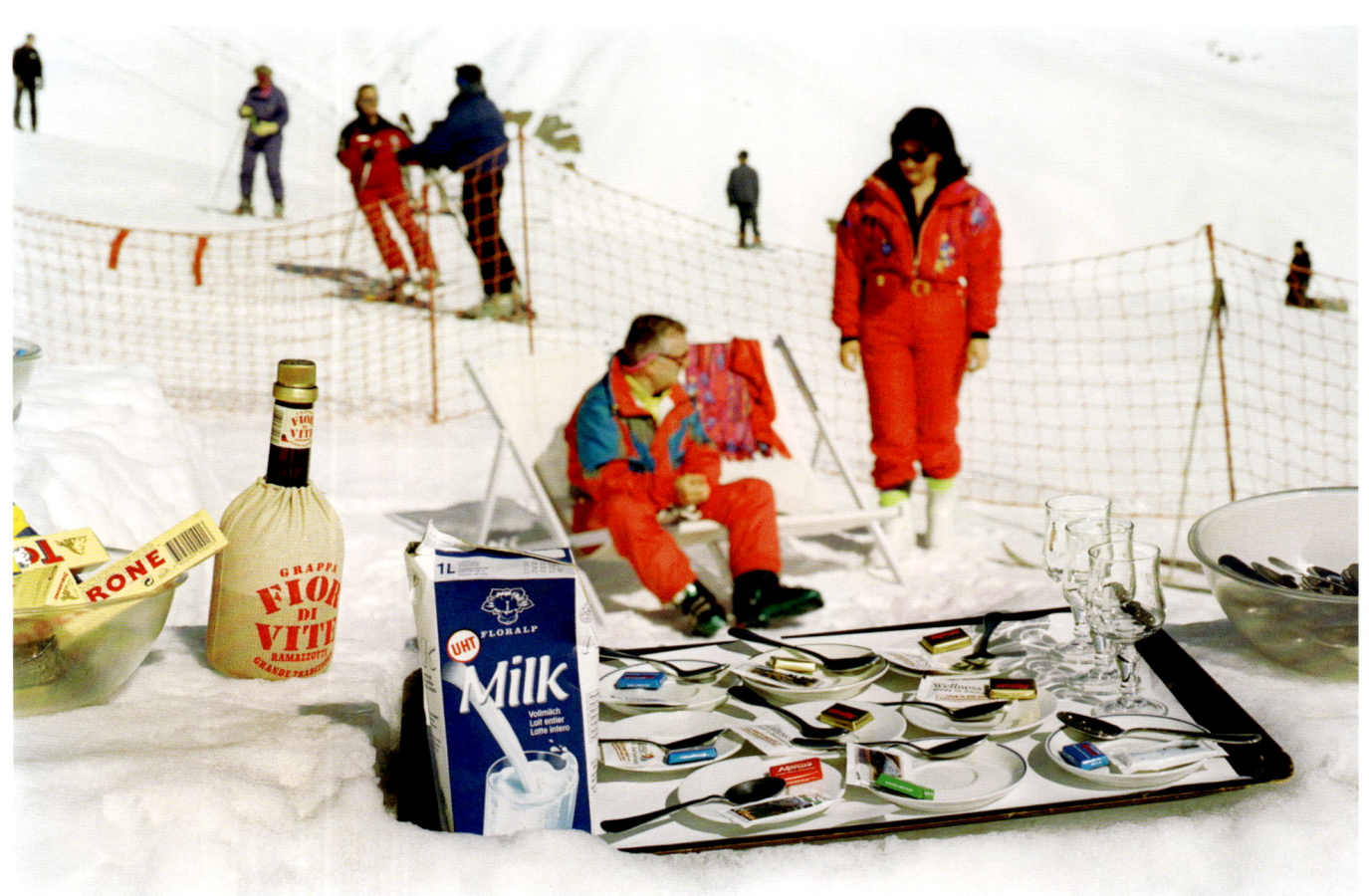

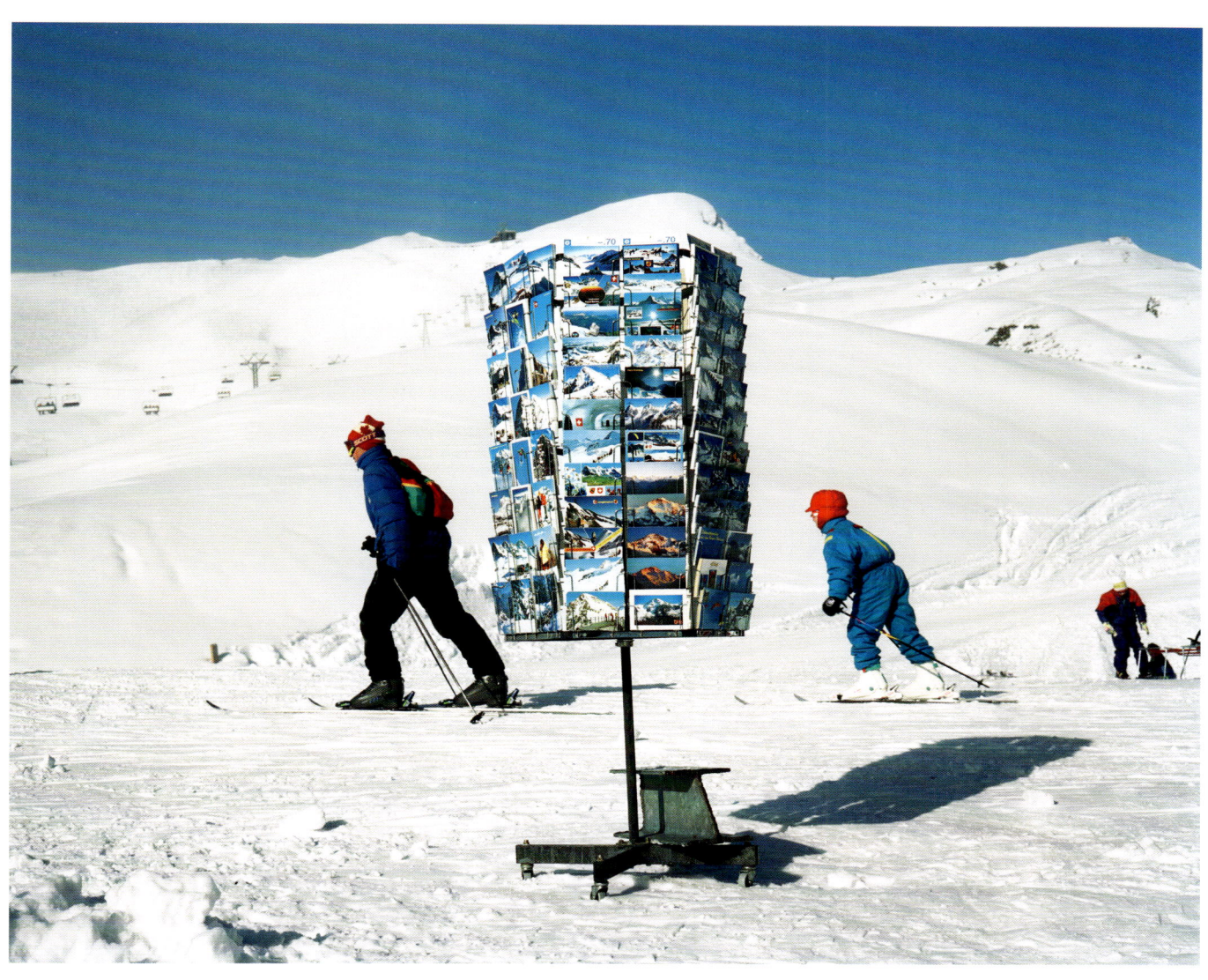

Opposite:
St. Moritz, Switzerland, 2003

Kleine Scheidegg, Switzerland, 1994

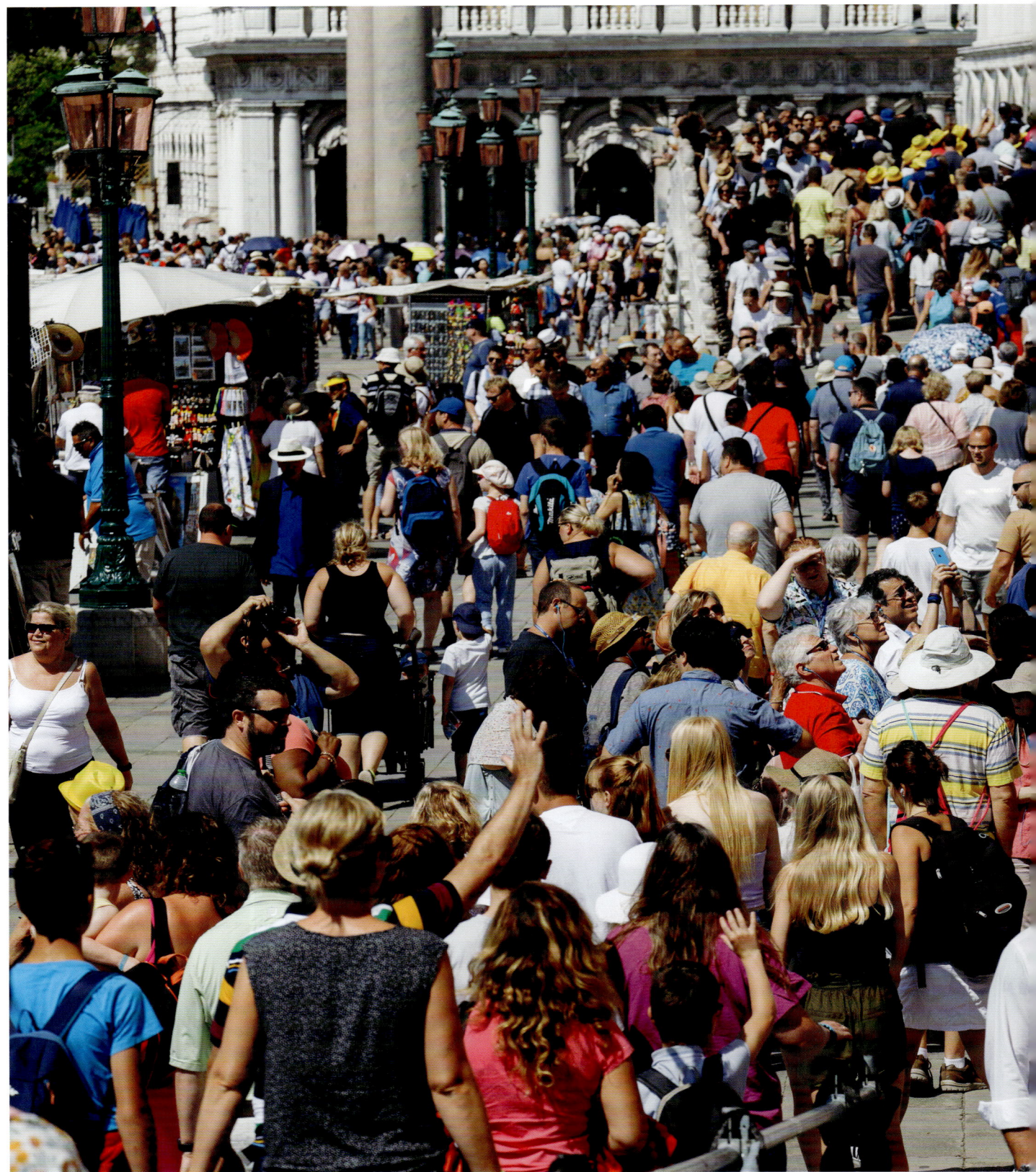

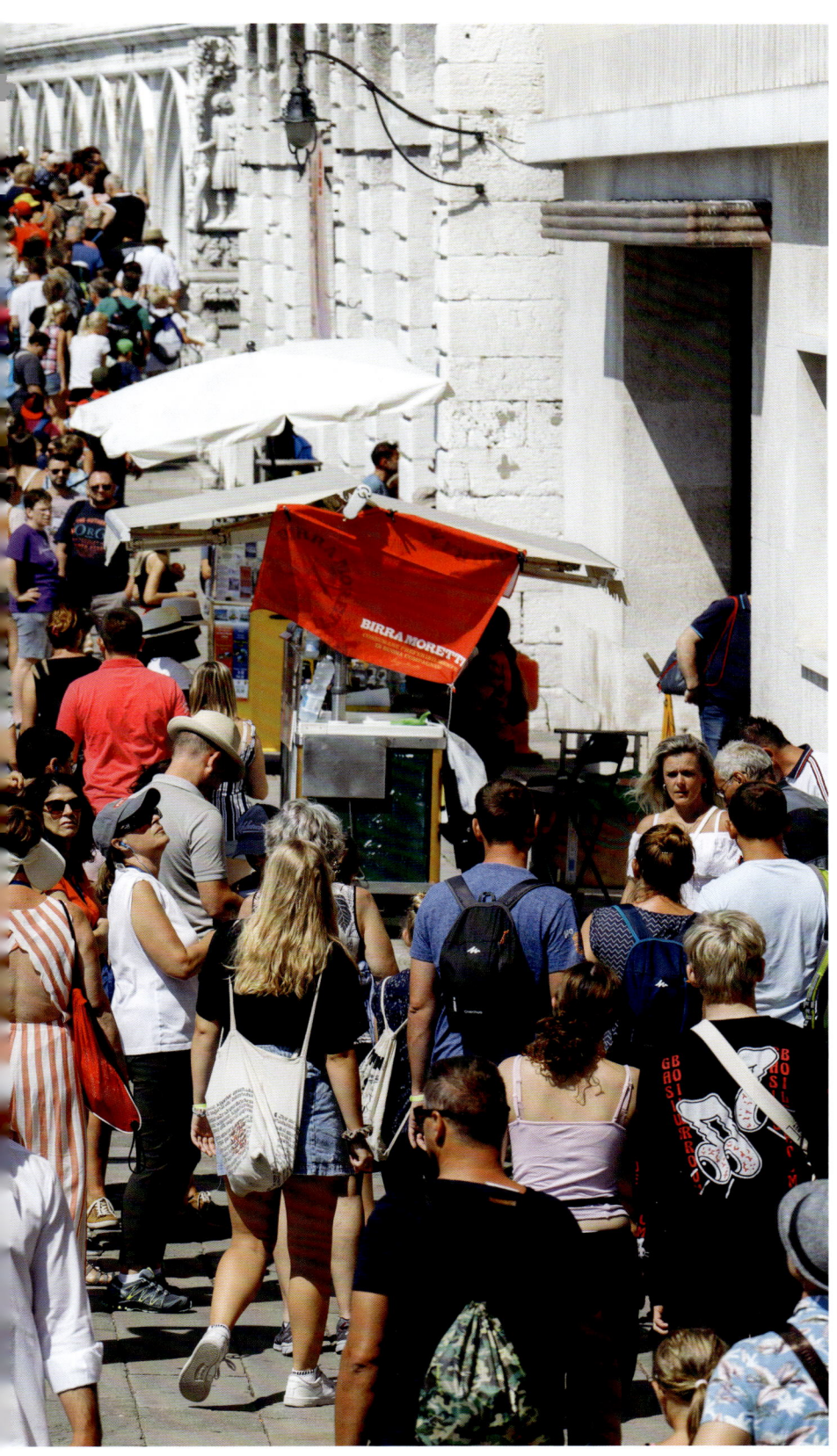

Venice, Italy, 2019

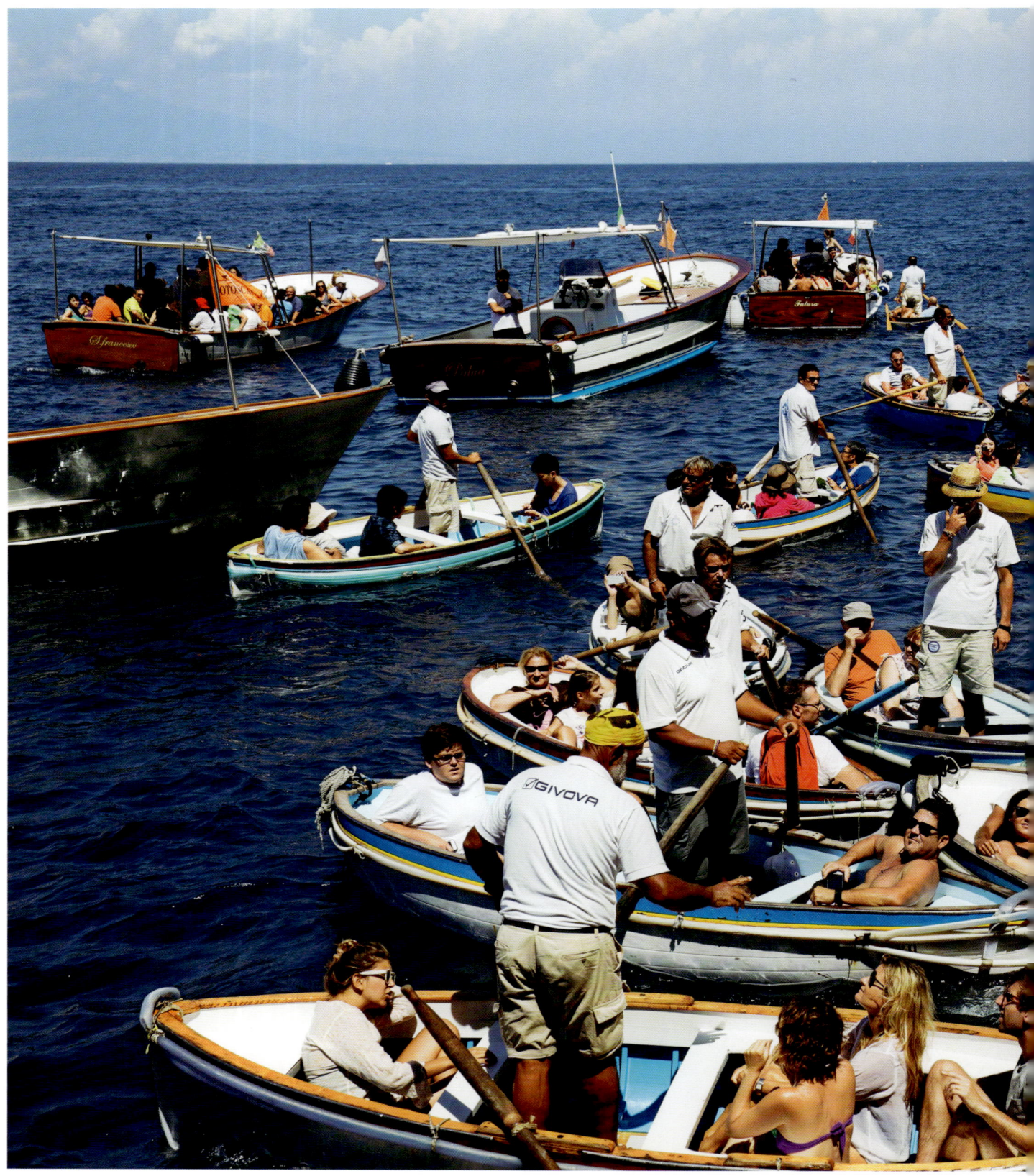

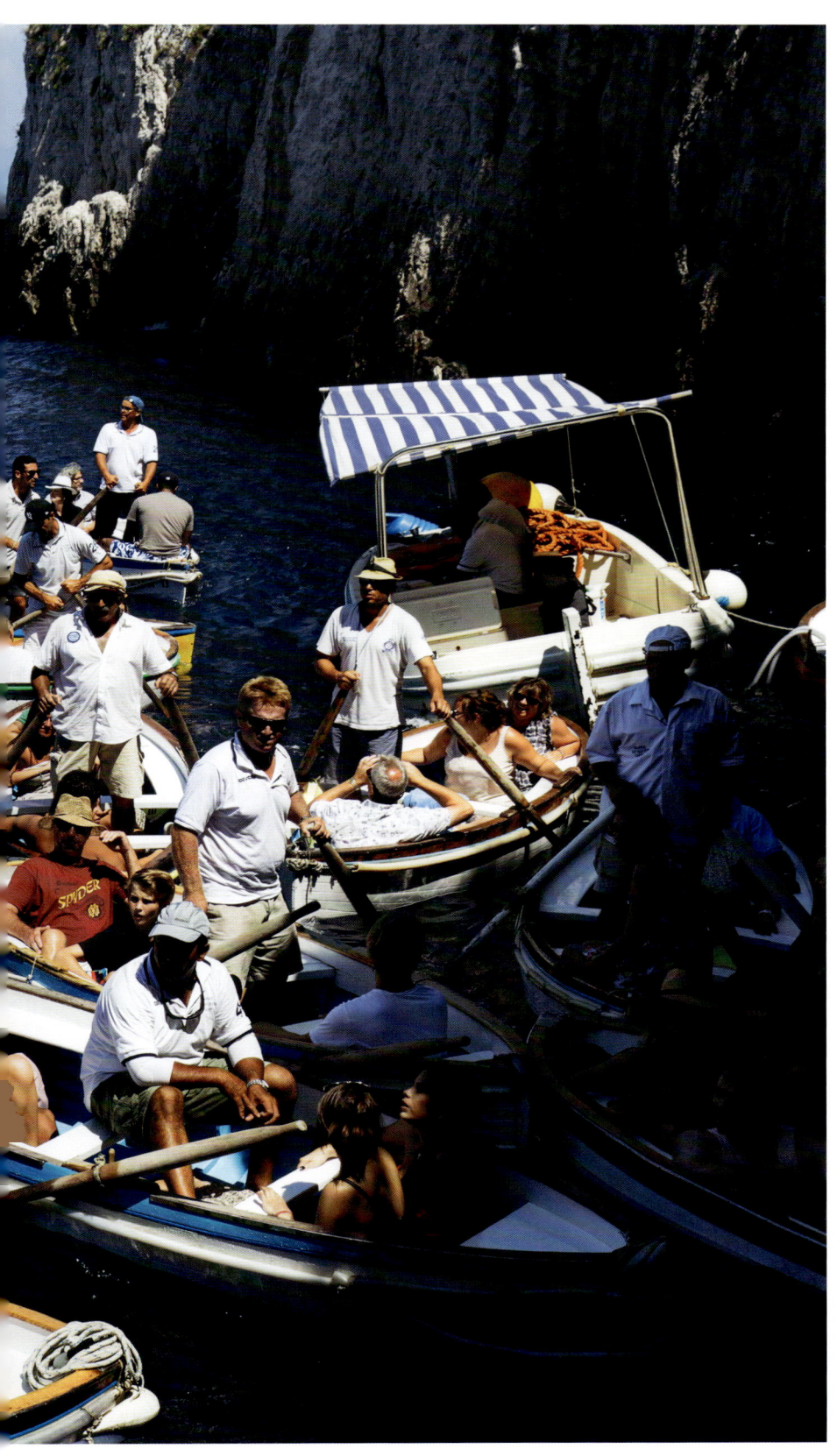

Blue Grotto, Capri, Italy, 2014

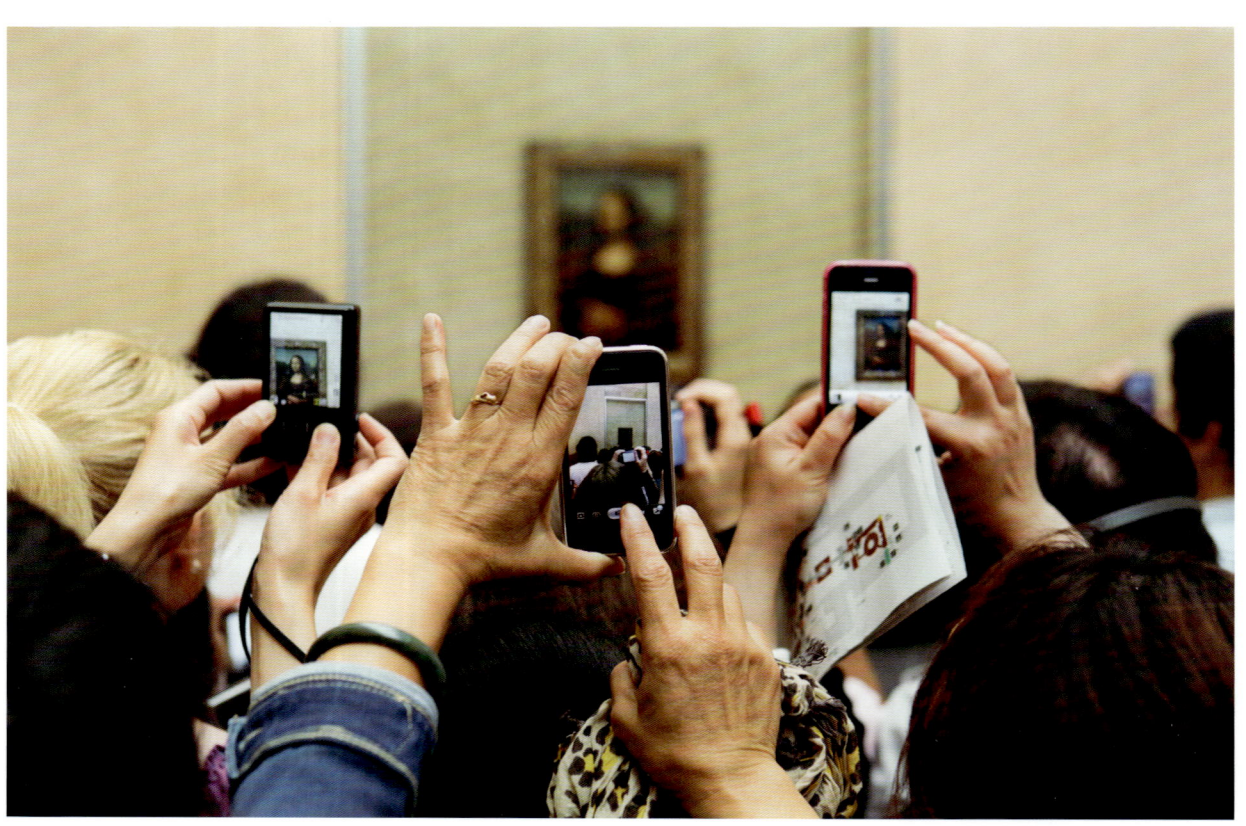

Musée du Louvre, Paris, France, 2012

Opposite:
Notre-Dame de Paris, France, 2012
Sistine Chapel, Vatican City, 2014

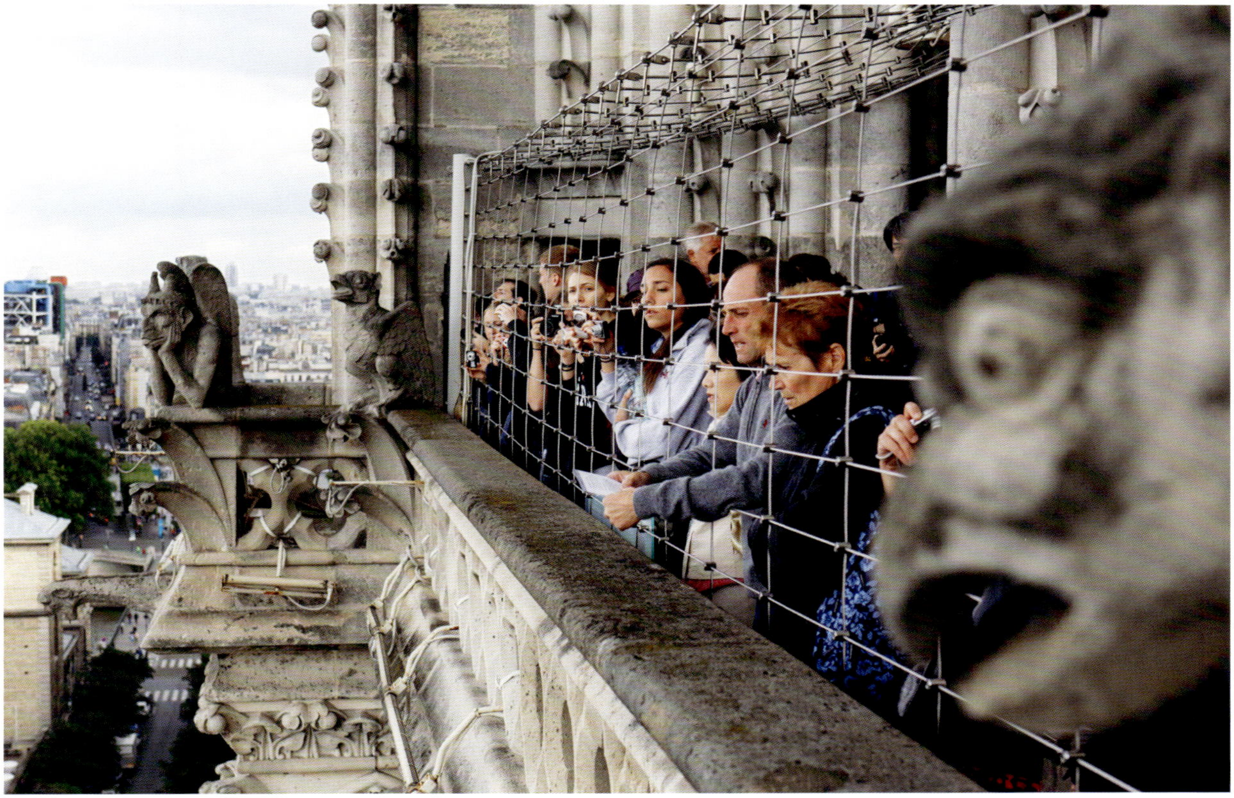

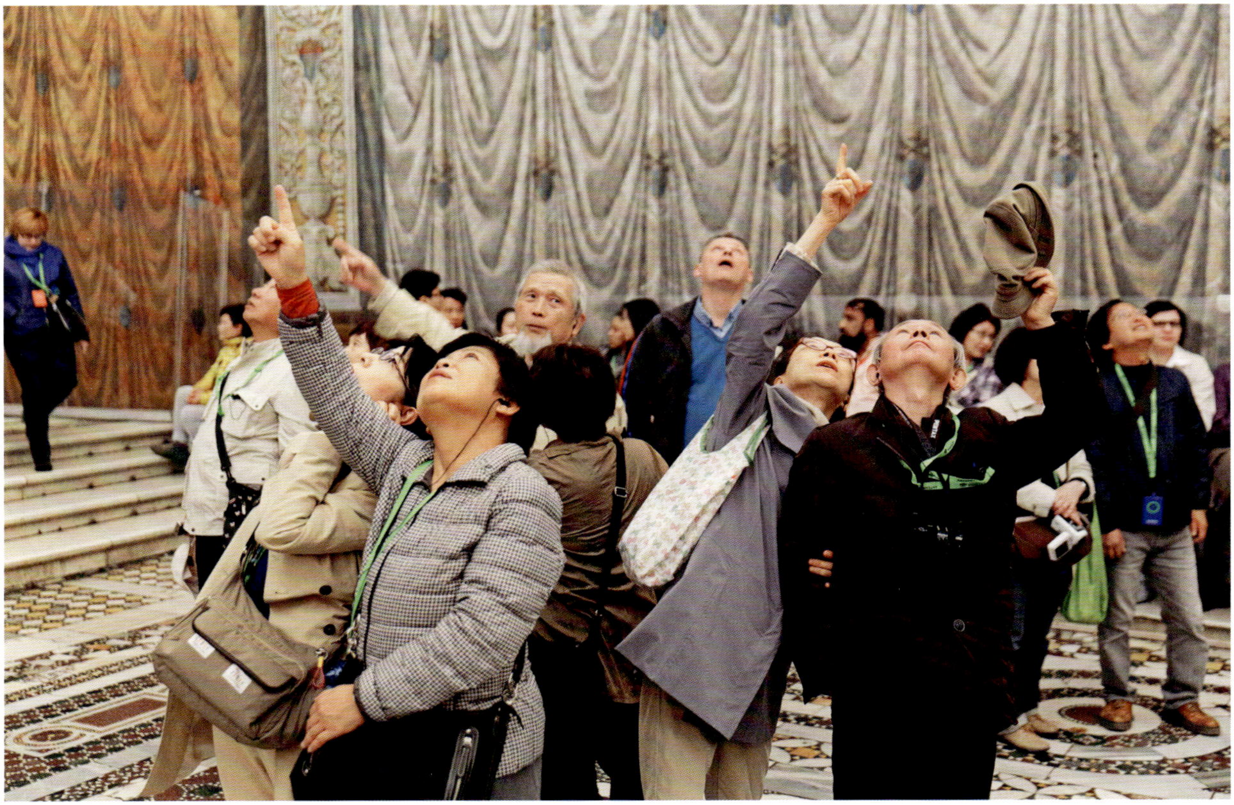

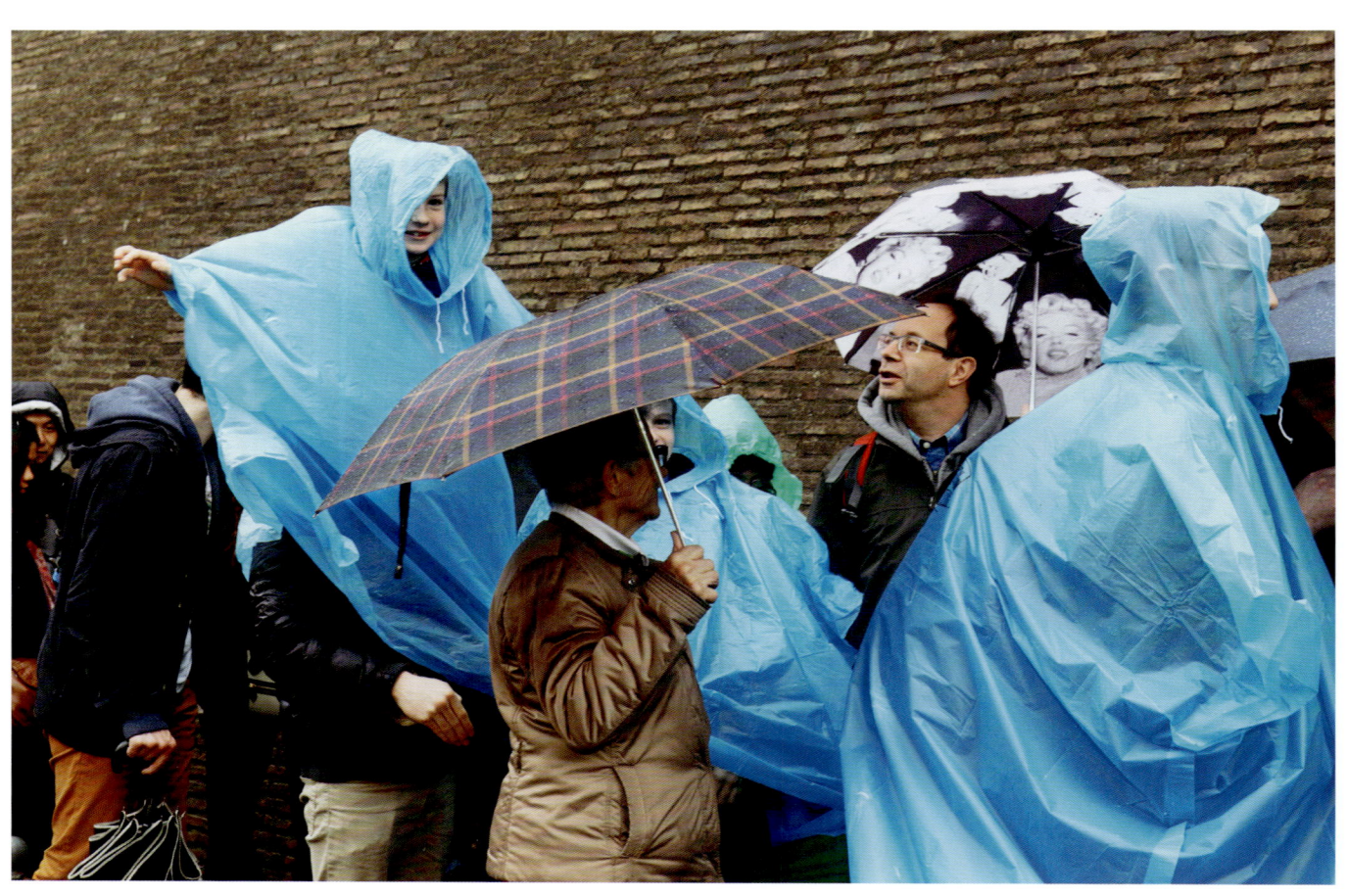

Vatican City, 2014

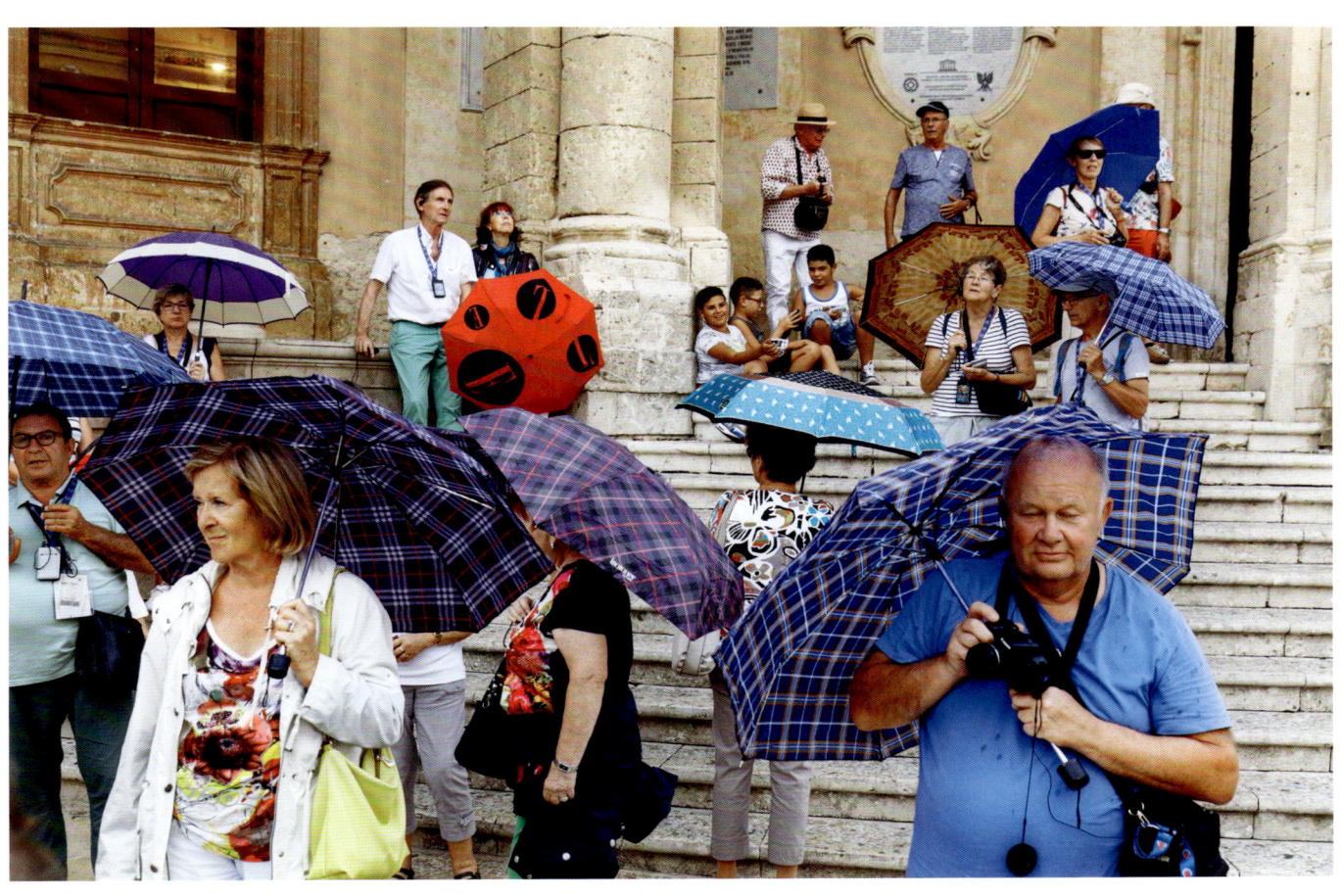

Noto, Sicily, Italy, 2016

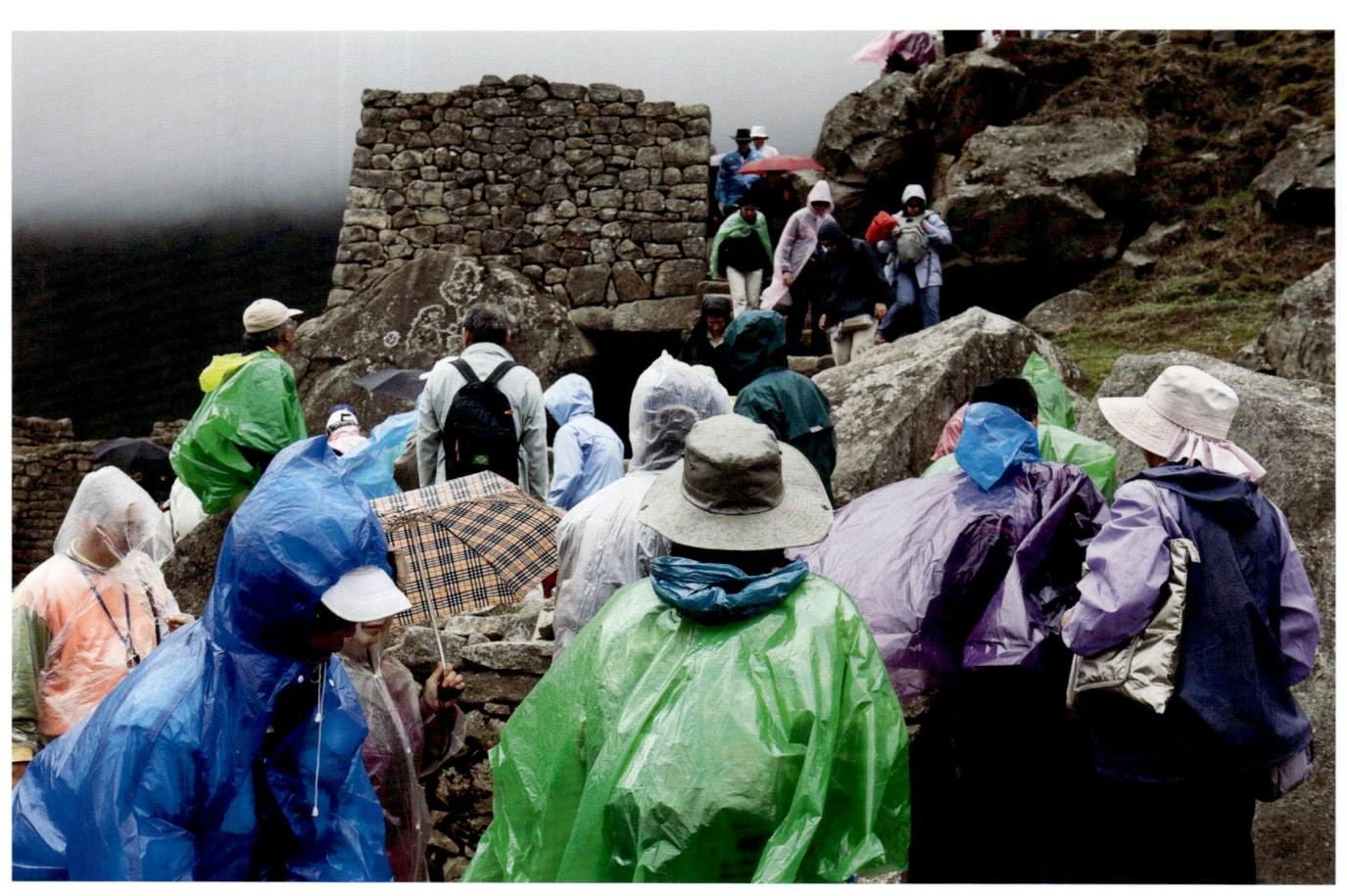

Machu Picchu, Peru, 2008

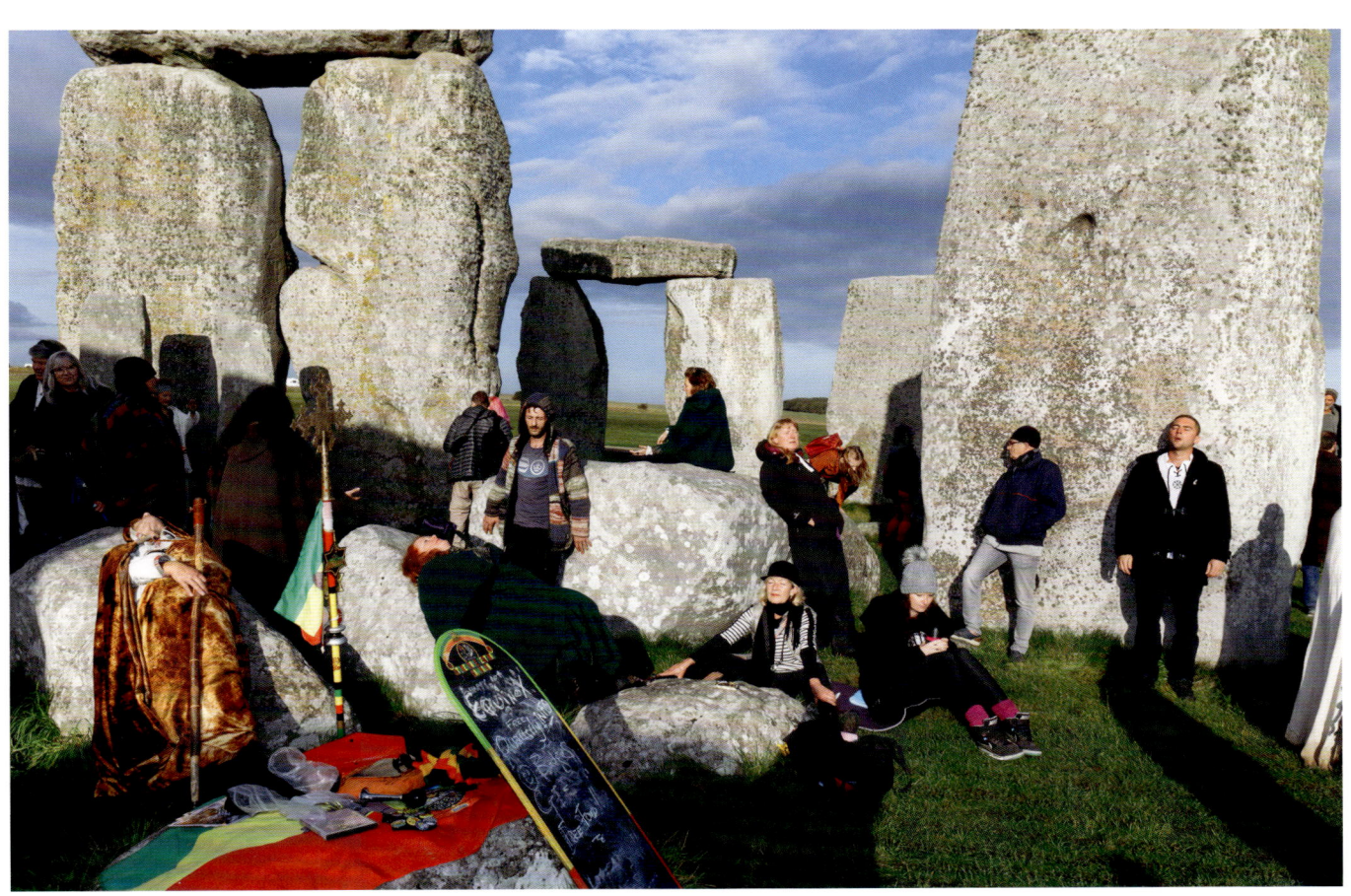

Stonehenge, Wiltshire, England, 2019

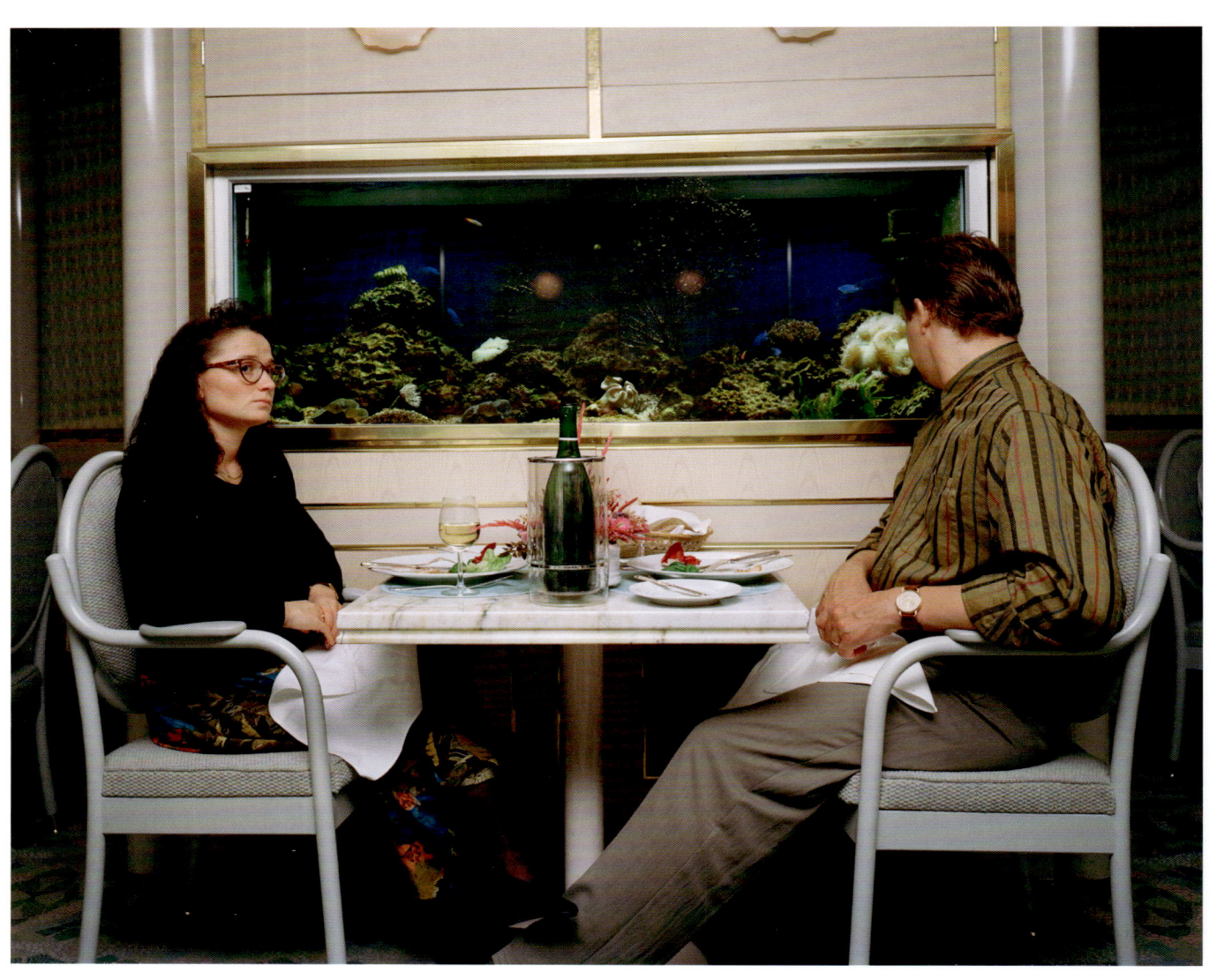

Ferry from Helsinki to Stockholm, 1991

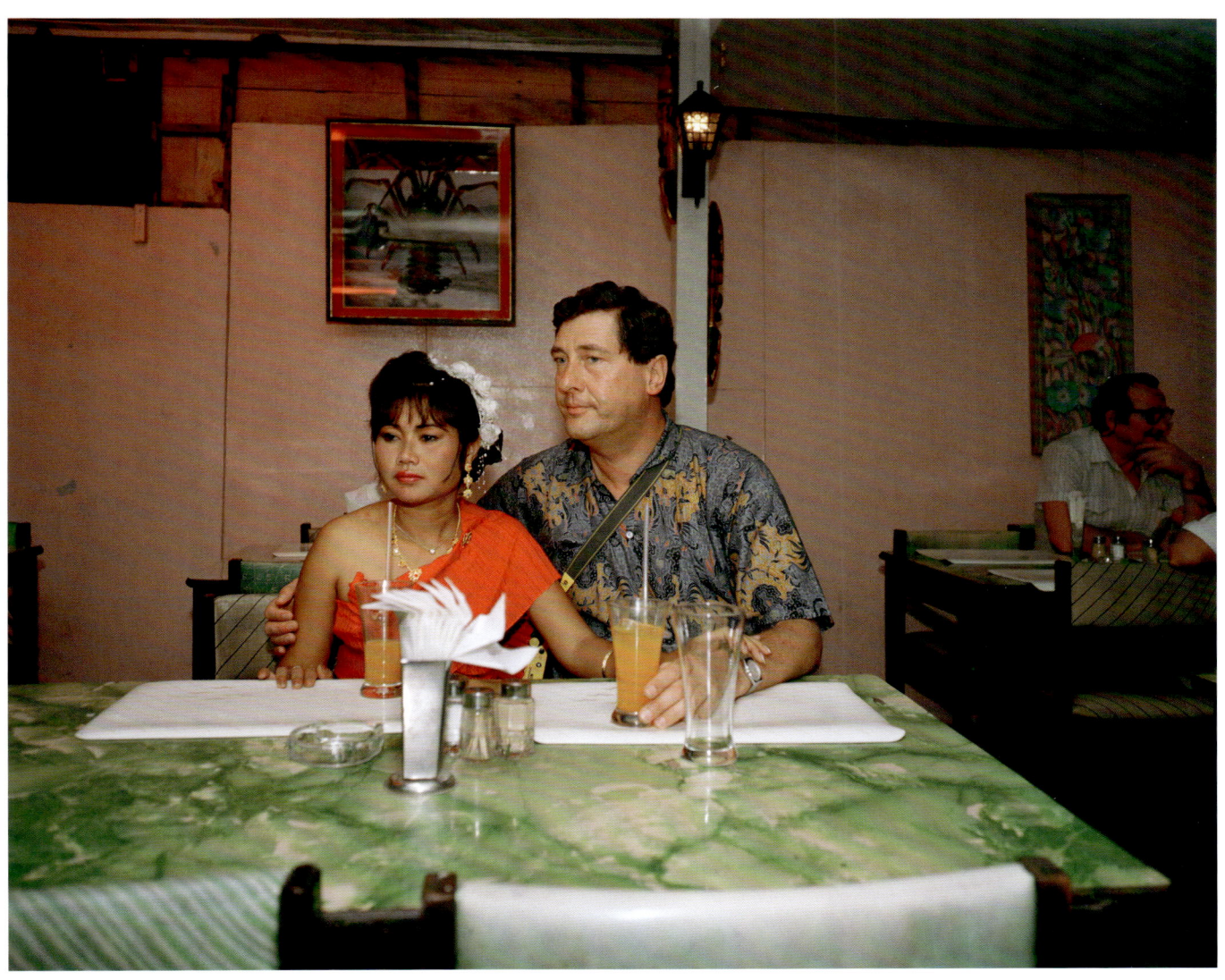

Pattaya, Thailand, 1993

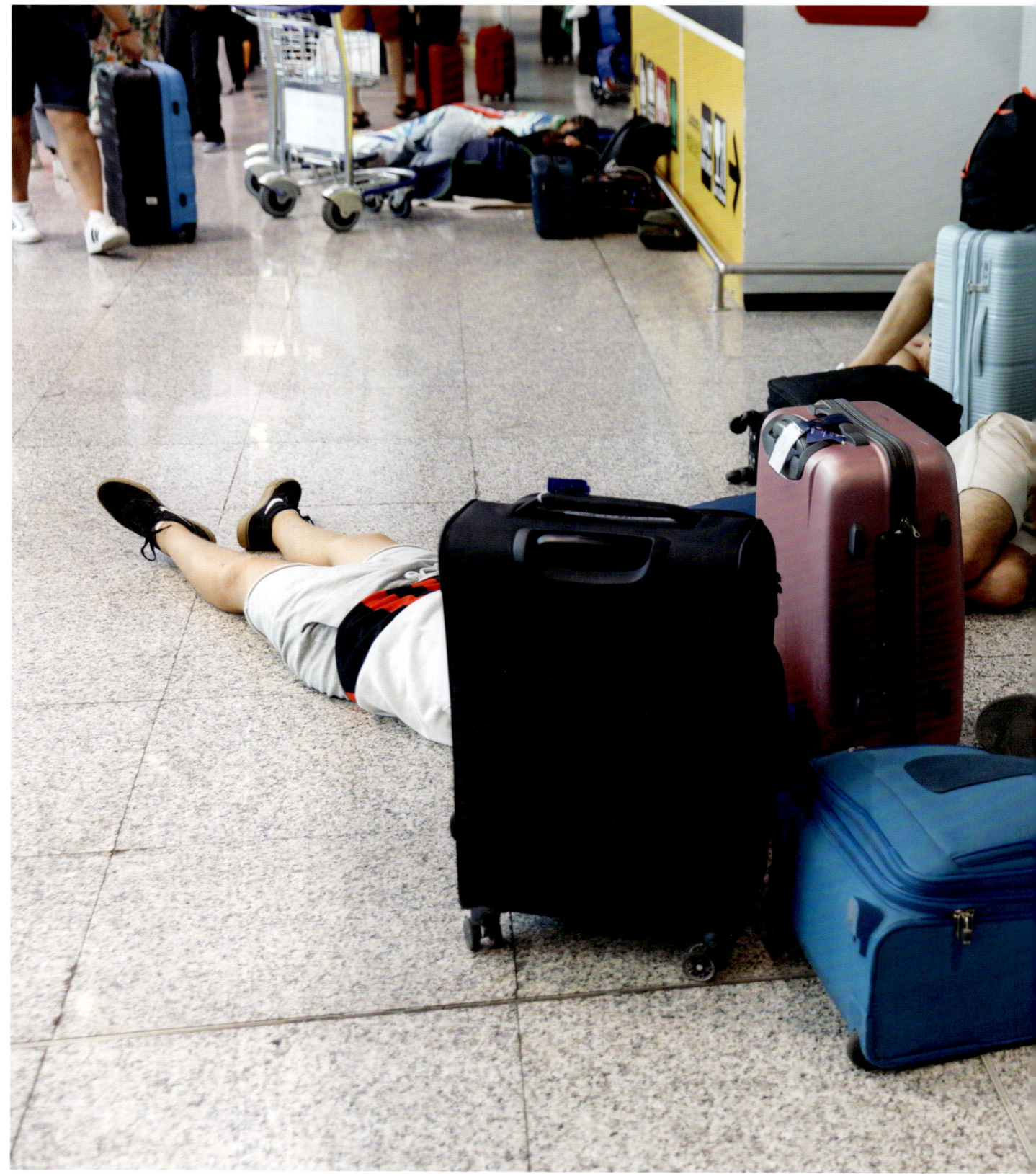

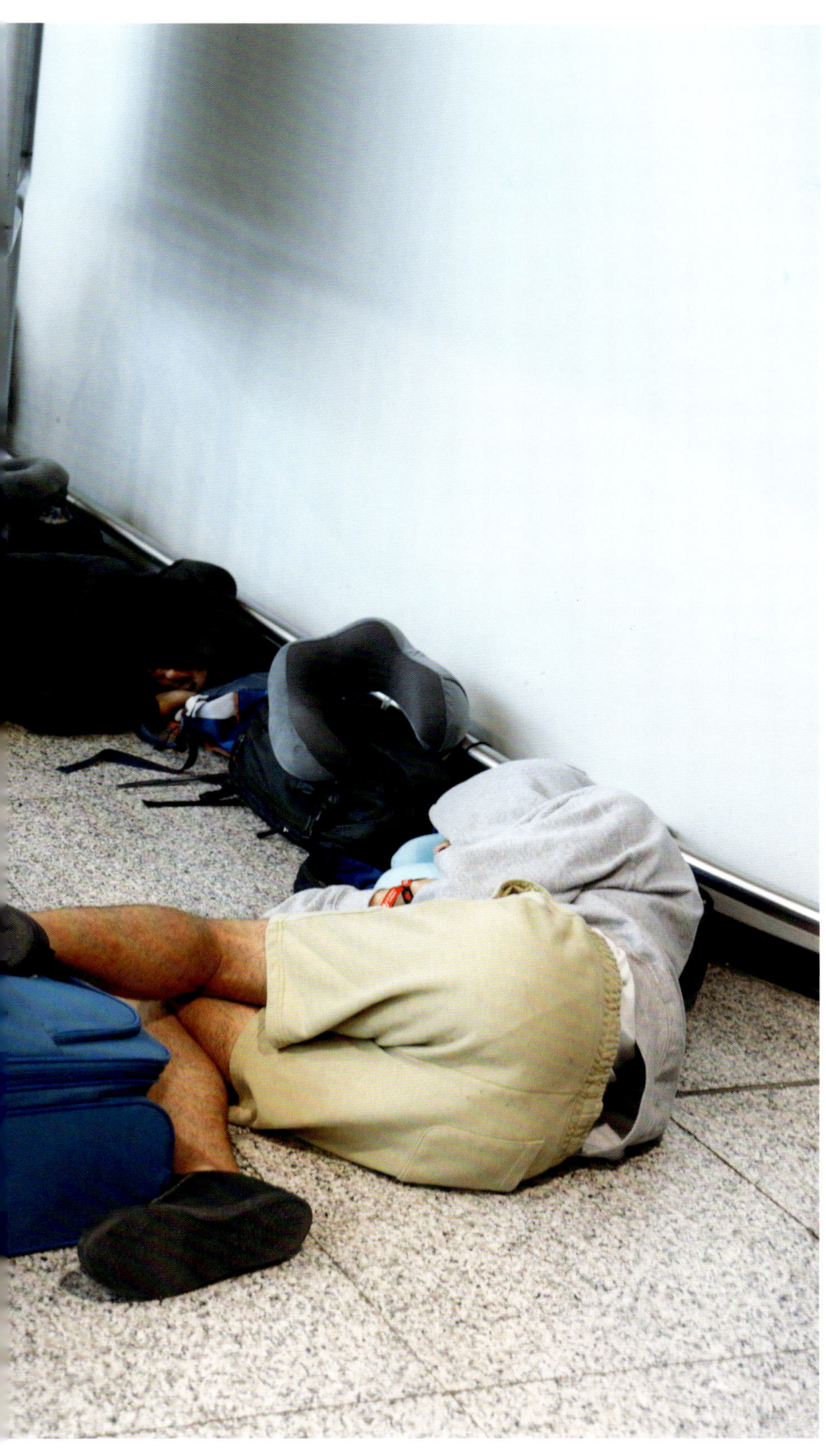

Rome, Italy, 2024

LAST CHANCE TO BUY!

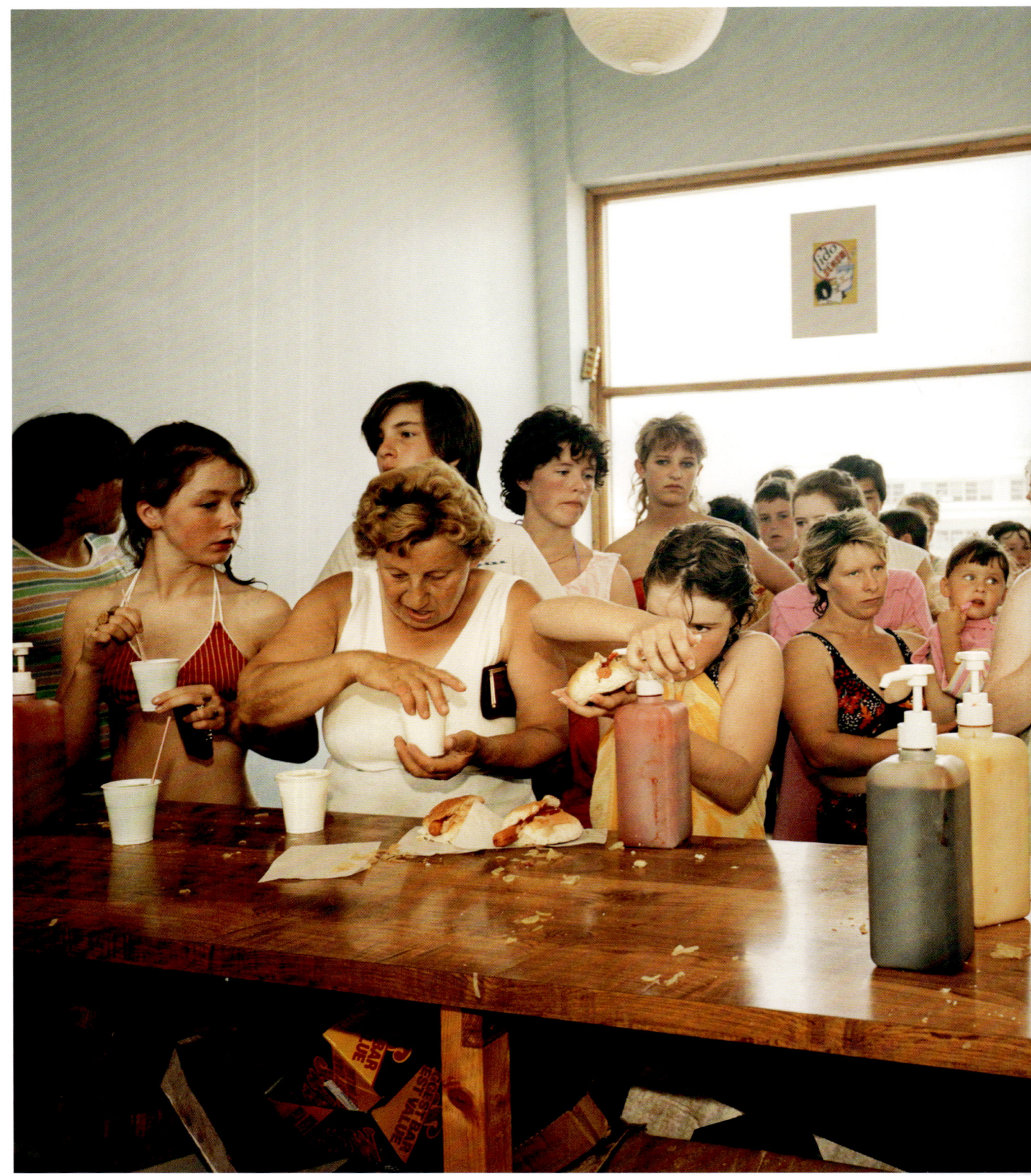

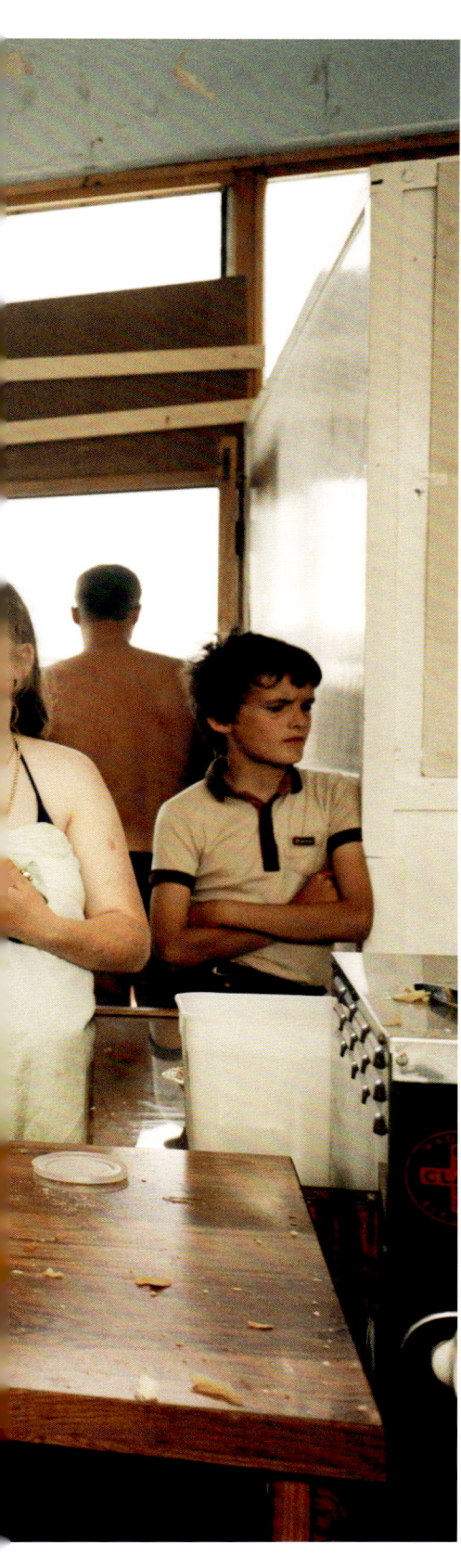

New Brighton, England, 1983–5

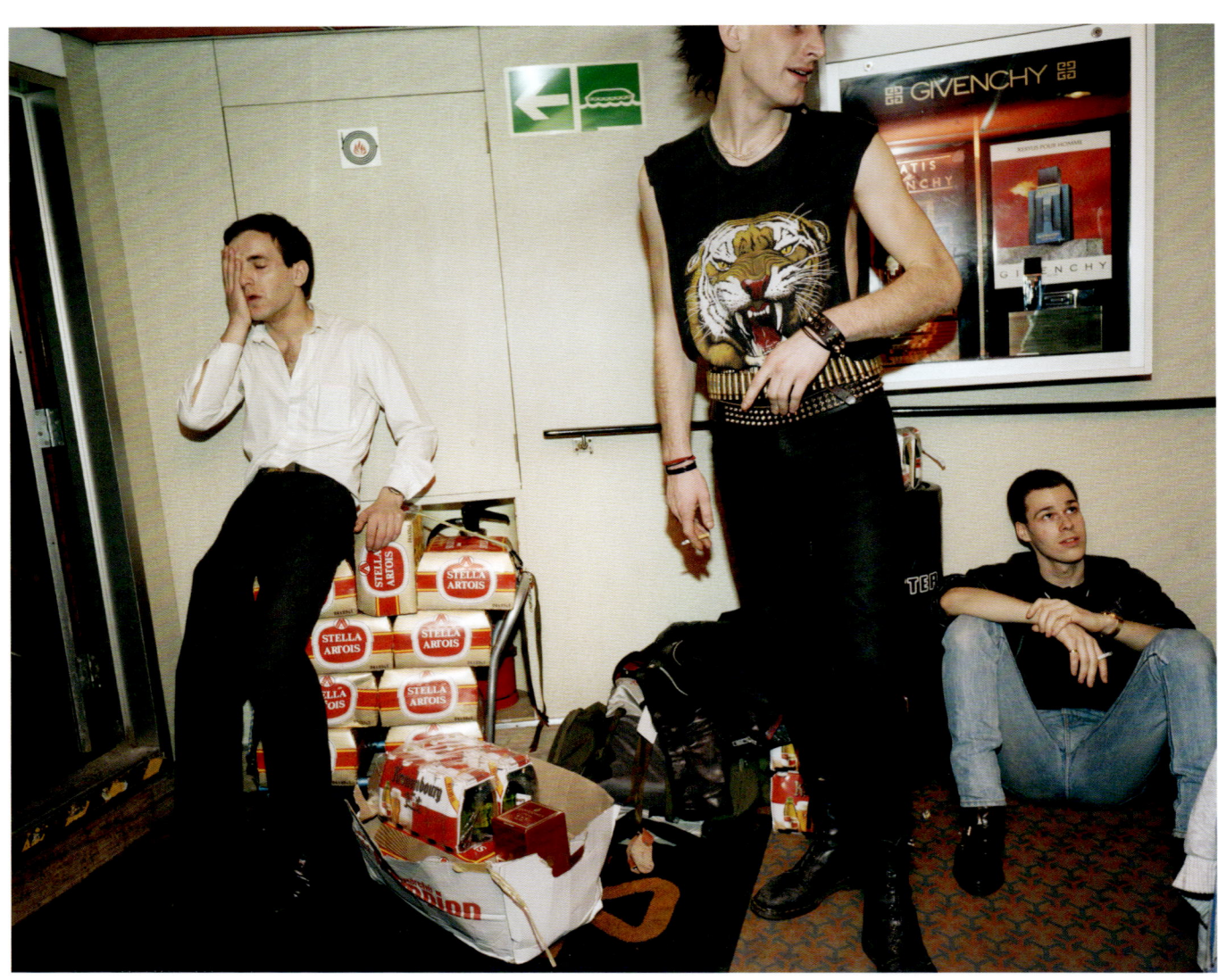

Boulogne-sur-Mer, France, 1988

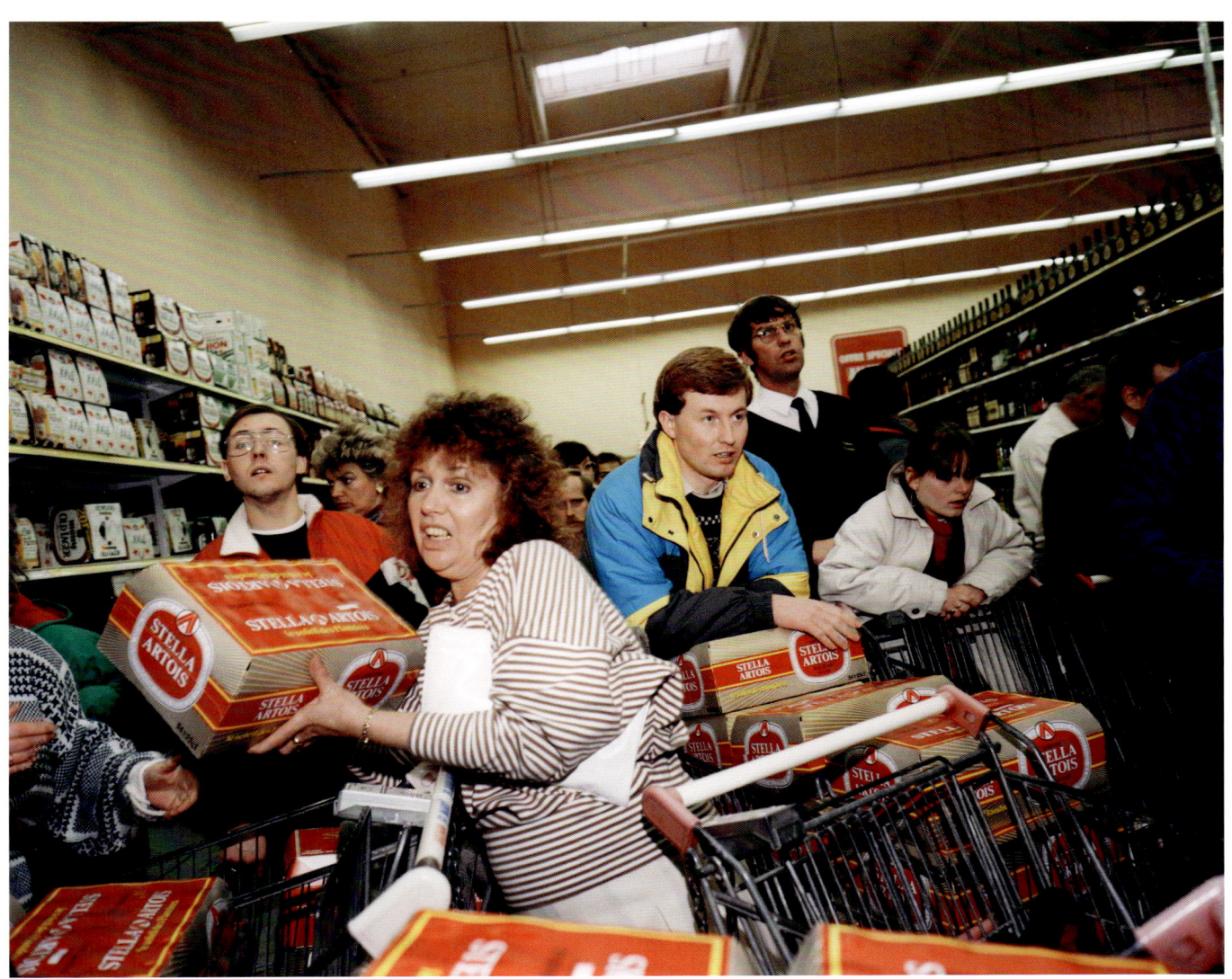

Calais, France, 1988

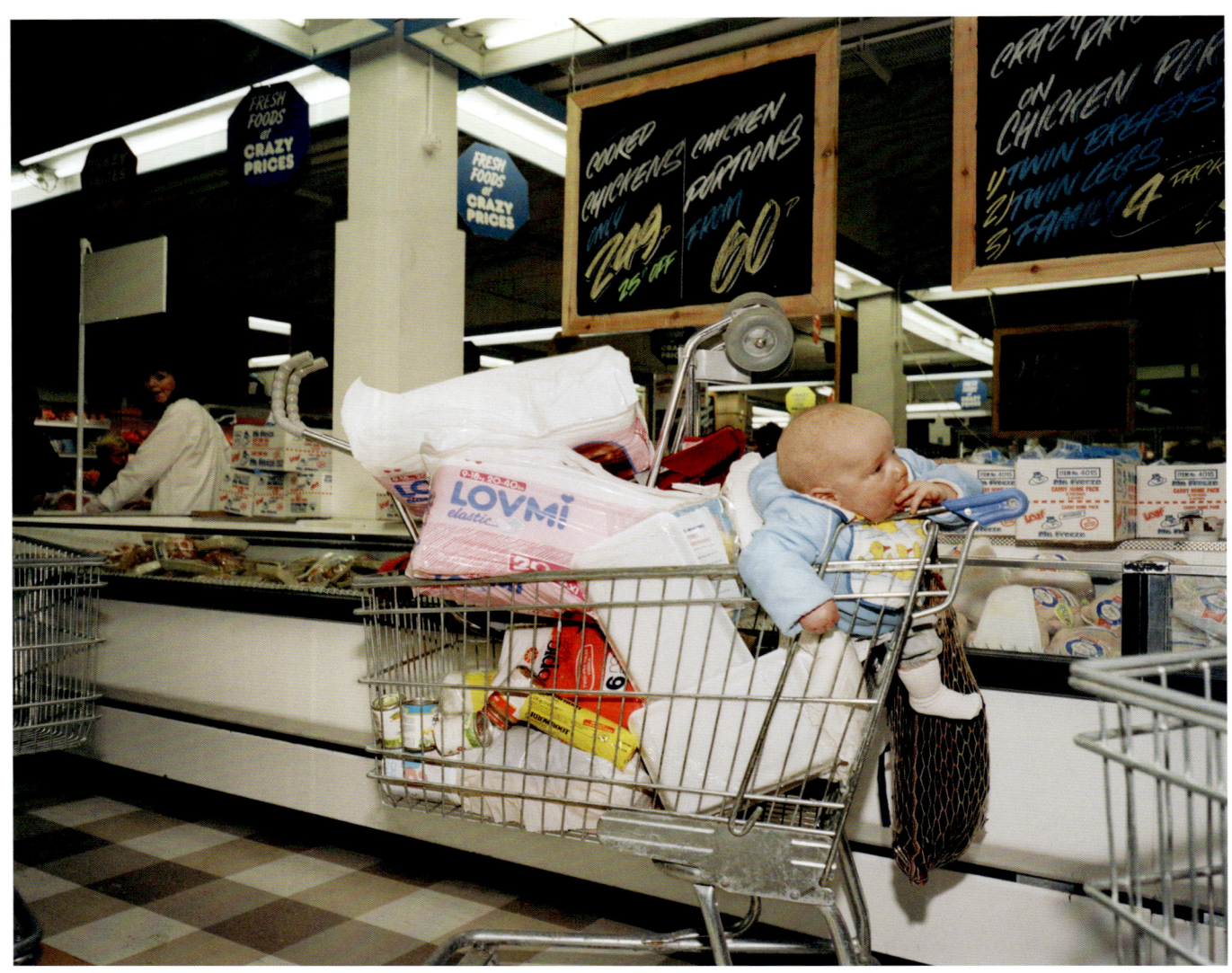

Dublin, Ireland, 1986

Opposite:
Prescot, England, 1984

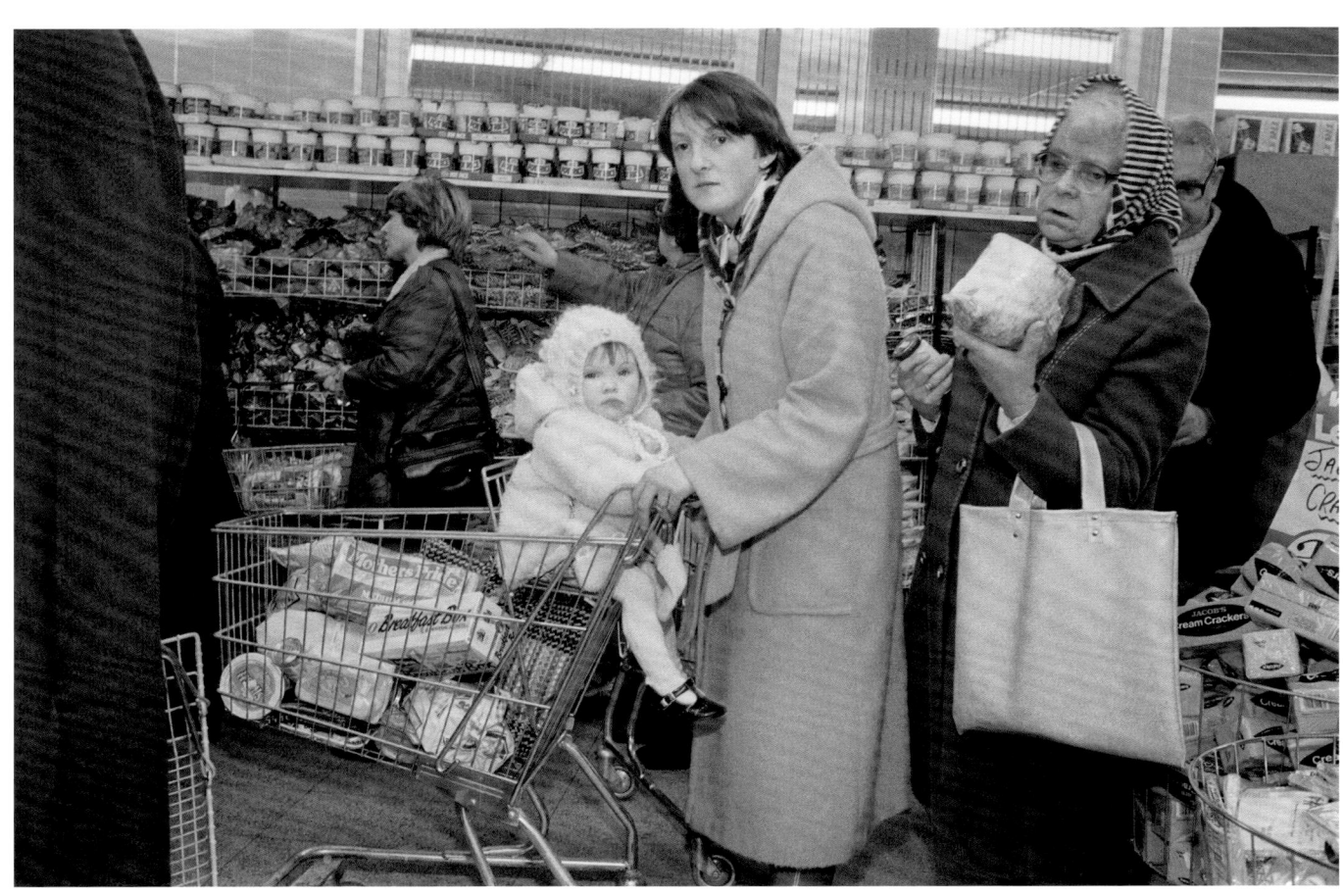

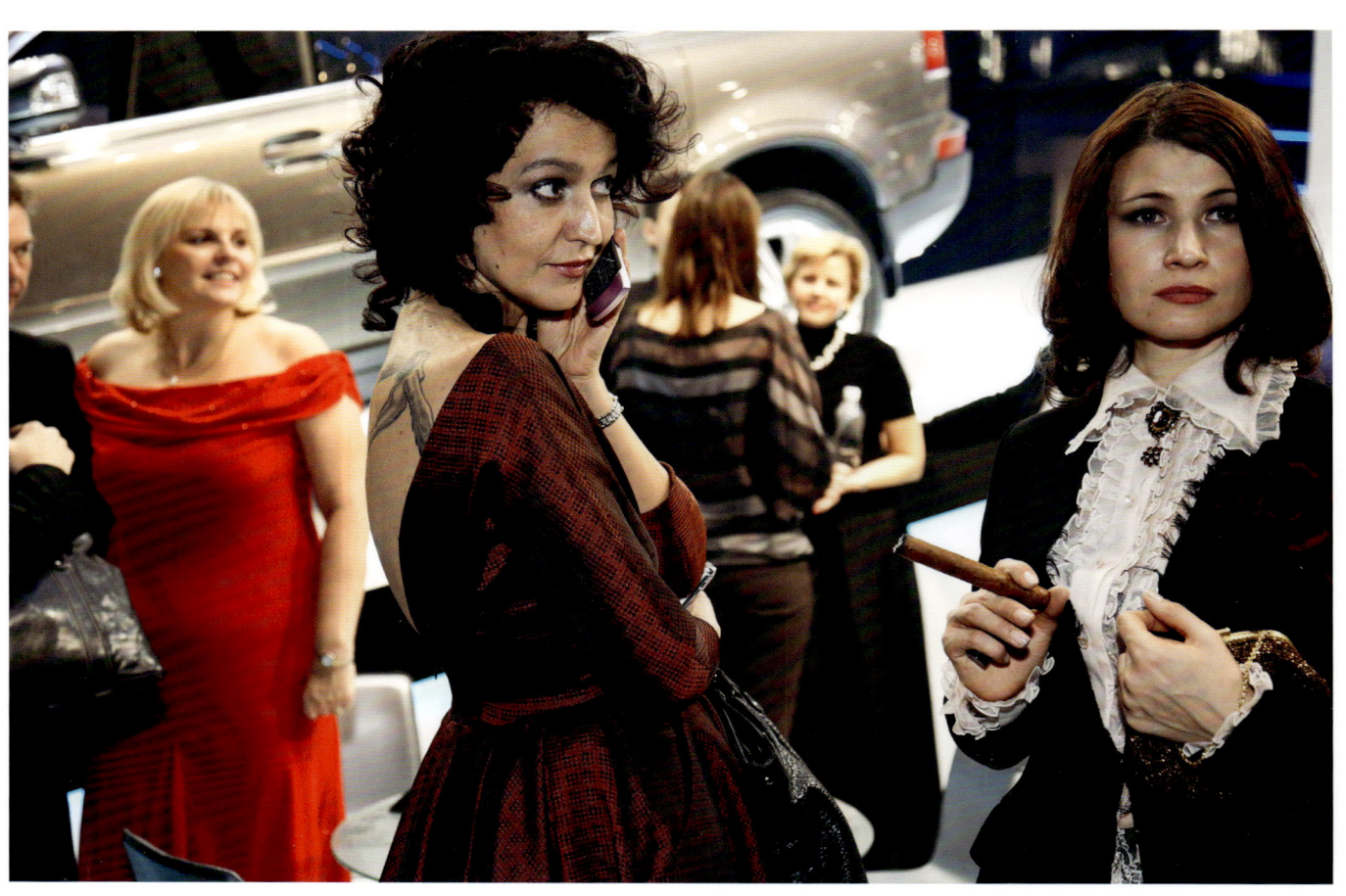

Moscow, Russia, 2007

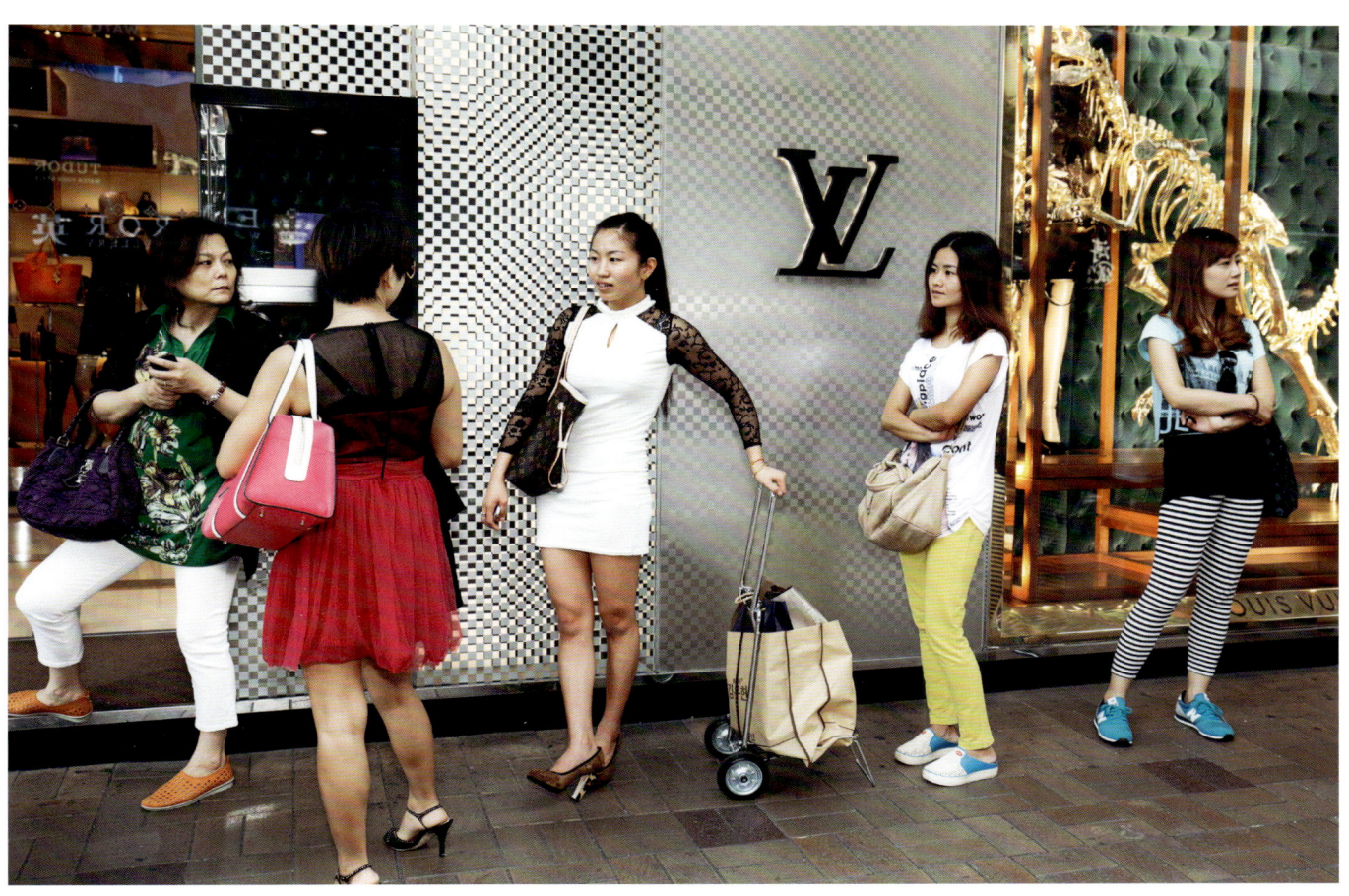

Hong Kong, China, 2013

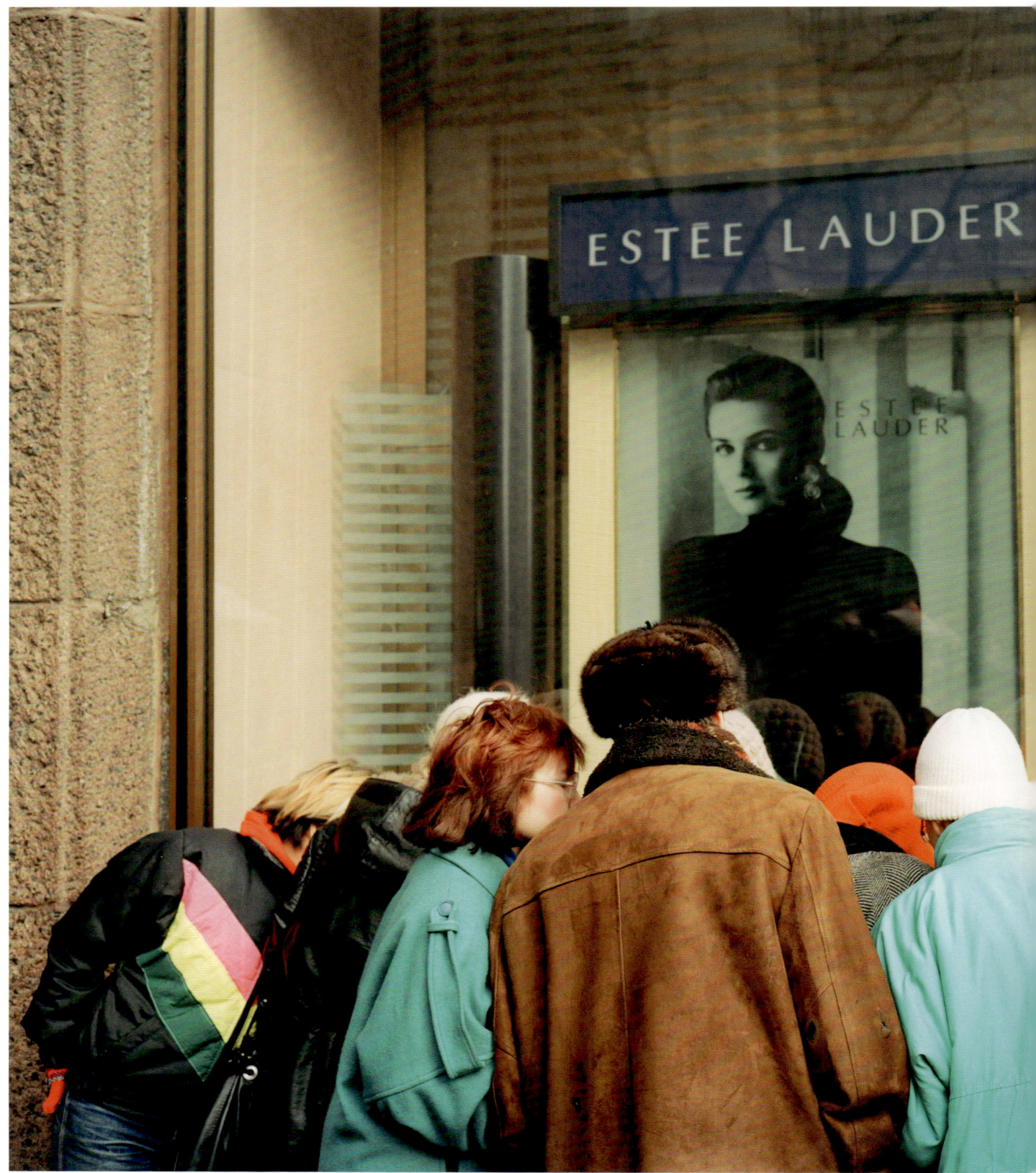

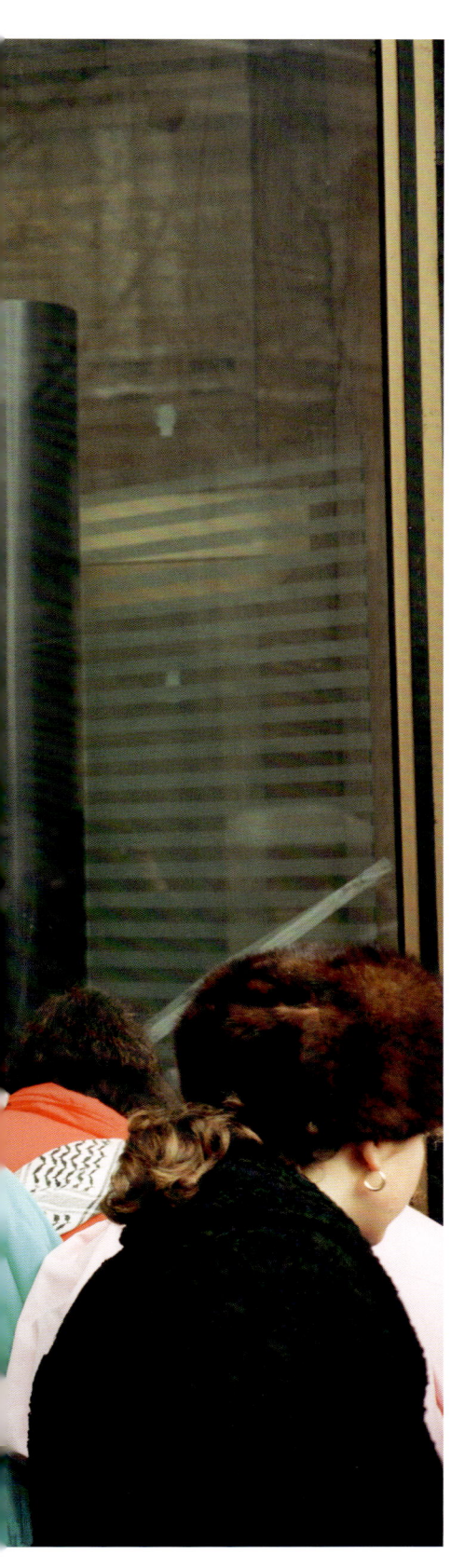

Moscow, Russia, 1992

105

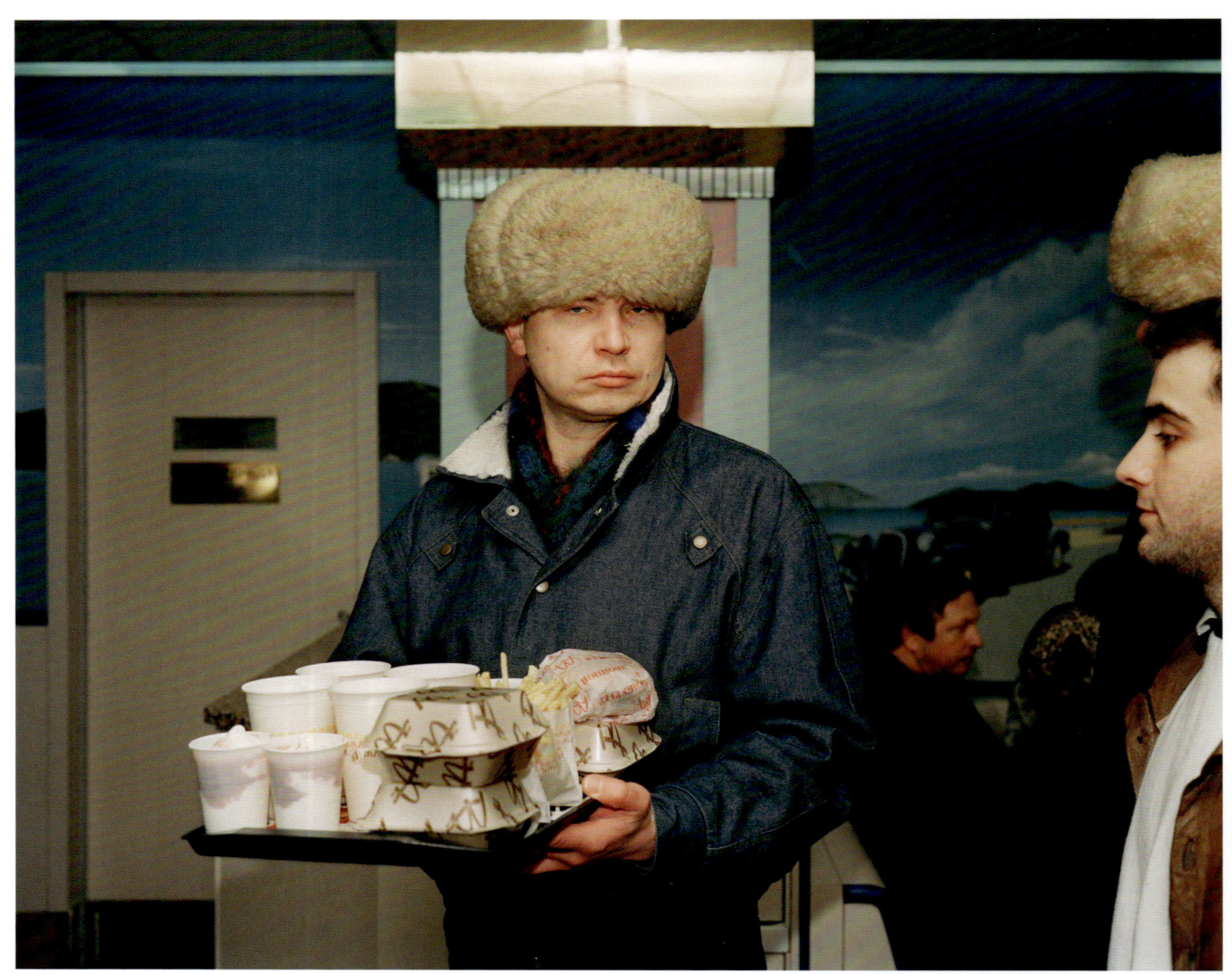

Moscow, Russia, 1992

Opposite:
Kent, England, 1986–9

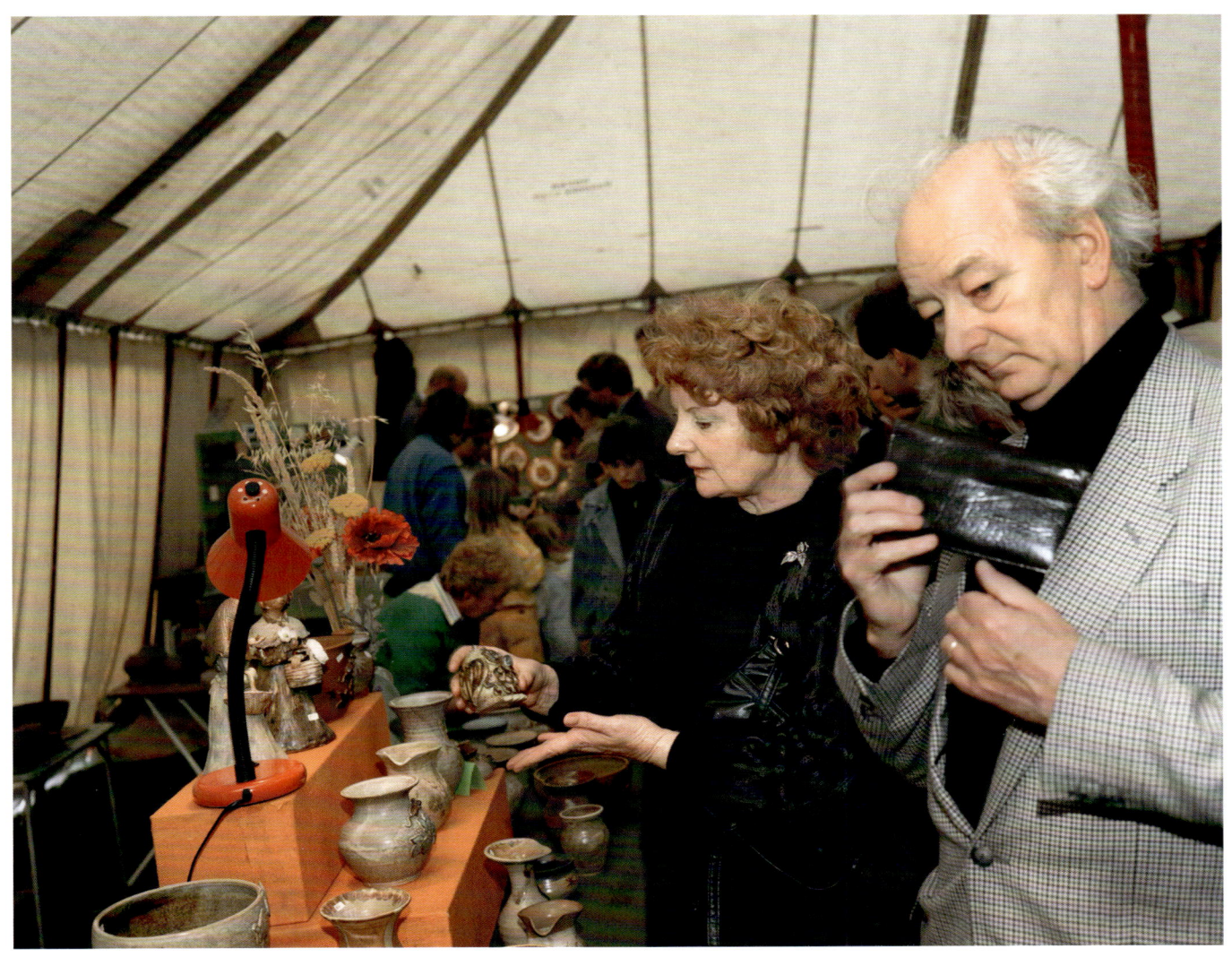

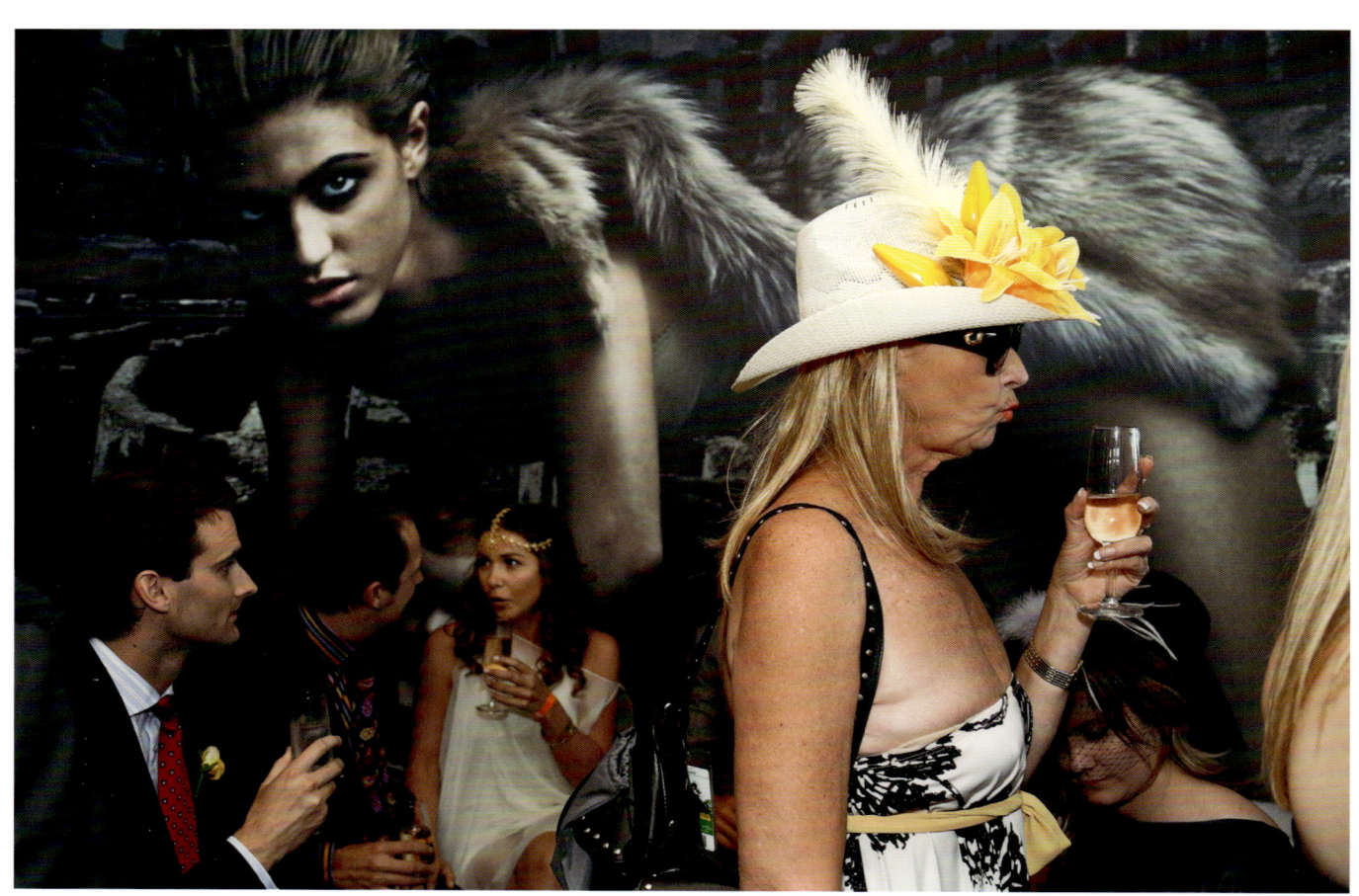

Melbourne, Australia, 2008

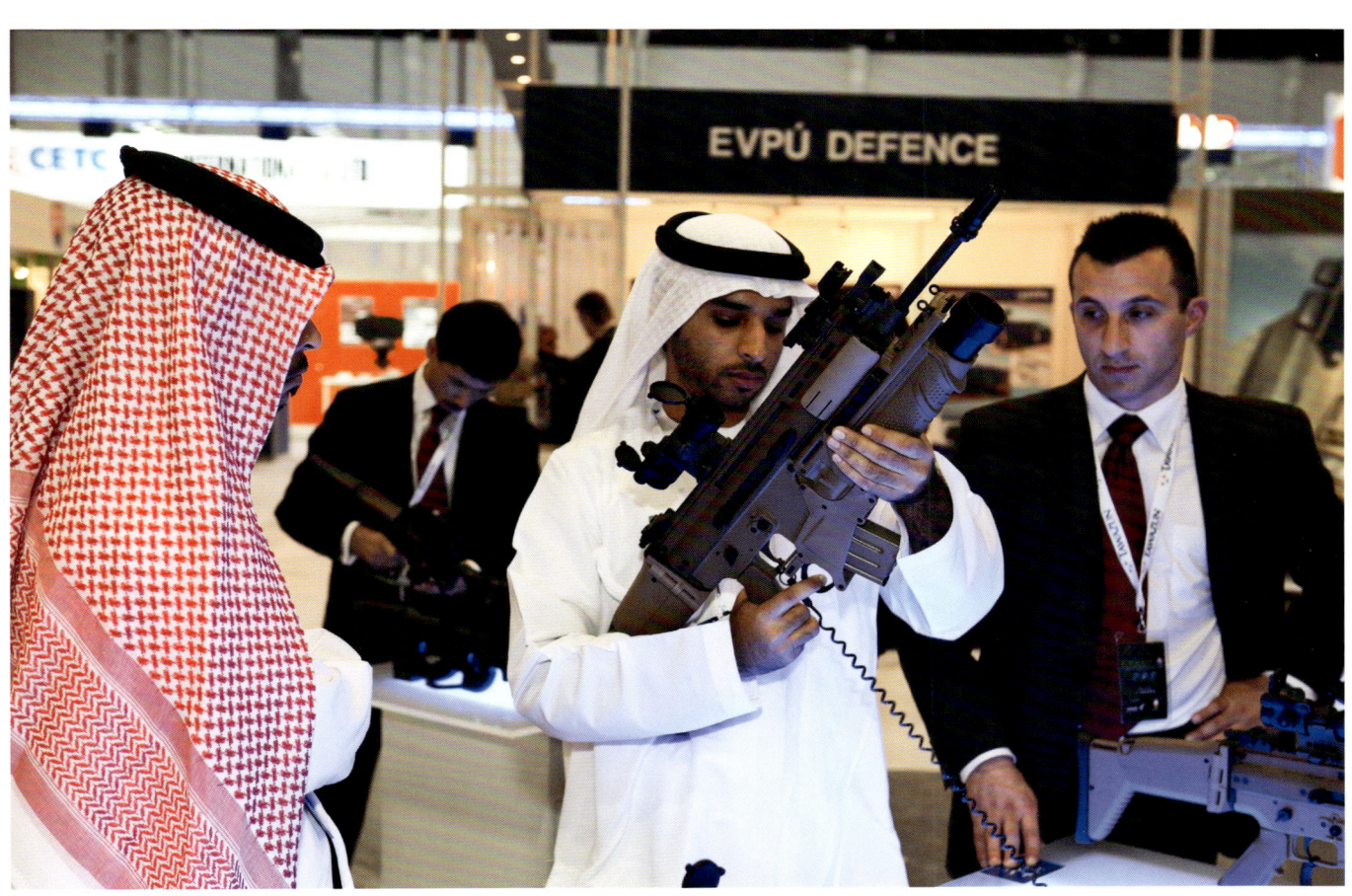

Abu Dhabi, United Arab Emirates, 2009

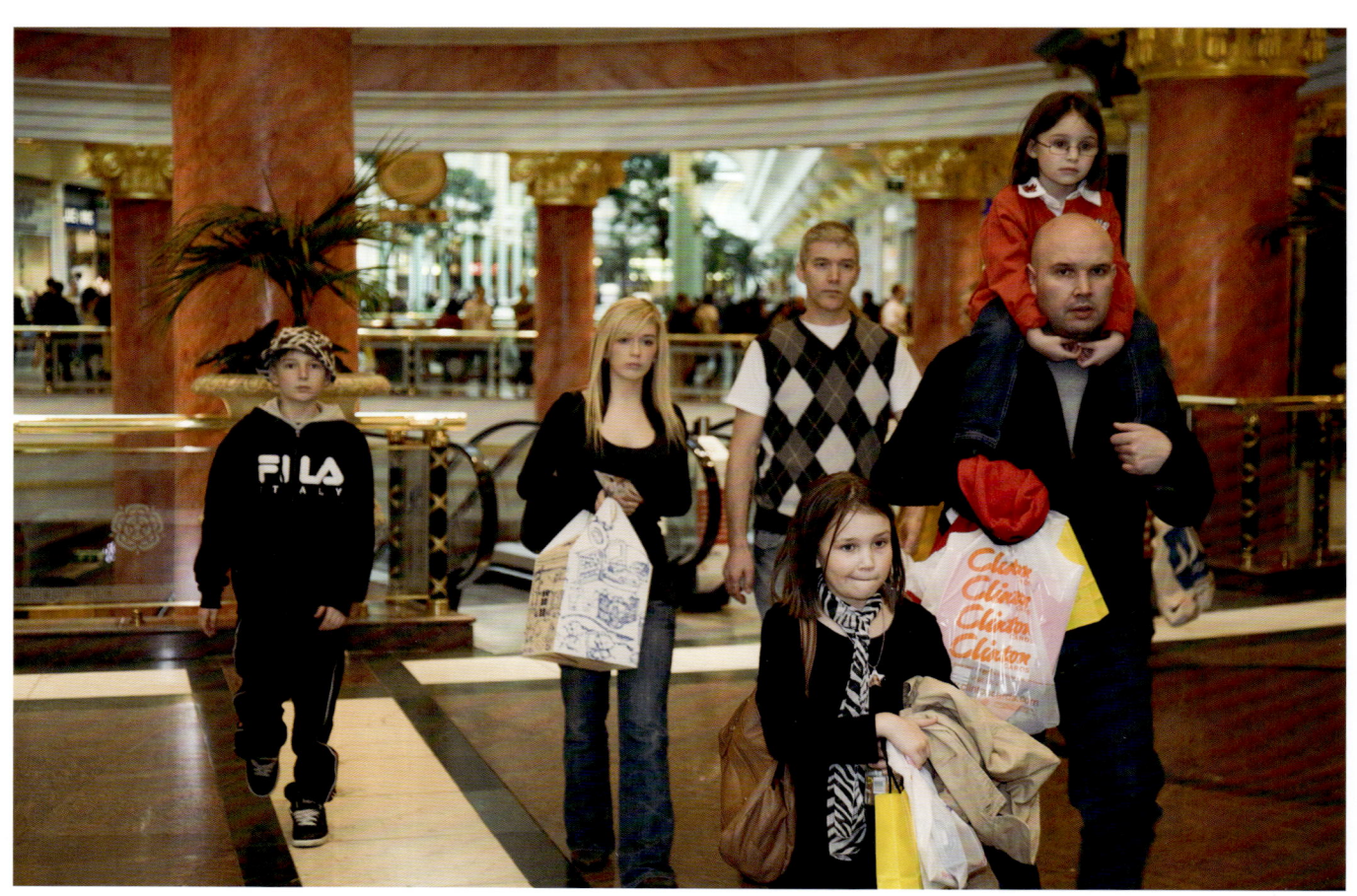

Manchester, England, 2008

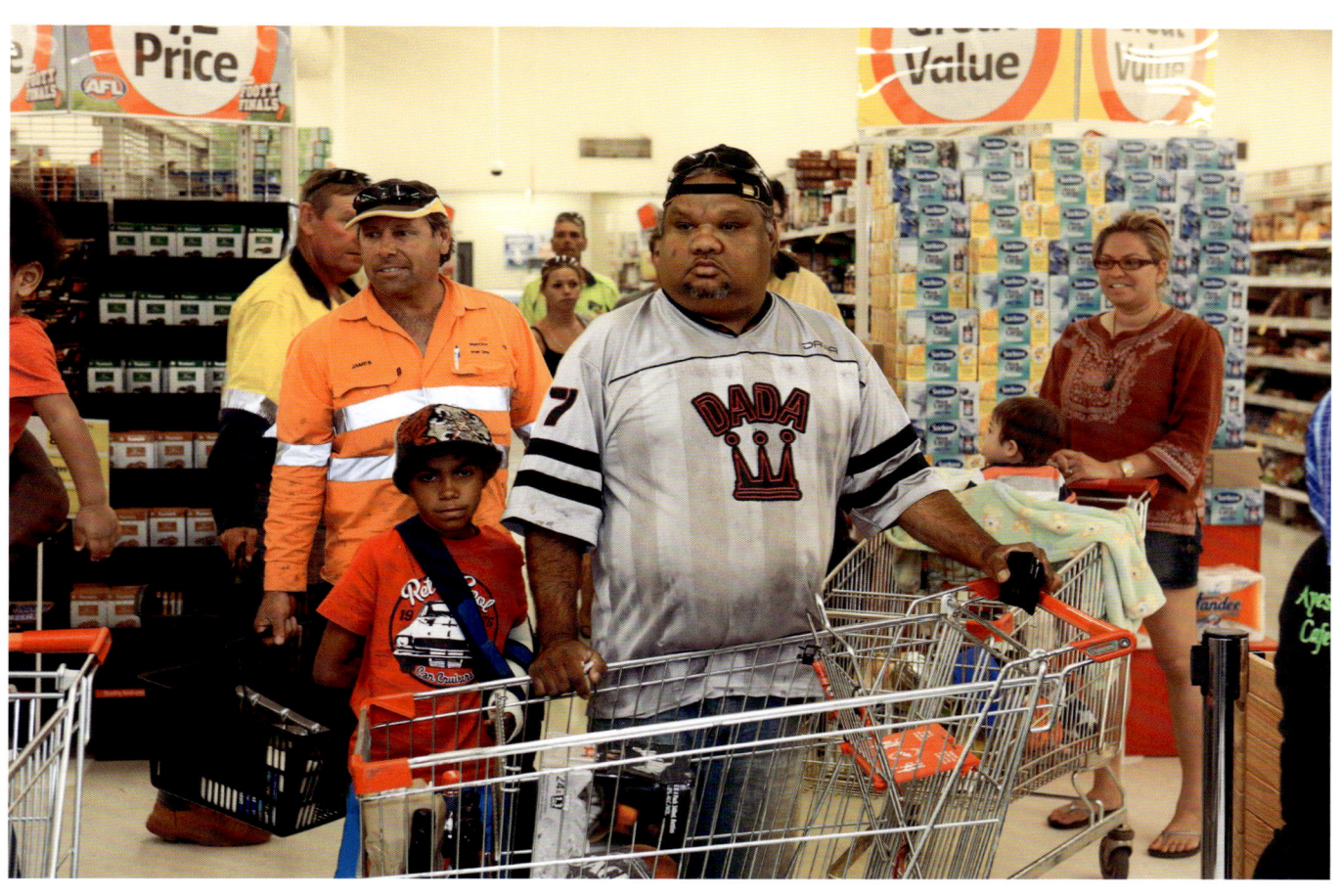

South Hedland, Australia, 2011

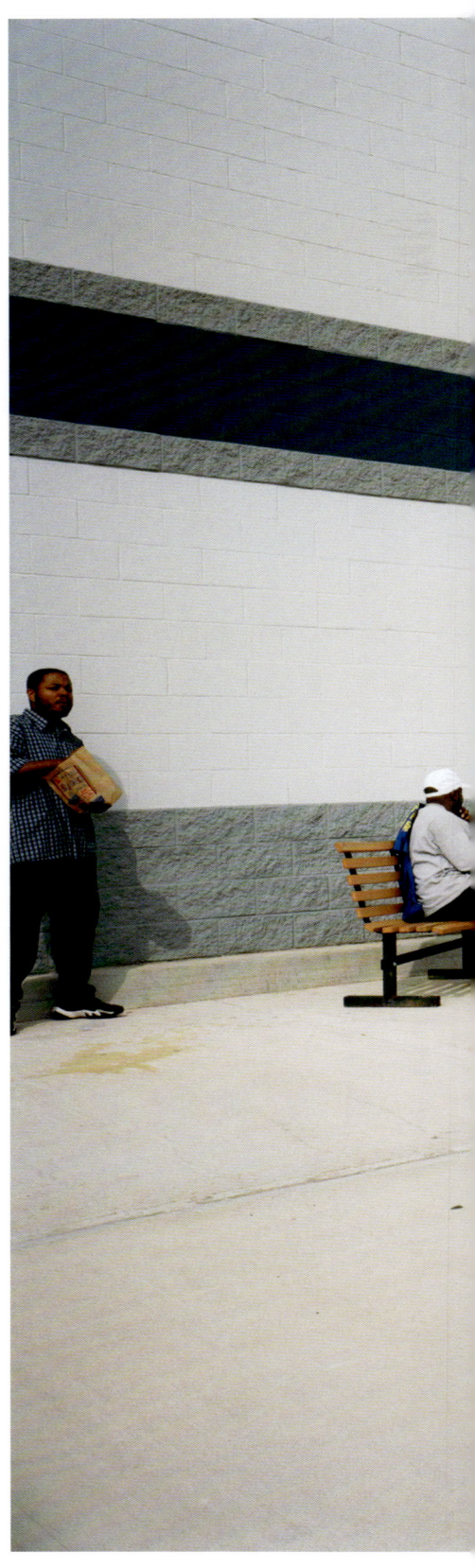

New Jersey, USA, 1998

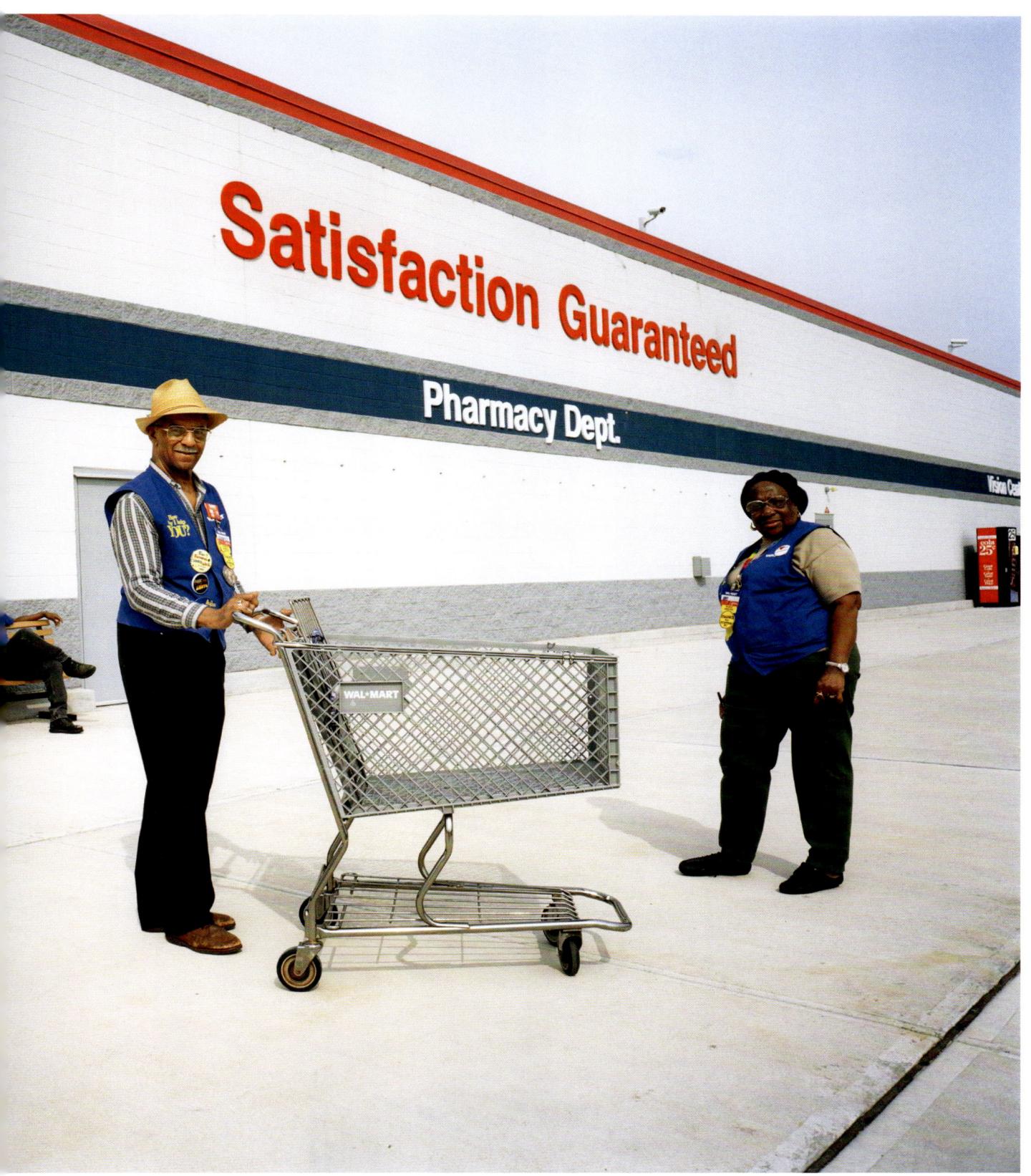

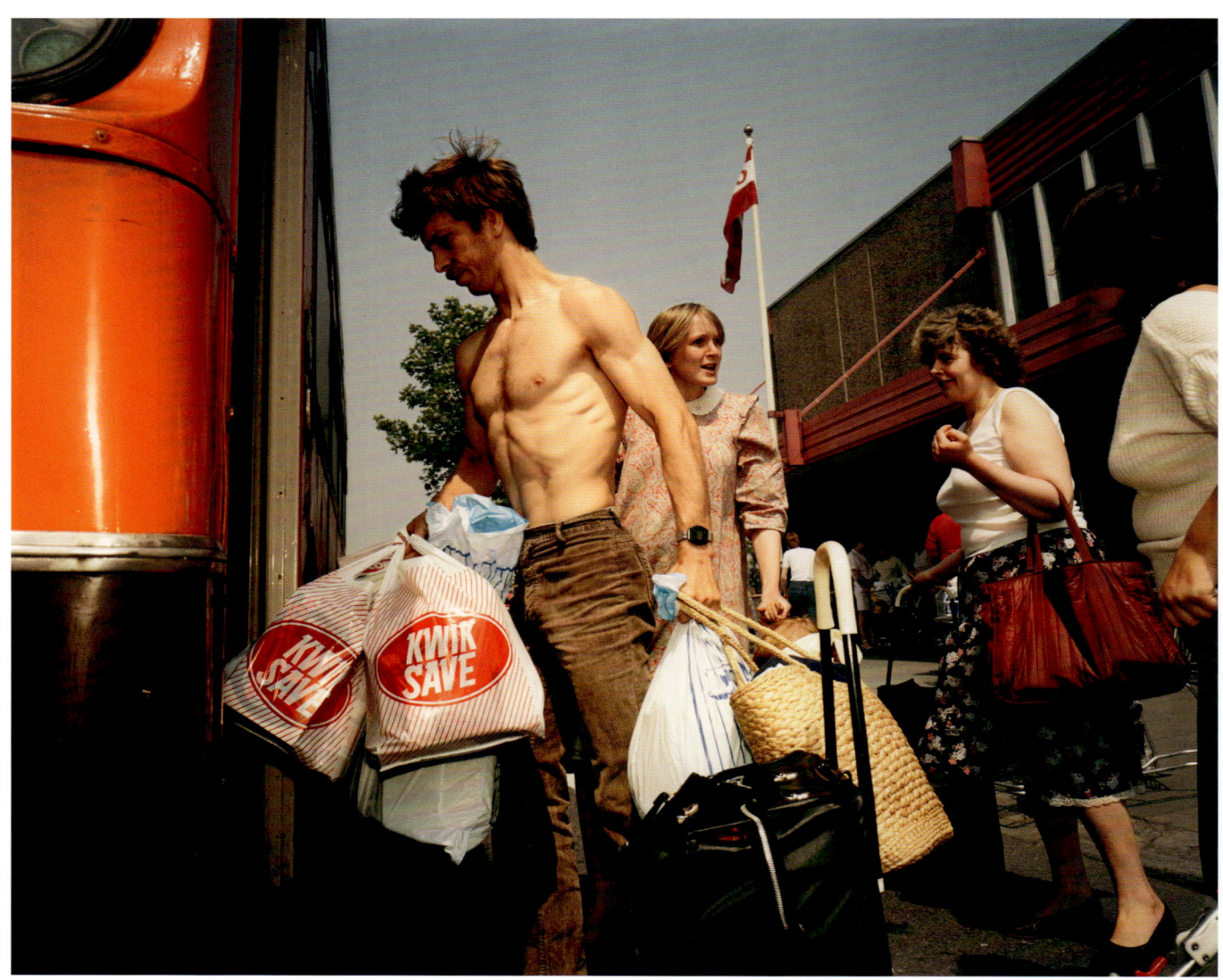

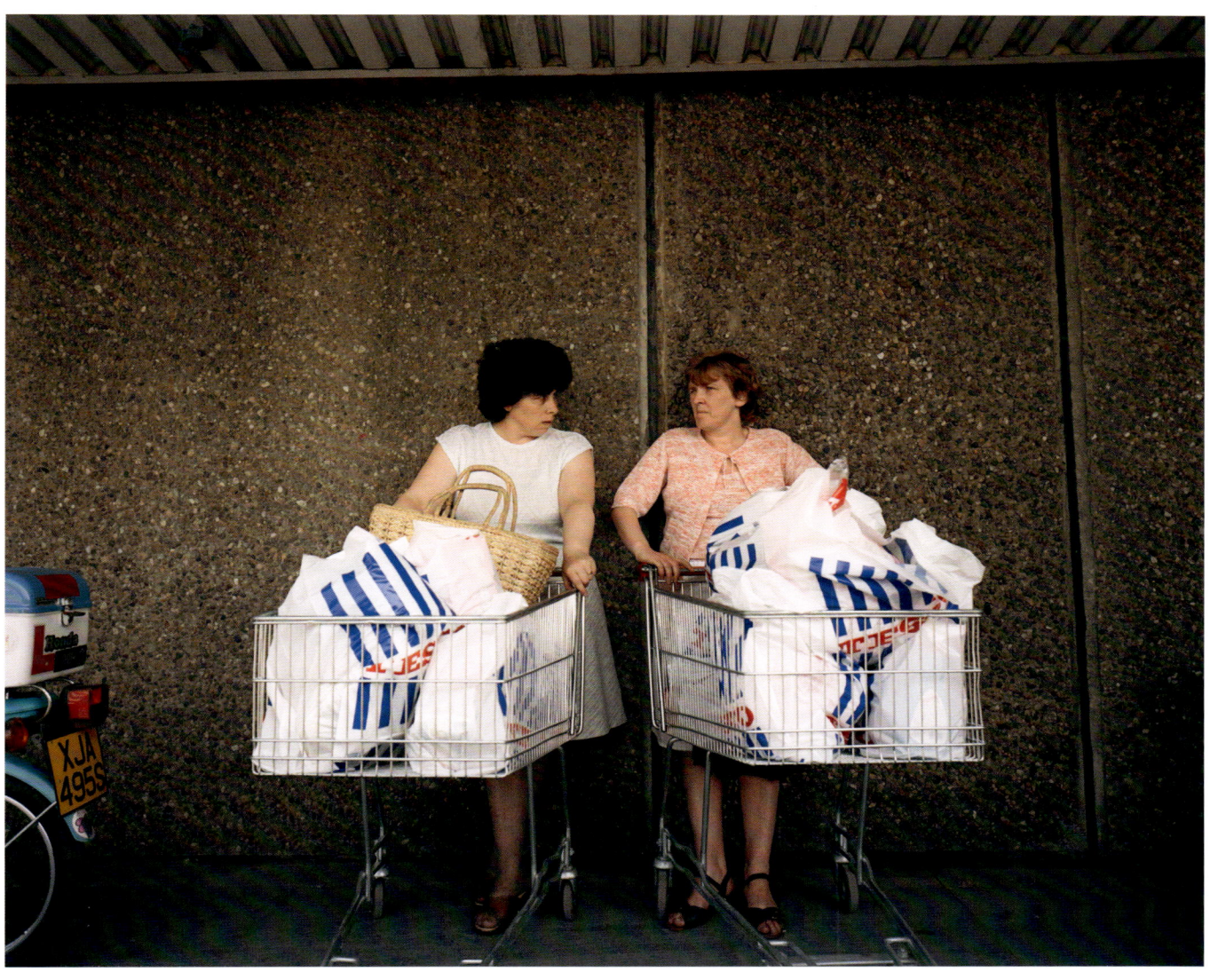

Opposite and above:
Salford, England, 1986

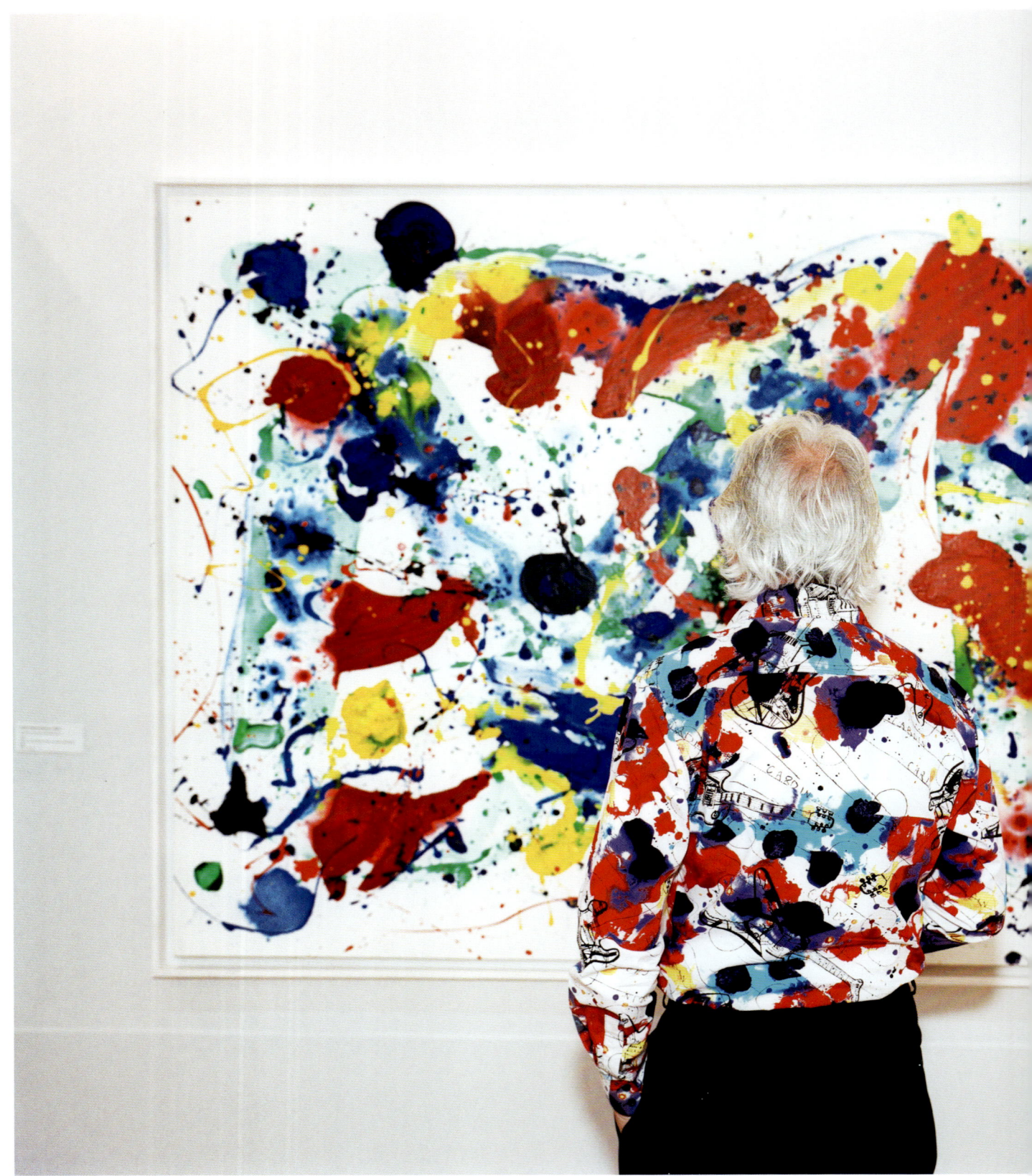

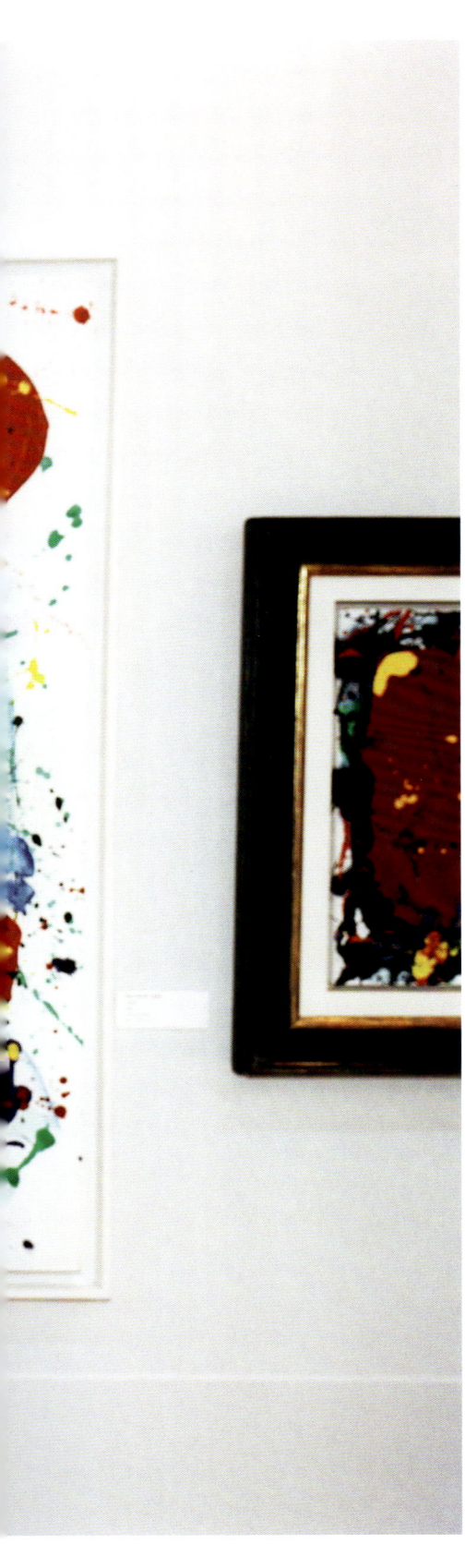

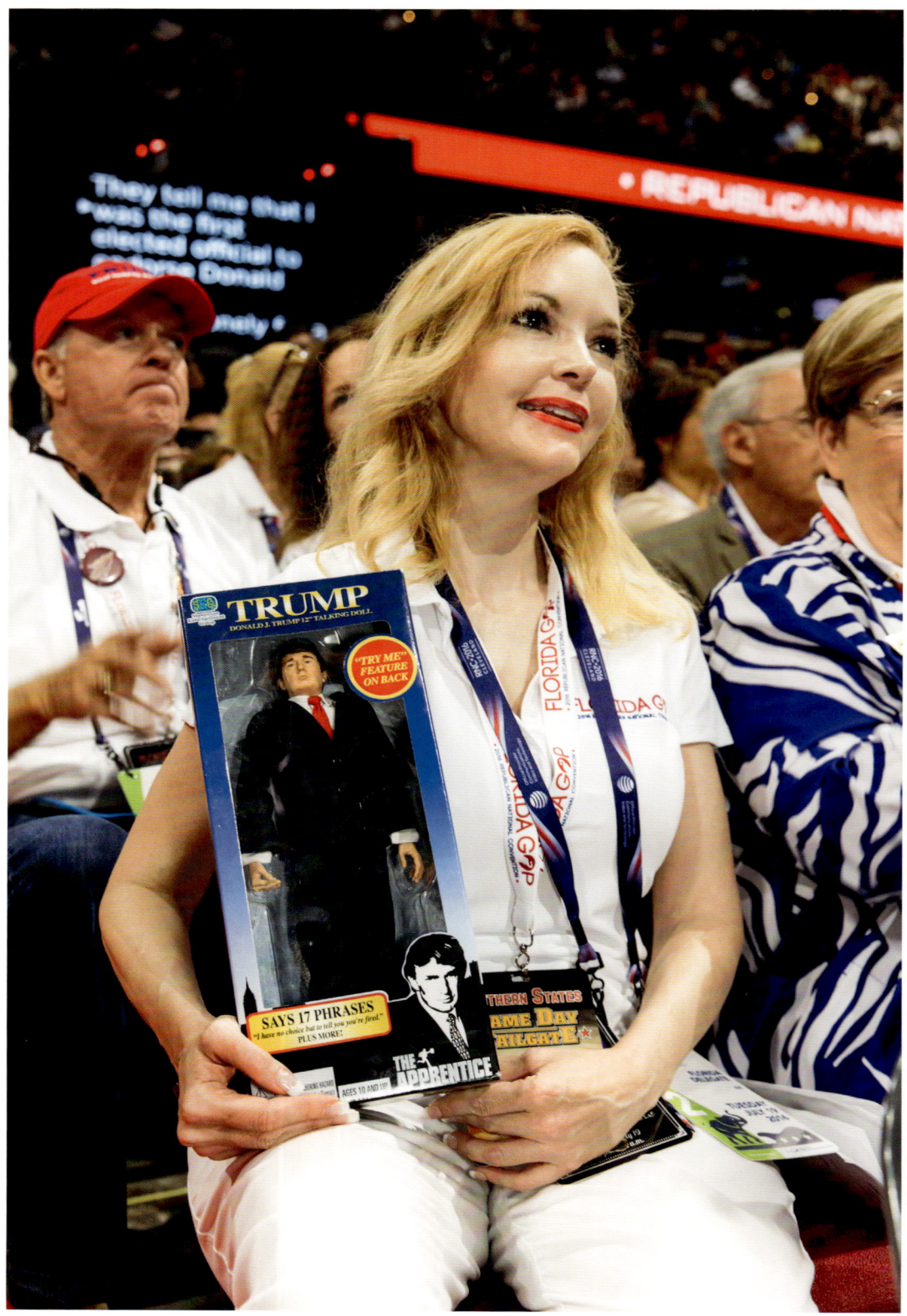

Cleveland, Ohio, USA, 2016

SHOP TILL YOU DROP!

BY
ROBERTA SASSATELLI

'Shop till you drop!' A phrase that is often repeated in our culture, it expresses a very specific psychic process: human beings throw themselves body and soul into the act of purchasing, accumulating, getting hold and hoarding of objects or, more often – as in the photographs of supermarkets dear to Martin Parr – a collection of objects. In all societies, the world of objects is an outstanding feature of human existence, offering us support and incitements and, at the same time, creating limits and difficulties. In a more general sense, the possibility that every way of life can be passed on to posterity – thus itself becoming a theme for reflection – is linked to our capacity to identify it with both material and cultural objects. In fact, it is thanks to these objects that any culture can expand well beyond the limits of the group that was originally its guardian. Nonetheless, the consumer capitalism defining the limits of contemporary society in the Global North implies a very special culture. Consumerism and its temples – supermarkets, shopping centres and fast-food outlets – connote the specific version of capitalism characterized by the dominance of consumption that was denounced in the critical works of numerous writers, such as Theodore Adorno, Hannah Arendt and Jean Baudrillard.[1] While it is true that notable forms of waste exist in all societies, indicating the symbolic domination of certain social groups, consumer capitalism generalizes acquisitive behaviour, allowing waste to become the order of the day.

This chapter of the catalogue opens with a picture showing a crowd of ravenous consumers who, with their fierce gestures and absent gaze, fill an anonymous space devoted to consumption where, in the foreground, there are now nothing more than the remains of a collective feast (see pp.96–7). Parr's picture is a reminder of the beginning of one of Italo Calvino's short stories in his book *Le città invisibili* (*Invisible Cities*), where one of the cities mentioned is Leonia, which is totally centred on consumption and its waste:

It is not so much by the things that each day are manufactured, sold, bought that you can measure Leonia's opulence, but rather by the things that each day are thrown out to make room for the new. So, you begin to wonder if Leonia's true passion is really, as they say, the enjoyment of new and different things, and not, instead, the joy of expelling, discarding, cleansing itself of a recurrent impurity.[2]

Thus, by focusing on the point of acquisition in its iconic omnipresence, Parr foreshadows our everyday Leonia: consumer capitalism, whose colourful goods seem to offer the final, definitive path to satisfying our desires; and whose rubbish, empty packaging, soiled and crumpled, recalls the frustration of those who, at the end of the day, are dissatisfied. Parr's vision expresses a form of cheerfulness that is, at the same time, emphatic, artificial and disconsolate: the saturated colours are a reminder of the invasion of plastic, with its profane convenience; the duller, blurred ones recall the evaporation of uncommodified nature that turns mankind into a decorative dust of organic matter.

Typically, the daily routine of capitalism is organized as a well-structured alternation of worktime and consumption time, which tend to correspond to different places: while worktime is necessary, recreation and fun are what really assume cultural centrality. Serving as an intermediary between these two periods of our lives – work and consumption – is the world of trade and exhcange. In fact, it is at the moment when we acquire things, especially in supermarkets, that we sense the key features of the emotional structure of consumer capitalism. A crowd of consumers, a traffic jam of trolleys, a woman in the foreground who grabs and holds aloft a pack of beer: this is one of the most significant pictures of a supermarket (see p.99). It is as if Parr were evoking the theme of the nymph-maidservant explored by the great art historian Aby Warburg in panel 46 of his last work, *Mnemosyne Atlas*. Warburg assembled a series of pictures from various periods in Western iconology portraying female figures – often nymphs or handmaidens – carrying objects on their heads or in their hands. This theme ranges from ancient Roman reliefs to Renaissance frescoes (for example, those of Ghirlandaio and Botticelli), concluding with a photograph of a peasant woman in Settignano, near Florence, taken by Warburg himself at the turn of the twentieth century.[3] This fundamental anthropological theme, which identifies human beings as a species that can pick up, carry and use objects, is expressed here by Parr from a consumerist point view: no longer the Olympian serenity of the aesthetics of the Italian Renaissance closely linked to the measured and calm concept of harmonious beauty, but rather a new type of female figure that is uncouth, askew and subject to spasms of emotion.

This picture is preceded – as in an inevitable nemesis – by a photograph of three young men tired of their purchases, waiting together, yet, at the same time, apparently distant from each other. Their expressions of mild astonishment remind us that, after shopping, there is a sense of emptiness and isolation that often ends up by predominating (see p.98). As Christopher Lasch argued in his classic work *The Culture of Narcissism*,[4] published shortly before Parr completed *The Last Resort*, consumer capitalism favours the development of 'weak personalities' withdrawn in themselves, continuously seeking gratification in things and likewise always doomed to disappointment. The pleasure that they crave in order to fill their inner void is, in fact, a sort of aggressiveness that does not recognize anything as sacred, instead reducing everything to interchangeable commodities. For Lasch, commodification is effectively a challenge to the humanity of individuals. Their sociality appears to shatter against the colourful collections of objects: by becoming consumers, human beings become a function (consuming – in other words, destroying – goods in order to make way for other goods) and a mass (thus contributing to the production of a variety of goods without contrasts).

In one way or another, what critical theory proposes is exactly what Hannah Arendt suggests in the chapter of *The Human Condition* entitled 'A Consumers' Society': a process of worldly alienation.[5] Arendt draws our attention to the way people are encouraged to focus not so much on the use of goods as on their purchase, in particular due to the lack of time to become accustomed to the things we buy and allow them to function so that we can feel truly at home with them in everyday life. In this respect, the quantity of our purchases appears to have grown so rapidly as to cause us to lose sight of their tangible meaning. As Hartmut Rosa, the last disciple of the Frankfurt School, writes, acceleration – evident in the crowds desperately seeking to do their shopping (see p.107) and get their hands on food and drinks (see pp.96–7, 106), and in the resulting waste materials (see pp.46, 48, 53) – is, in fact, the most significant feature of contemporary capitalist society.[6] The culture of objects flows more rapidly than the culture of subjects – that is to

say, the capacity of human beings to enrich objects with meaning. Thus, for Baudrillard, commodities have become an organized 'global, arbitrary and coherent' system of signs, according to the continuous and planned creation of innovation and obsolescence, and human needs depend on the commodity system rather than on the living relationship between subjects and objects.[7] In this commodified voracity, every purchase is always the last of an infinite series – and the last choice is always the best!

In the sequence of works on display here, the photograph itself is a consumer object, but Parr's aim is certainly more subtle than that. In this book, the image the camera lens focuses on serves as a mirror showing not so much a reflection of reality as an emotional laceration that tears apart the veil of our carefree connivance in what Nancy Fraser has described as 'cannibal capitalism'.[8] This is a form of capitalism that tends to transform consumption into a myth; that is to say, 'it is a statement of contemporary society about itself... Just as medieval society was balanced on God and the Devil, so ours is balanced on consumption and its denunciation.'[9] Thus, we are invited to take a fresh look at the brand new topos of commercial modernity: the child in a shopping trolley (see pp.100–101). In these pictures, which are perhaps the most memorable of them all from an anthropological point of view, we see a baby in a supermarket trolley, as if it were just one of the items on sale. Whether in black and white, as in the older photograph, or in colour, as in the more recent shot, Parr focuses our attention on the way in which, in an increasingly objectified world, even the most tender human being is mingled with commodities. And, in this mixture, there is the possibility, for us as spectators, of a melancholic estrangement, of a mocking smile, of some critical distance.

If the reduction of the human being to a commodity is a general and recurring theme in the present volume – a theme that can be found on several levels, whether by aesthetic analogy (see p.116) or by transforming Donald Trump into a toy (p.118) – although often reflecting the British identity, the photographs were taken over a number of decades in a variety of locations, with an oblique reference to the American model. In the years following the Second World War, the developments in consumer capitalism in Europe and then, more recently and especially after the end of the Cold War, in other countries in the south and east of the world, have been interpreted as a form of Americanization of our lifestyle. Supermarkets (but also mass tourism or fast-food restaurants) reflect the emergence of American influence as that 'of a great imperium with the outlook of a great emporium'.[10] And Parr reveals not only the ceaseless intermingling of goods and people in a hybrid system that commodifies human beings and humanizes commodities, but also the endless process of redefining tastes and values that this system implies.

Hence it is the progressive triumph of a consumerist culture – the essence of which is constituted by speed, quantity and superficiality – that is most evident in the pictures presented here.

Often women play a leading role in this culture: in both the West and the East they are culturally and socially constructed as consumers par excellence. Consumer capitalism has exploited their capacities, offering them a space for action where other spheres, such as politics or business, were less accessible. And it is through their quest for pleasure and refinement, and fashion and freedom, among other things, that consumption becomes not only a standardized opportunity for greed, but also a job in its own right that needs preparation, especially for the middle classes, by paying careful attention to positional and symbolic objects. Some items, such as designer handbags, may be difficult to obtain immediately, but are still much sought after by many women so that they can be one up on their girlfriends. And they are things that, like an animistic god, are all branded and we do not see them portrayed as such, but for which, as one of Parr's most telling photographs demonstrates, it is necessary to patiently queue up outside a luxury store (see pp.104–5).

This was the predominant, global mentality, especially in the second half of the twentieth century, when we were perhaps labouring under the illusion that war had finally been replaced with consumption. The *pax consummatio* (consumer peace) combines the features of the sacred that were previously associated with religion. The final pictures in this chapter contain ironic references to the 'last day' – in other words, to transcendence as the key feature of every religion.[11] In the Judaic-Christian tradition, the last day is the Apocalypse: not just destruction, but also revelation, judgement and the beginning of a new supersensual reality. This eschatological vision calls to mind the passage from the limits of the human condition to a divine, higher dimension. In the centre of this scenario there is often a profoundly human gesture: the shared meal. Parr juxtaposes its representation as an explicit gesture of Christian solidarity with that of the profane 'last day' of the sales. But the meal eaten with others is a sign that, despite the judgement, there is still hope: that of a saved community, gathered in the presence of the sacred. In consumer culture, on the other hand, from the last-day sales to the advertising countdowns, the eschatological language is recycled in order to produce a sense of urgency in the purchases, rather than in spiritual conversion. Transcendency is replaced by the eternal present in which, rather than being sublimated, desire is consumed. Certainly, in consumer capitalism, the sacred offers an opportunity for selling, yet even here one catches a glimpse of simple, direct and authentic desires: the need for community, the search for meaning, nostalgia for what lies beyond. Perhaps, in the tension between the sacred and

the market, there is opportunity for asking questions about what 'end' really means, what is really worth saving and what, on the contrary, should be abandoned.

In consumer capitalism, every value may become a means for commodification: the logic of individual enjoyment – hedonism – is subject to the circulation of goods. After all, even weapons are only commodities. And here is a photograph – even more challenging now that peace has been violated twice over for Europe, which is currently between two inescapable fires – demonstrating that even a machine gun can arouse those desires on which the market is based (see p.109). The passion for shopping, where everything is the same thanks to the great leveller, money, mixed cocktails and weapons in a sampling procedure that is both hedonistic and macabre. Eros and Thanatos, the two principles that fascinated Sigmund Freud, the drive towards life and death facing each other in their double need to exist and dissolve, are not simply created through war and violence, but also through commodities that goes so far as to propose the desire for death as the principle of commercial satisfaction.[12] And yet, consumption is perhaps – to a limited extent, at least – a way of exorcizing death, as Don DeLillo demonstrates in *White Noise*. When, at the end of the novel, the supermarket shelves have been rearranged, unexpected anxiety is aroused: yet the protagonist soon realizes that the world has been saved because the mechanism that gives value to goods functions regularly:

The terminals are equipped with holographic scanners, which decode the binary secret of every item, infallibly. This is the language of waves and radiation, or how the dead speak to the living. And this is where we wait together, regardless of age, our carts stocked with brightly colored goods.[13]

All in all, this chapter of Parr's work plays on the centrality of the shopping trolley: whether it is full or empty is of little import – the trolley is our main way of reaching a highly imaginative and incessant Cockaigne.[14] Unlike Banksy's famous Trolley Hunters, created for the first time in 2006 and published in conjunction with the exhibition entitled 'Barely Legal' held in Los Angeles in the same year, here the trolley does not take the place of the prey. For Parr, present-day consumers do not have to face an absurd hunt for the trolley, emulating their ancestors who obtained food by hunting animals of various sizes; modern consumers have to deal with a new sacred symbol. The empty trolley at the centre of the photograph dominated by the slogan 'Satisfaction Guaranteed' (see pp.112–13) is a mystical and cold portal towards the promised, obligatory satisfaction. And, in the sequence of pictures proposed, the trolley takes the role of a fetish: the family laden with bags proceeds through the mall with fixed and astonished stares (see p.110), expressing astonishment; they are followed by a photo of a father and son pushing a trolley containing only a few products in a crowded supermarket (see p.111), and then the staff members who, standing next to an empty trolley outside the store, seem to be consulting us with quizzical expressions. The family thins out and disappears; the work that lies behind commerce frames the trolley, which seems to be telling us it is ready to be loaded up. But Parr takes us by the hand and invites us to continue the journey: two trolleys are now overflowing with goods; two lady shoppers proceeding side by side, look at each other and talk, comparing the pile of overflowing bags filling them up (see p.115). Or again, women exchanging glances and comments, leaving a young man to take charge of the huge supermarket bags (see p.114). Thus, the human factor returns in this pictorial journey that Parr proposes through its places and times, not so much to fill up the trolleys as to make them significant in our daily interaction: this is a form that may be banal, but is an incredibly way of existing as subjects in society today. Inevitably, this reminds us of what Parr himself stated in an interview regarding his work of the 1980s:

New Brighton was in fact a political photographic project. Thatcherism celebrated the new-found greatness of the nation, which was particularly vexing for those living in Liverpool, at that time one of the poorest and shabbiest cities in the United Kingdom. Even so, in this dismal scenario, people continued to go about their normal lives: they went to the seaside, played with their children, ate ice-cream, all the things you usually do by the sea. This was the contrast that I wanted to highlight in my project.[15]

Thus, the progressive and inexorable commodification of the world corresponds with a similarly continuous activity on the part of consumers in order to stimulate the logic of personal relations: one of the paradoxes of our society is the fact that we must necessarily translate the commodities we use in terms of everyday banality. In other words, we must somehow appropriate them and decommodify them if we want our activities to have a meaning for us as human beings.[16]

While the behaviour patterns that the photographs depict in a disenchanted manner are ubiquitous, Parr seems to be telling us that it is not necessary to be oppositive in order to be critical: for that matter, resistance, as Michael Foucault put it, is always the result of power, accompanying it and, at times, ending up by nourishing it.[17] Thus it is more effective to enter, like a visual ethnographer, the everyday routine of consumer capitalism in order to be transferred to the other part of the stage, from the point at which its face becomes a mask, which speaks of us of what we take for granted, of

what we ask to give us satisfaction and plenitude. It is a gaze that, in some ways, is in abeyance, an epoché – a suspension of judgement – that is both welcoming and critical, implying, as Parr himself put it, 'the maximum receptiveness before the complexity of phenomena',[18] which results in the 'ironic heroization of the present', associated by Charles Baudelaire with the *flâneur*: 'you have no right to despise the present.'[19] This is why the documentary angles and the immediacy of snapshots are in contrast with the strong polychromatism of the pictures: this colour effect, which plays such an important role in advertising imagery, is the dominant feature of these photographs, which are meant to be an immoralist critique, capable of truly expressing, from close at hand, the experience of mass consumption and, starting from there, suggesting what might be a possible alternative. It is as if these pictures were telling us that we cannot opt out of consumer capitalism, but that we can, from within, explore its pleasures and limits, and imagine possibilities of transcendency through the capacity to understand the ambivalence of consumption and the way it remains – despite everything – a domain for action that it is difficult to abandon.

1   Theodor Adorno, 'On popular music', in *Studies in Philosophy and Social Sciences Studies in Philosophy and Social Sciences*, 9 (1), pp.17–48, New York City, The Institute of Social Research, 1941; Hannah Arendt, *The Human Condition*, Chicago, University of Chicago Press, 1958; Jean Baudrillard, *The Consumer Society: Myths and Structures*, London, Sage, 1998 (original French ed. 1970).

2   Italo Calvino, trans. William Weaver, *Invisible Cities* (*Le città invisibili*), San Diego, New York and London, Harcourt Brace & Company, 1974.

3   Georges Didi-Huberman, *Il passo leggero dell'ancella. Sul sapere eccentrico delle immagini*, Bologna, EDB, 2020. See also: www.warburg.library.cornell.edu/panels/panel-46/.

4   Christopher Lasch, *The Culture of Narcissism*, New York, Norton, 1979.

5   Arendt, *The Human Condition*.

6   Hartmut Rosa, trans. Jonathan Trejo-Mathys, *Social Acceleration: A New Theory of Modernity*, New York, Columbia University Press, 2013.

7   Baudrillard, *The Consumer Society*, 1998.

8   Nancy Fraser, *Cannibal Capitalism: How Our System Is Devouring Democracy, Care and the Planet — and What We Can Do About It*, London and New York, Verso, 2022.

9   Baudrillard, *The Consumer Society*.

10 Victoria De Grazia, *Irresistible Empire: America's Advance through Twentieth Century Europe*, Cambridge, Massachusetts, and London, Belknap Press of Harvard University Press, 2005.

11 François Gauthier and Tuomas Martikainen, eds., *Religion in Consumer Society: Brands, consumers and markets*. Farnham and Burlington, Vermont, Ashgate, 2013.

12 Sigmund Freud, trans. James Strachey, *Civilization and its Discontents*, New York and London, W. W. Norton & Company, 1961; Herbert Marcuse, *Eros and Civilization: A Philosophical Inquiry into Freud*. Boston, Beacon Press, 1955.

13 Don DeLillo, *White Noise*, New York, Viking Penguin, 1985.

14 Piero Camporesi, 'Carnevale, Cuccagna e giuochi di villa', in *Studi e problemi di critica testuale*, 10, Pisa and Rome, Fabrizio Serra Editore, 1975, pp.57–97.

15 Martin Parr and Quentin Bajac, trans. David Stanton, *Intervista a un fotografo promiscuo*, Rome, Contrasto, 2012. Originally published in: Quentin Bajac, Amsterdam, Schilt Publishing & Gallery, 2011.

16 Roberta Sassatelli, *Consumer Culture, History, Theory and Politics*, London, Sage, 2007.

17 Michel Foucault, *La volontà di sapere*, Milan, Feltrinelli, 1976 (Eng. ed.: *Lectures on the Will to Know*, ed. Arnold Davidson; trans. Graham Burchell, New York City, St Martin's Press, 2014).

18 Martin Parr and Quentin Bajac, *Intervista a un fotografo promiscuo*.

19 Michel Foucault, 'What is Enlightenment?', in *The Foucault Reader*, ed. Paul Rabinow, New York City, Pantheon Books, 1984, pp.32–50. *Cf.* Charles Baudelaire, 'On the Heroism of Modern Life,' in *The Mirror of Art*, London, Phaidon, 1955.

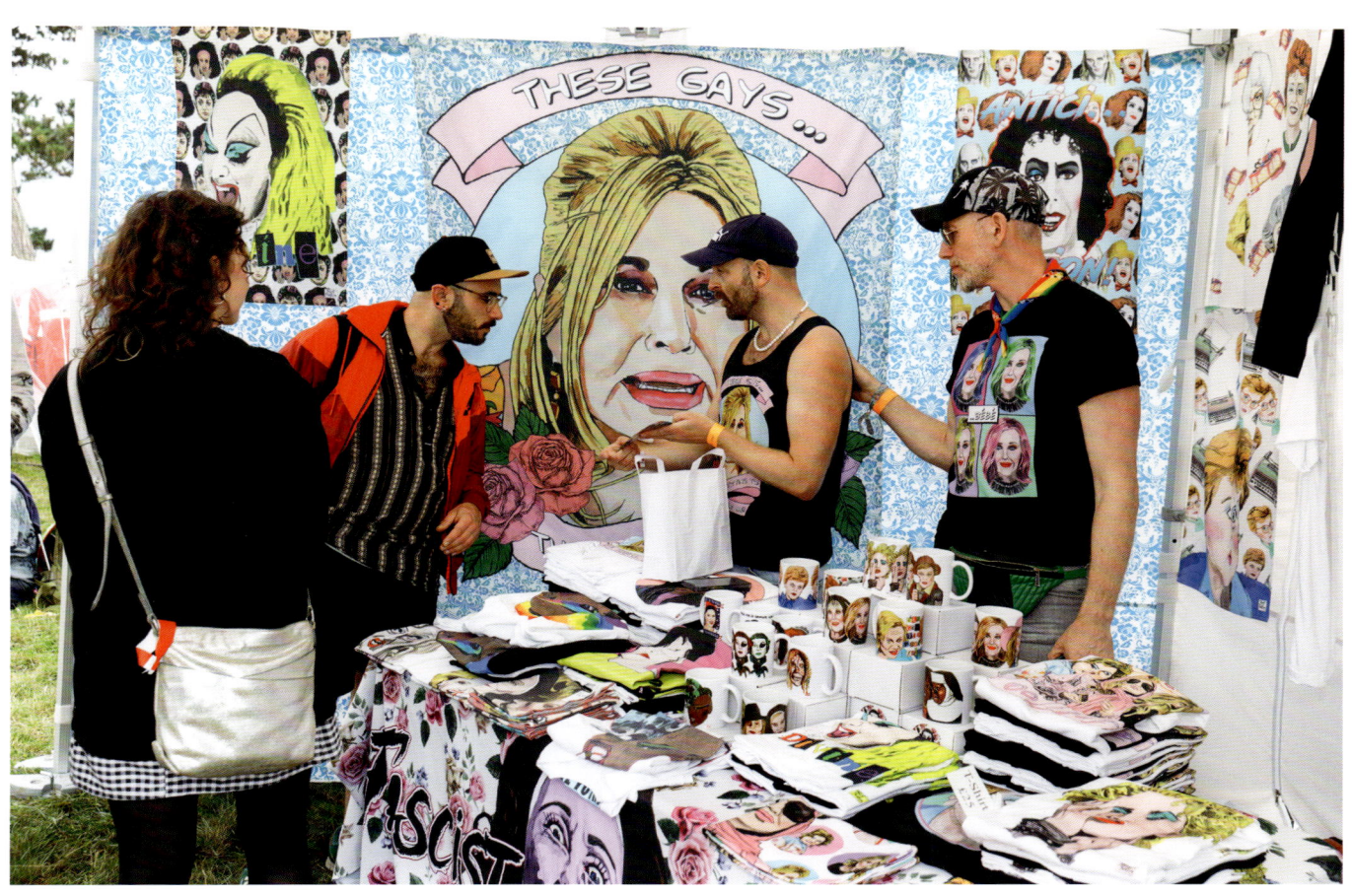

Pride, Bristol, England, 2023

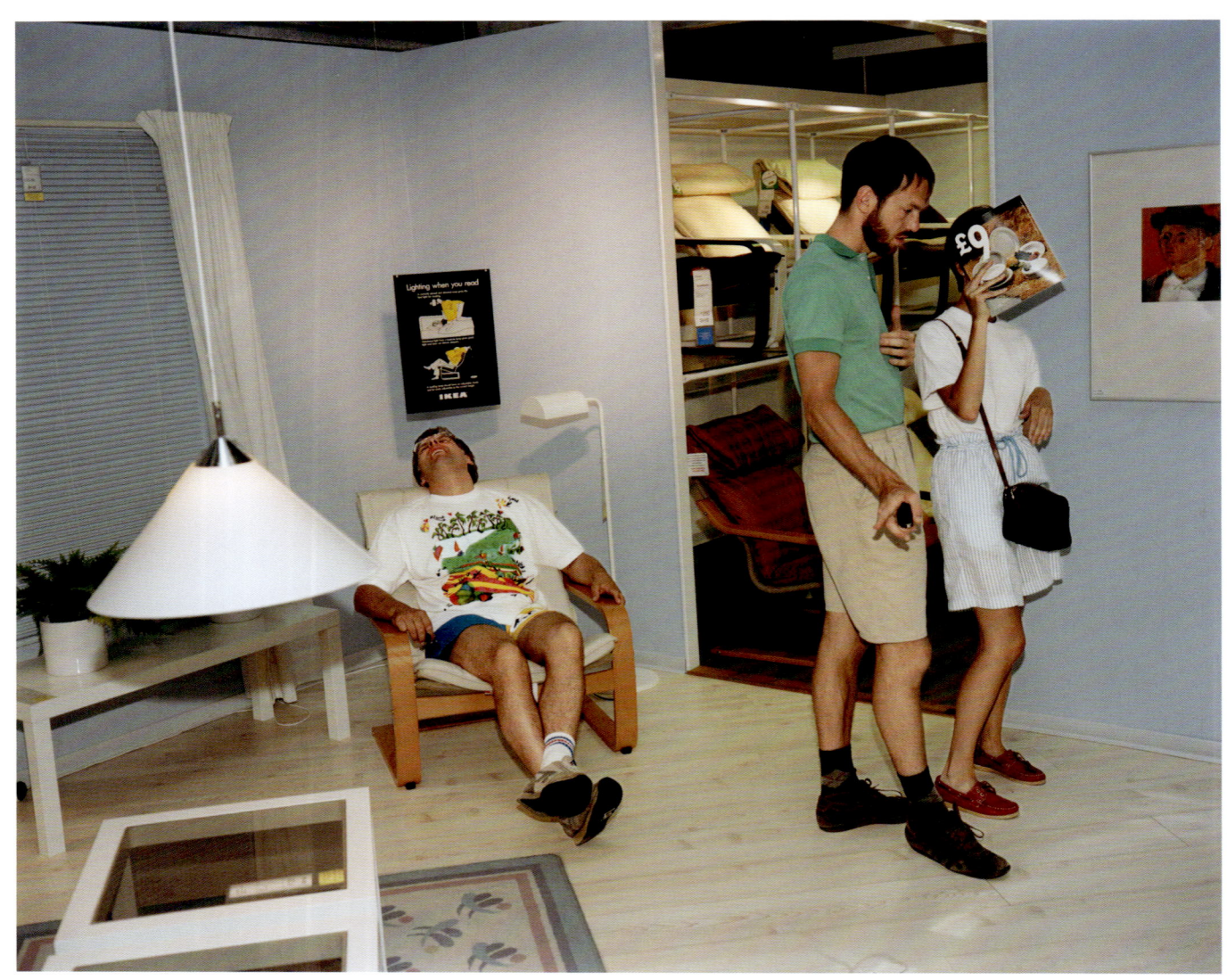

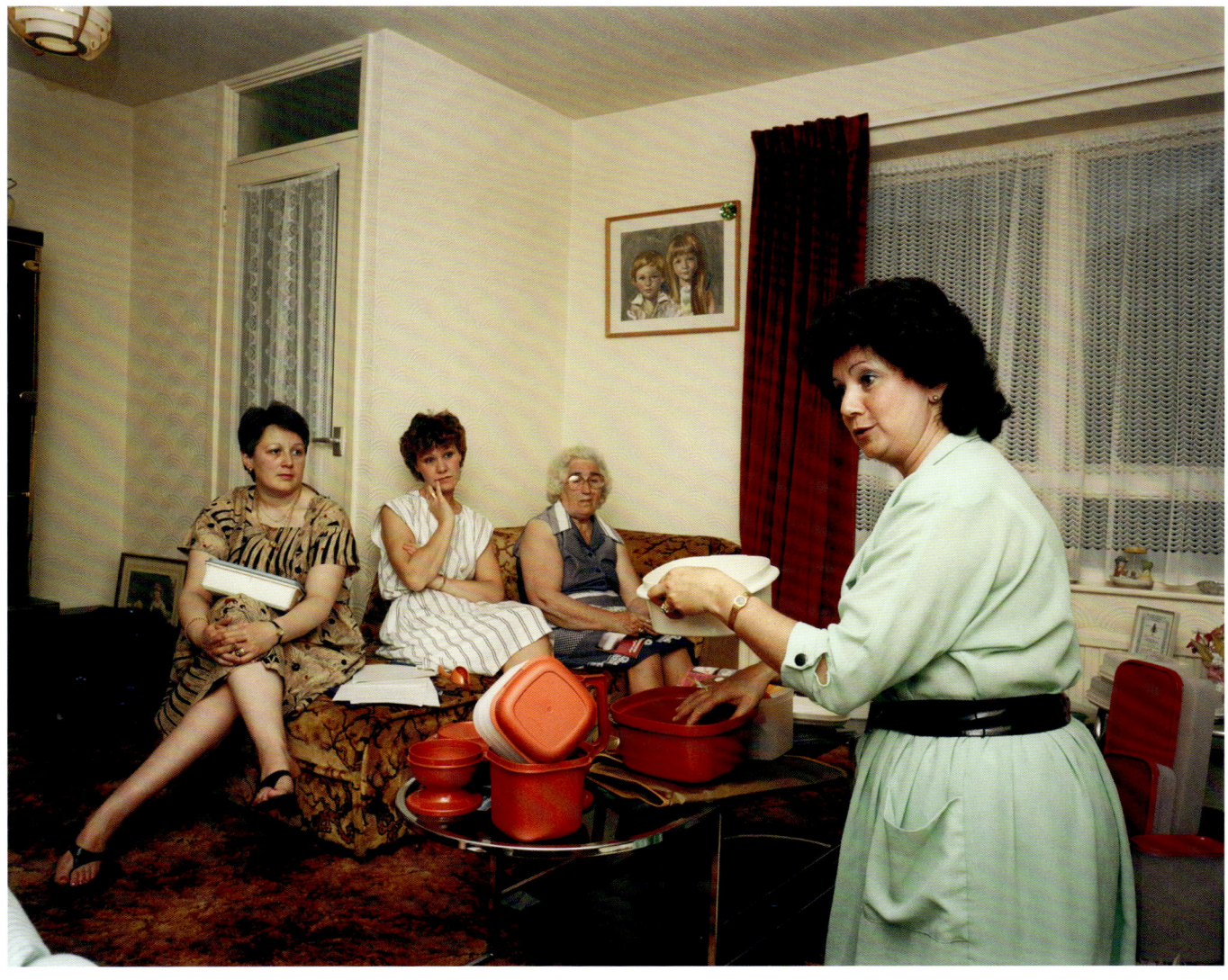

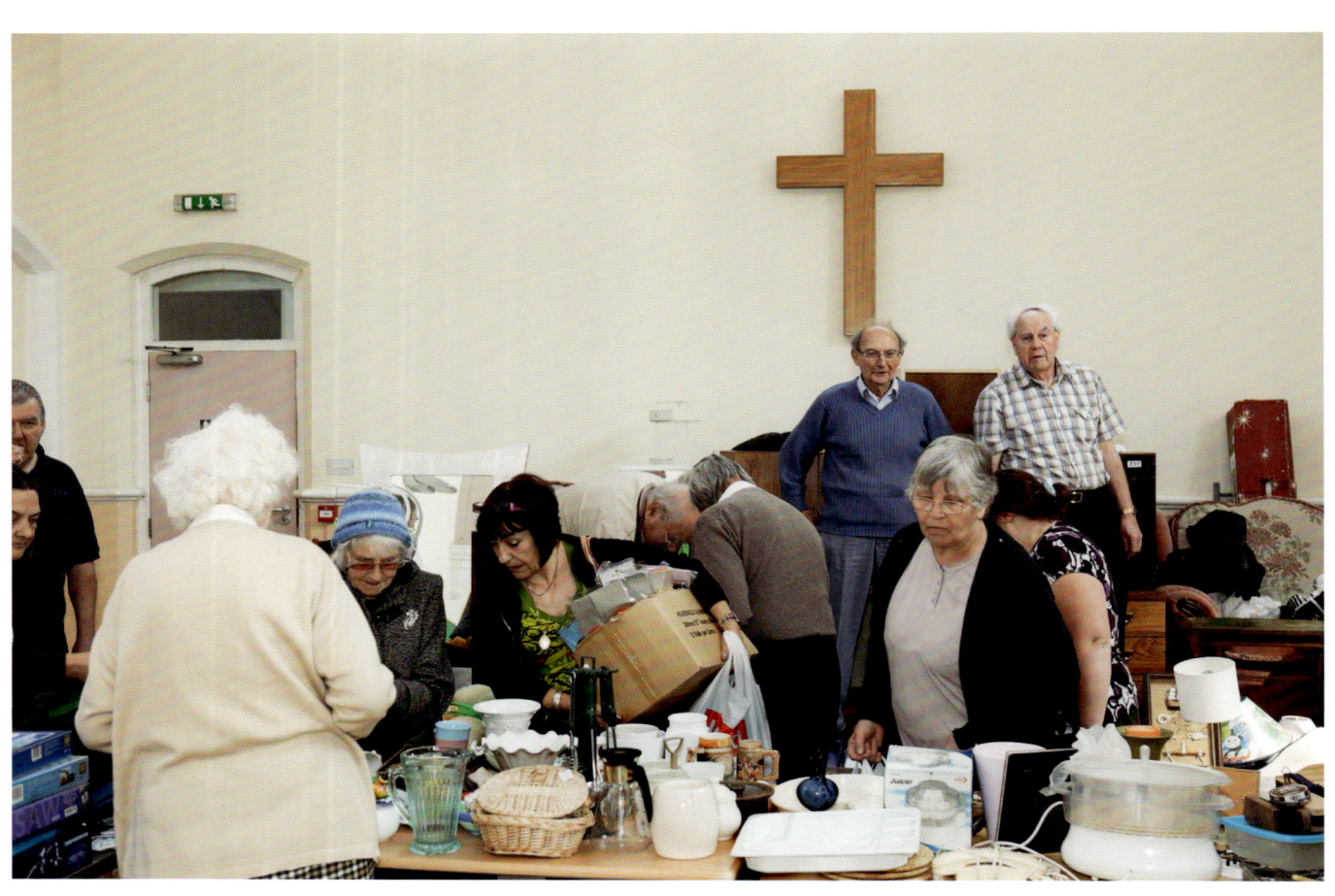

Walsall, England, 2011

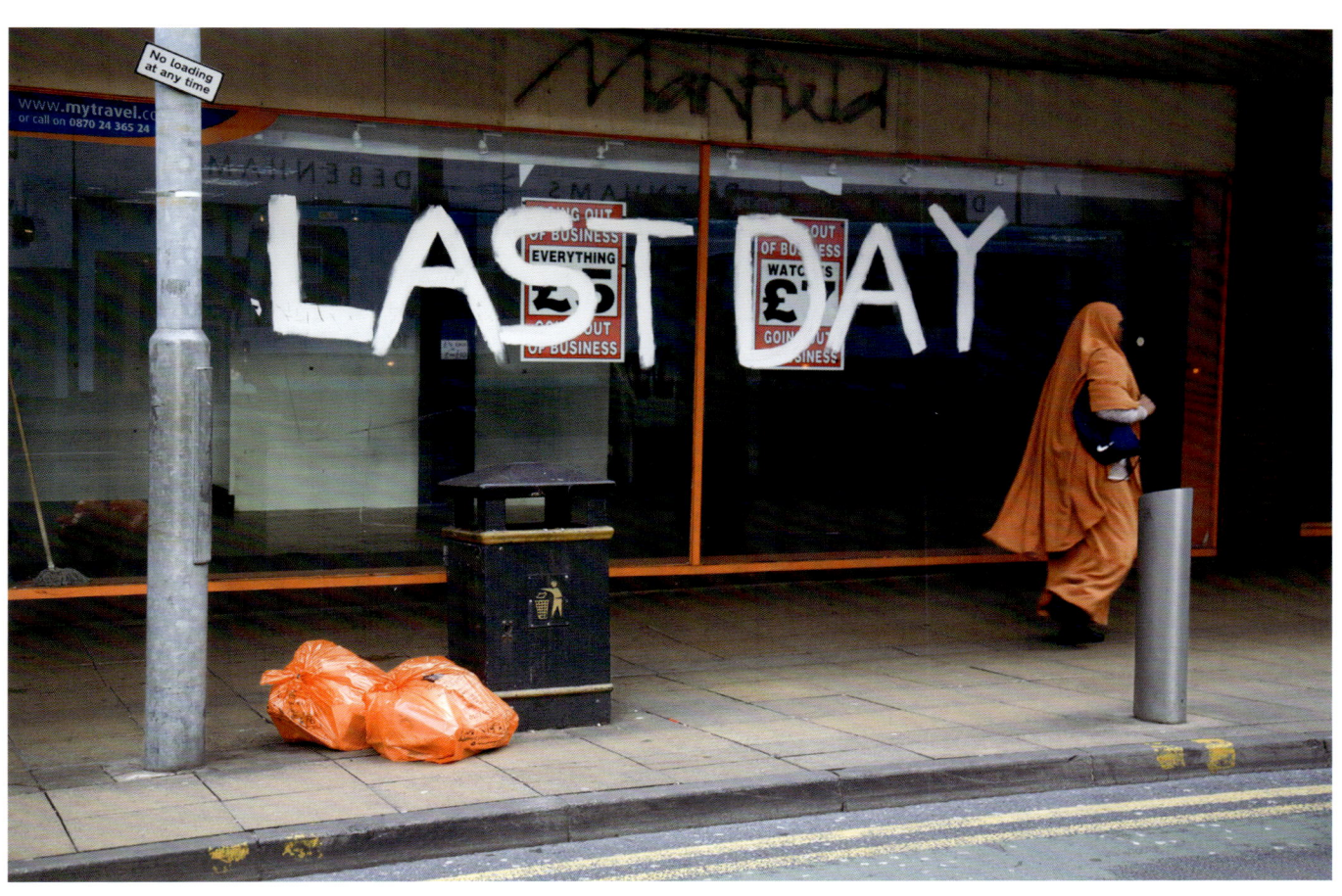

Manchester, England, 2008

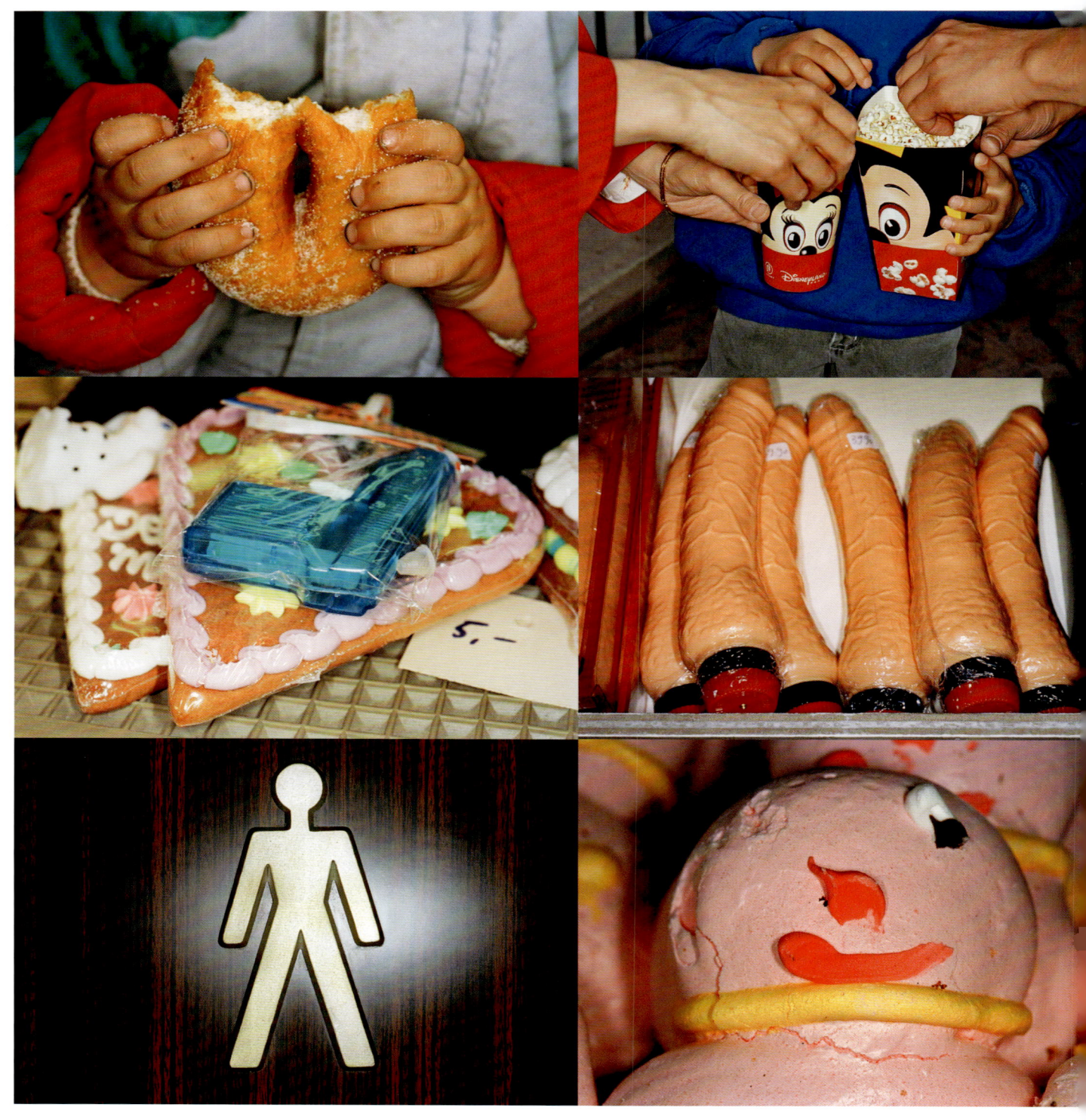

Top: Ramsgate, England, 1996 and Disneyland Paris, Marne-la-Vallée, France, 1998
Middle: Munich, Germany, 1997 and Amsterdam, the Netherlands, 1997
Bottom: Budapest, Hungary, 1998 and Taunton, England, 1998

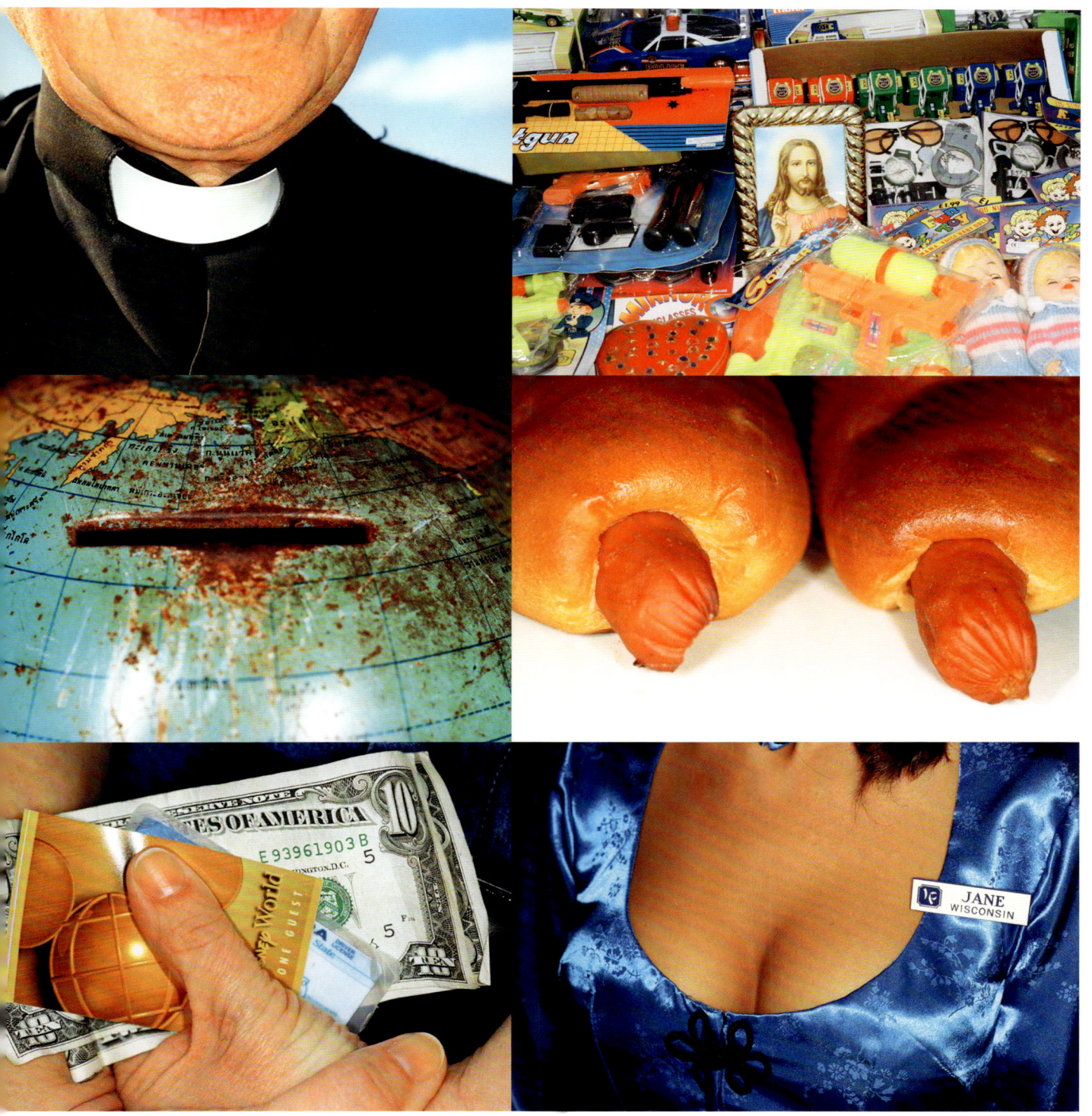

Top: **Allihies, Ireland, 1997** and **Dingle Races, Ireland, 1997**
Middle: **Zurich, Switzerland, 1997** and **Tokyo, Japan, 1998**
Bottom: **Florida, USA, 1998** and **Las Vegas, Nevada, USA, 1998**

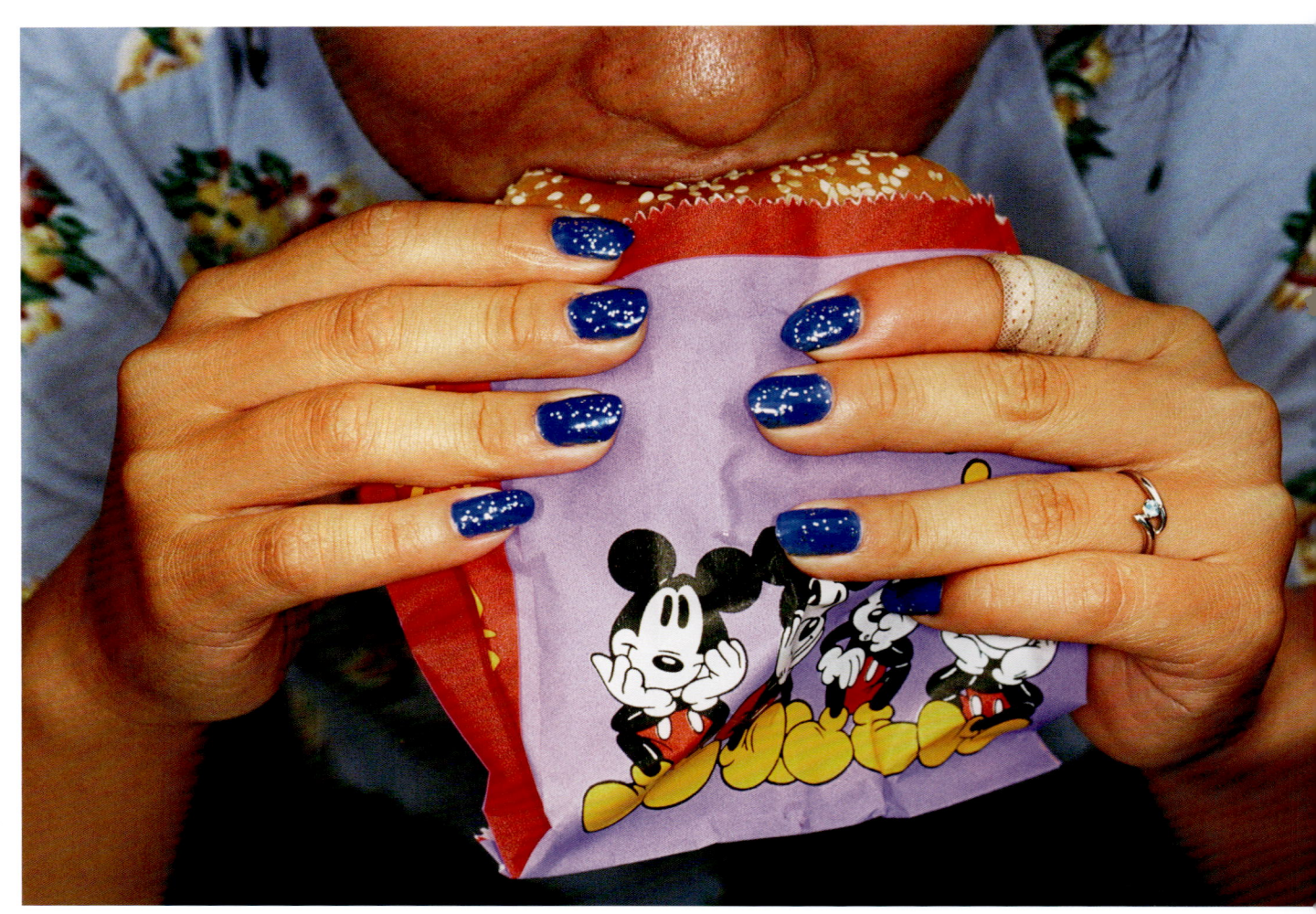

Tokyo Disneyland, Japan, 1998

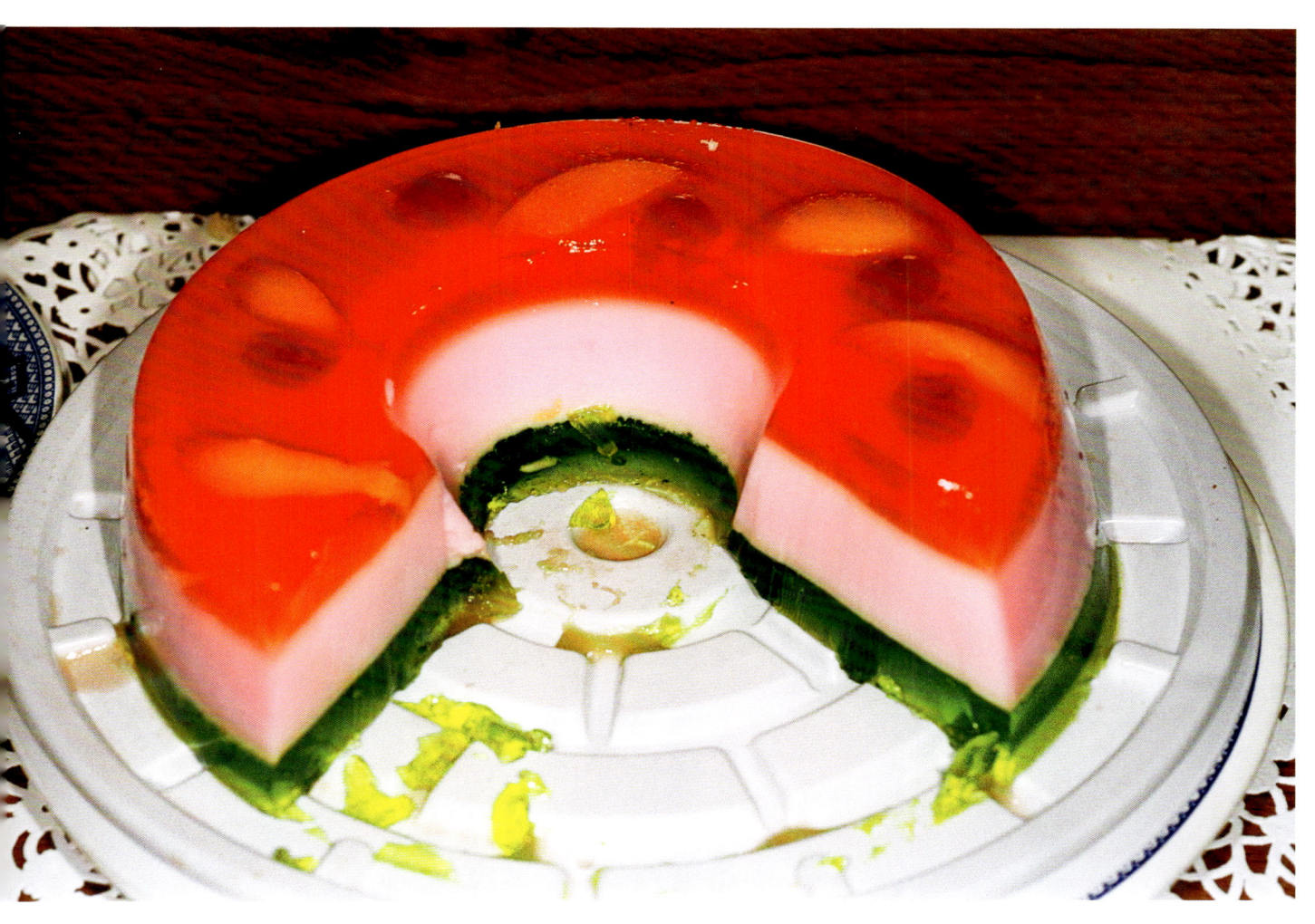

Tijuana, Mexico, 1993

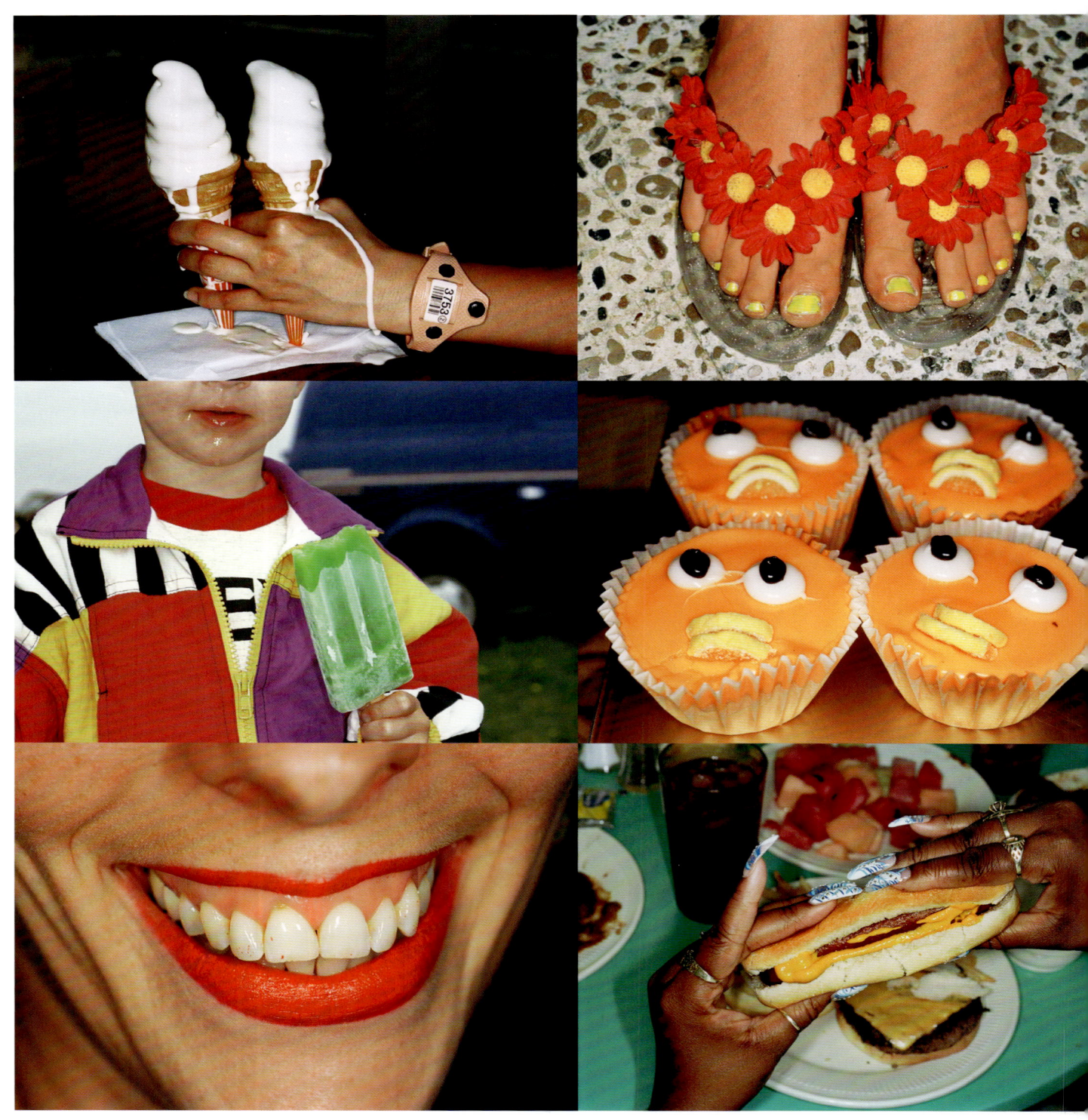

Top: **Tokyo, Japan, 1998** and **Benidorm, Spain, 1997**
Middle: **Bristol, England, 1995** and **Glasgow, Scotland, 1999**
Bottom: **Zurich, Switzerland, 1997** and **Cruise Ship, USA, 2002**

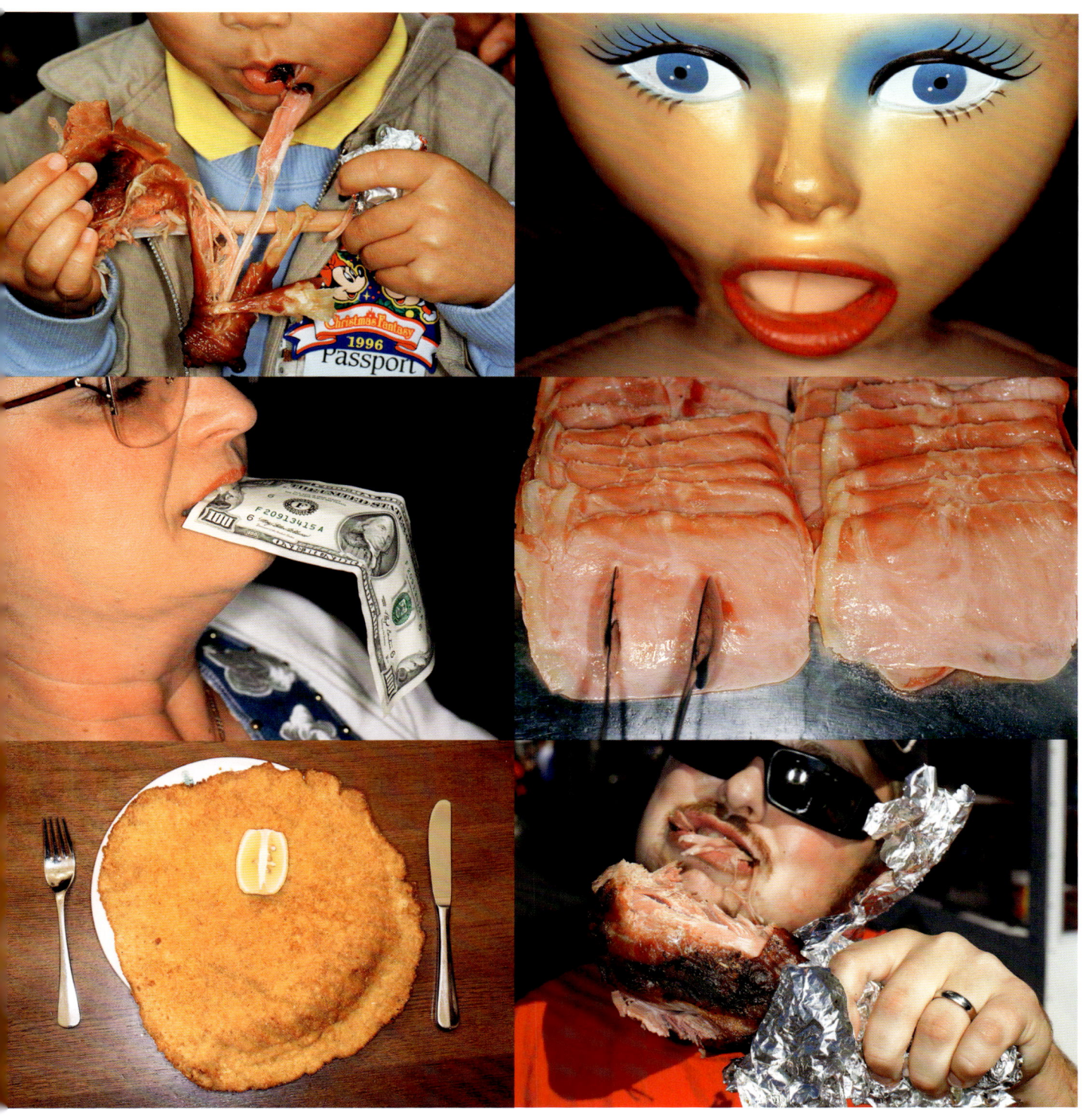

Top: **Tokyo Disneyland, Japan, 1998** and **Amsterdam, the Netherlands, 1998**
Middle: **USA, 1998** and **Benidorm, Spain, 1997**
Bottom: **Vienna, Austria, 2016** and **Atlanta, Georgia, USA, 2010**

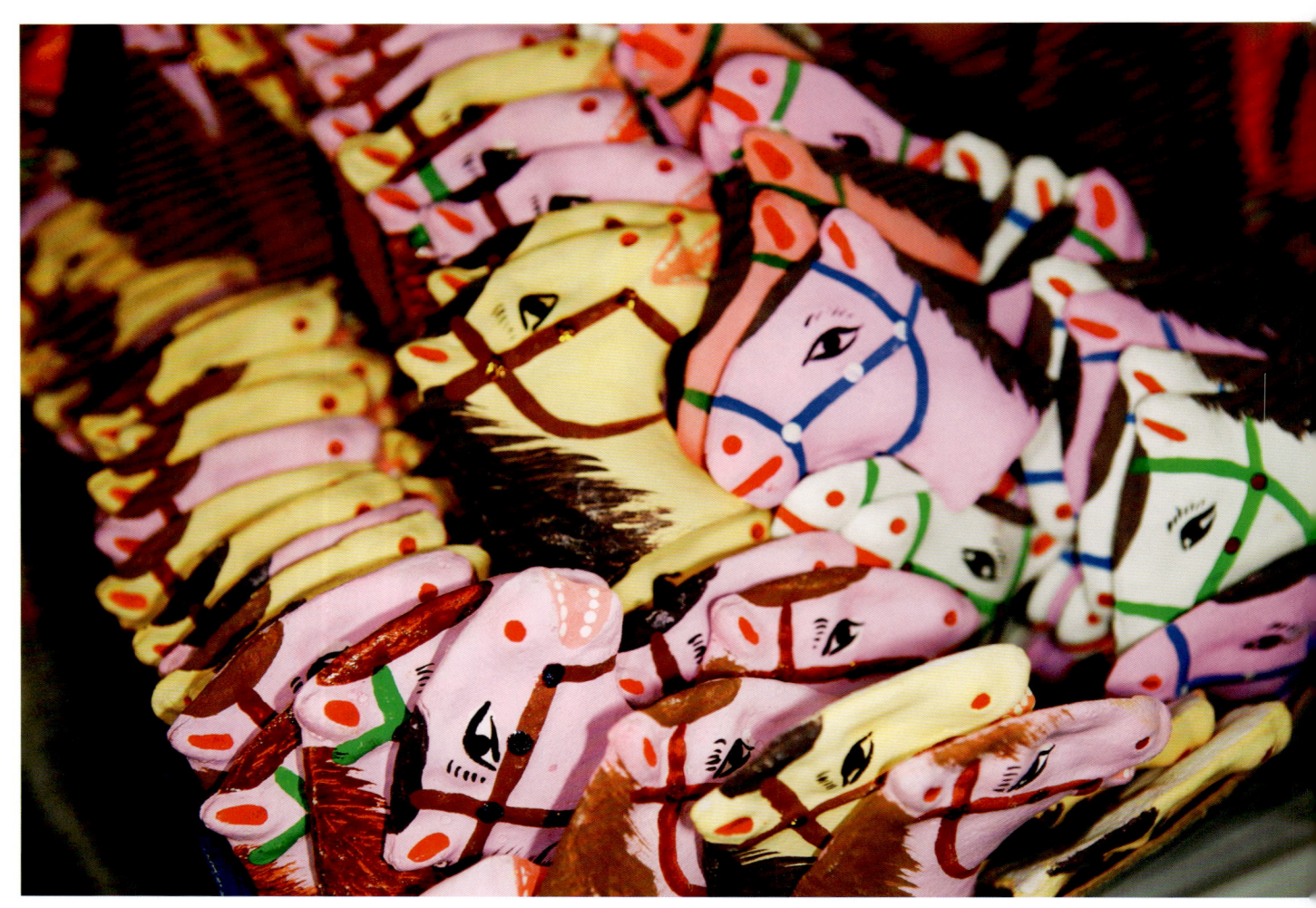

Cuzco, Peru, 2008

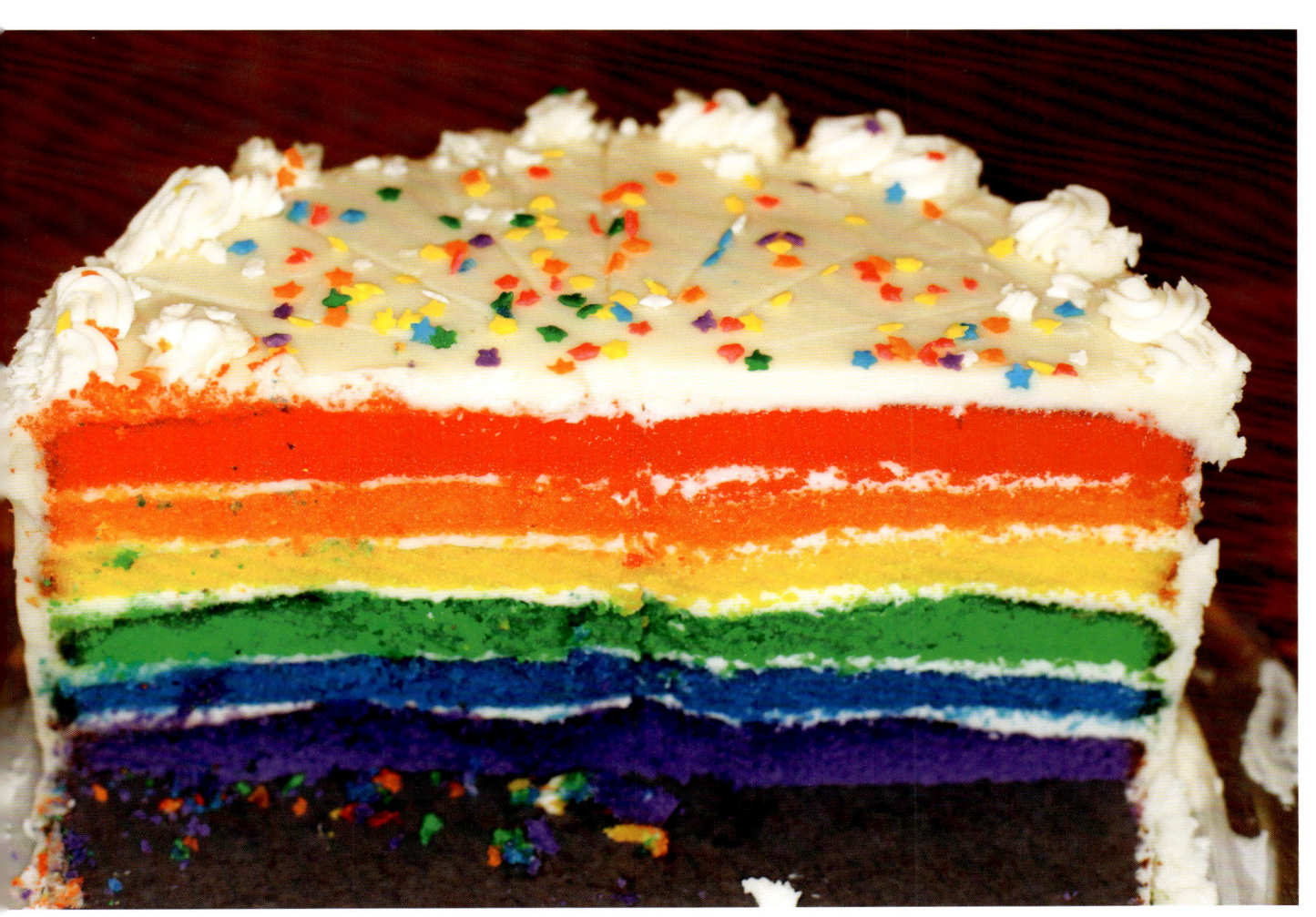

Atlanta, Georgia, USA, 2010

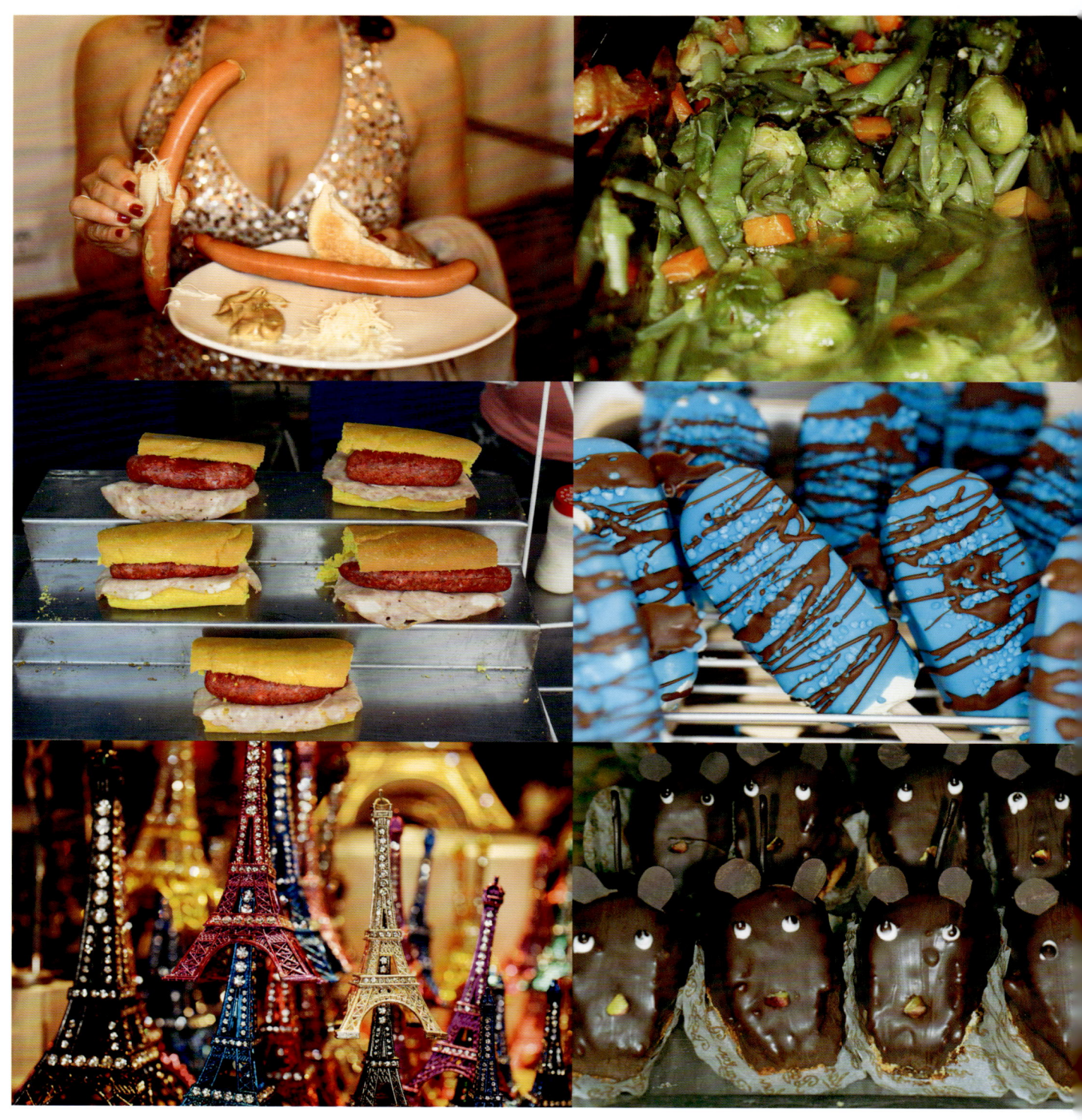

Top: **Vienna, Austria, 2016** and **Benidorm, Spain, 1997**
Middle: **Trinidad, Cuba, 2017** and **Tayto Park, County Meath, Ireland, 2019**
Bottom: **Paris, France, 2012** and **Istanbul, Türkiye, 2002**

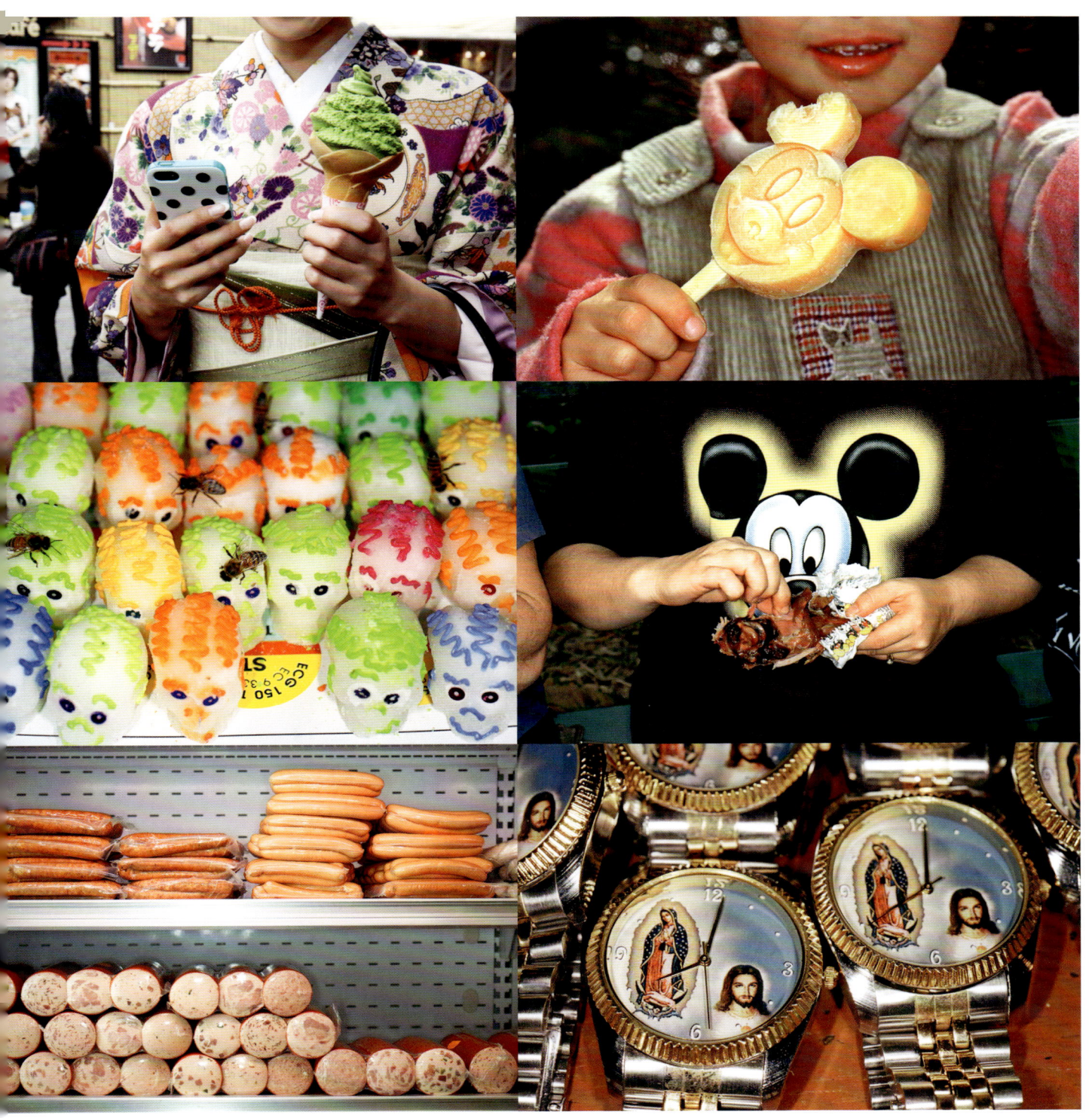

Top: **Kyoto, Japan, 2013** and **Tokyo Disneyland, Japan, 1998**
Middle: **Mexico City, Mexico, 2003** and **Tokyo Disneyland, Japan, 1998**
Bottom: **Zermatt, Switzerland, 2012** and **Mexico, 2003**

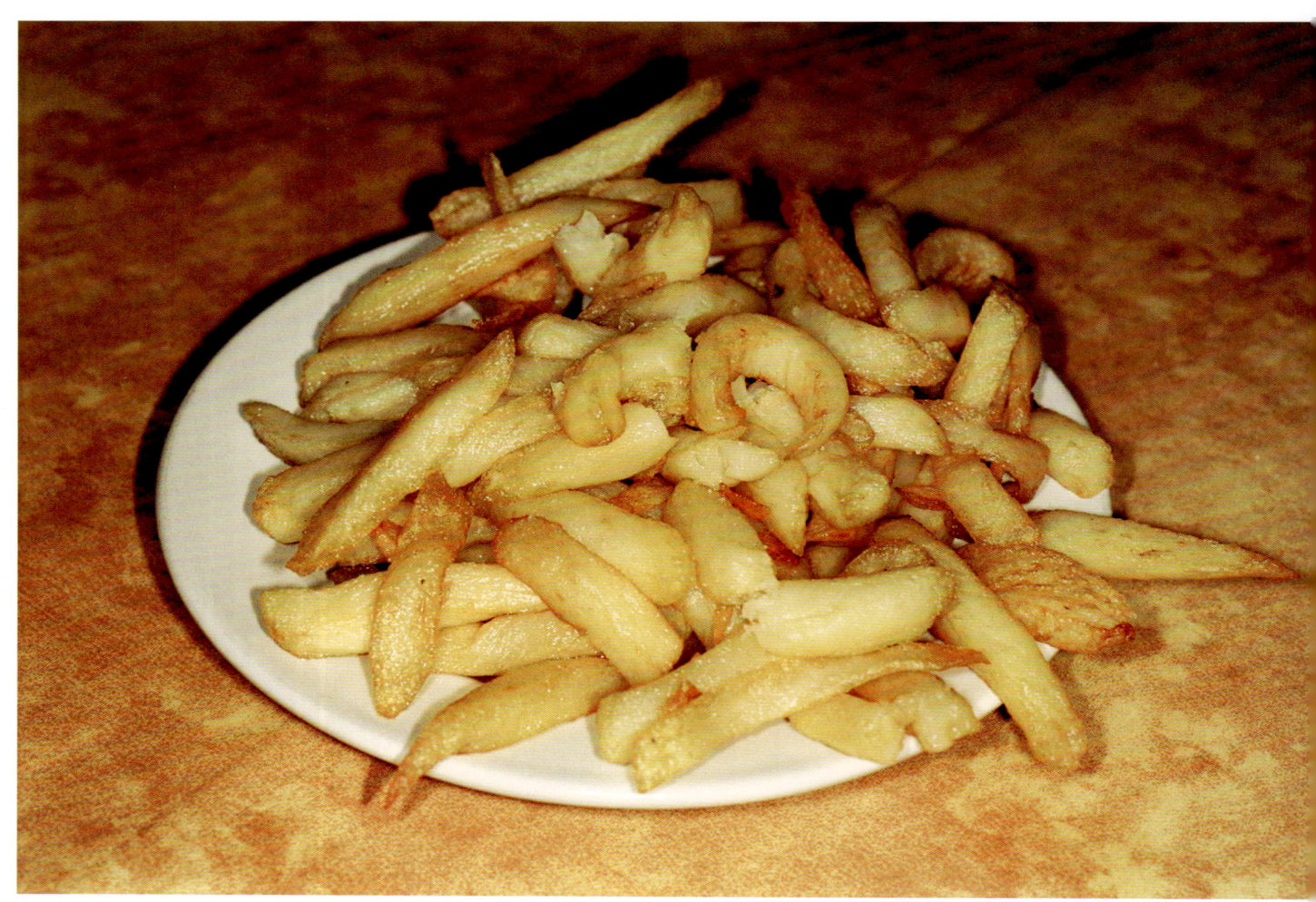

Majorca, Spain, 2003

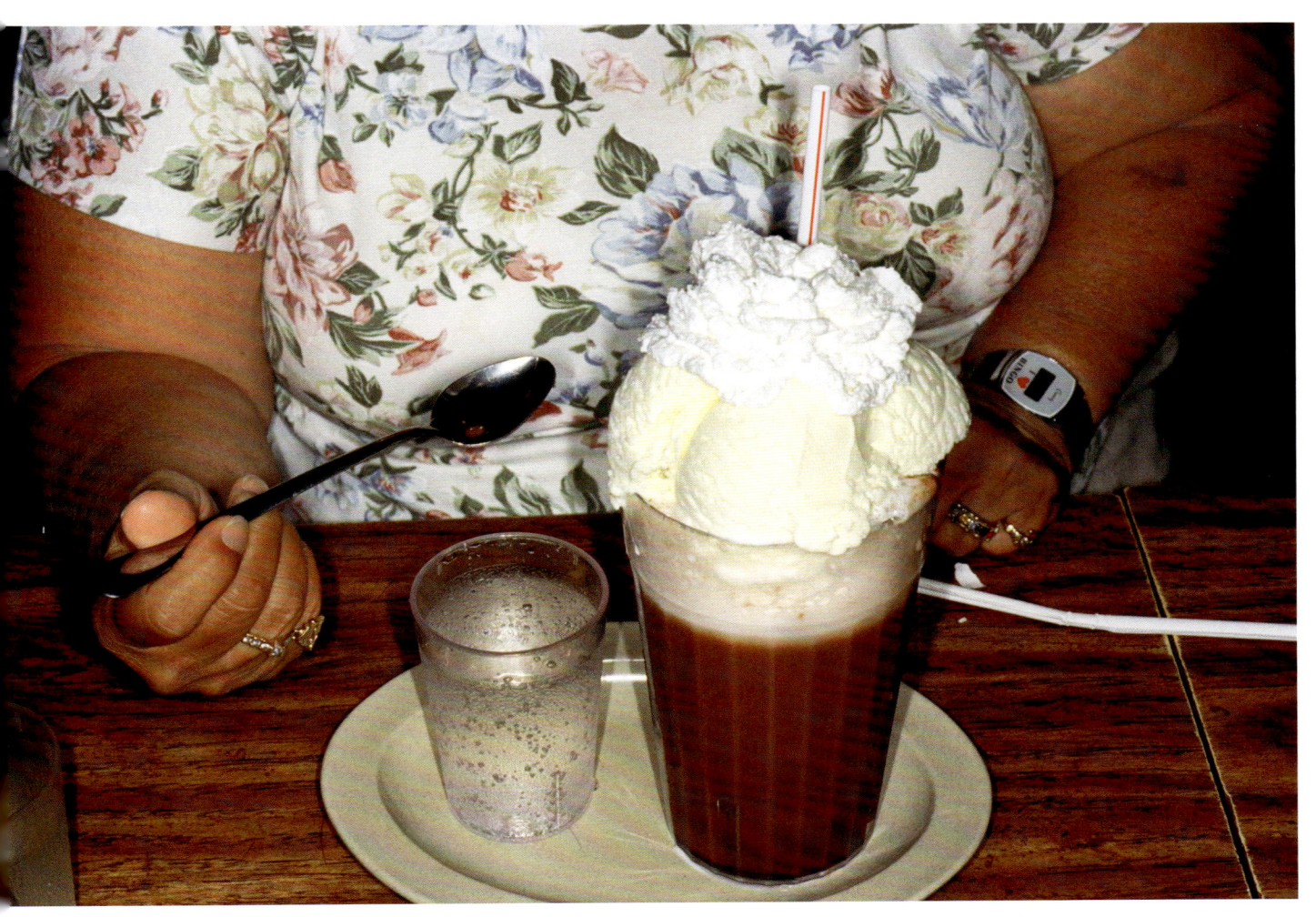

Florida, USA, 1998

THE
ANIMAL
KINGDOM

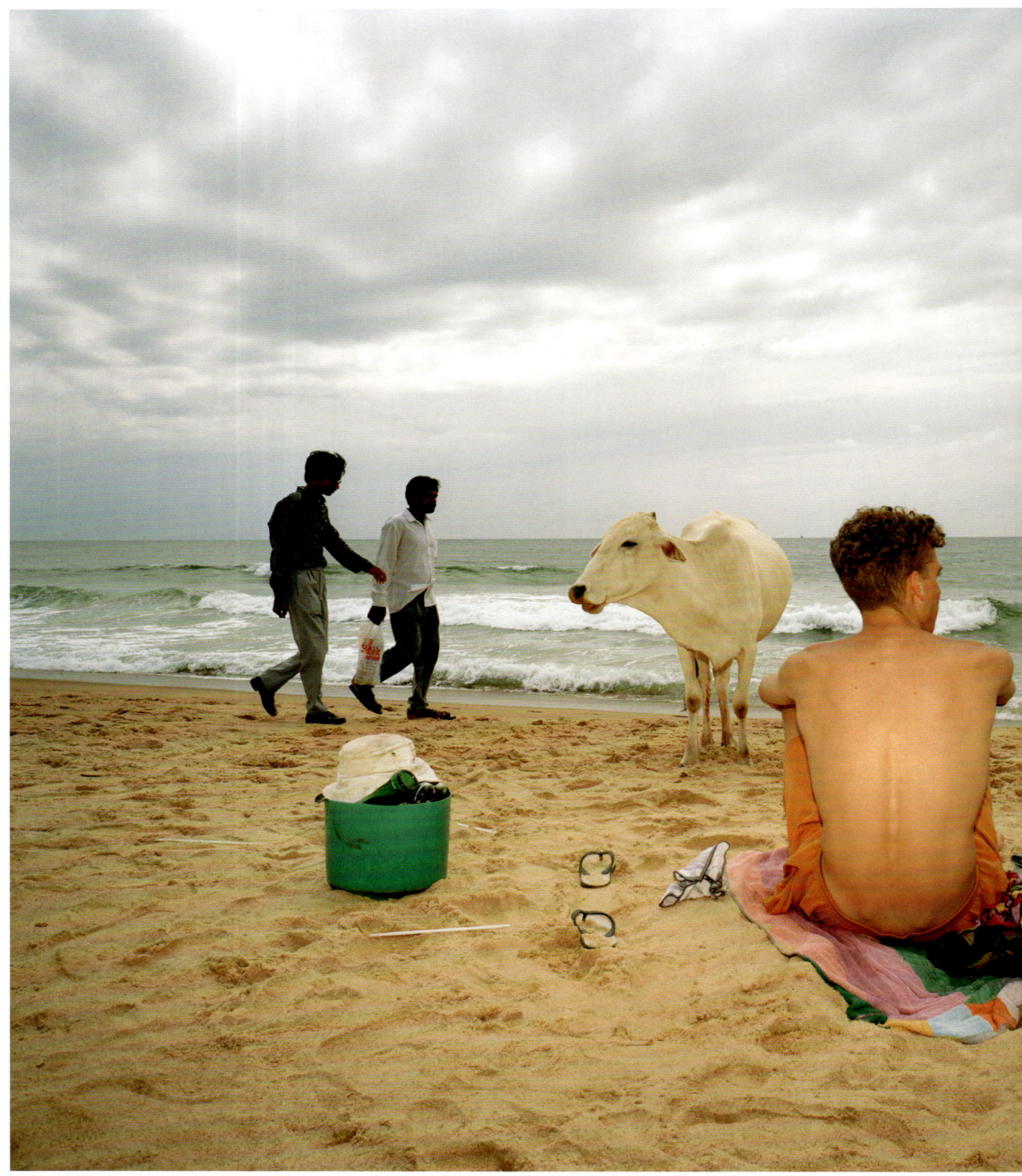

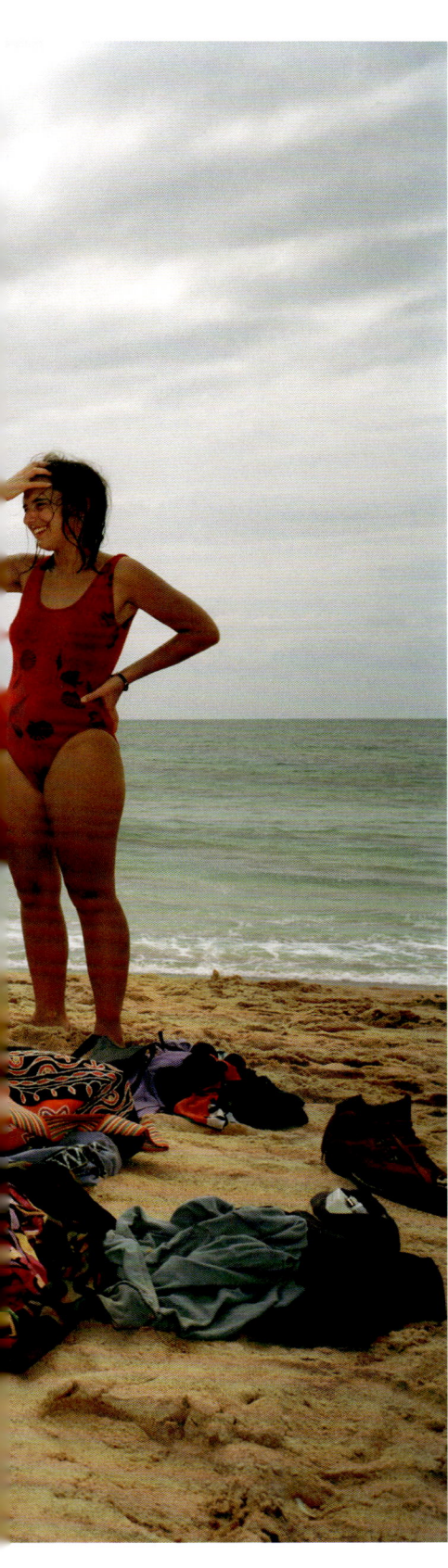

Goa, India, 1993

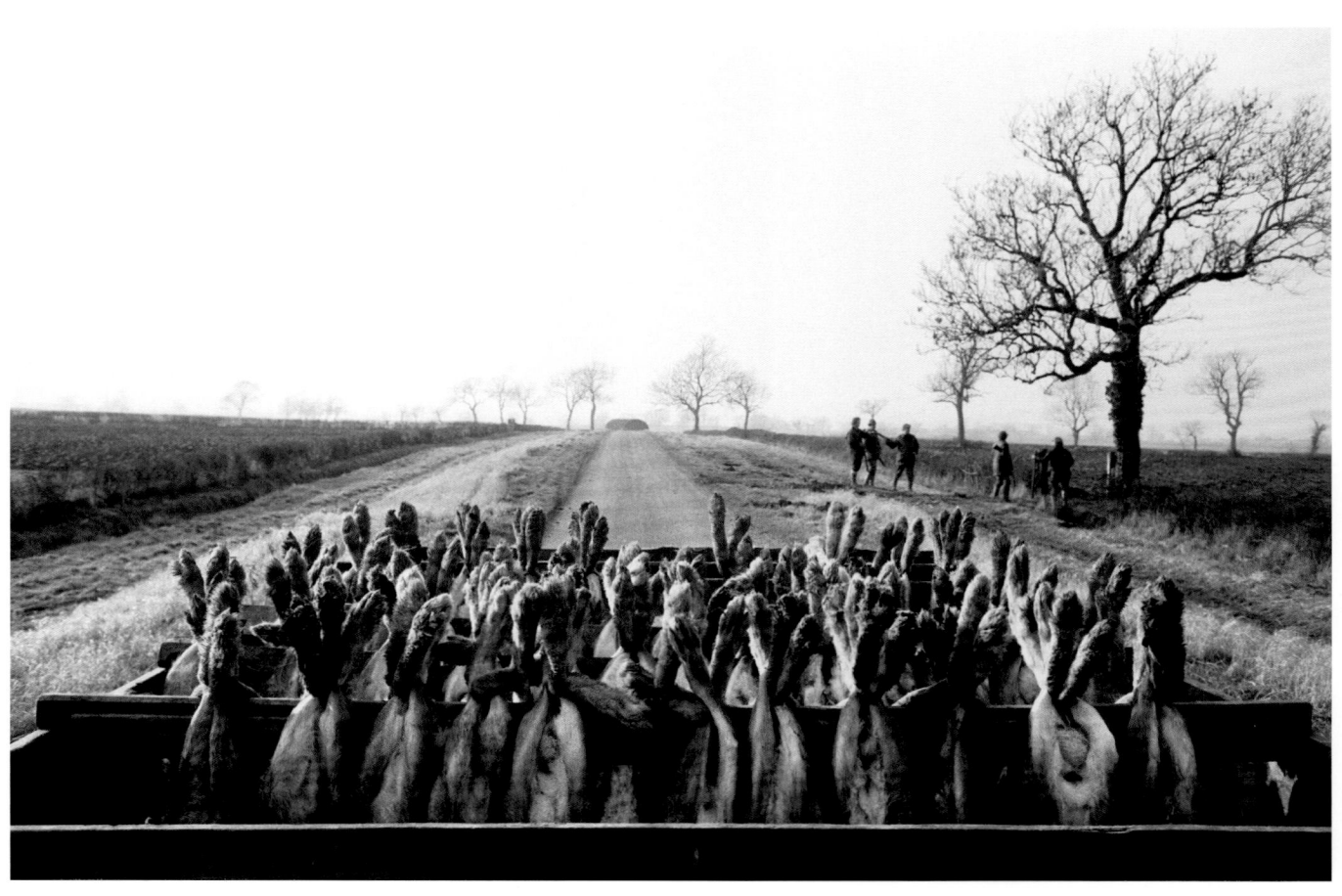

Near Stamford Bridge, East Yorkshire, England, 1981

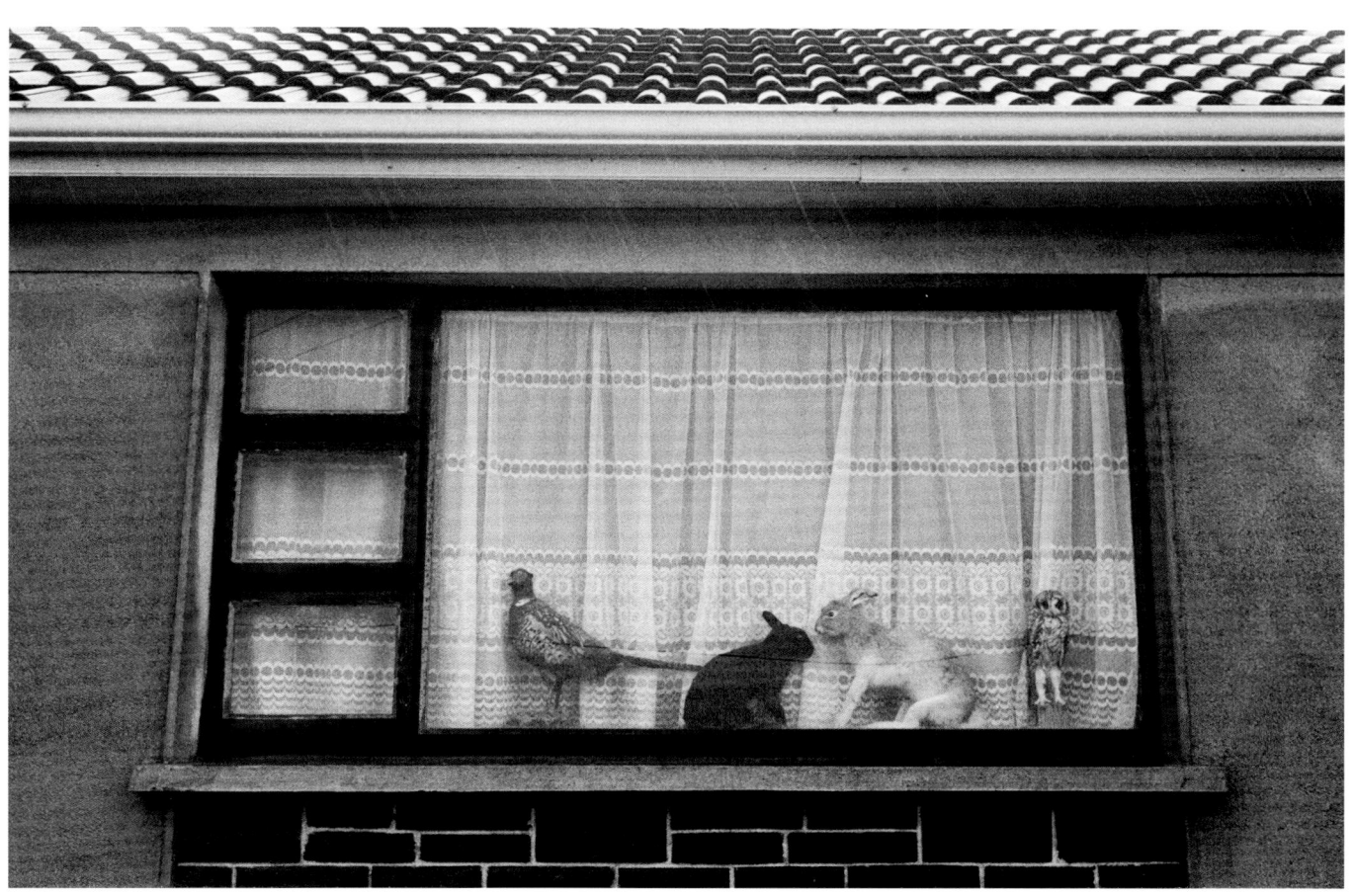

Castlerea, Ireland, 1981

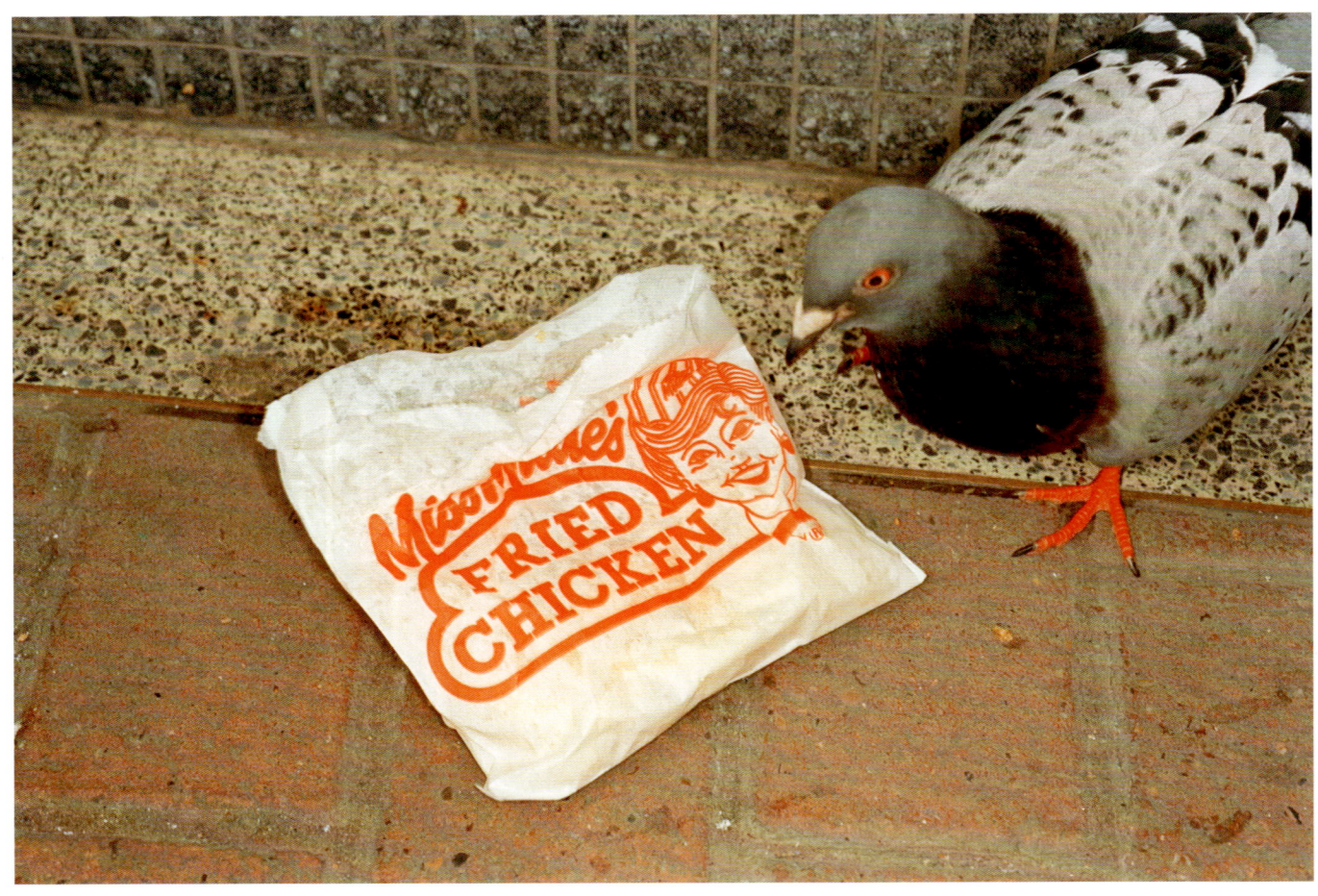

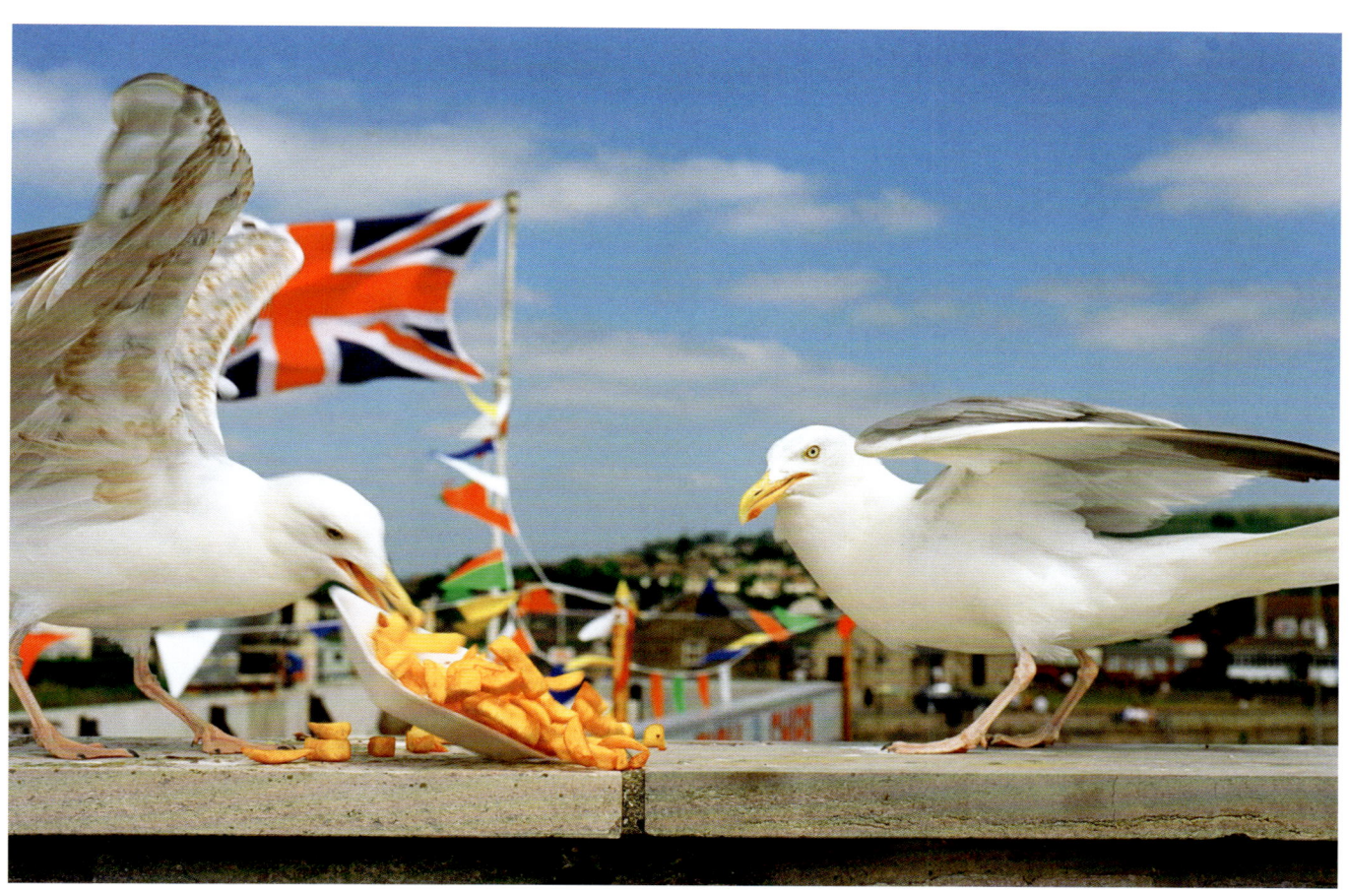

West Bay, England, 1996

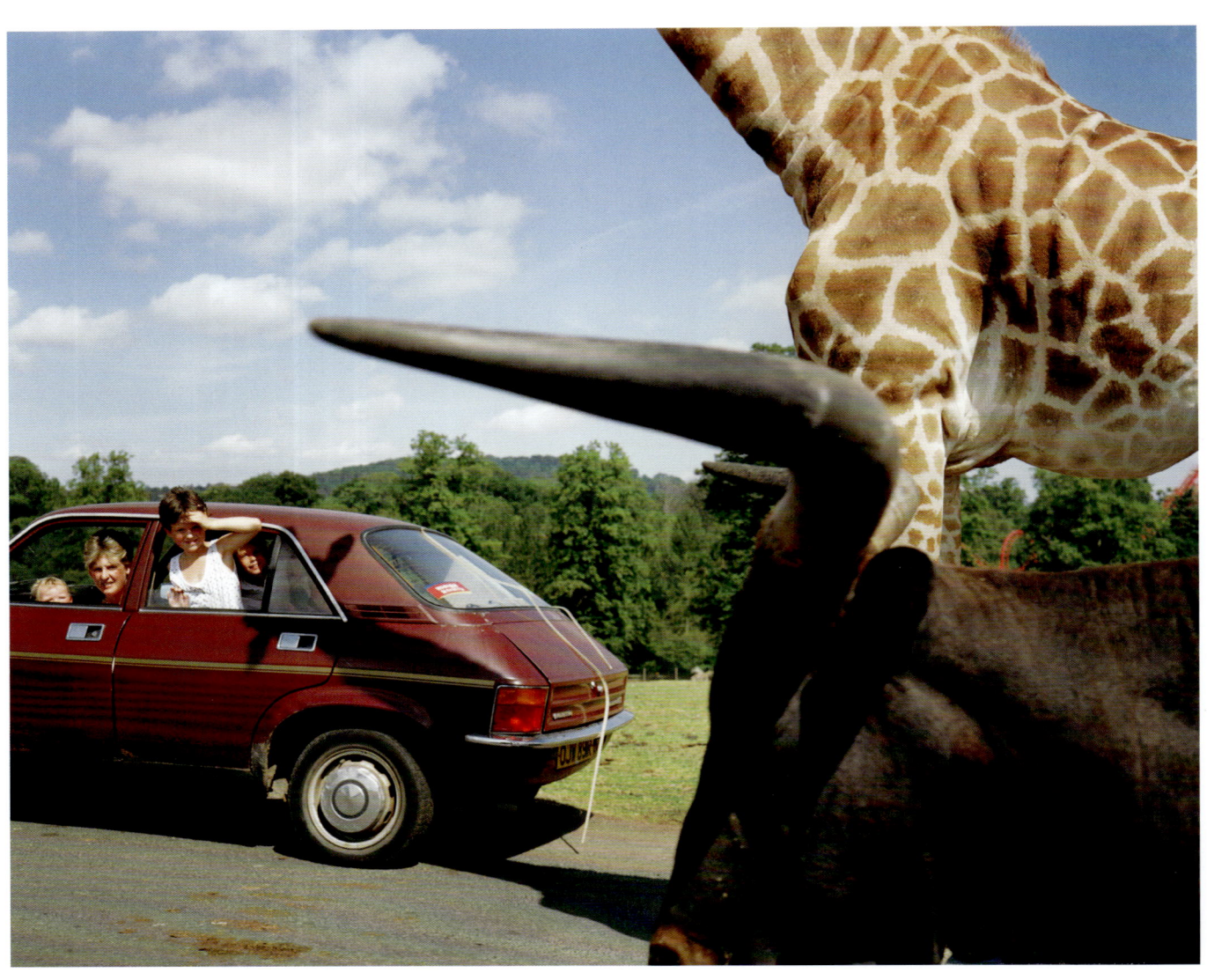

West Midlands Safari Park, England, 1990

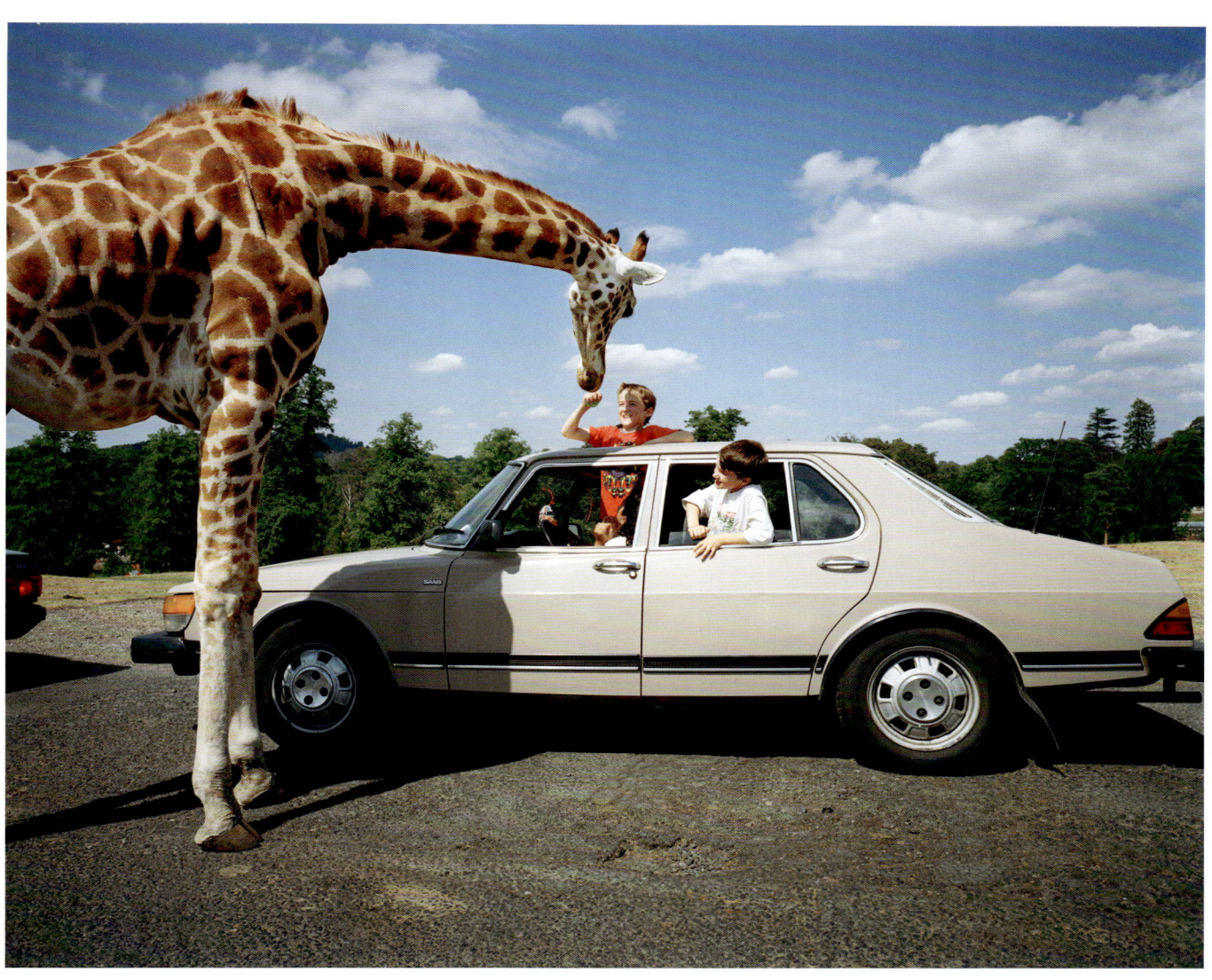

Longleat Safari Park, England, 1994

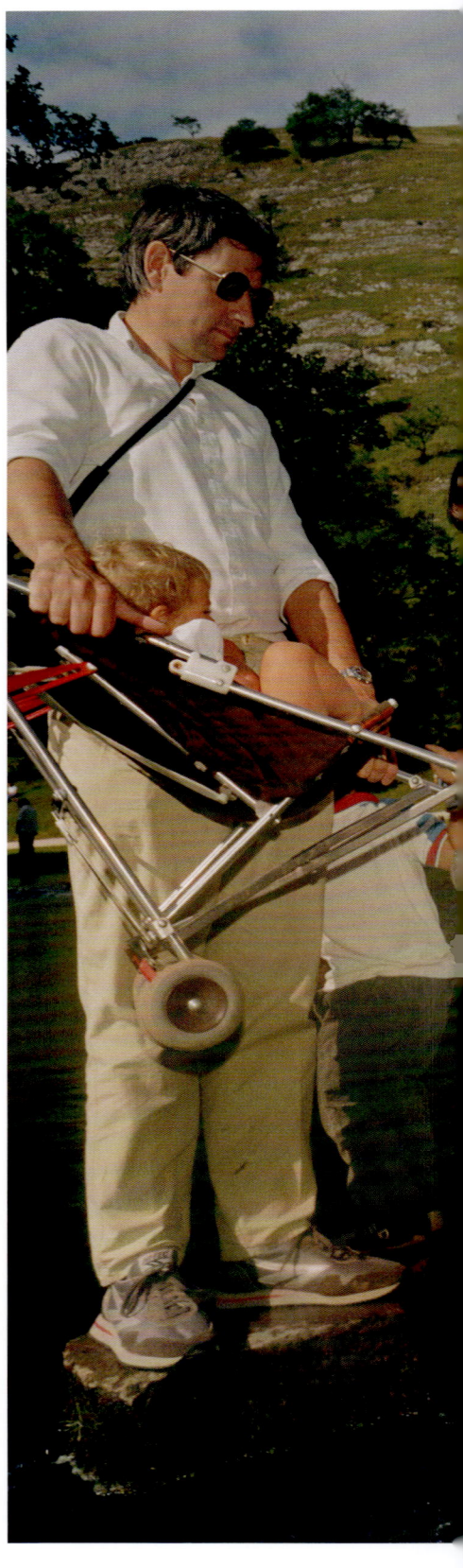

Dovedale, England, 1989

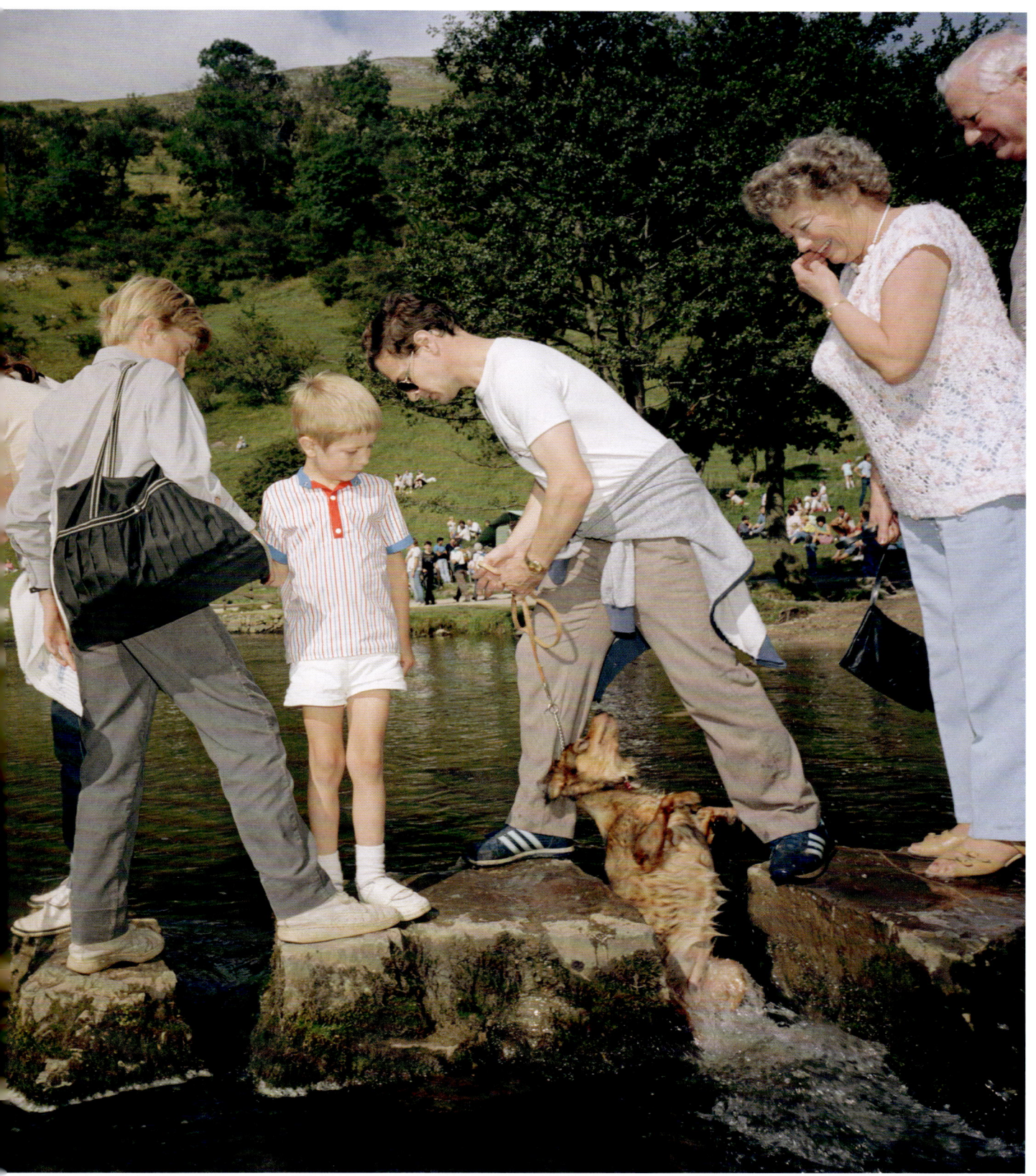

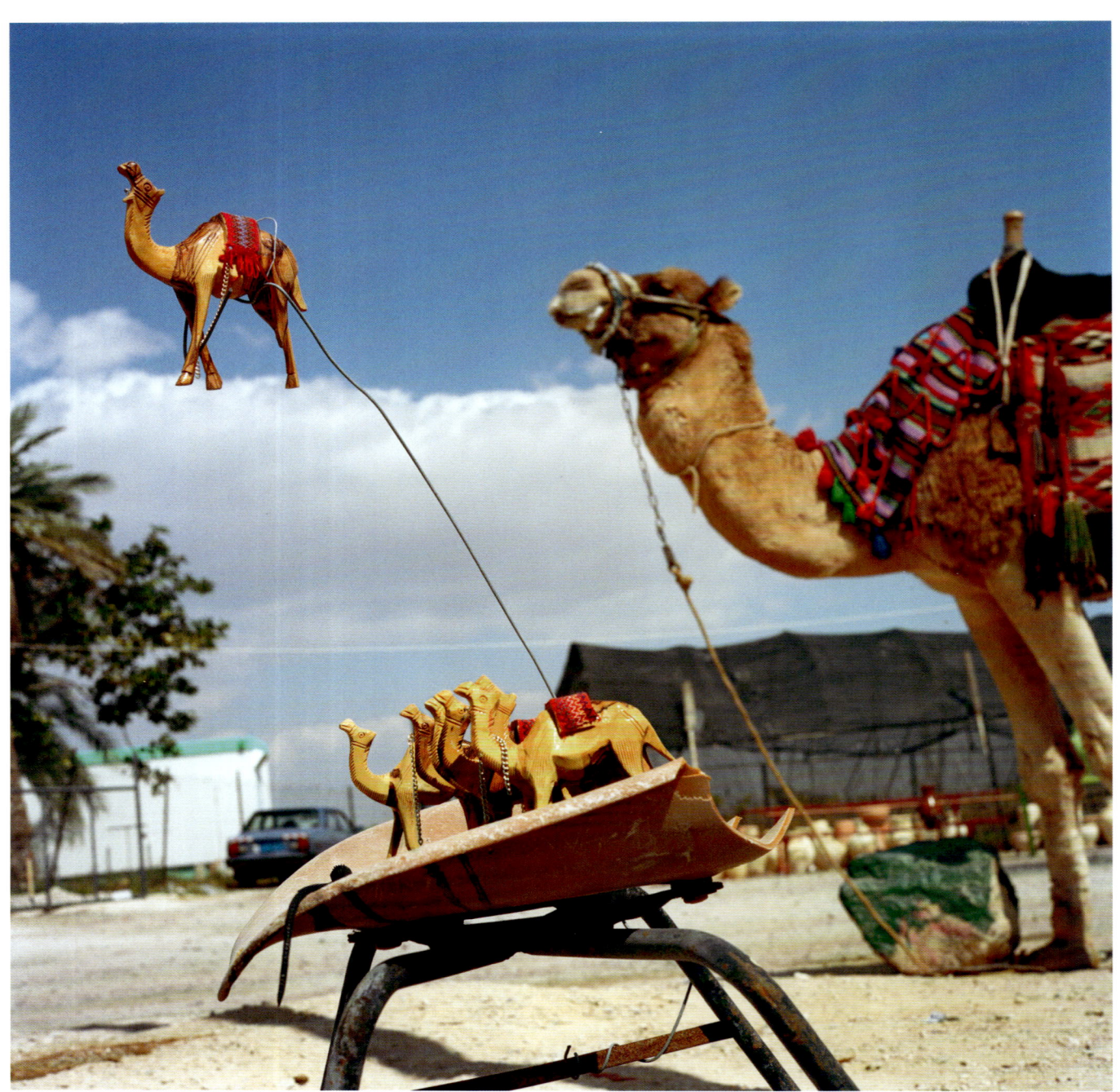

Jerusalem, Israel, 1995

WHERE HAVE THE ANIMALS GONE?

BY

VIOLETTE POUILLARD

The globalization of commercial transactions since the early modern era, and the subsequent emergence of nineteenth-century industrial capitalism, relied heavily on non-human animals (referred to hereafter as 'animals'), who, from then on, came to be both destroyed and protected as resources. In the twentieth century, the rise of consumer society completed a profound shift in anthropozoological relations. Given that Martin Parr documents consumer habits and their global spread,[1] it is no surprise that animals should have a strong presence in his work.

Animals as Mass Consumer Goods

For the most part, the animals in Martin Parr's images – like those in our daily lives – have been rendered invisible as they are manifested as consumer goods. In the sterilized, sanitized, blood-stained buffet of the series *Common Sense*, and other photos, they are found as sausages, ham, deli meat, hamburgers, hot dogs, steaks, rinds, thighs, breaded, roasted, sliced or set in aspic. At times, they are hinted at through their pasteurized products like meringue, cheese, ice cream, whipped cream and so on (see pp.96–7, 106, 128–39). Elsewhere, they lurk in the quiet ubiquity of skins and hides in handbags, shoes, clothing, accessories and rugs or upholstery (see pp.103, 124). This predominant way of interacting with animals is not inherent, but rather the result of contingent historical choices in a globalized world, demanding the constant flow of domesticated and wild animals both near and far, dead or alive. The wet markets of Hong Kong – a hub of the animal trade (see p.167) – literally teem with wild or farmed animals who are imported from Southeast Asia, where they are sold for local consumption and for export as food, for medicinal purposes or to supply zoos, labs and dealers. Between 2006 and 2010, the US imported 3.6 million amphibians from Hong Kong, while the EU, between 2010 and 2019, brought in anywhere from 814 to 2,000 million, mostly from Asia, all to satisfy Europe's appetite for frog legs.[2]

In the complex, interconnected web of globalization, the boundaries between *elsewhere* and *here*, like the dividing line between junk food and gastronomy, are disintegrating. The temptation to retreat to the local – to *terroir* and tradition – does not offer a clean break from any of this. Even in the cheerful countryside of early 1980s rural England, ensnared in Thatcherite policies, one could already observe hunts whose excess, enabled by advanced technologies, required meticulous planning to avoid the piling-up of bodies that results in a radical negation of the individual (pp.144, 167).

Nowhere and Everywhere: The Disappearance of Animals

In his seminal article, published in 1977 and still relevant today, art critic John Berger identifies the disappearance of animals from daily life that came with the rise of industrial society as a turning point in human-animal relations. He notes that this also coincided with an increase in animal imagery – pictures and likenesses – in popular culture, as well as the theatrical display of animals in the context of mass leisure activities.[3] Martin Parr's work captures this infinite multiplication of animal imagery and productions, with the Disney industry being one of the most extreme examples (see pp.30, 62, 128, 130, 137). For more than twenty years, Parr himself has collected Soviet space-dog ephemera and memorabilia in the form of watches, clocks, lamps, cigarette cases, sweet tins or figurines.[4] The exemplary case of the Cold War canine cosmonauts – Laika, Belka and Strelka – reflects the dissolution of animals' individual experiences behind a mask of images that fuel narratives of their submission or self-sacrifice for human ends, thereby validating the latter. As Berger points out, rather than fostering human-animal relationships, animals' shift into images merely underscores their radical marginalization.[5]

Their exclusion is even more manifest in the theatrical arrangements of taxidermy. Whether modest and personal or grandiose and public, such displays are always inseparable from hunting culture and its appetite for trophies that retain the hollow form of what once was and has since been destroyed (see pp.145, 166). This culture flourished particularly within colonial states, where the destruction of animals hit a peak, supported by the foundations of colonial ideology itself.[6] Like countless colonial museums, the Prince of Wales Museum – founded in Bombay (now Mumbai) in 1905 and renamed Chhatrapati Shivaji Maharaj Vastu Sangrahalaya in 1998 (see p.166) – houses sections dedicated to both art and natural history. The latter focuses on regional fauna,[7] in contrast to metropolitan museums and zoos that capitalize on an exoticism modelled primarily on imperial geography. Set in the heart of India's economic capital, the museum now welcomes visitors – both urban and rural, Indian and foreign[8] – who smile next to menacing carnivores that are no longer a menace: the Asiatic lion was driven to the brink of extinction by nineteenth-century British colonialists with the assistance of Indian farmers. Today, only a few hundred individuals remain in the Gir Forest and the surrounding areas, who have become a symbol of Gujarat's identity.[9]

Touching Animals[10]

Even outside cities, actual encounters with living animals are rare, found neither in the sequestered world of the industrial farms that supply fast-food chains, nor amid the gunfire of rural hunting culture. Proximity must be sought elsewhere: in the time-honoured tradition of the household pet, now common across social classes, as well as by conjuring what no longer exists *here* in some fantasized *elsewhere*, which zoos – in the broad sense of places that enable encounters with captive animals – excel at providing. Exoticized animal rides have become a regular feature of tourist itineraries since Western zoos began phasing them out in the mid-twentieth century, in response to changing attitudes towards animals and growing criticism. On the Mount of Olives outside Jerusalem, camel rides (see p.152) are a tourist staple even though the agricultural, transport and pack uses of camels have steadily declined since the end of the British Mandate in Palestine in 1948, and the dominance of motorized transport signalled their demise as a means of travel.[11] In Southeast Asia and India, elephant rides are one of the most popular tourist activities. In Jaipur, a hotspot of elephant tourism (see p.160), Martin Parr (perhaps mounted on a pachyderm himself) captures tourists who, seeking immersion in a fantasy of ancient royalty with its colourfully clad elephants, usually balk at the intrusion of other tourists into their photos. However, a globalized world does not allow us to find *elsewhere* what has been lost *here*. The kingdoms have died out, and tourism is a mass industry whose mahouts are not immune to the economic jolts this entails. But above all, the romantic notion of a lost ancestral harmony between animals and humans unravels from the animals' point of view: while elephant exploitation has hit new heights since the colonial era, these intensive uses are piled onto age-old – and intrinsically violent – methods of capture and training.[12]

Since the emergence of modern zoological gardens in the early nineteenth century, the fabled *elsewhere* has also been recreated in the hearts of Western cities and suburbs, aided and abetted by the import and captivity of wild creatures. Beginning in the 1930s, and with renewed vigour in the 1960s, Europe's lush countryside became the stage of safari parks (see pp.148–9), gathering species mainly from (former) colonial states in Africa in settings designed to mask all traces of artifice: fences, cages, enclosures, cables and electrical wiring are all neatly tucked out of sight. Seeking nature from the comfort of their cars, visitors experience a sense of liberty inside the animals' very enclosure, and capture an illusory closeness with animals;[13] like the tourists in Jaipur – but unlike Martin Parr – they strive to exclude other cars and their occupants from their pictures.

Is it because it is constantly thwarted that this dream of communing with animals continues to resurface? Is this what we see in Venice, Piazza San Marco (see p.161), where flocks of pigeons, tamed over centuries, feralized and now reduced to the status of pests, alight on tourists who feed them and engage briefly in avian communion? Martin Parr captured this fleeting reversal of relationship in photos that – for once – might almost be confused with the sort of snapshot sought by tourists. But a rude awakening came in 2008 when the mayor of Venice, turning the exception into the rule, abruptly banned feeding the pigeons that had adapted their behaviour to conform to human expectations and thus become a tourist attraction.[14]

Before, after and often during the sought-for communion, animals find themselves surrounded yet alone, trapped by a human-imposed dependence that creates their vulnerability.[15] When they are not busy performing or interacting, Jaipur's elephants are chained up, safari-park animals are locked in their enclosures, and pigeons are shooed away or killed.

Remodelling Animals

The Western lowland gorilla named Nico was born in Africa in 1962. Captured and removed from his group and his mother (who was certainly killed), he was brought to Hanover Zoo in 1964, then transferred to Rapperswil in Switzerland in 1966, and finally to Longleat Safari Park in Wiltshire, England, in 1986. The gorilla was loaned to Bristol Zoo in November 1991 and returned to Longleat in March 1992,[16] where Martin Parr took his portrait a few years later. On 4 August 1996, *The Independent* newspaper published an article entitled 'For the Gorilla with Everything', illustrated by two of Parr's photos, one featuring Nico in his night enclosure (see p.157).[17] In the article, the journalist never deviates from the conceptual framework of wildlife domestication: Nico and his 'partner' Samba are depicted as a couple attended by thoughtful caregivers who allow the gorillas – after a tough day of roaming their island gathering food – to return to the warmth of their 'bijou Japanese-style residence' and kick back in front of the TV with a glass of Ribena (a blackcurrant soft drink). The interviewed keepers describe Nico's favourite programmes, which he watches while eating, 'just like we do', as well as the documentaries he is shown – including some referred to as 'gorilla porn', to encourage him and Samba to get 'romantic'. The article ends with a reassuring anthropomorphic statement about how the solitary gorillas, 'like many humans, have to resort to their television for a sense of community'.[18]

The gorillas' forced insertion into the human realm – which attempts to convince us that the boundary between animals and humans has been erased, while in fact simply reinforcing it (the submission of animals to human will and frame remains the defining feature of their relationship) – masks the hypervisible element revealed by Parr's photo: three quarters of the intrinsically prison-like image is filled by bars that prevent the gorillas from escaping, changing channels or even enjoying an unimpeded view of their TV programme. The photo undermines the rhetoric of zookeepers, press officers – and journalists – who, since the early twentieth century, have sought to conceal the disciplinary nature of confinement that compromises the desired human-animal relations. Only by reading between the lines of the article in *The Independent* do we realize that the gorillas are imprisoned in their cell from closing time until the zoo reopens the next morning and perceive the solitude (or artificial coupledom) imposed upon gregarious creatures, as well as the psychological impoverishment engendered by captivity that must be compensated for by television.

The nagging questions surrounding the nature of human-animal relations under the care of the former surfaces even in the case of pets. From the nineteenth century onwards, the relationship between humans and dogs, the first animals to be domesticated, have reached a climax of control and power through a threefold historical process of suppression-domestication-remodelling. The first of these consisted of the mass extermination of stray dogs, who were captured then poisoned, hanged, drowned, slaughtered or smothered. In New York, between 1894 and 1908, the American Society for the Prevention of Cruelty to Animals killed over 1.5 million dogs and cats. Even today, many pounds and shelters euthanize in cases of overpopulation, or when animals are deemed 'unadoptable'. This went hand in hand with the reshaping of pet dogs to meet modern expectations, under threat of the pound, through the widespread use of the age-old muzzle, leash and collar (see pp.150–151), as well as through confining them to private property. A dog's only access to the outside world now occured in the company of his master. This double process coincided with the first dog shows in England and the United States in the 1860s,

designed to evaluate the excellence of breed and conformity to standards achieved through genetic purity. The remodelling of canine bodies led to an increasing control over dogs, who have become at once consumer goods, objects of affection and ostentatious attributes – a process reflected in specific practices and gestures – notably grooming and, outside of dog shows, apparel (see pp.162–3).[19]

Nahuelito: Animals Are Looking
Where have animals gone? The individual animals that bring us back to ourselves? John Berger underscores the crucial role of the animal gaze and its negation:

Animals are always the 'observed'. The fact that they can observe us has lost all significance. They are the objects of our ever-extending knowledge. What we know about them is an index of our power, and thus an index of what separates us from them. The more we know, the further away they are.[20]

Martin Parr's realist panorama challenges this epistemological paradox by emphasizing the impossibility of fully removing ourselves from the animal gaze. Though we may pile toads into baskets like pieces of fruit, individuals still look out at us from the heap, even if we no longer look back (see p.167). Though we may hide our dogs' eyes behind dark glasses (see p.162), blur their vision in a cloud of hairspray (see p.163) and drag them along hastily even on leisure outings (see pp.150–1), their eyes are still glued to us. Though we may dismember our quarry, rip off their heads (see p.165) and outfit them with glass eyes (see p.166), they still still seem to be staring at us.

Animal agency does not emerge in an ethereal, ahistorical world free from domination and power asymmetries. Rather, it is shaped within the very tightened mesh of the ever-denser and far-reaching net woven by consumer society – or within its interstices. Animals in human custody use whatever space they are allowed (see pp.142–3, 186). Still others live with us yet without us – in the margins of our lives, in our abandoned vehicles (see p.188–9), on our surfeits of sugar, unused goods, trash, bins overflowing with food; they observe us casually, on the sly, as they please (see pp.137, 146–7).

And in Mar del Plata, Argentina, when the fiendish head of the fabled Patagonian sea monster Nahuelito (see pp.168–9), or some other beast, is conjured from the sand with our hands, it serves as a mischievous reminder that animals still intrude. When the sea recedes (did Martin Parr await the moment?), when all that remains of mythical marine beasts are fragments, when the joke is over and when we are left to our solitude and introspection and our canine companion comes trotting to the rescue, he reminds us that this encounter washes almost anything away.[21]

Martin Parr's photos cannot be reduced to colourful images for animal lovers. By exposing consumer society in the making – subverting the conventions of tourist photography, revealing the flip side of spectacle, dwelling on the piling-up of bodies – Parr goes against the grain of the prevalent animal representations within consumer society, which tend to conceal domination to leave us only with agency and affection, which are thereby insufficient and misleading.

We may smile at the most obvious quirks that such domination brings about (see p.164) and at the ostentatious excesses it permits (see p.158) – such as recomposed birds (see p.159), ersatz versions of whole carcasses once worn on nineteenth-century hats, now scorned by over a century of harsh criticism. But Martin Parr is also speaking about himself, perhaps riding an elephant, or with us on safari, or else covered in pigeons in Piazza San Marco. And in truth we are smiling at ourselves, riddled with contradictions (vegans are still rare, even as veganism becomes another mode of consumption that has not escaped Parr's keen eye), terribly violent in our pacifism, caught in a globalized community that reassures us even while it leaves us implacably alone.

1 Martin Parr views himself as a documentary photographer: see Martin Parr, *Le Mélange des genres. Entretien avec Quentin Bajac*, Paris, Textuel, 2010, p.65.
2 Michael A. Webster, 'Hong Kong's Trade in Wildlife', *Biological Conservation*, vol. 8, 1975, pp.203–11; Jonathan E. Kolby et al., 'First Evidence of Amphibian Chytrid Fungus (*Batrachochytrium dendrobatidis*) and Ranavirus in Hong Kong Amphibian Trade', *PLoS ONE*, vol. 9, no. 3, 2014 (online: www.doi.org/10.1371/journal.pone.0090750); Sara Boss et al., 'Serotypes, Antimicrobial Resistance Profiles, and Virulence Factors of *Salmonella* Isolates in Chinese Edible Frogs (*Hoplobatrachus rugulosus*) Collected from Wet Markets in Hong Kong', *Foods*, vol. 12, no. 1, 2023 (online: www.oi.org/10.3390/foods12112245).
3 John Berger, 'Why Look at Animals?', *About Looking*, London, Writers' & Readers' Publishing Co-op, 1981 [1977], pp.1–26.
4 Martin Parr and Richard Hollingham, *Space Dogs. The Story of the Celebrated Canine Cosmonauts*, London, Laurence King Publishing, 2019. I would like to thank Julia Chiron for sharing this reference.
5 Berger, 'Why Look at Animals?'.
6 Andrew C. Isenberg, *The Destruction of the Bison. An Environmental History, 1750–1920*, Cambridge, Cambridge University Press, 2000.
7 S. F. Markham and H. Hargreaves, *The Museums of India*, London, The Museums Association, 1936.
8 Savia Viegas, 'Rich Men's Collections, A Nation's Heritage, and Poor Men's Perceptions', *Teaching South Asia*, vol. 1, no. 1, 2001, pp.12–22.
9 'Asiatic Lion', Chhatrapati Shivaji Maharaj Vastu Sangrahalaya website (online: www.csmvs.in/collections/asiatic-lion/); Mahesh Rangarajan, 'Animals with Rich Histories. The Case of the Lions of Gir Forest, Gujarat, India', *History and Theory*, vol. 52, no. 4, 2013, pp.109–27.
10 The title is borrowed from Nigel Rothfels, 'Touching Animals. The Search for a Deeper Understanding of Animals', in Dorothee Brantz (dir.), *Beastly Natures. Animals, Humans, and the Study of History*, Charlottesville and London, University of Virginia Press, 2010, pp.38–58.
11 Penny Johnson, 'Take My Camel: The Disappearing Camels of Jerusalem and Jaffa', *Jerusalem Quarterly*, no. 53, 2013, pp.28–41.
12 Martha Chaiklin, 'Ivory in Early Modern Ceylon: A Case Study in What Documents Don't Reveal', *International Journal of Asian Studies*, vol. 6, no. 1, 2009, pp.37–63; Jonathan Saha, *Colonizing Animals. Interspecies Empire in Myanmar*, Cambridge, Cambridge University Press, 2021; Jennah Green, Jan Schmidt-Burbach and Lindsay Hartley-Backhouse, 'Giants in tourism: captive conditions, industry trends, and animal welfare implications for Asian elephants in tourism from 2014 to 2020', *Frontiers in Ethology*, no. 4, 2025 (online: www.doi.org/10.3389/fetho.2025.1532995). I would like to thank Elisabeth Vermandere for her information on Jaipur.
13 Éric Baratay and Élisabeth Hardouin-Fugier, *Zoo. A History of Zoological Gardens in the West*, London, Reaktion Books, 2002; Andrew J. P. Flack, 'Lions Loose on a Gentleman's Lawn: Animality, Authenticity and Automobility in the Emergence of the English Safari Park', *Journal of Historical Geography*, no. 54, 2016, pp.38–49.
14 Colin Jerolmack, *The Global Pigeon*, Chicago/London, University of Chicago Press, 2013.
15 John Kinder, *World War Zoos. Humans and Other Animals in the Deadliest Conflict of the Modern Age*, Chicago, University of Chicago Press, 2025.
16 Thomas Wilms et al., *International Studbook for the Western Lowland Gorilla* Gorilla g. gorilla, Frankfurt, Frankfurt Zoo, no. 962, 2011.
17 Matthew Sweet, 'For the Gorilla With Everything', *The Independent*, 3 August 1996, pp.36–7. The photo in the article differs slightly from the one shown on p.157.
18 *Ibid*.
19 Michael Worboys, Julie-Marie Strange and Neil Pemberton, *The Invention of the Modern Dog. Breed and Blood in Victorian Britain*, Baltimore, Johns Hopkins University Press, 2018; Chris Pearson, *Dogopolis. How Dogs and Humans Made Modern New York, London, and Paris*, Chicago and London, University of Chicago Press, 2021.
20 John Berger, 'Why Look at Animals?', p. 14.
21 I would like to thank Sylvestre Pouillard for the Nahuelito hypothesis. For more on this, see María Inés Palleiro, 'La dama fantasma y el monstruo del lago: Narración, ciencia y creencias en actuaciones discurcovas', *Runa*, 2011, vol. 32, no. 2.

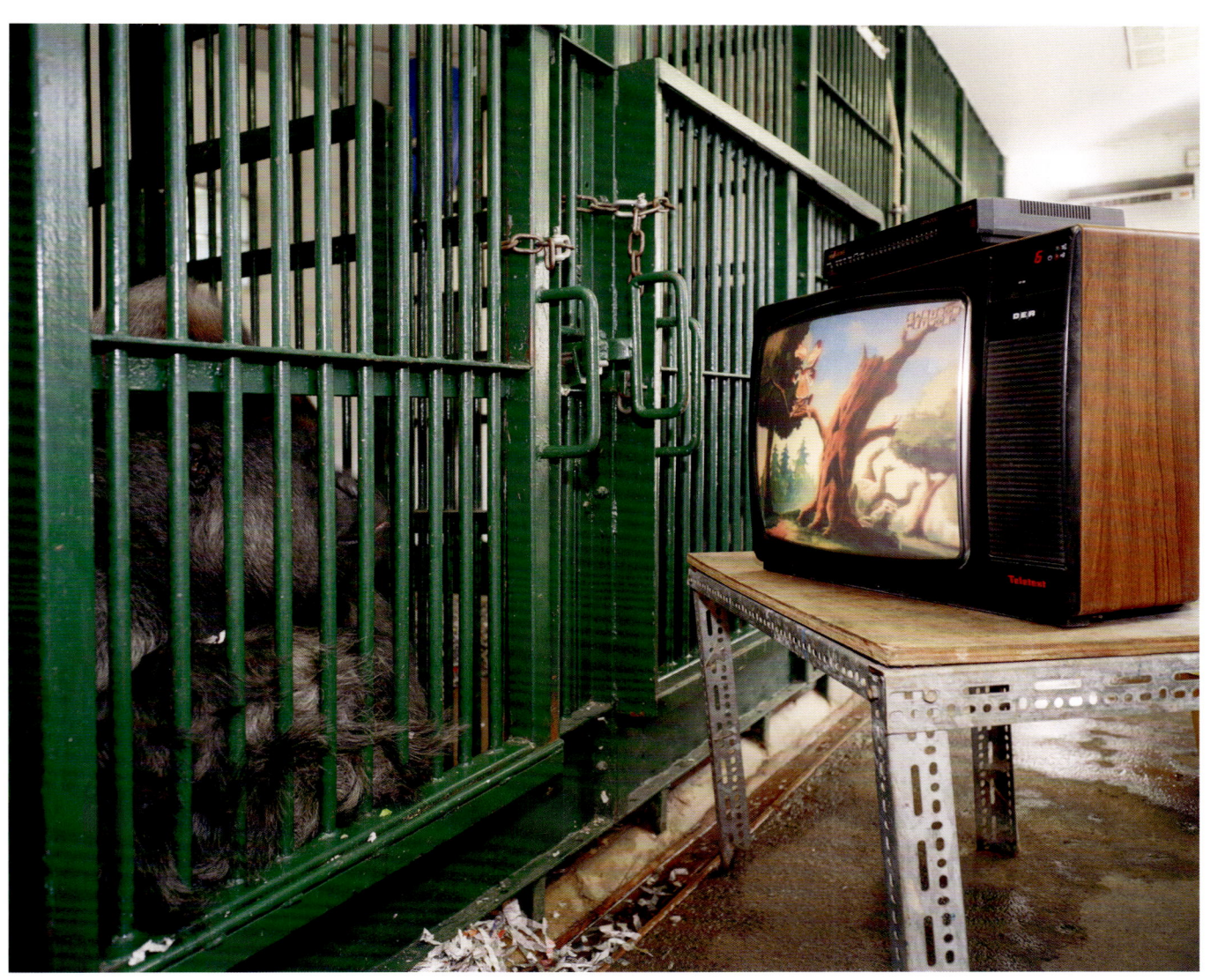

Longleat Safari Park, England, 1998

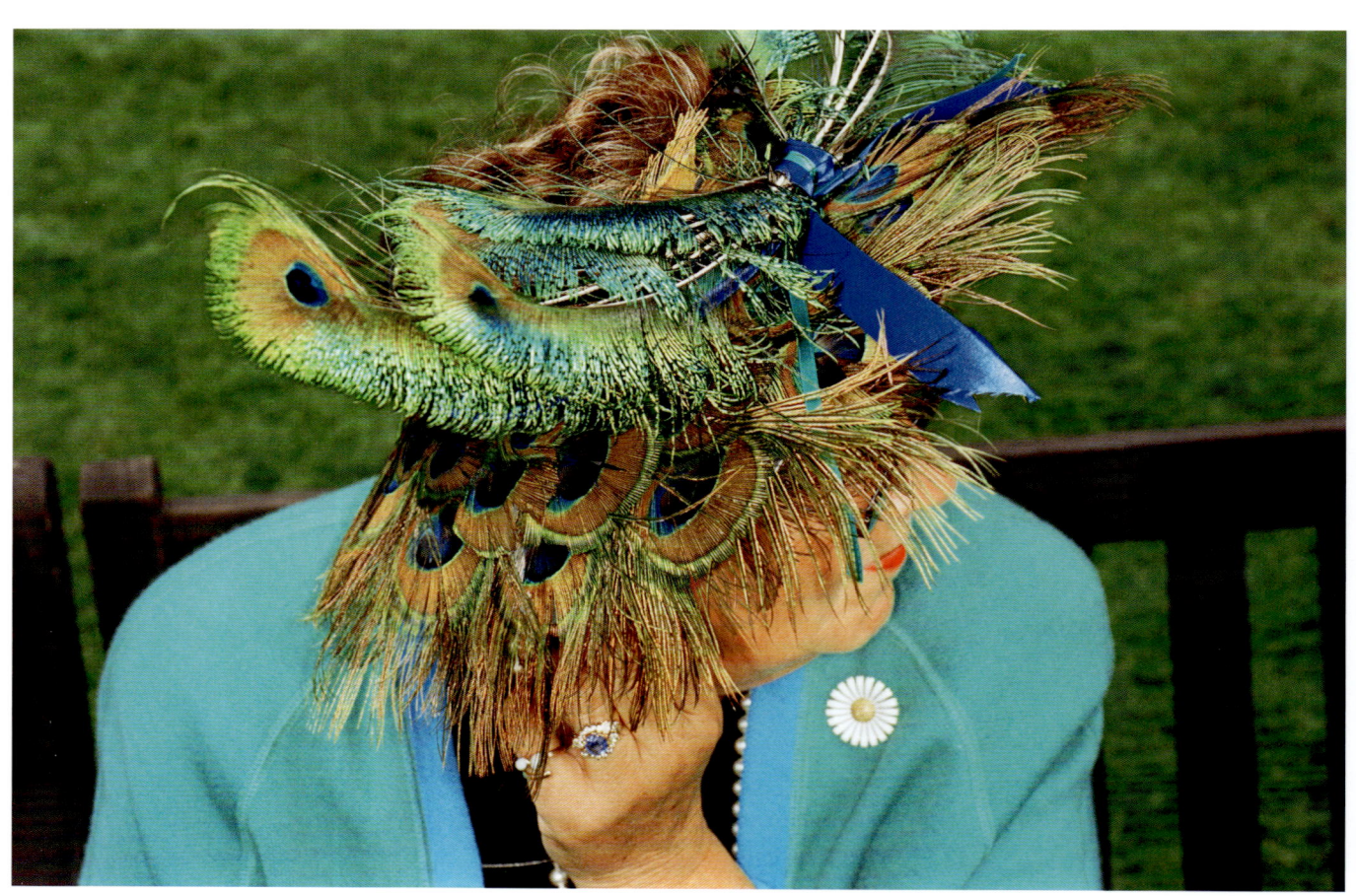

Ascot, England, 1999

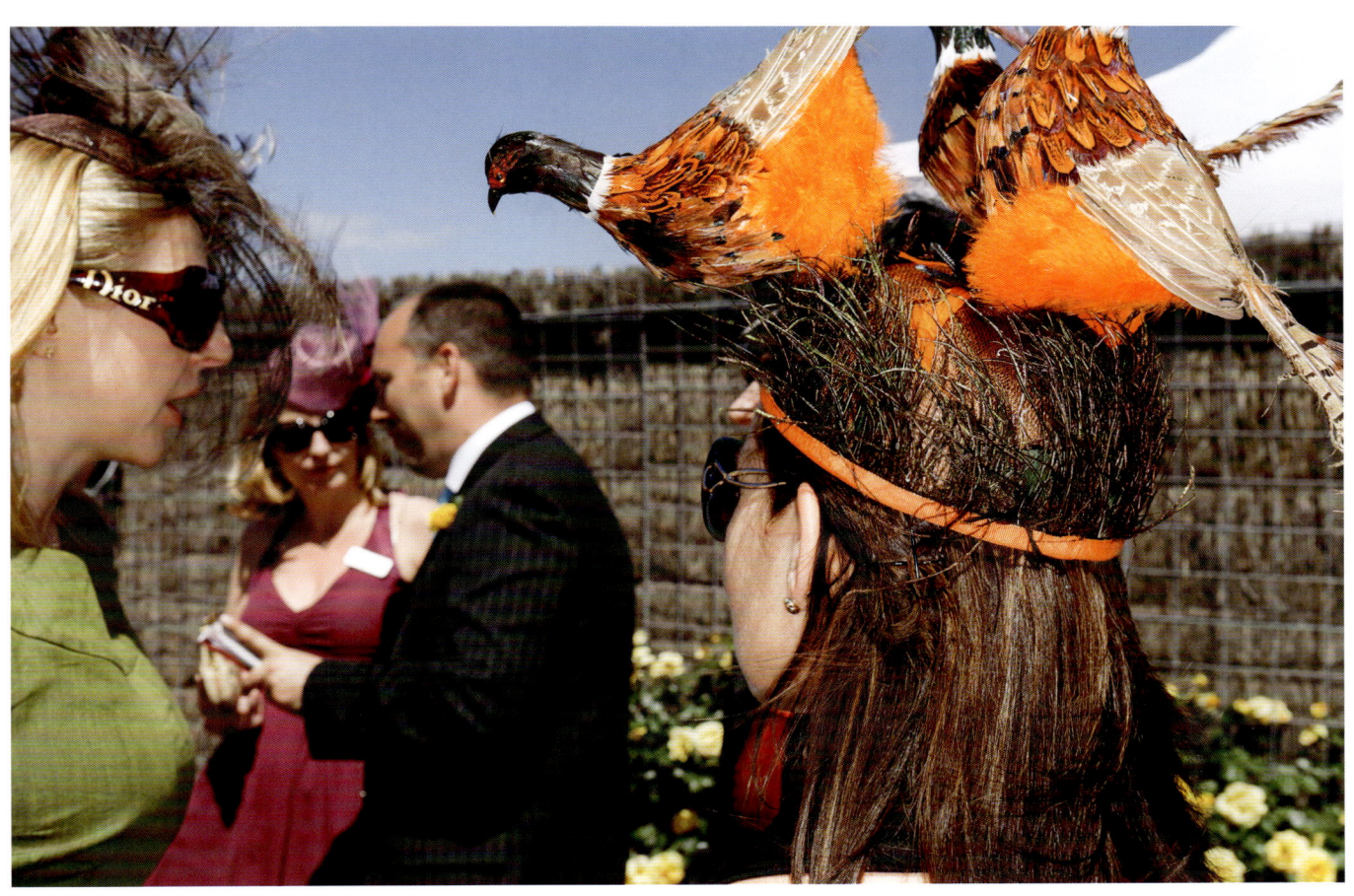

Melbourne, Australia, 2008

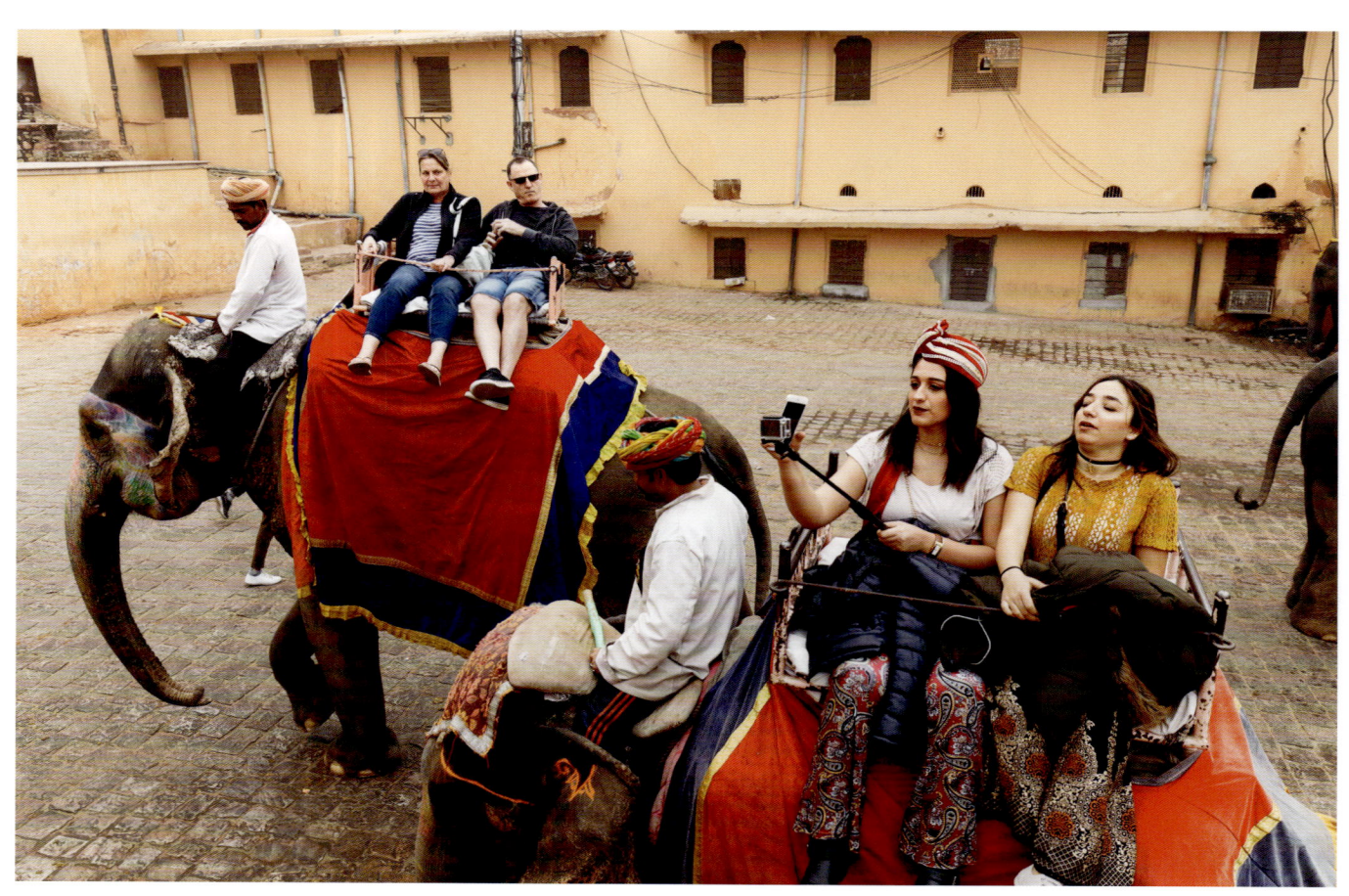

Amer Fort, Jaipur, India, 2019

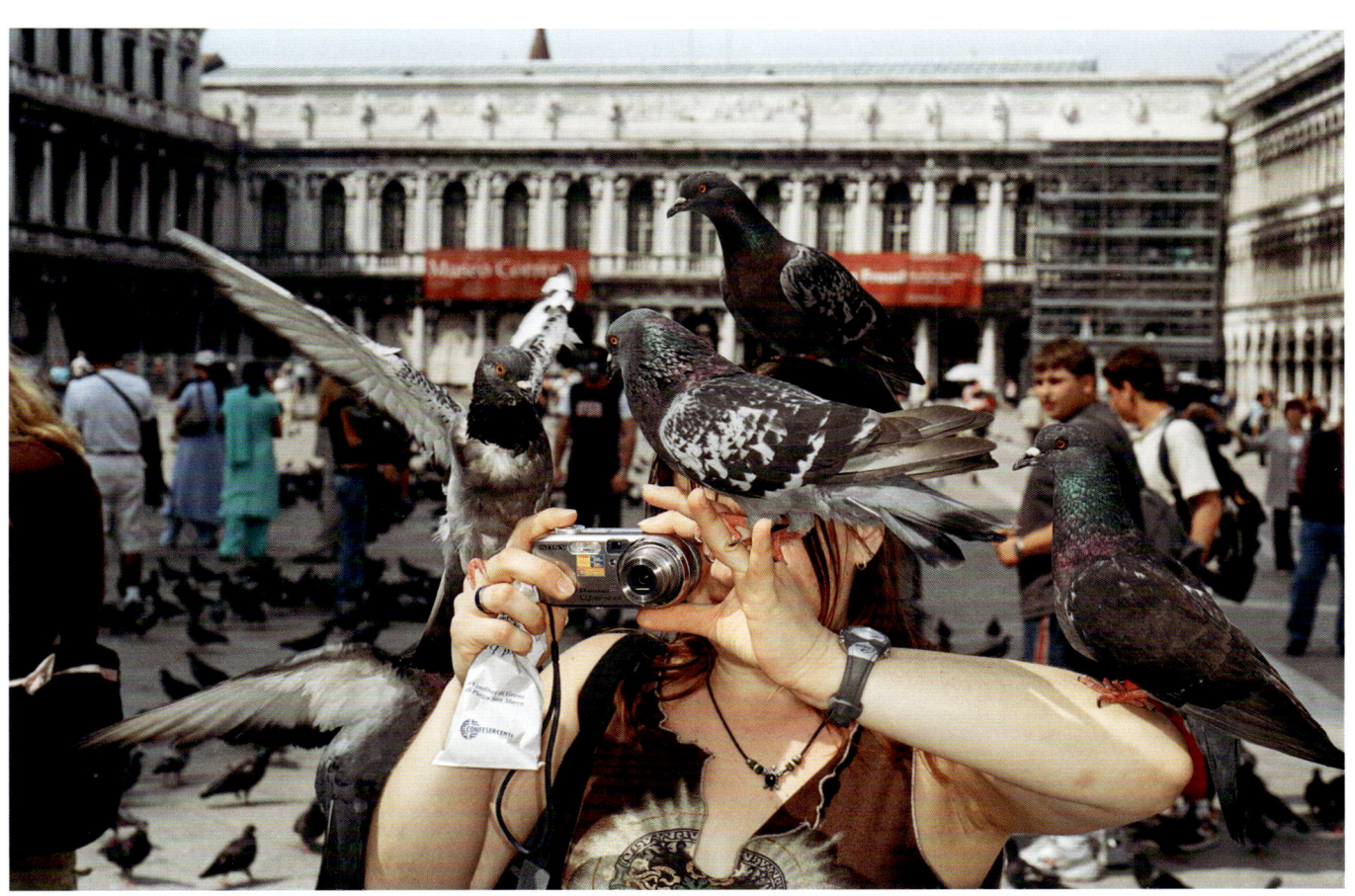

Venice, Italy, 2005

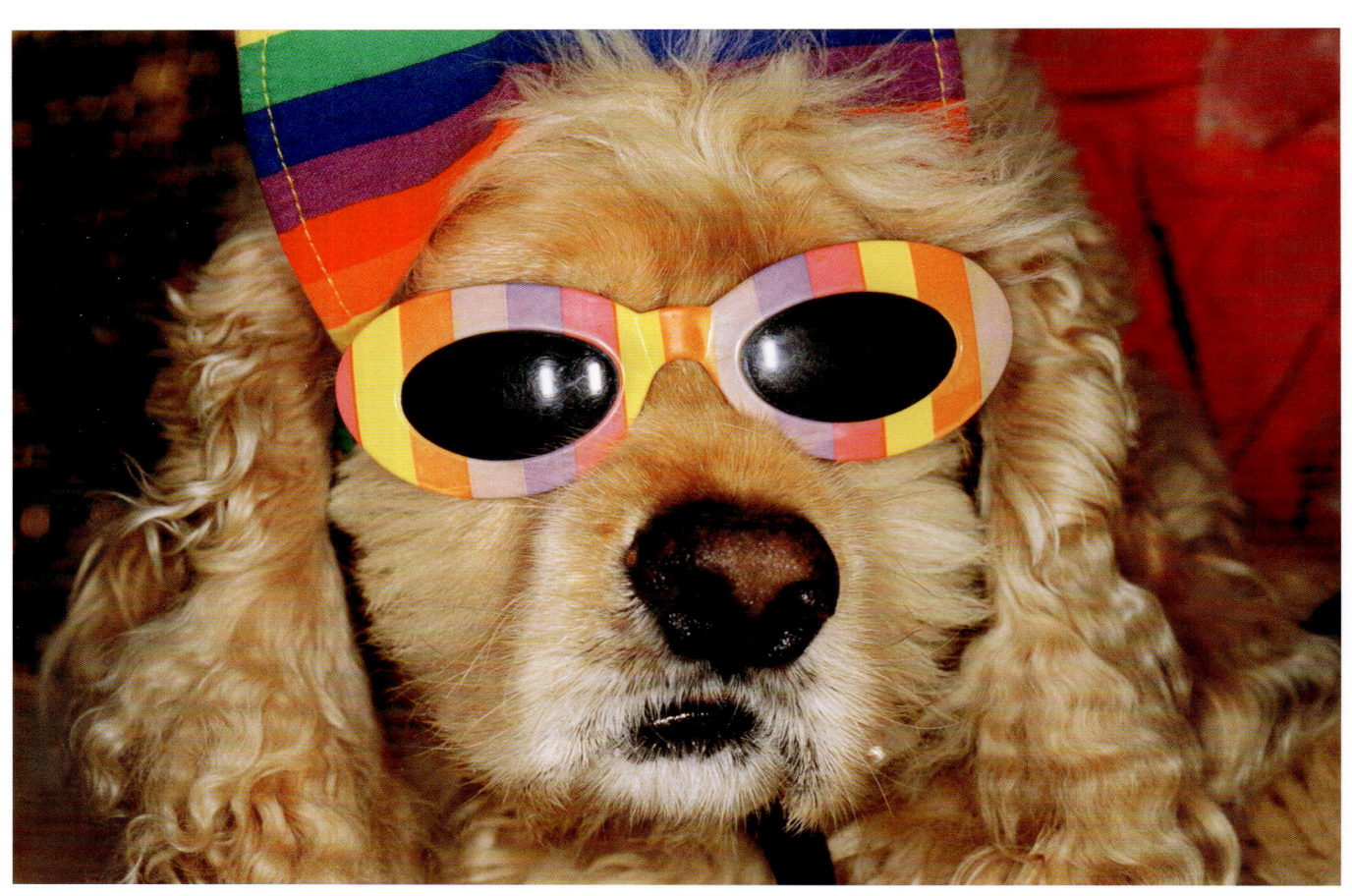

Venice Beach, California, USA, 1998

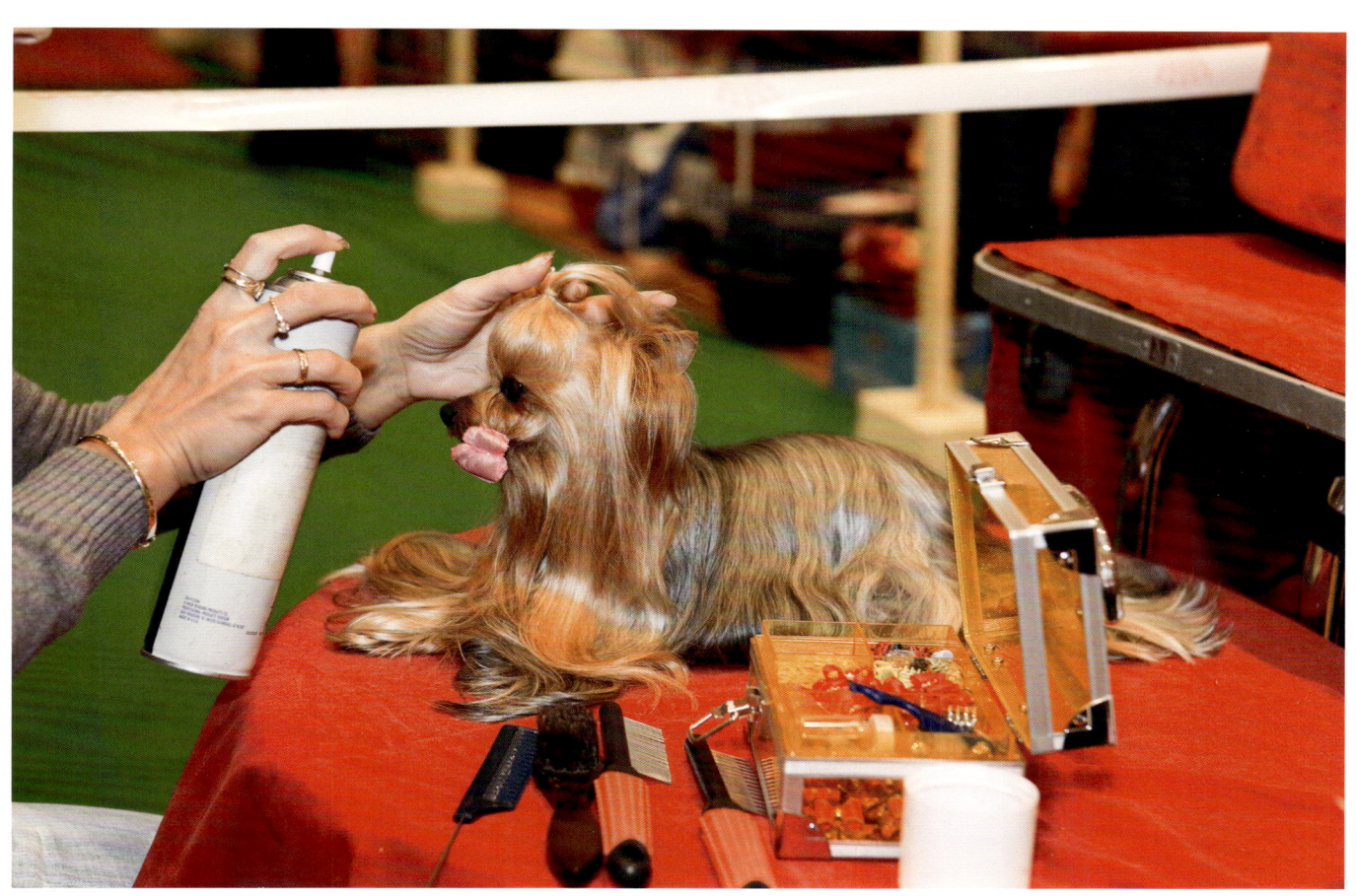

Neumünster, Germany, 2009

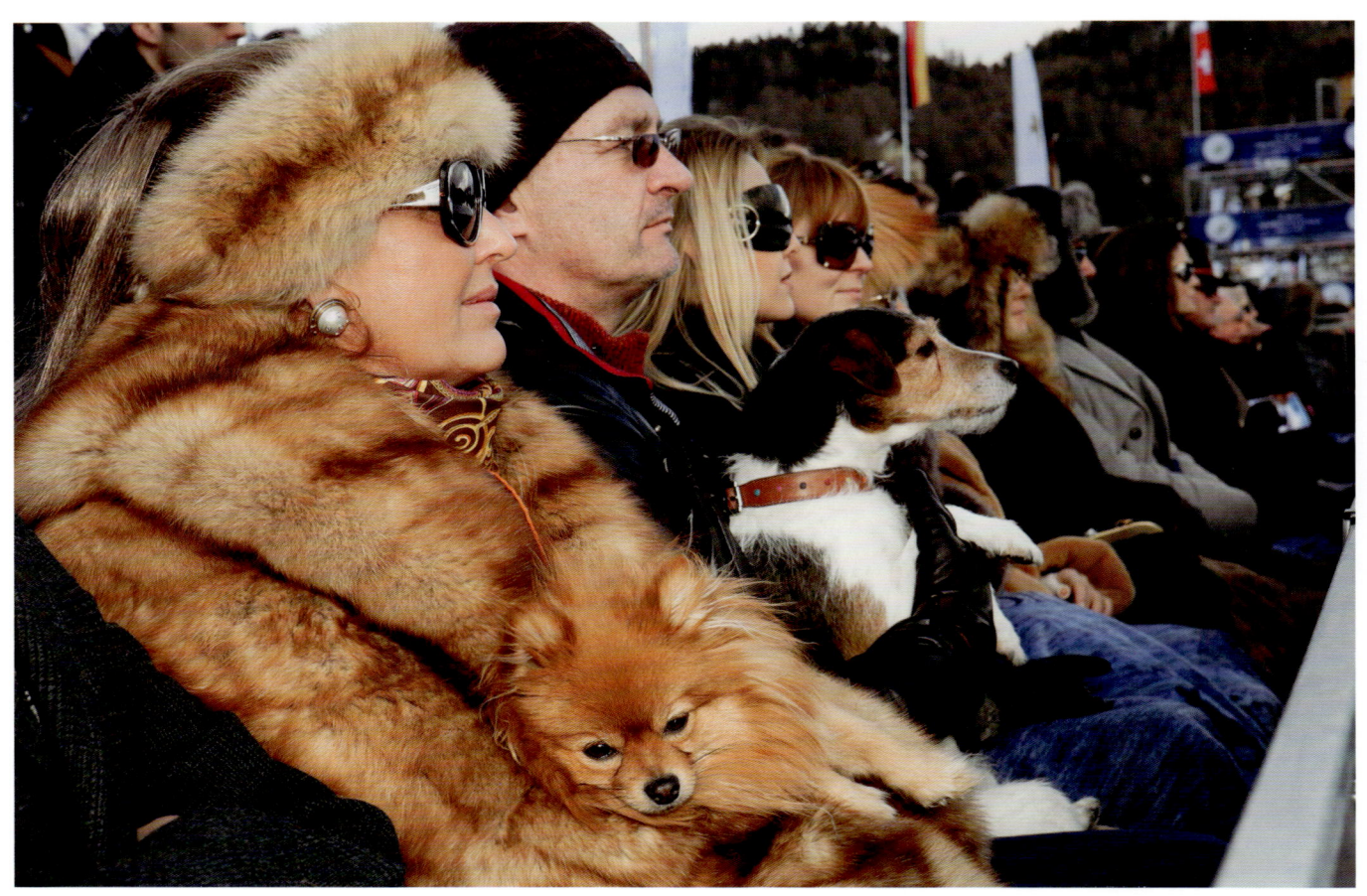

St. Moritz, Switzerland, 2011

Opposite:
Vienna, Austria, 2015

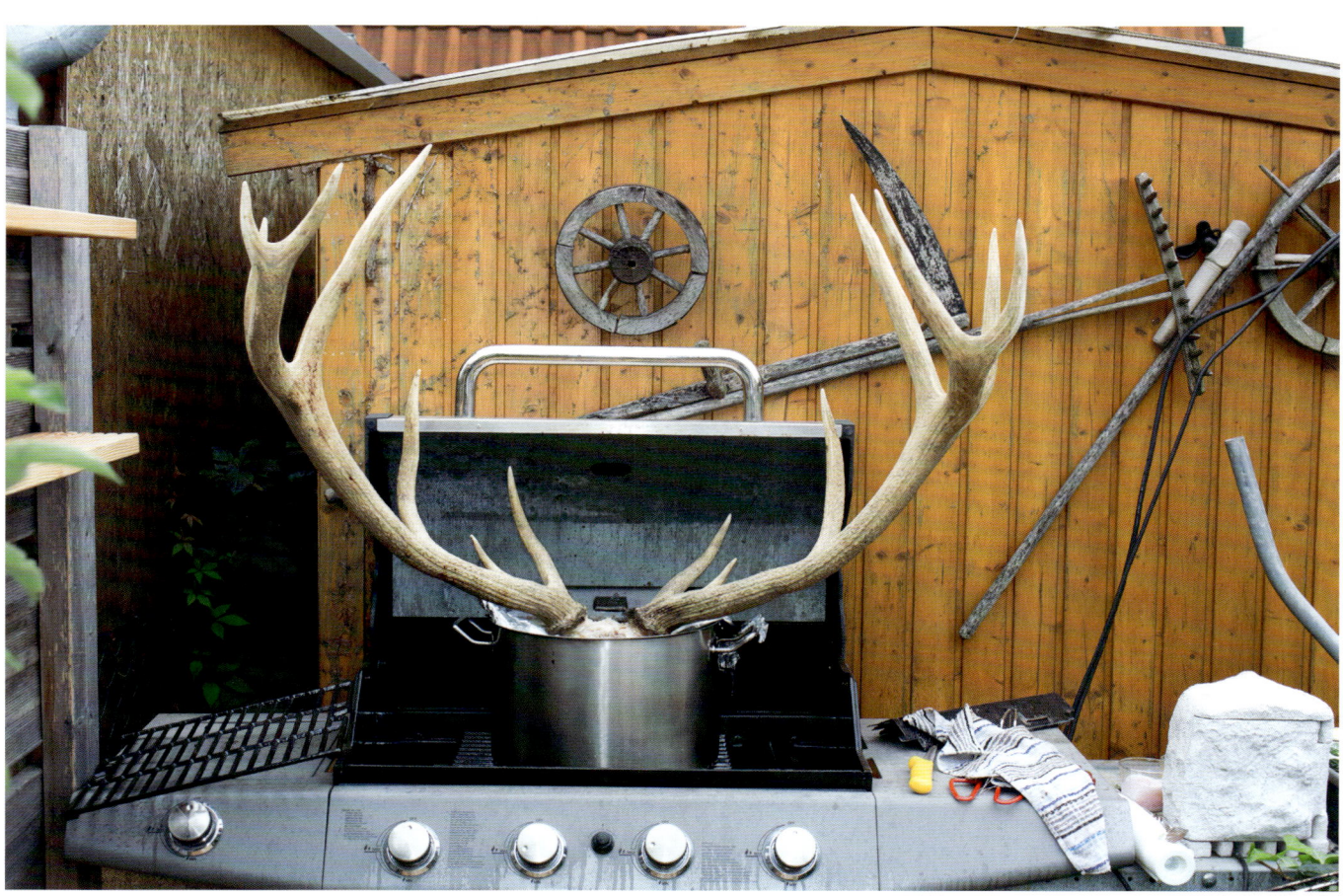

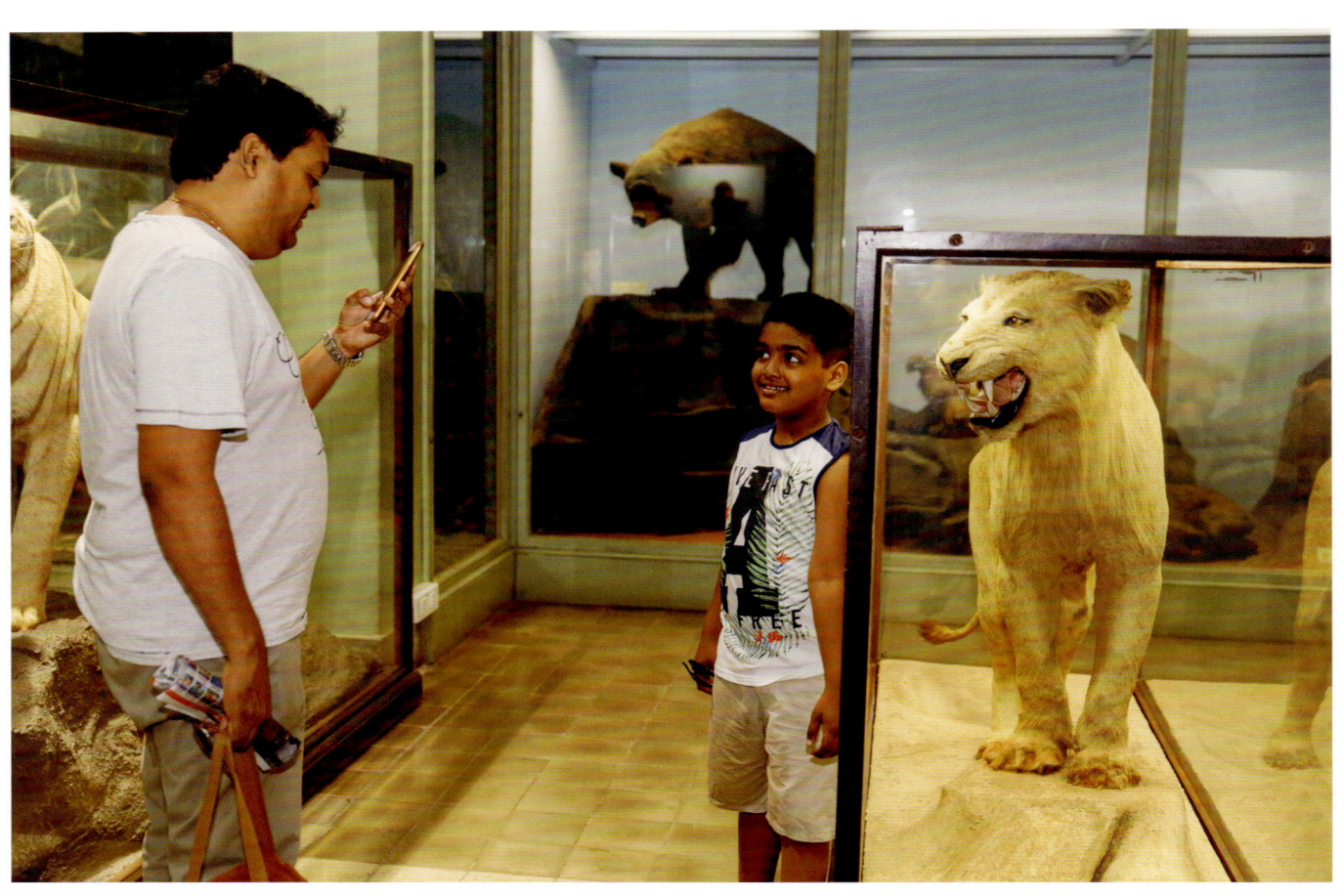

Prince of Wales Museum, Mumbai, India, 2019

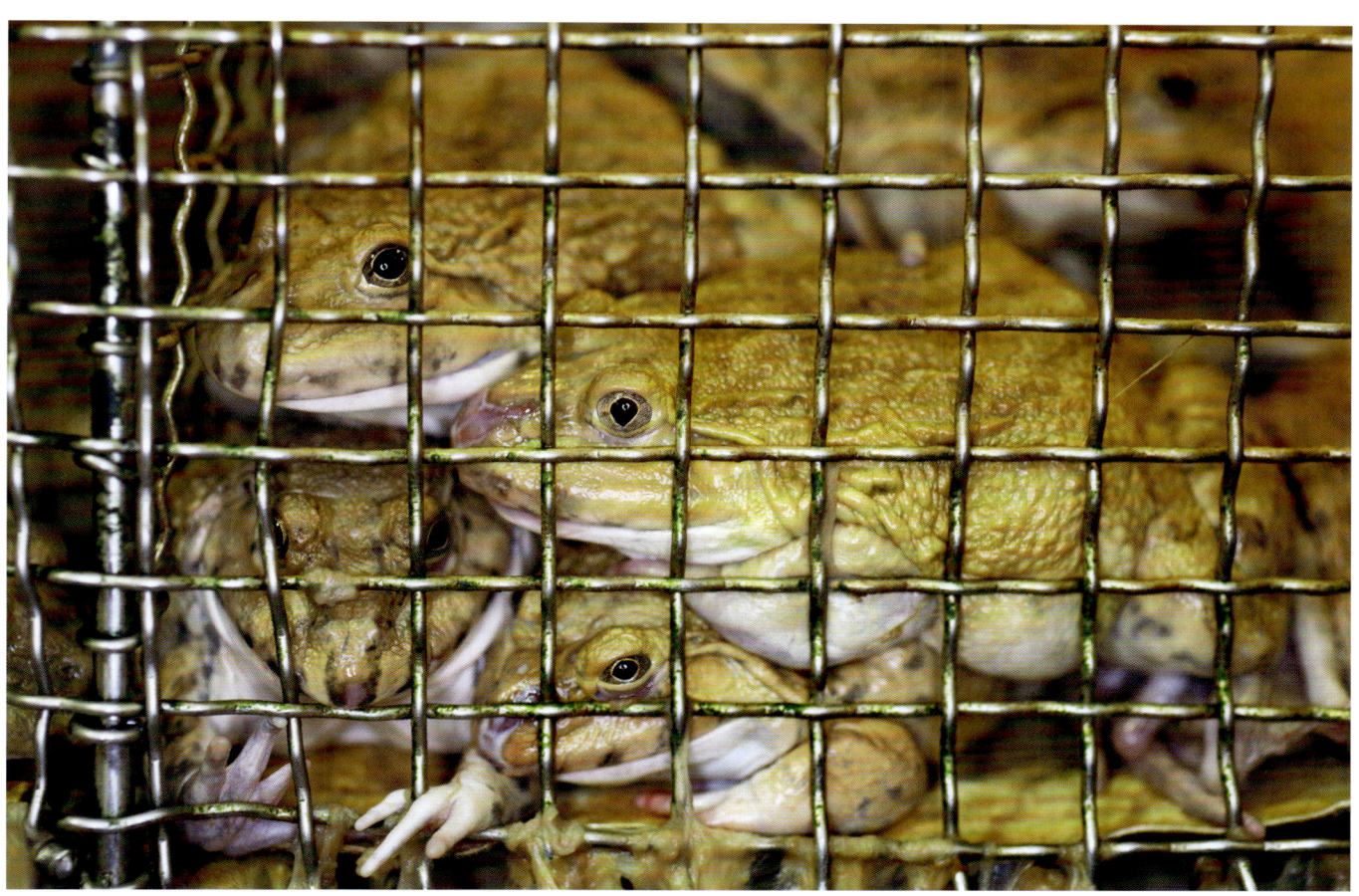

Hong Kong, China, 2013

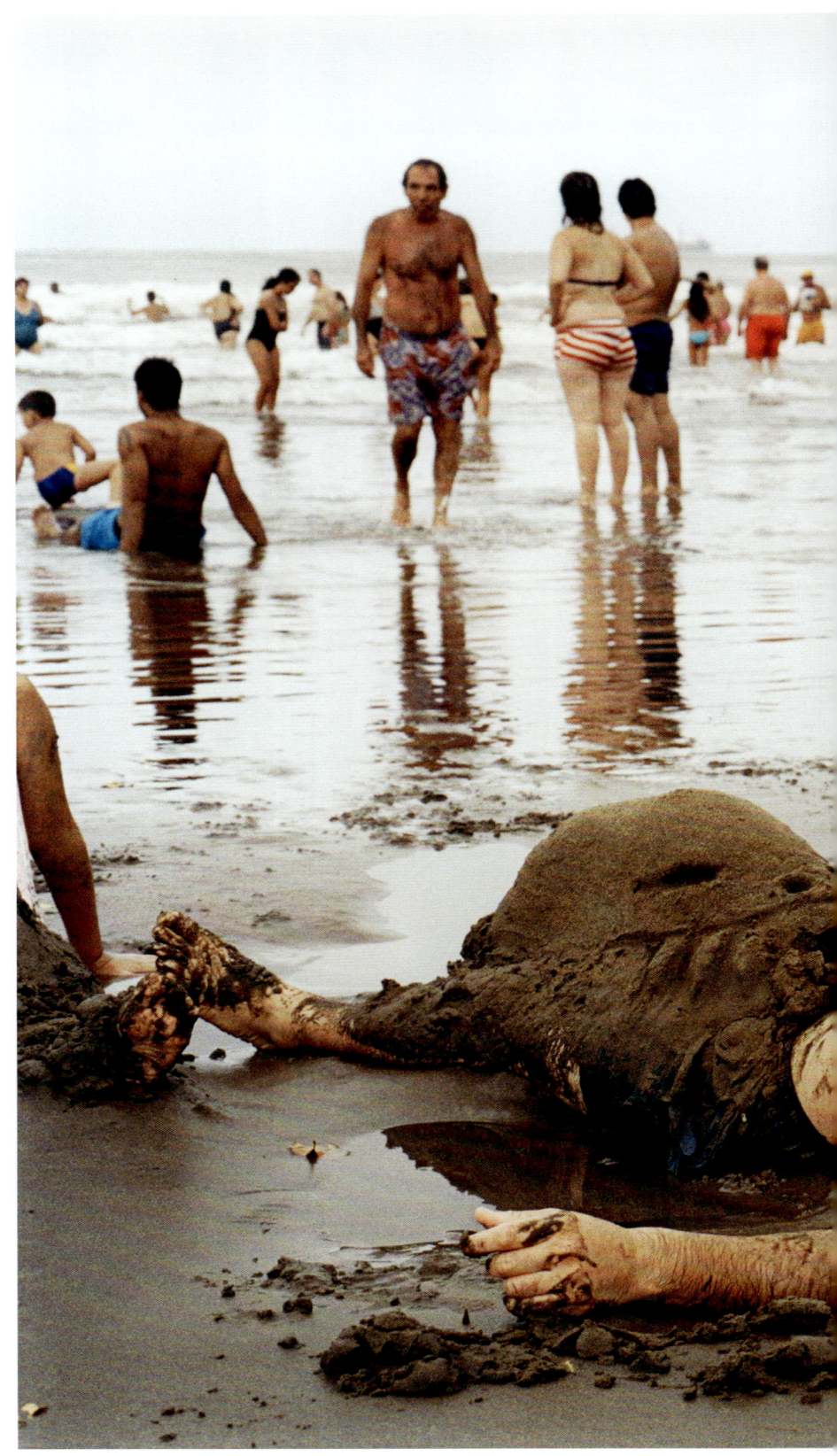

Mar del Plata, Argentina, 2007

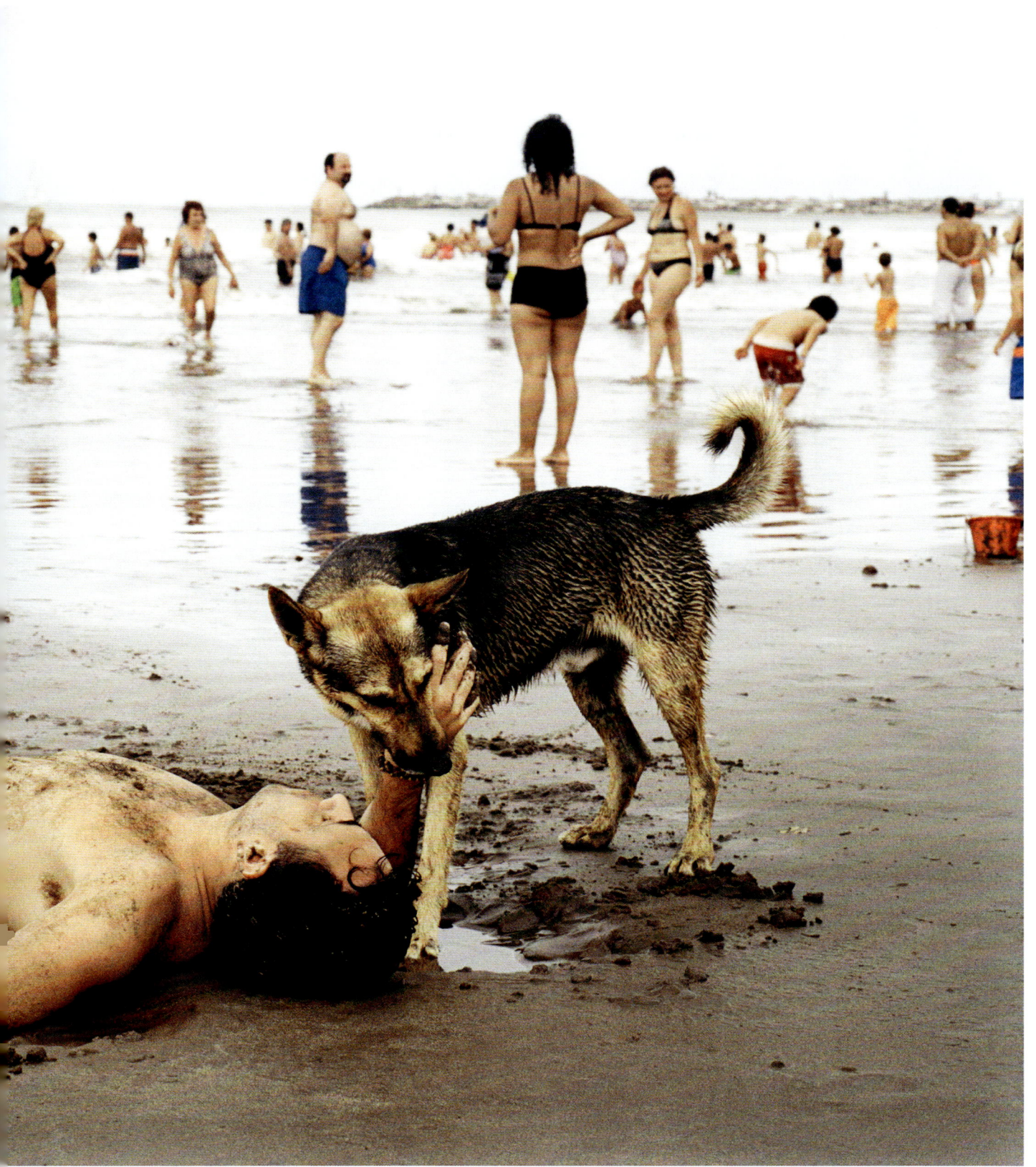

TECHNOLOGY ADDICTION

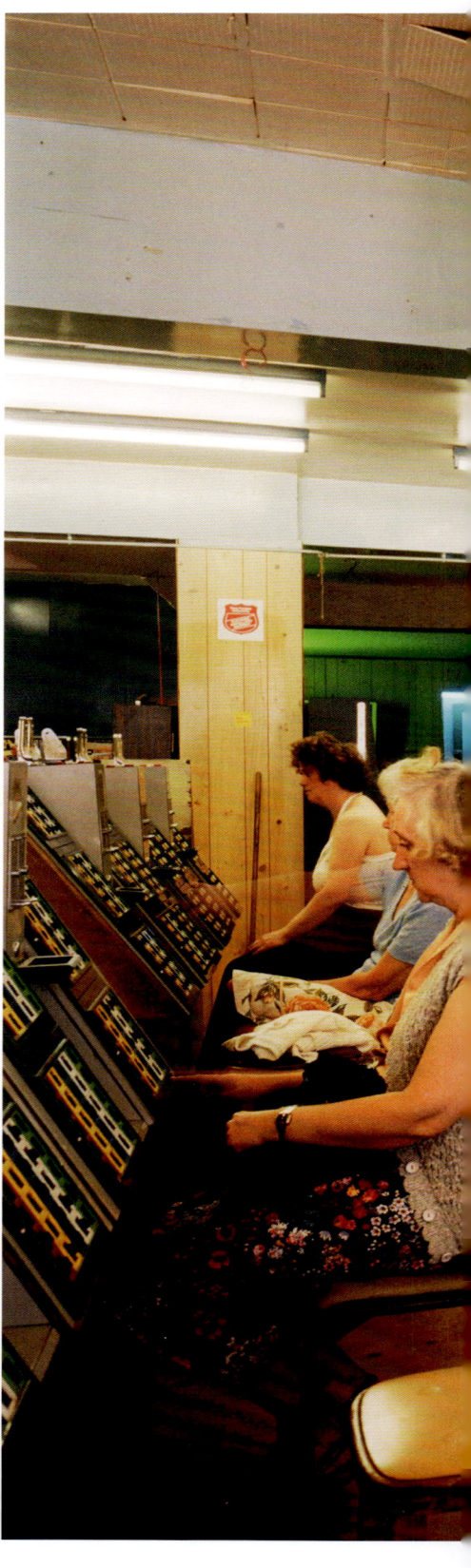

New Brighton, England, 1983–5

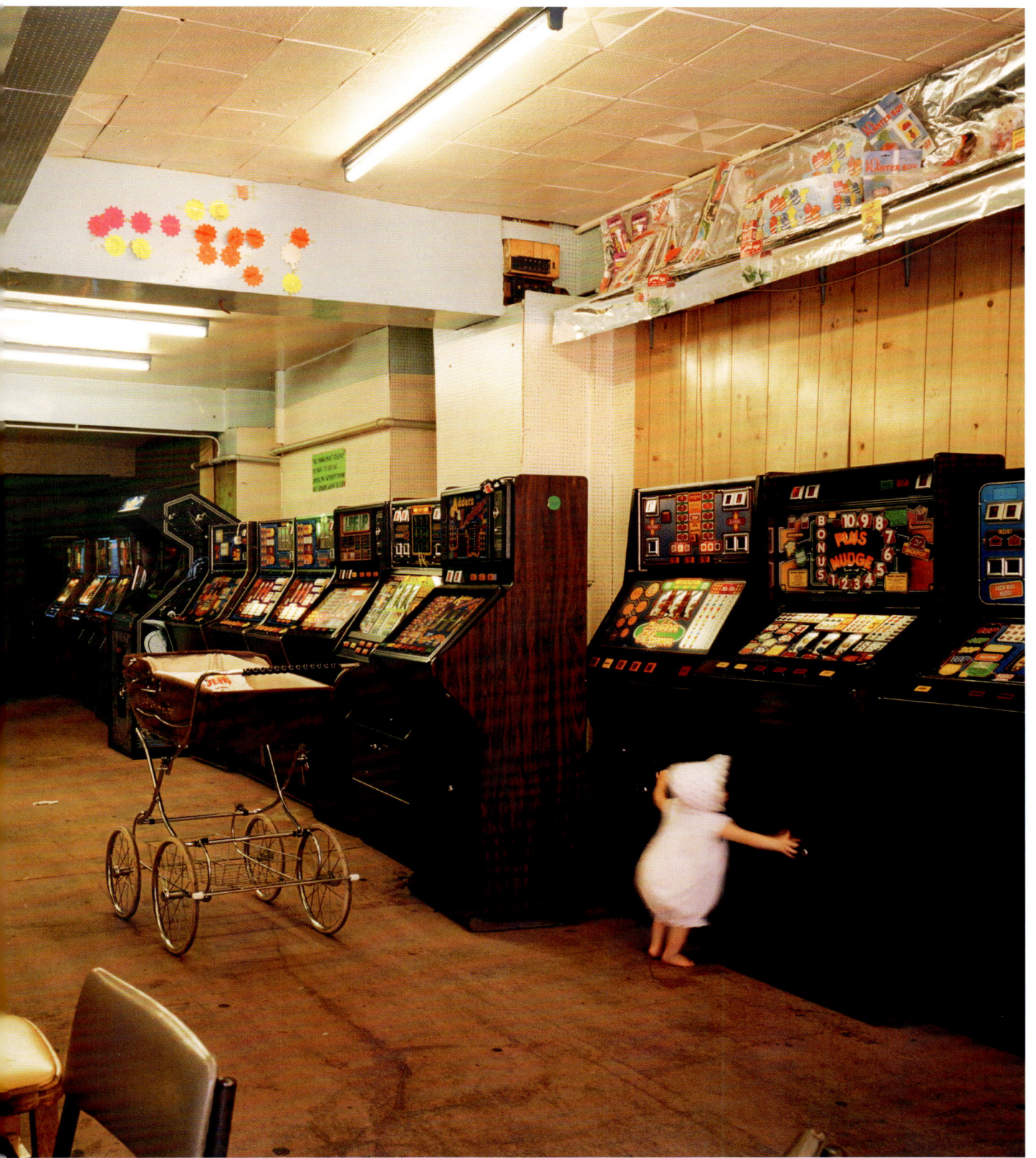

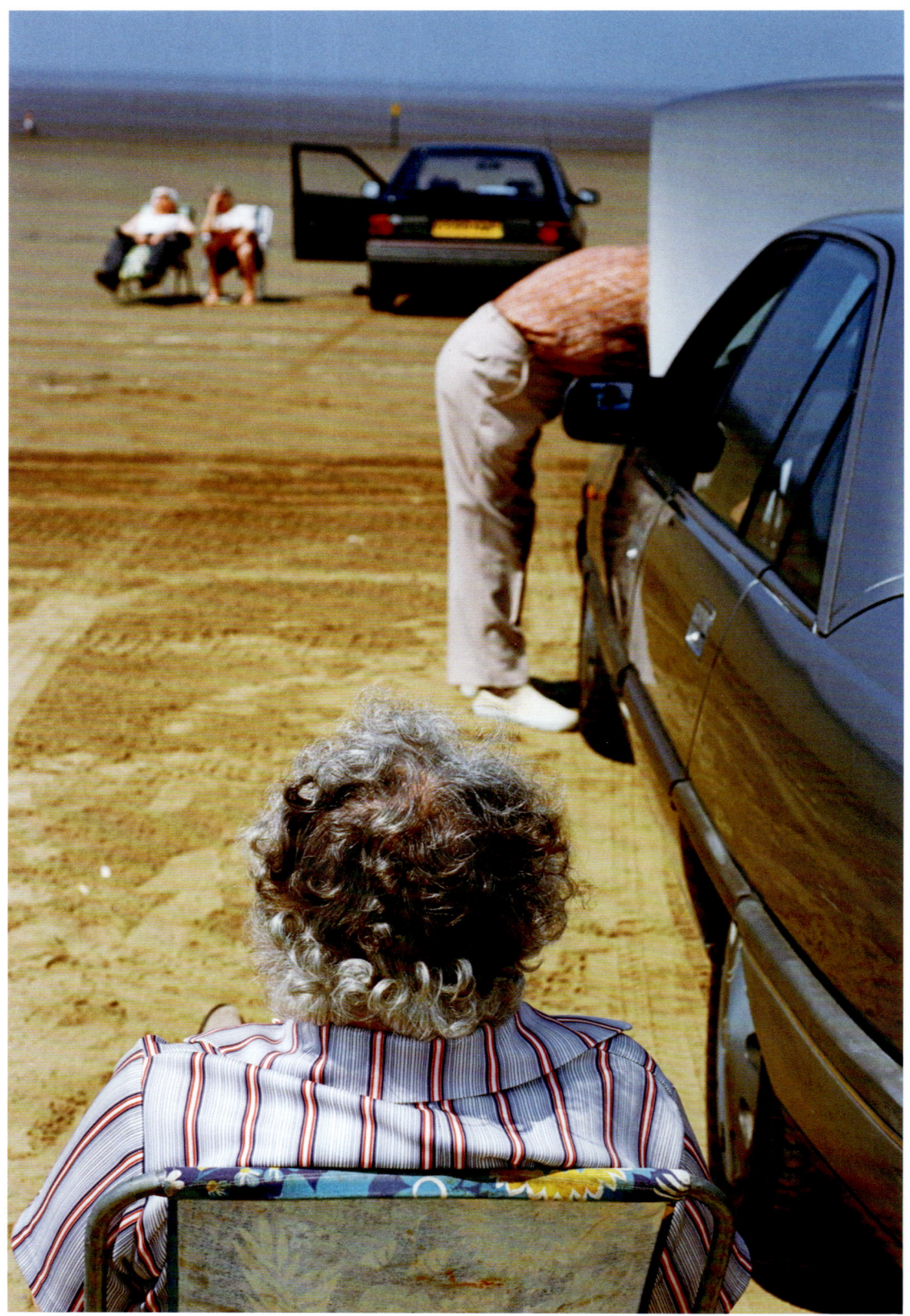

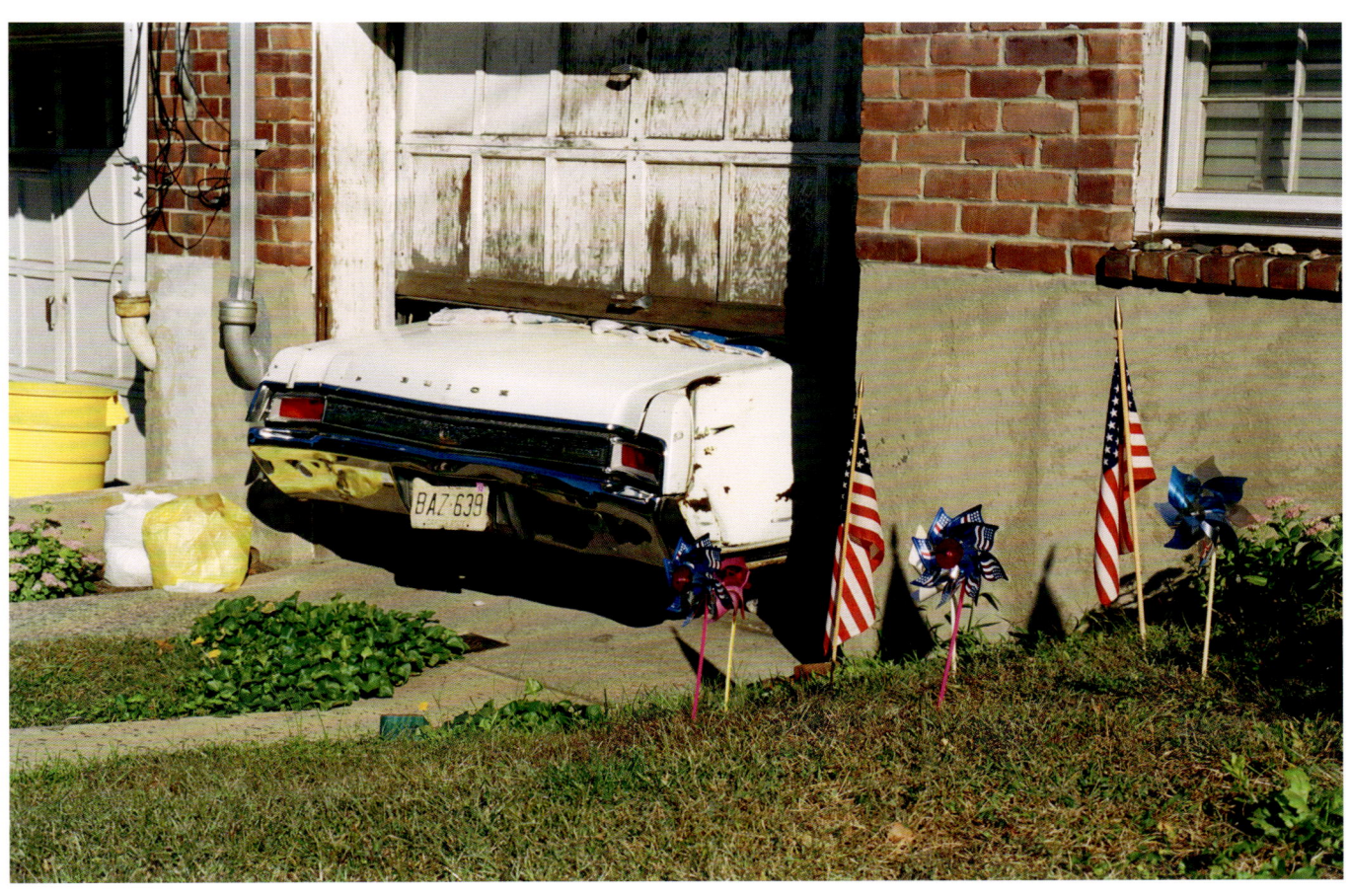

Opposite:
Weston-super-Mare, England, 2000   **Newark, New Jersey, USA, 2001**

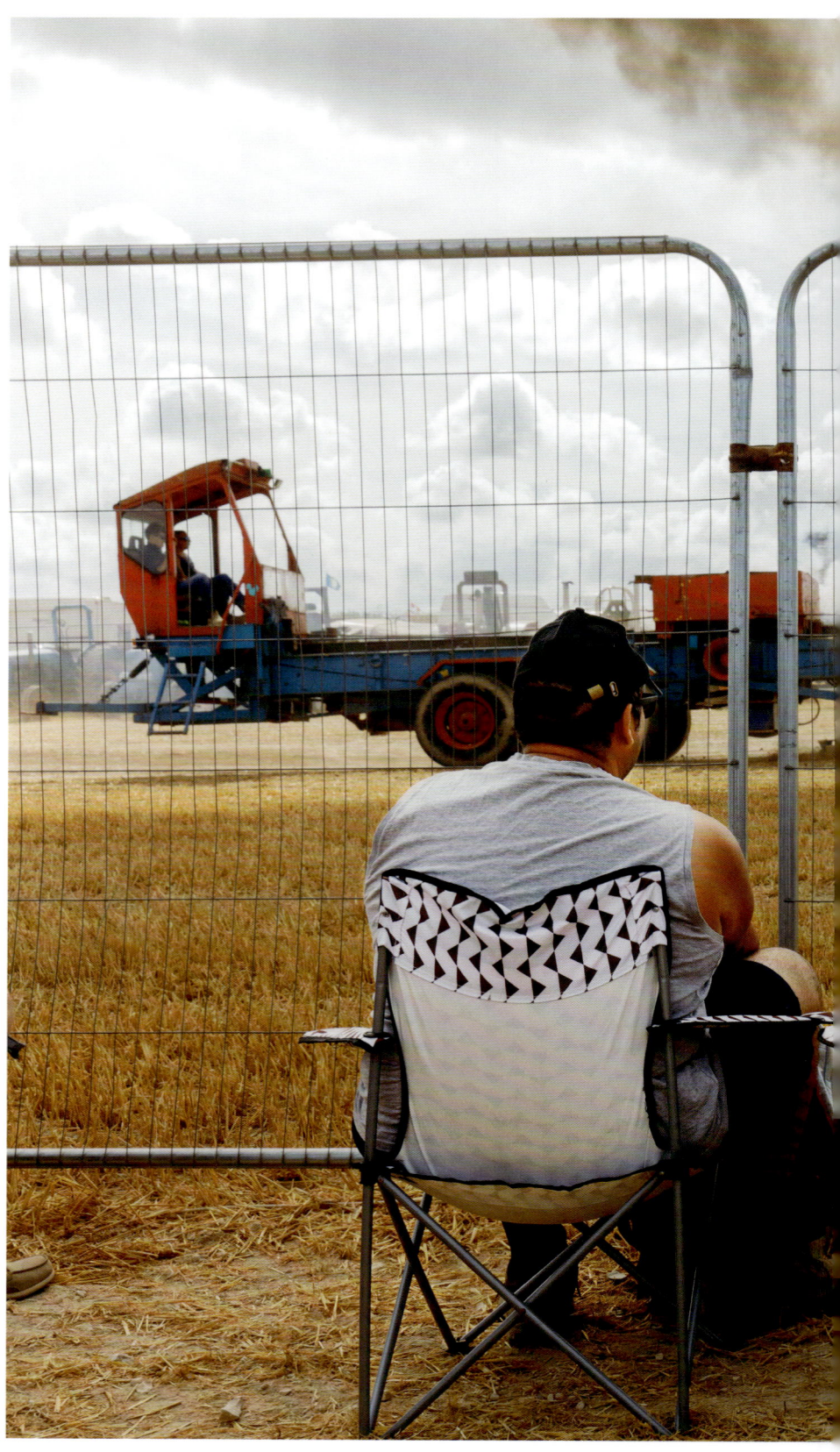

Dorset, England, 2022

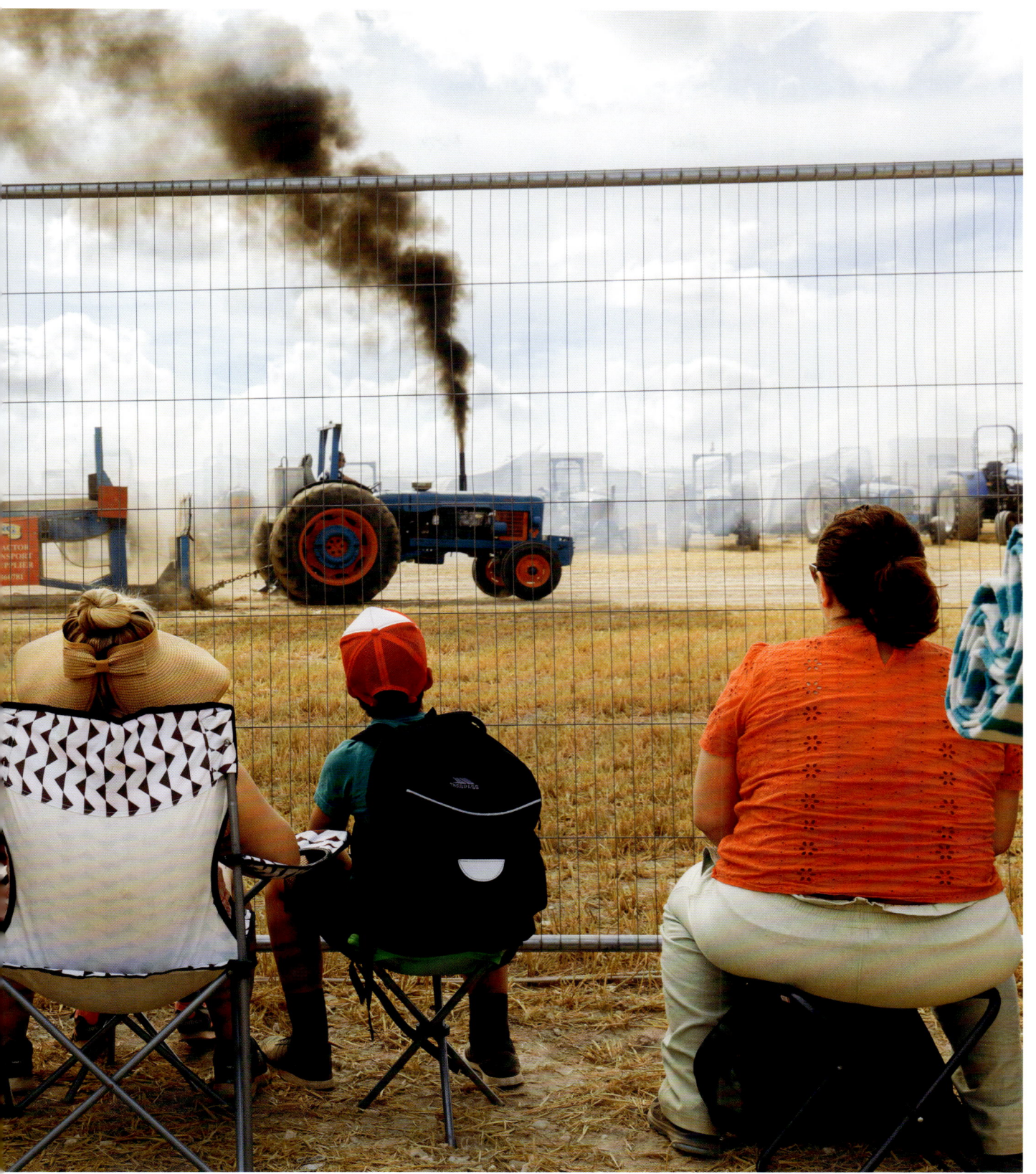

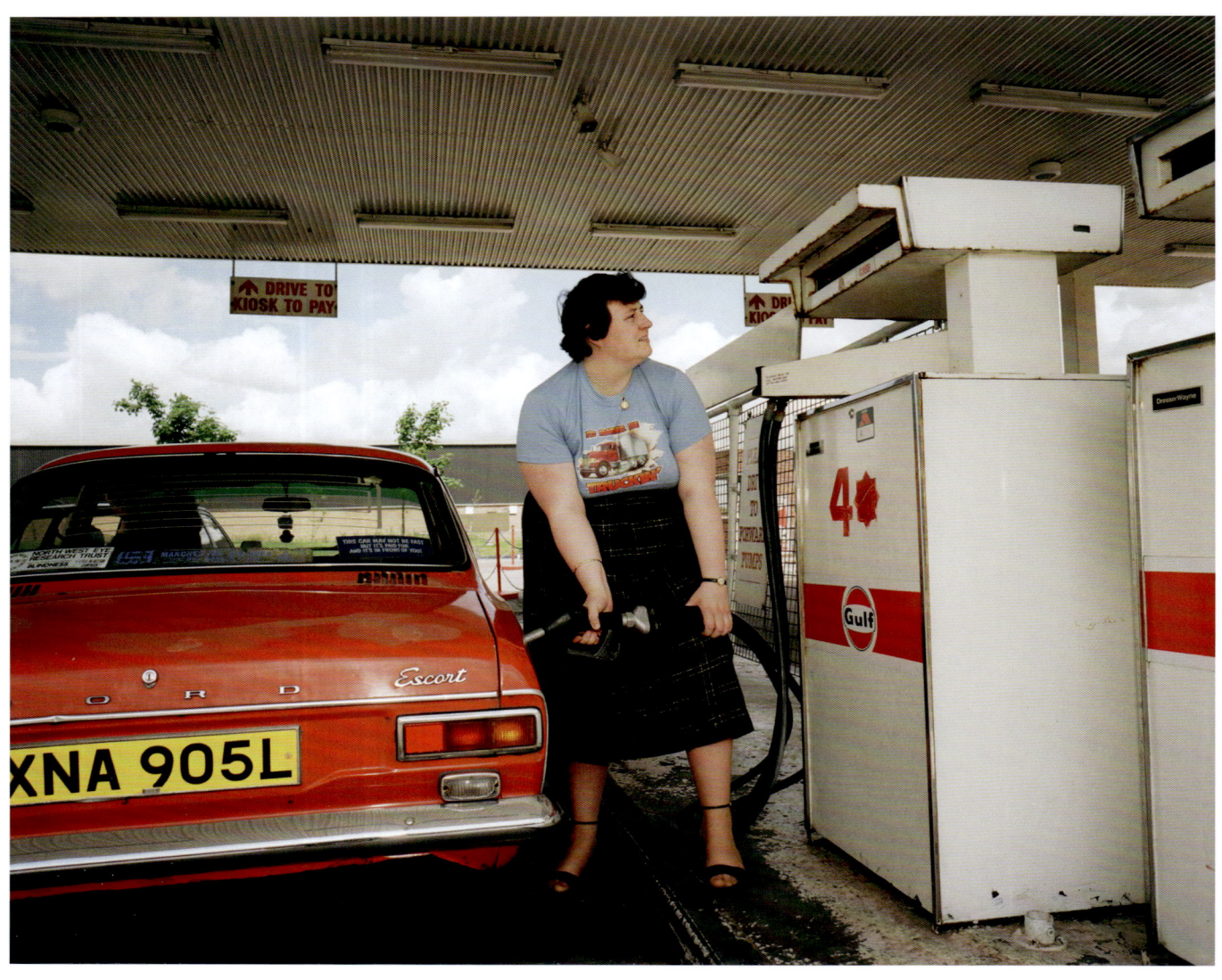

Salford, England, 1986

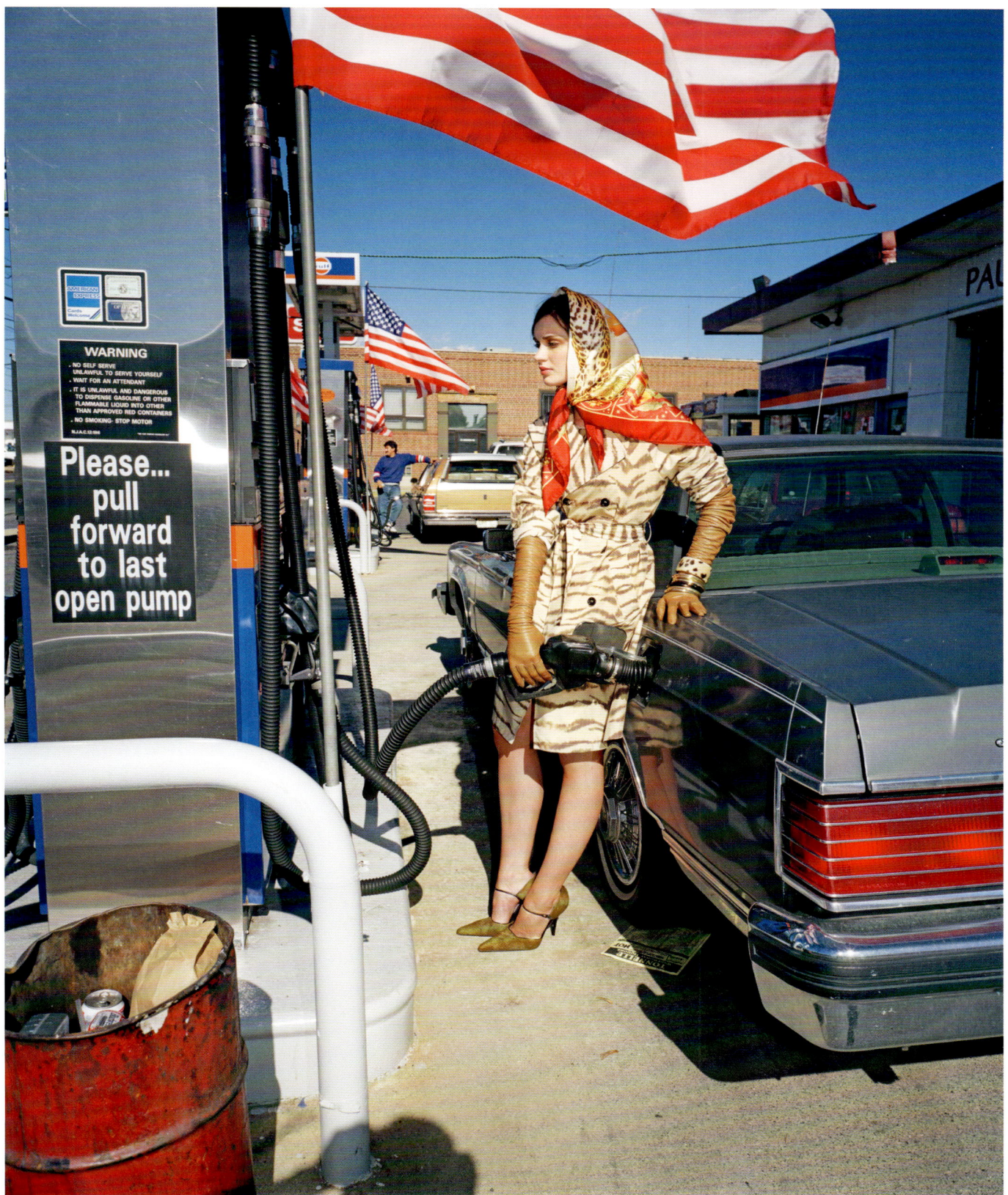

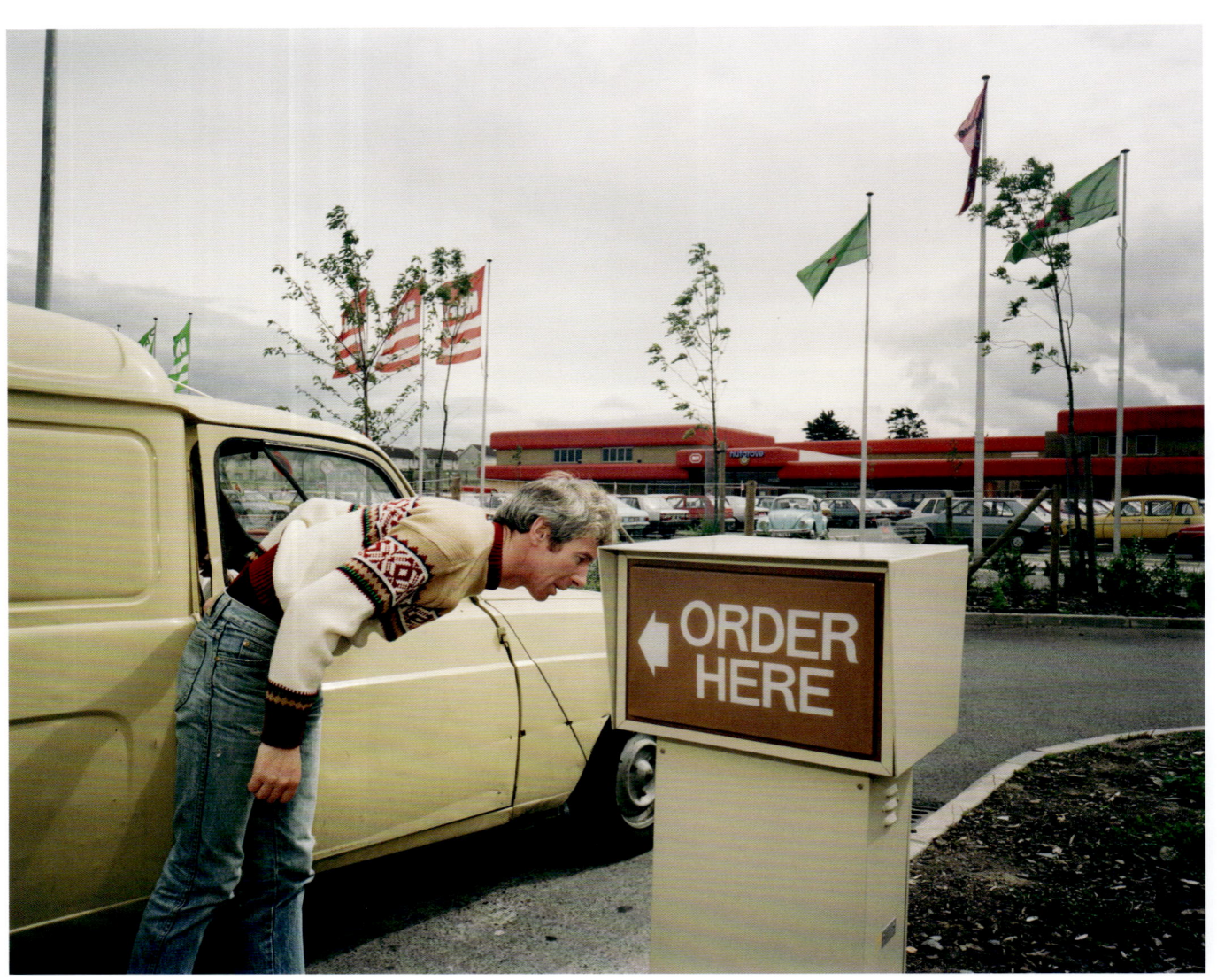

Dublin, Ireland, 1986

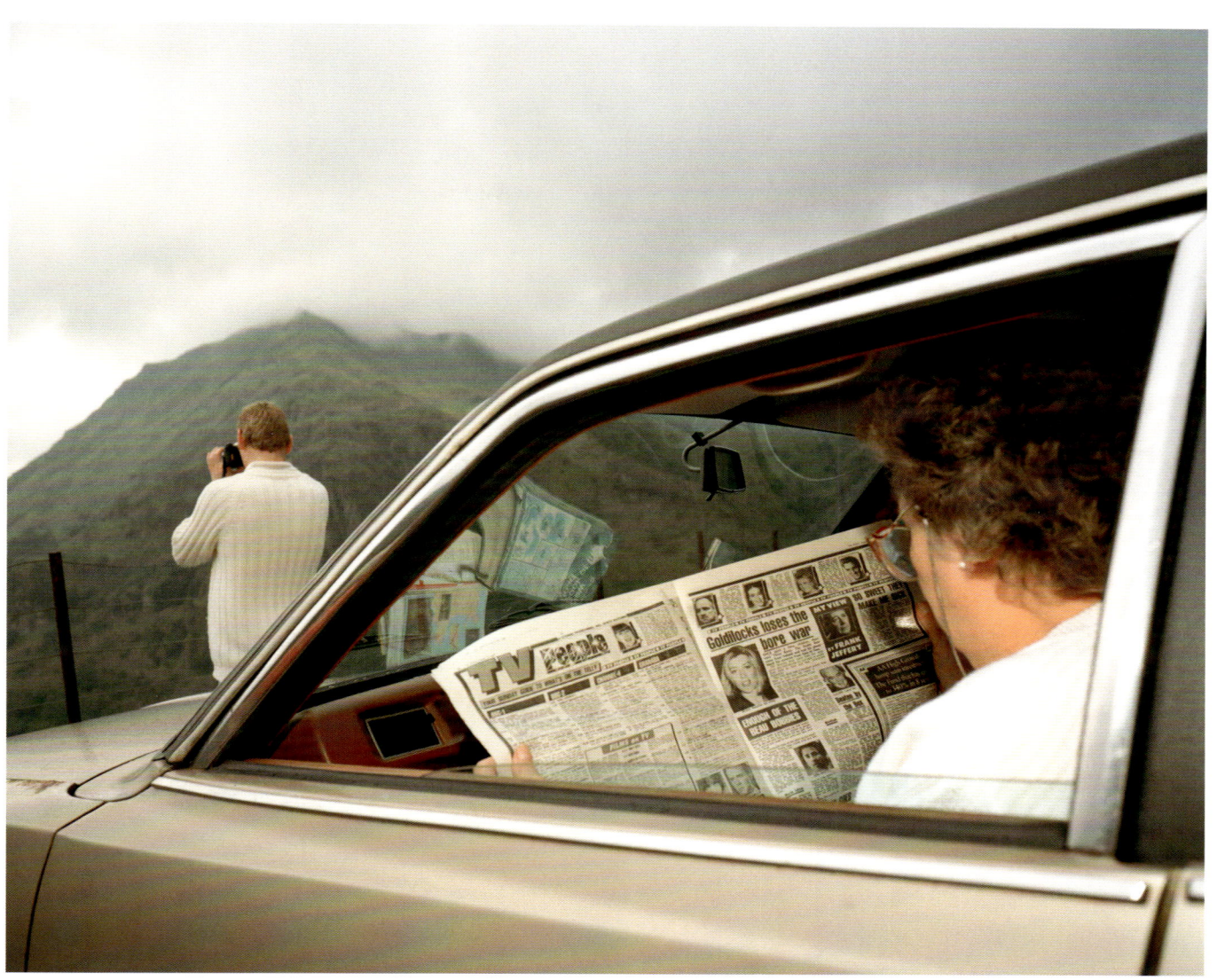

Snowdonia, Wales, 1989

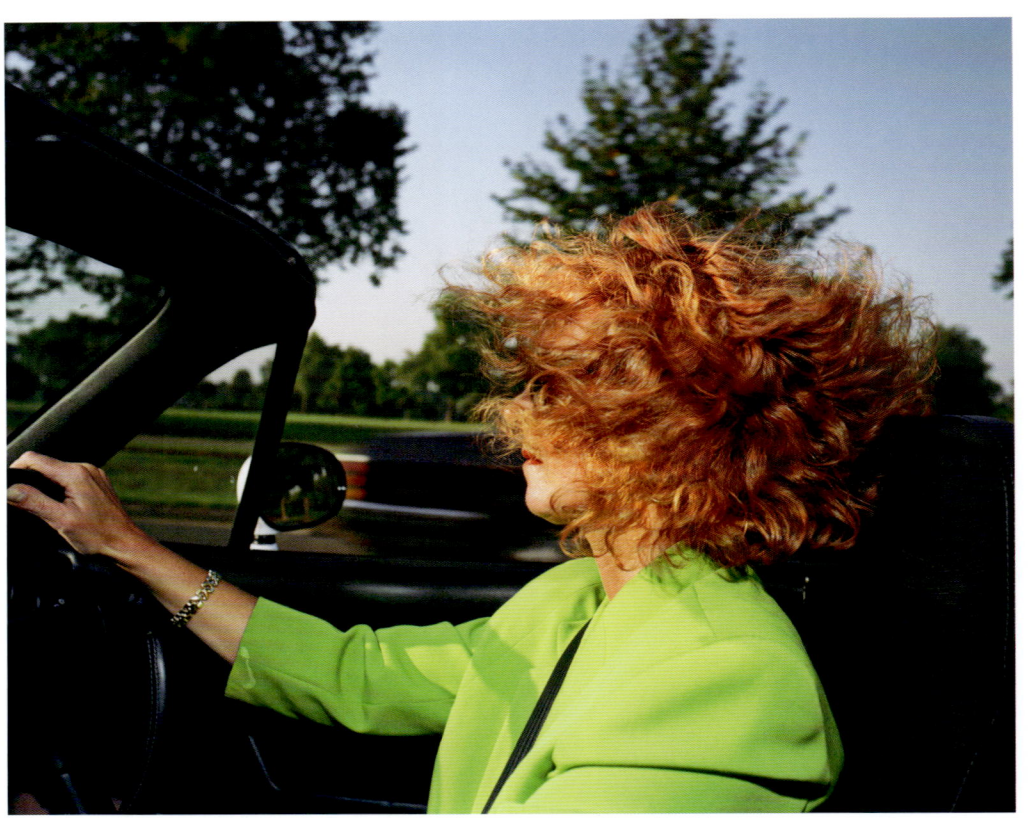

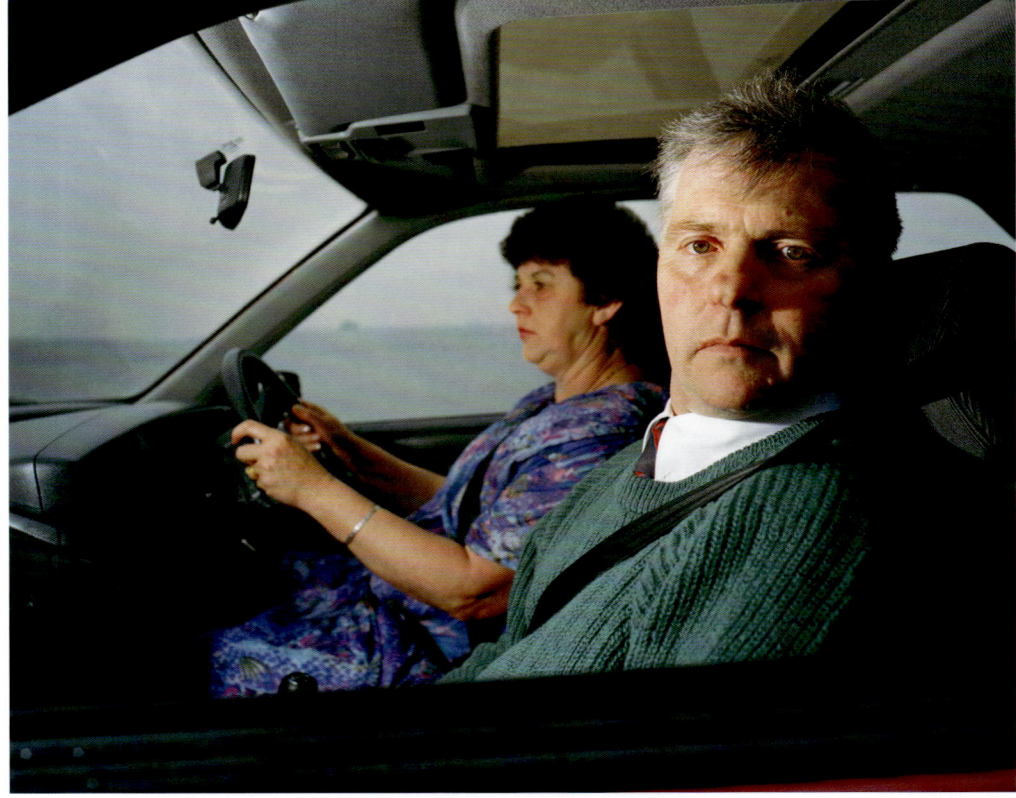

England, 1994

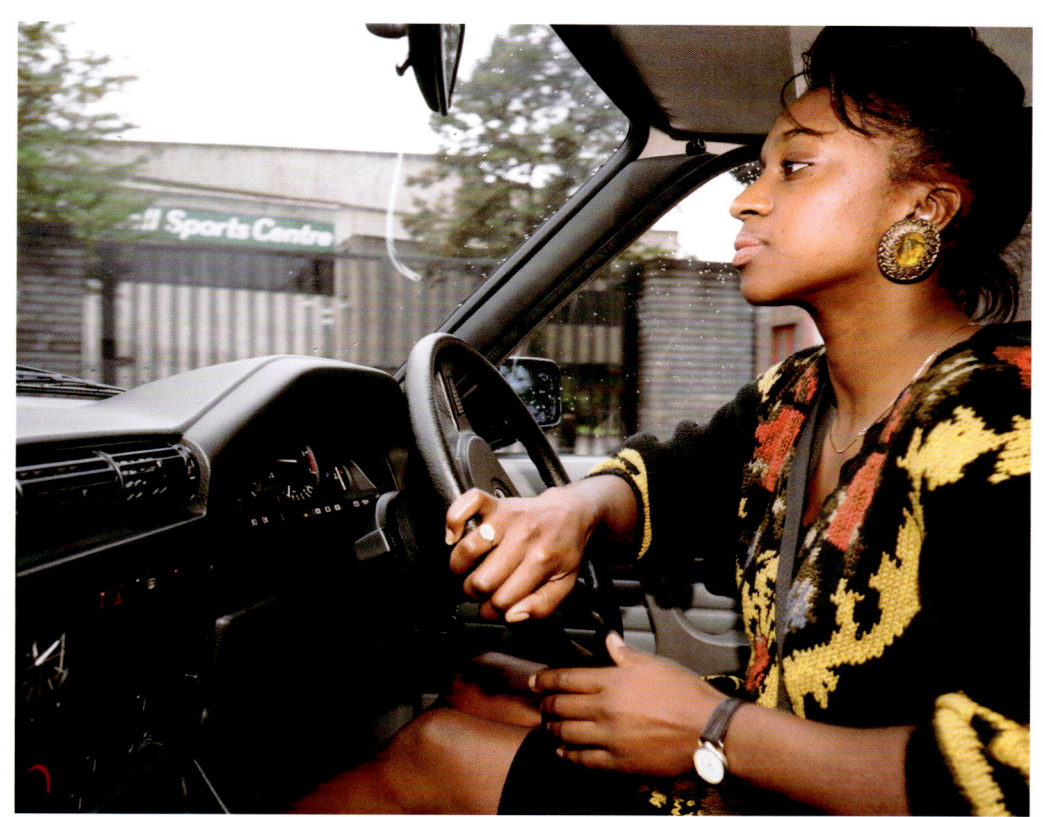

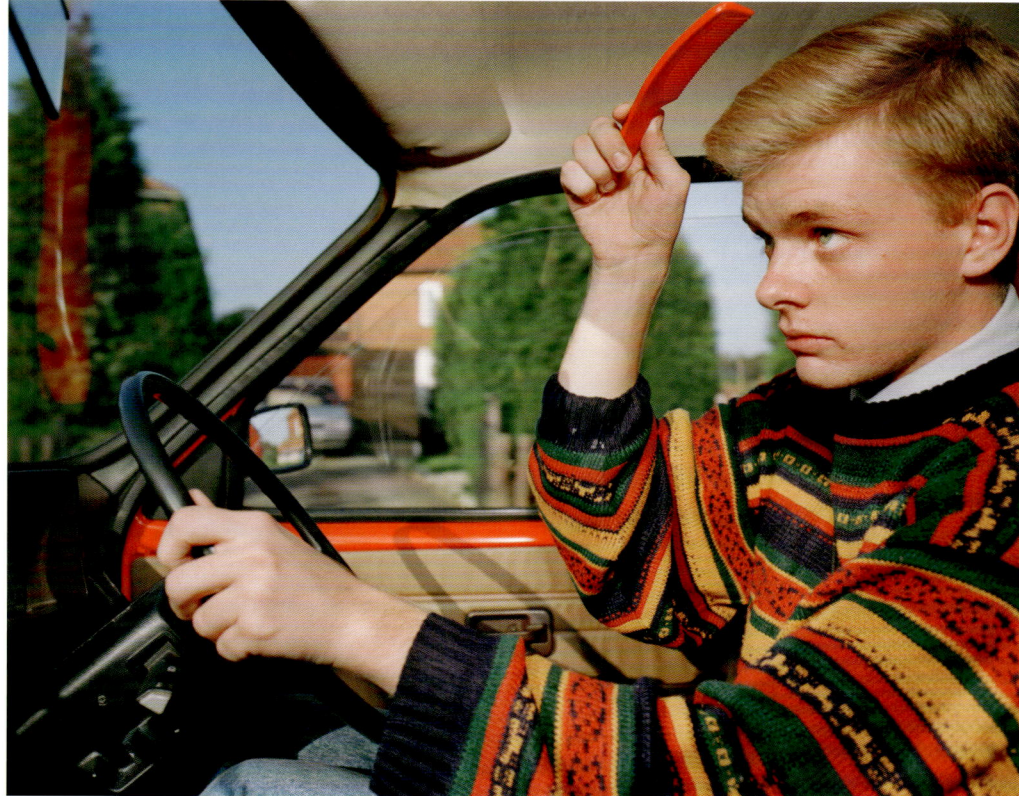

England, 1994

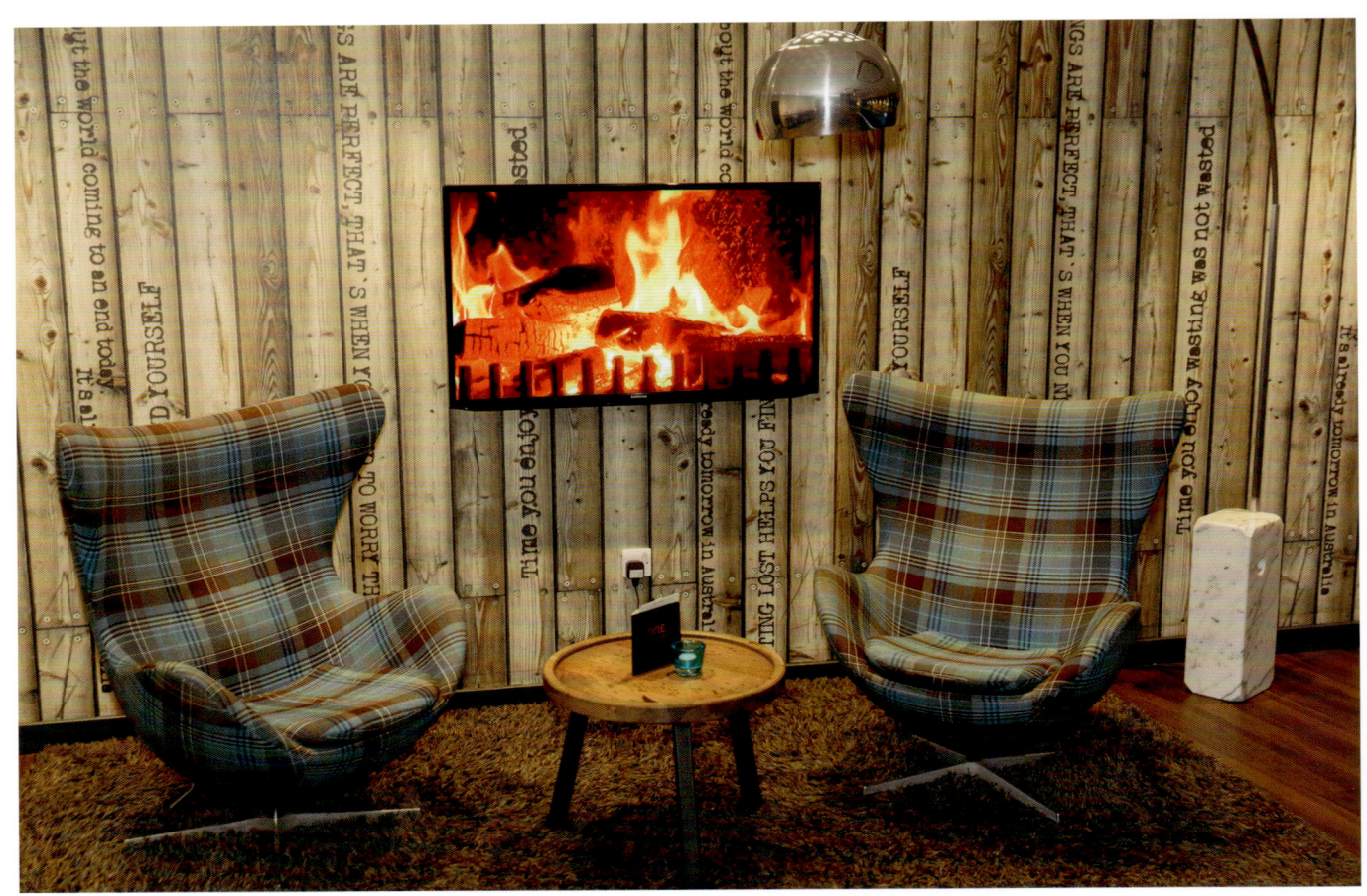

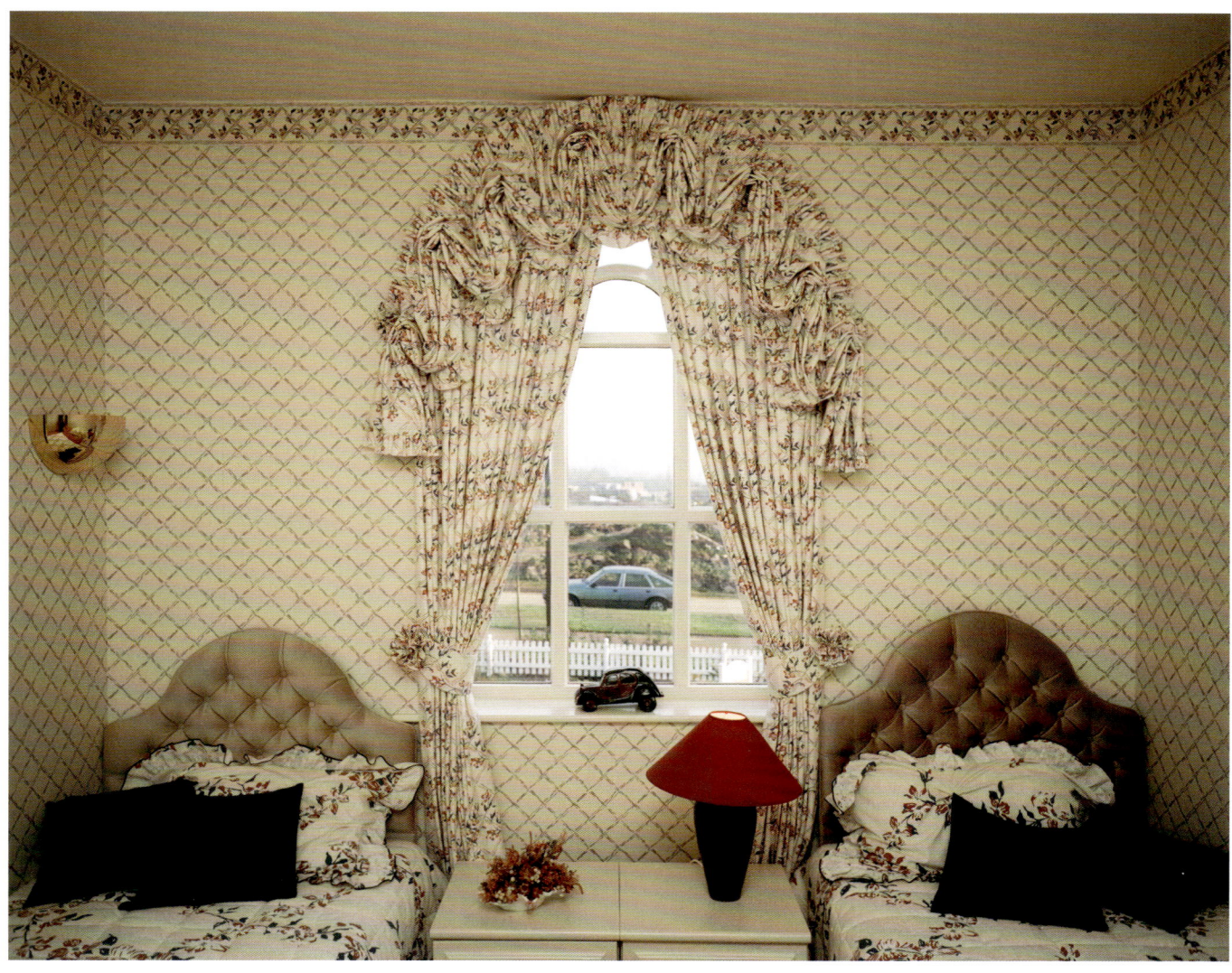

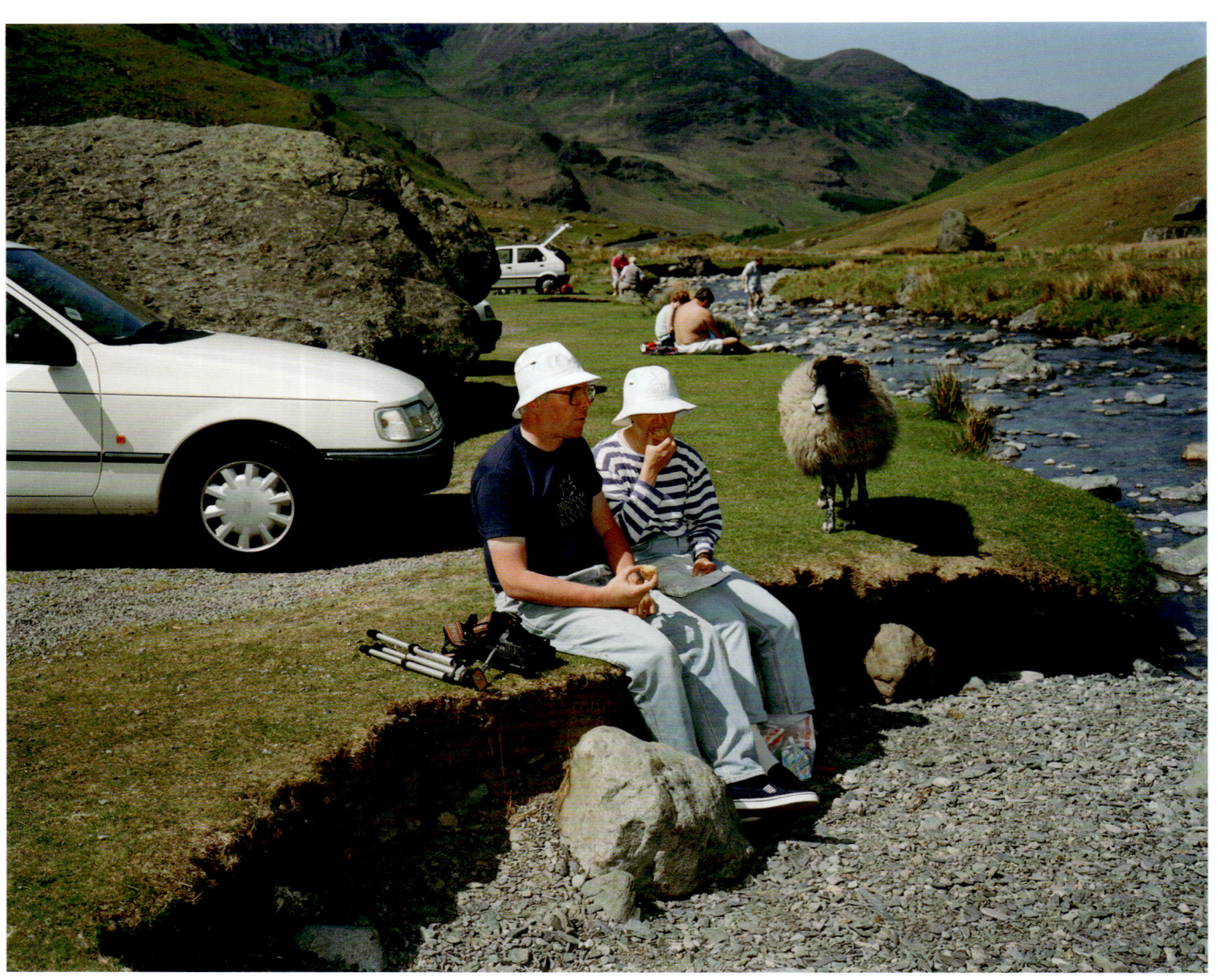

Honister Pass, England, 1994

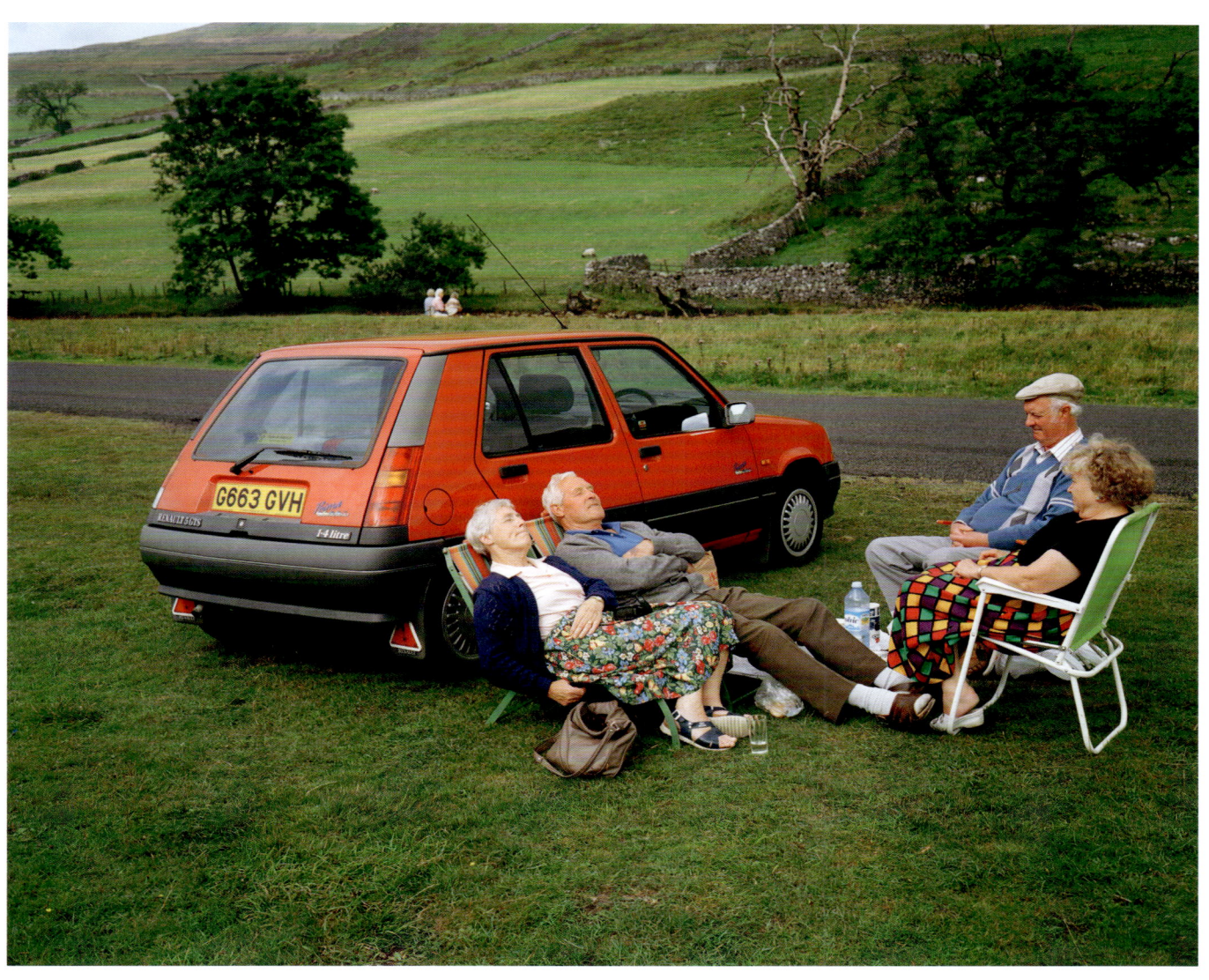

Yorkshire Dales, England, 1994

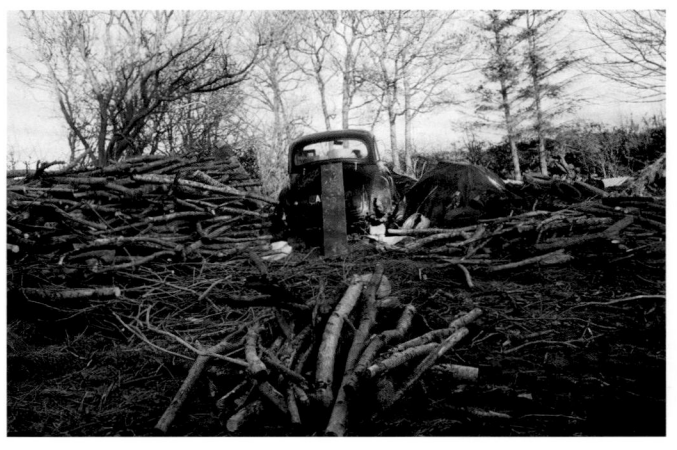
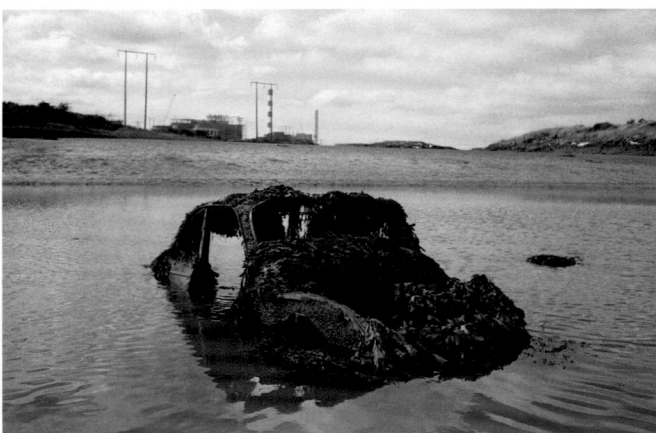
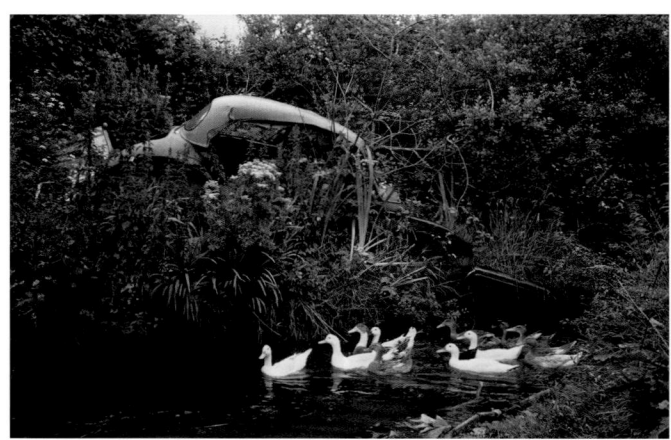
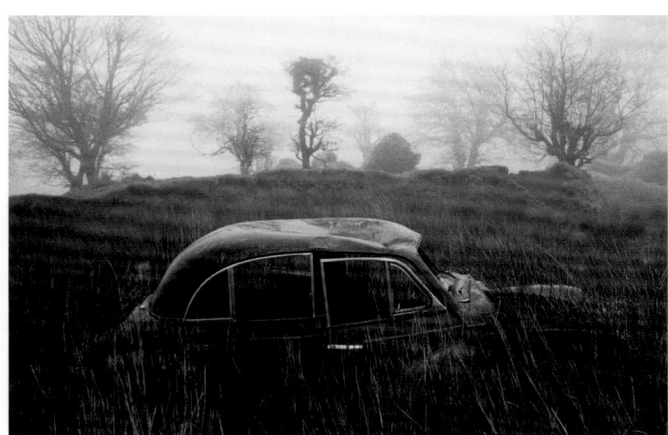

Ireland, 1980–83

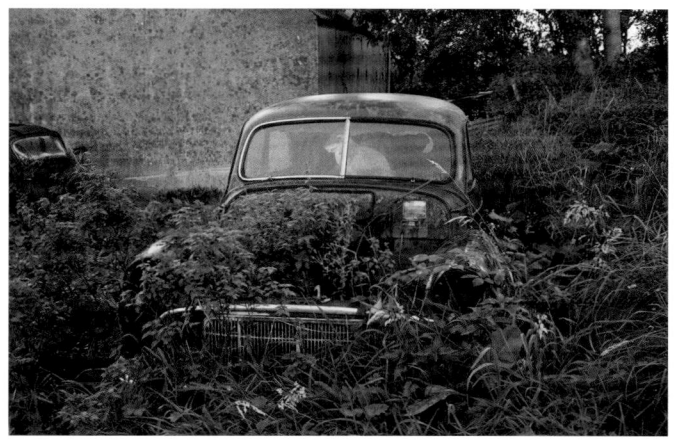
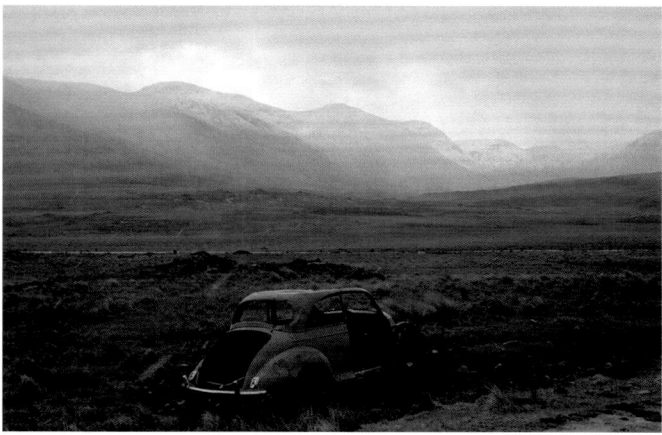
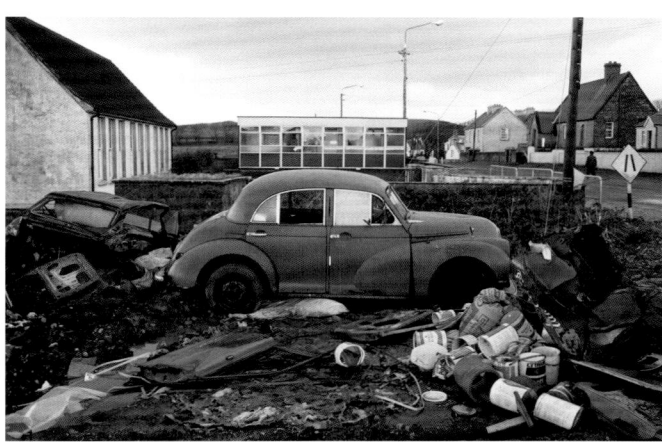
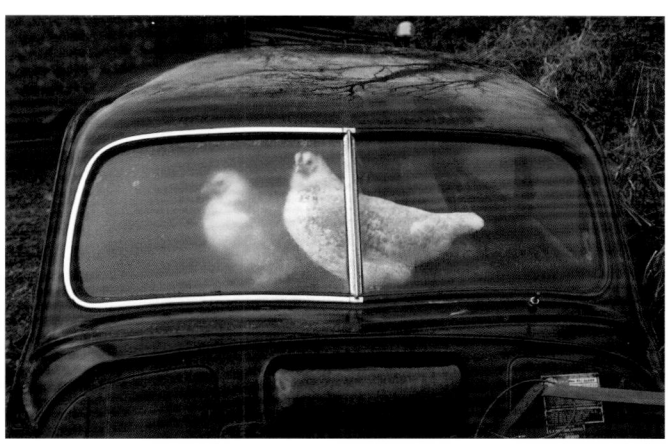

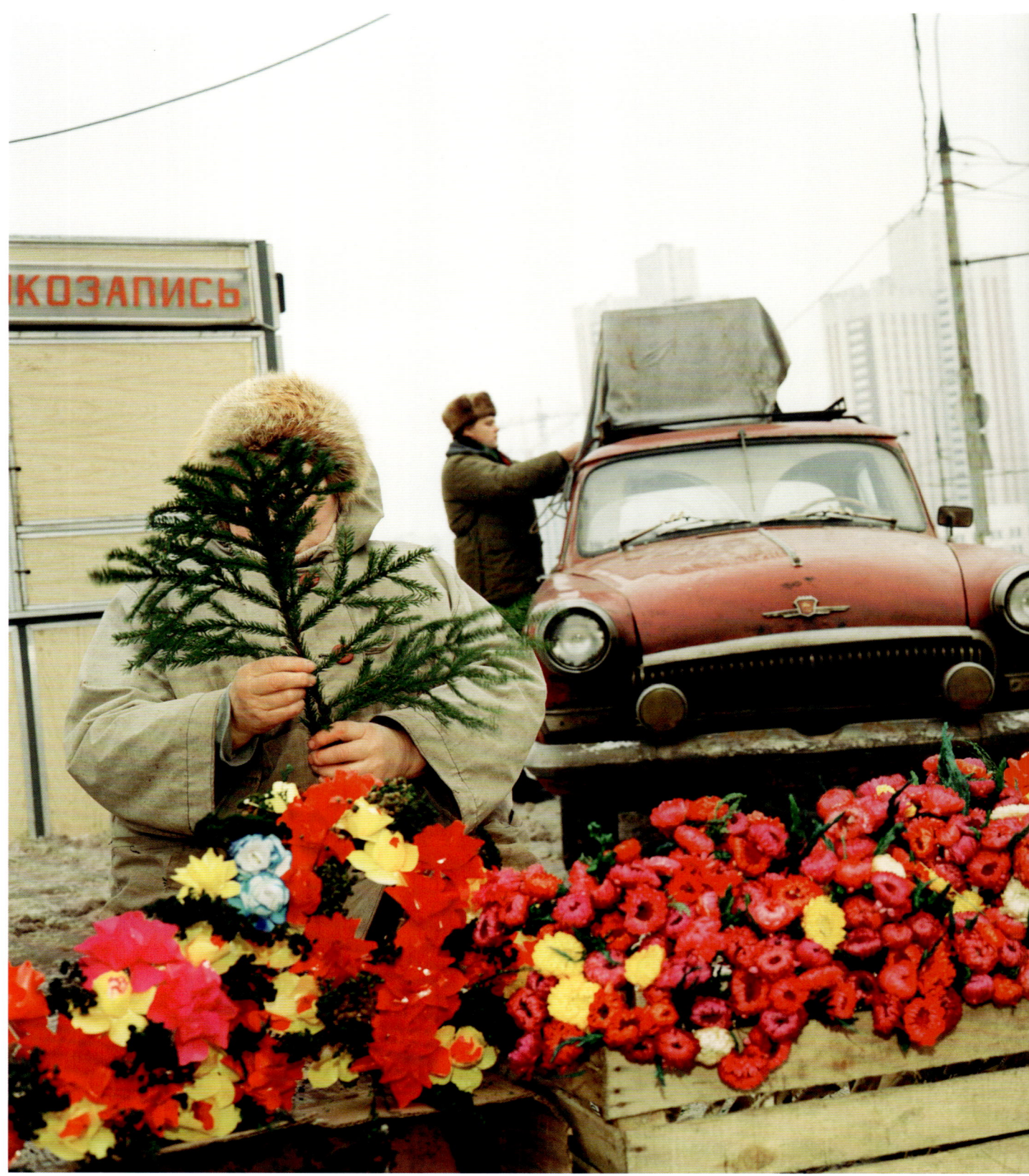

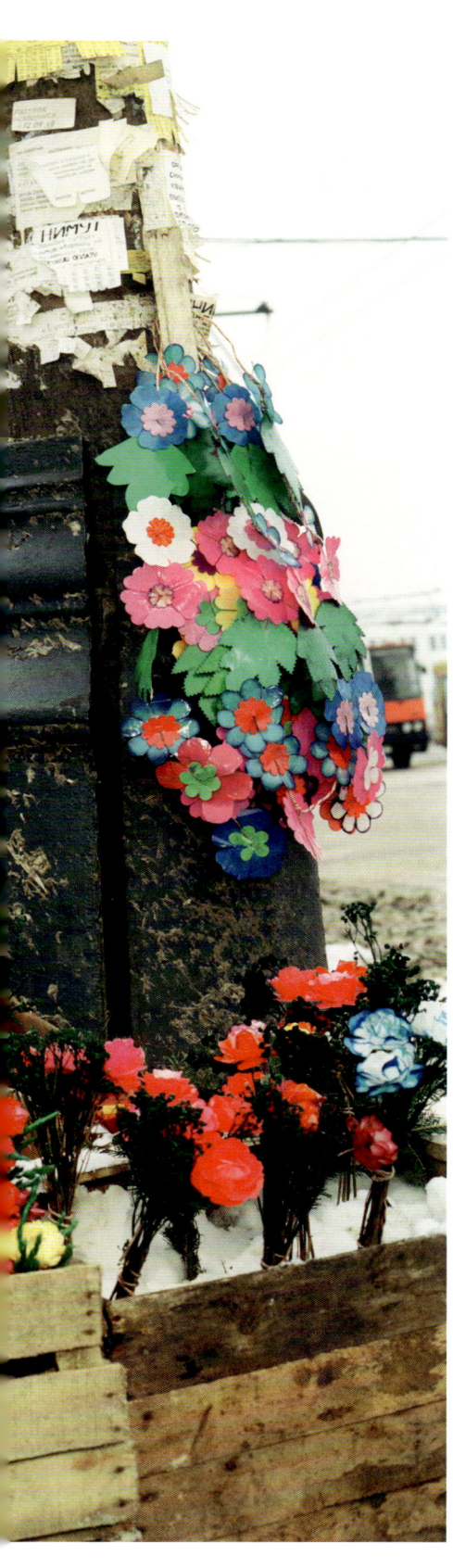

Moscow, Russia, 1992

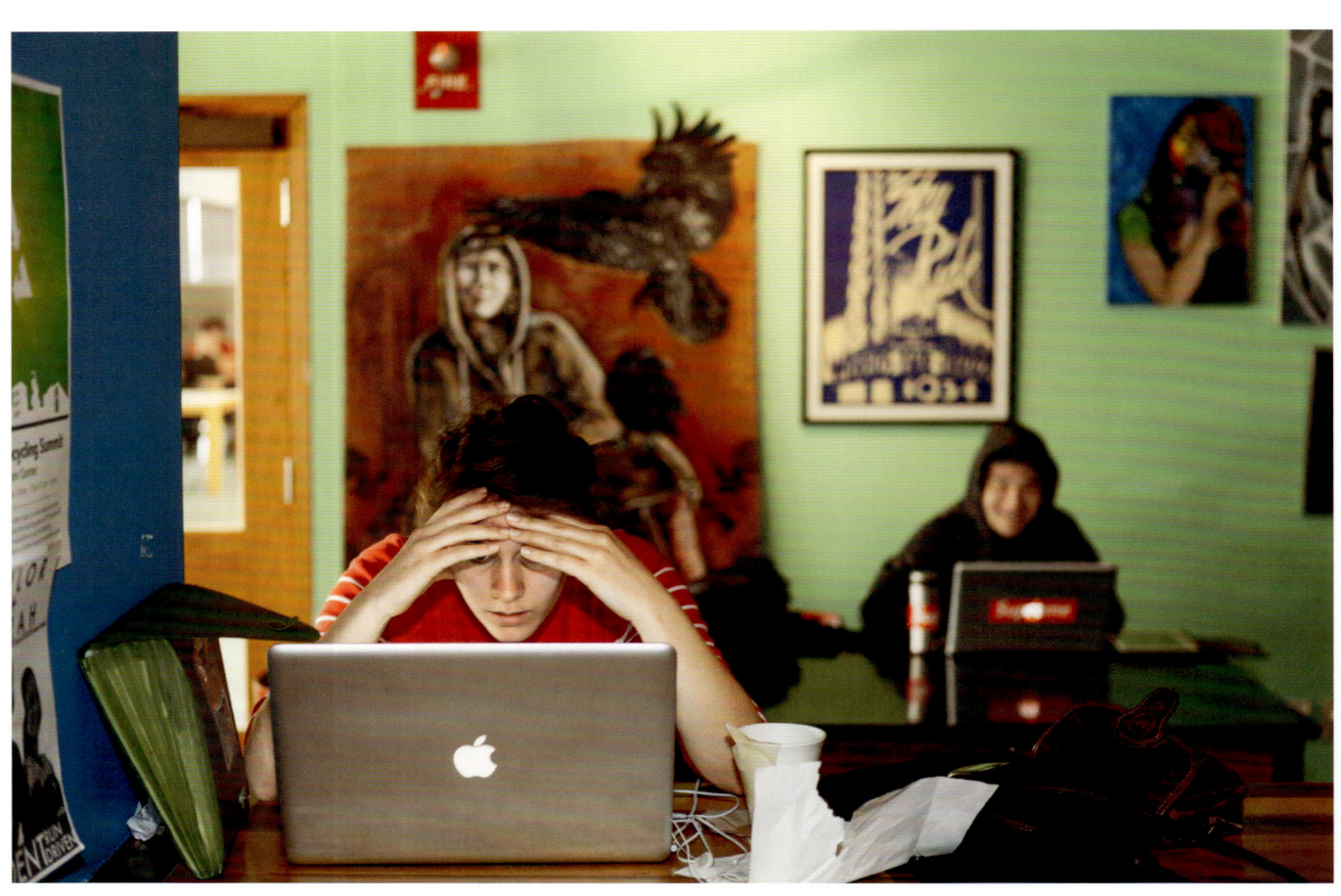

Rochester, New York, USA, 2012

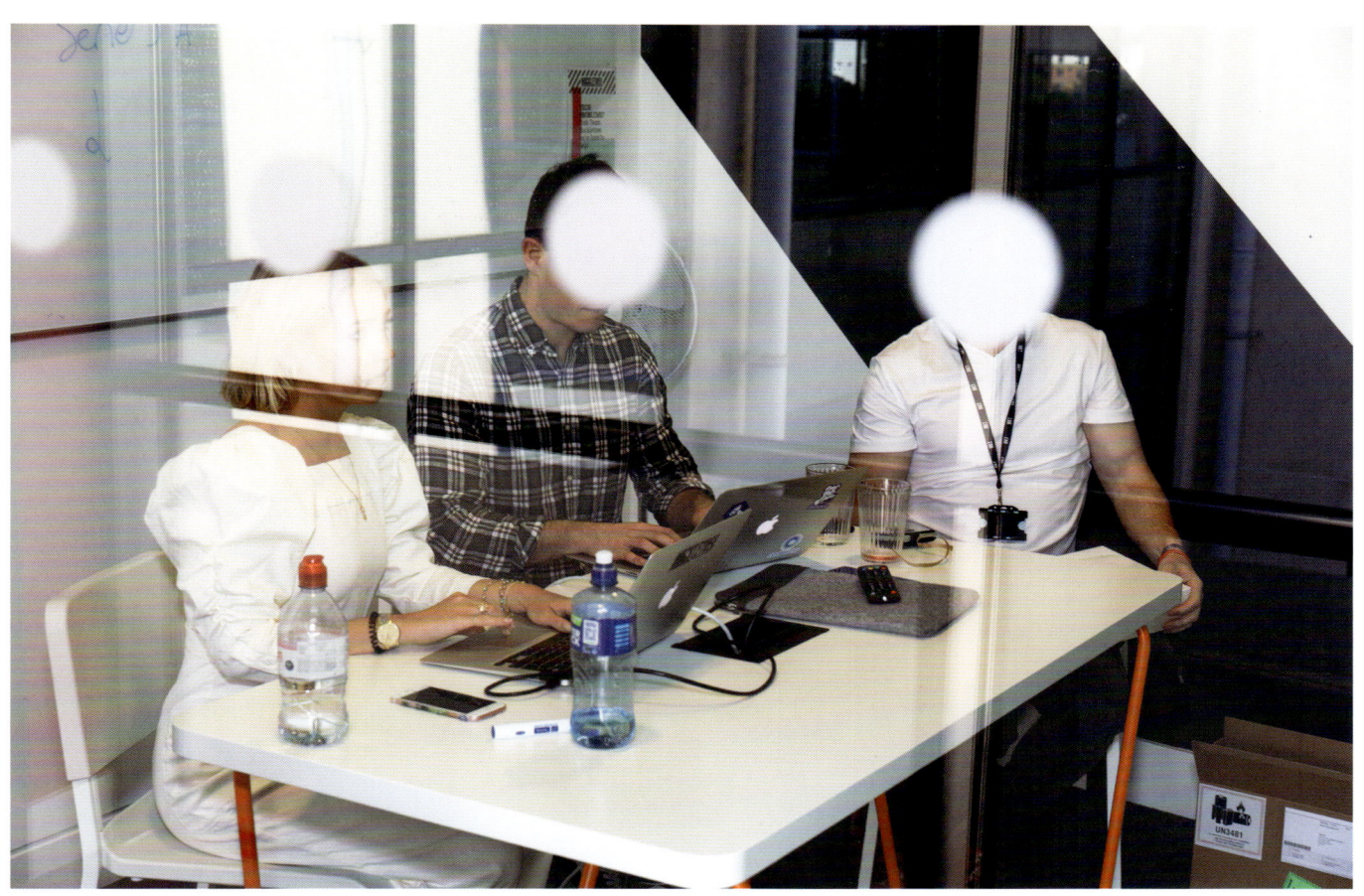

Dublin, Ireland, 2019

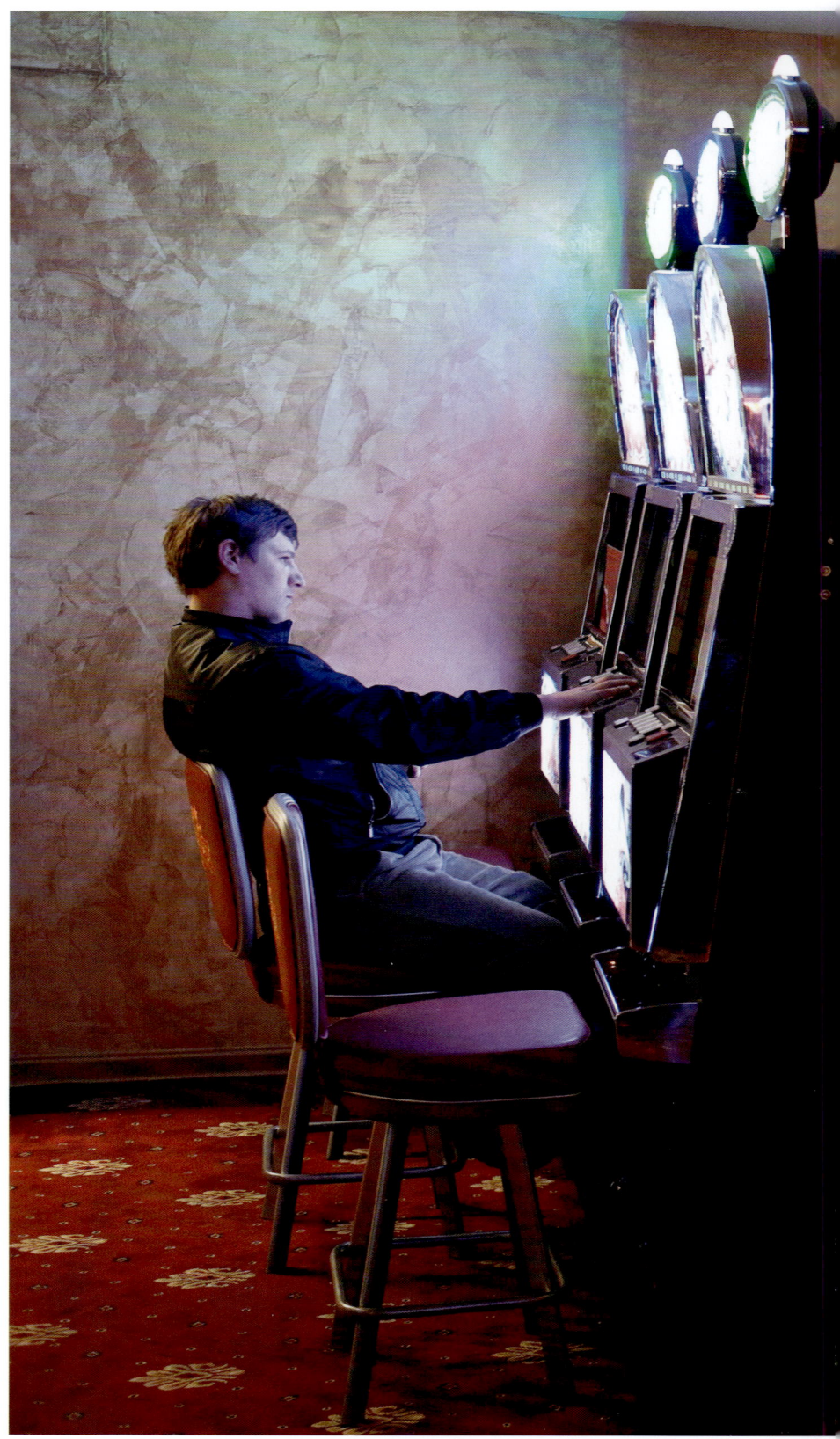

Tbilisi, Georgia, 2009

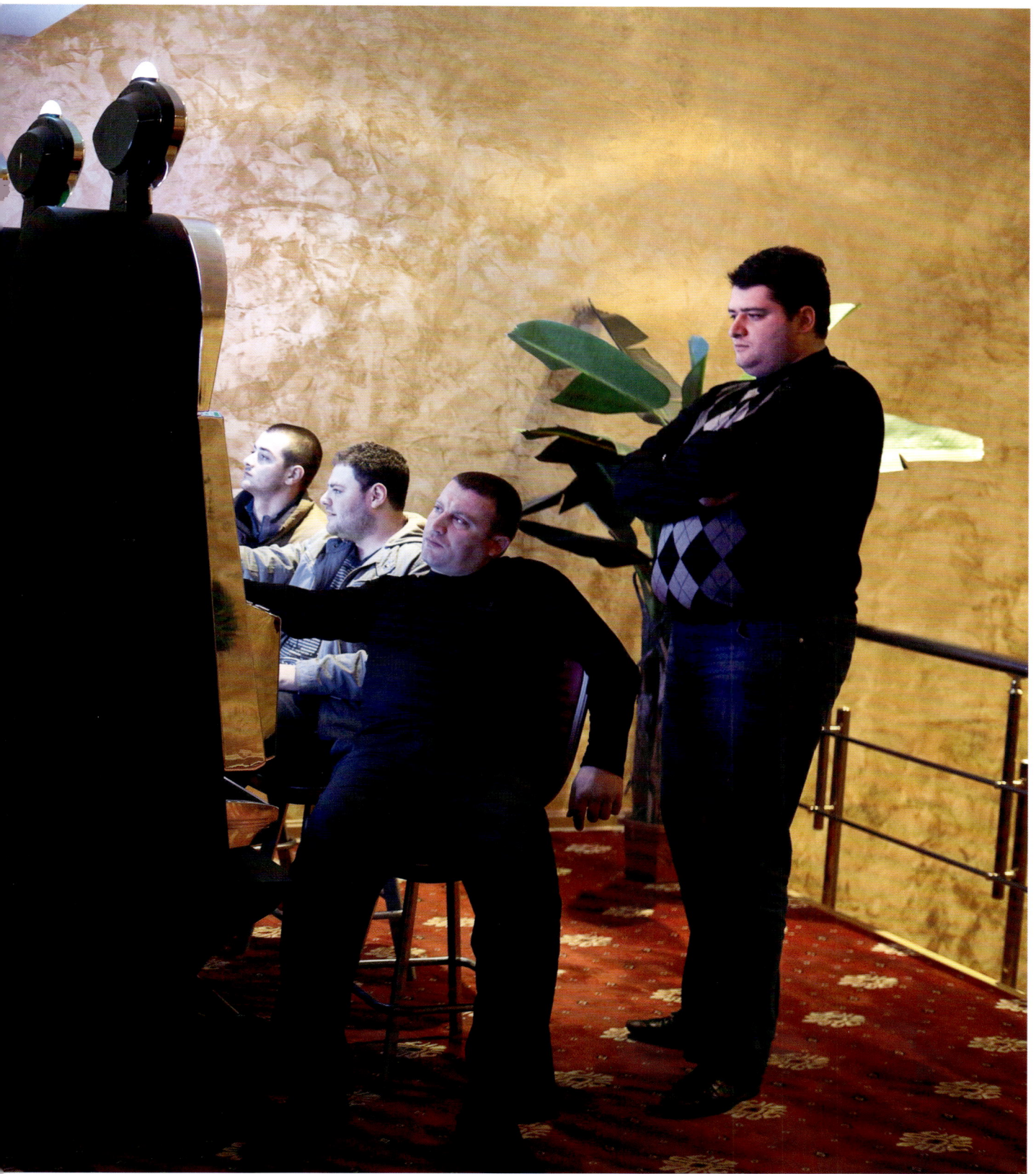

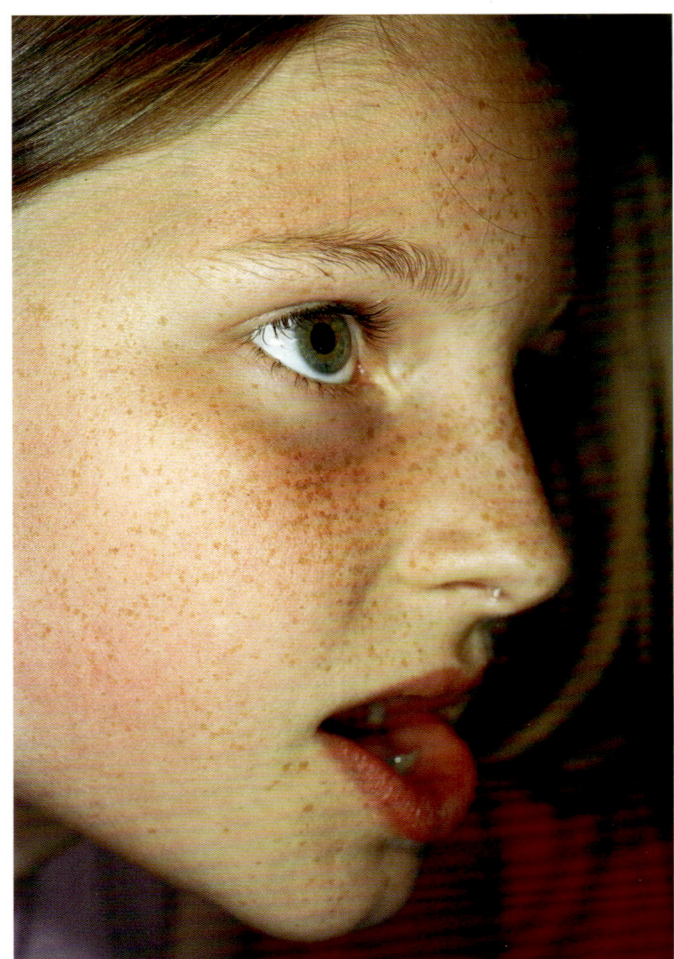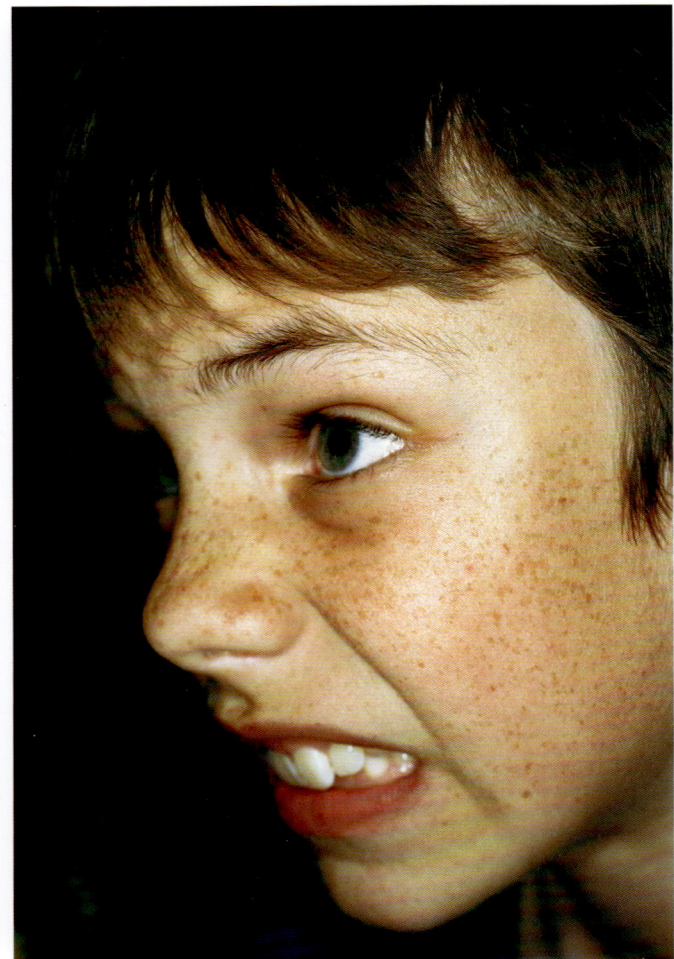

Sony Playstation advertisement, England, 2003

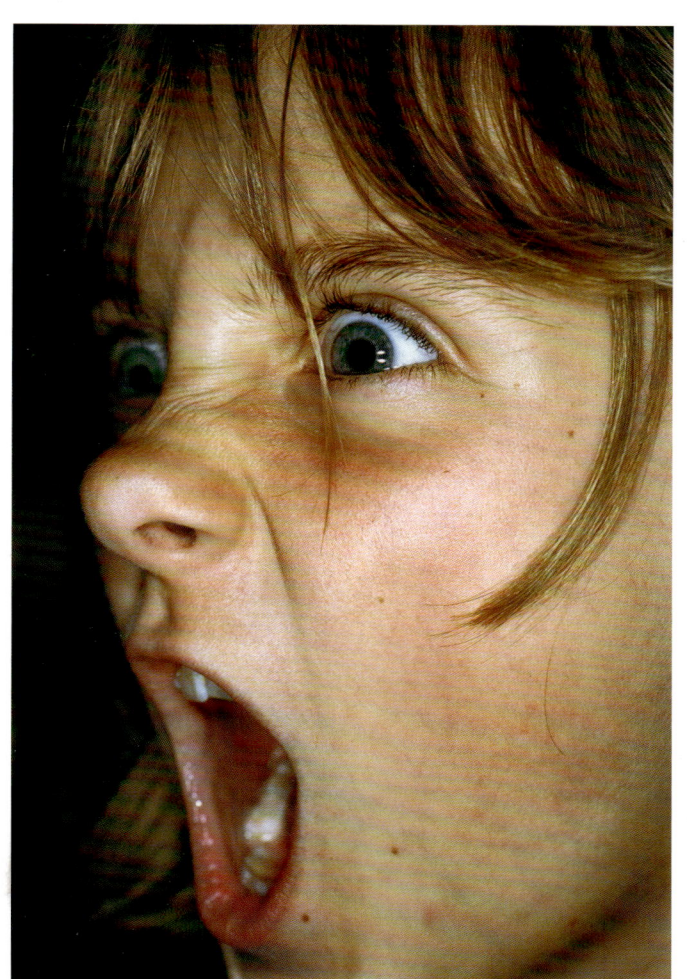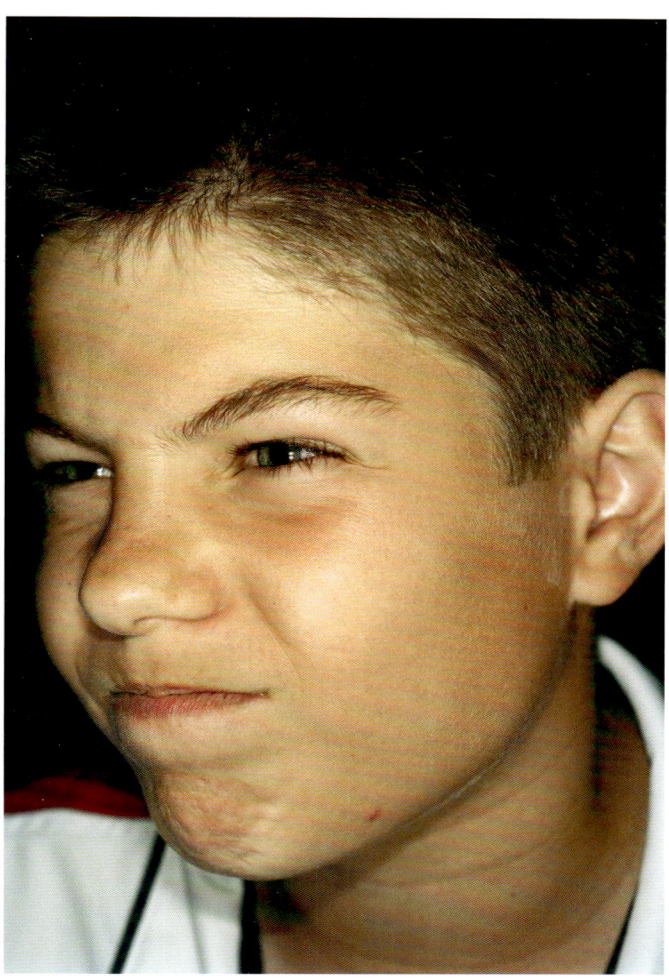

Overleaf:
Tokyo, Japan, 2000

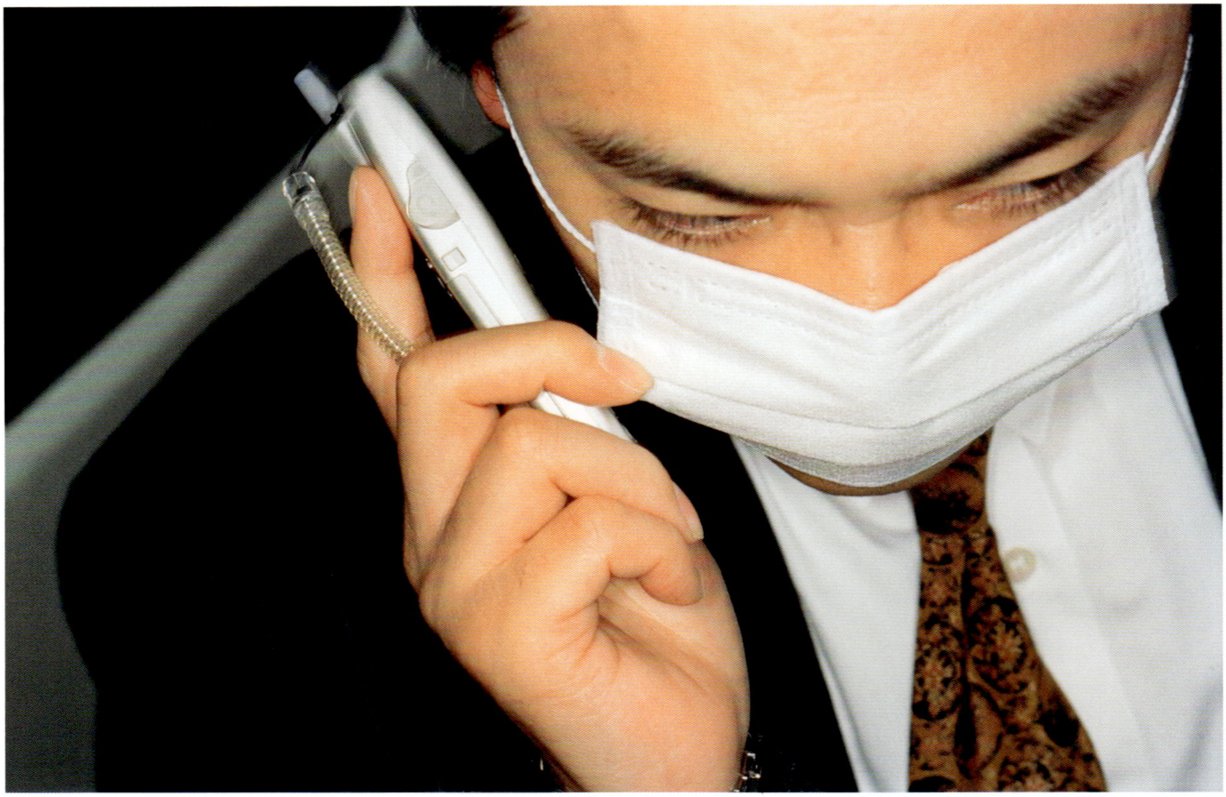

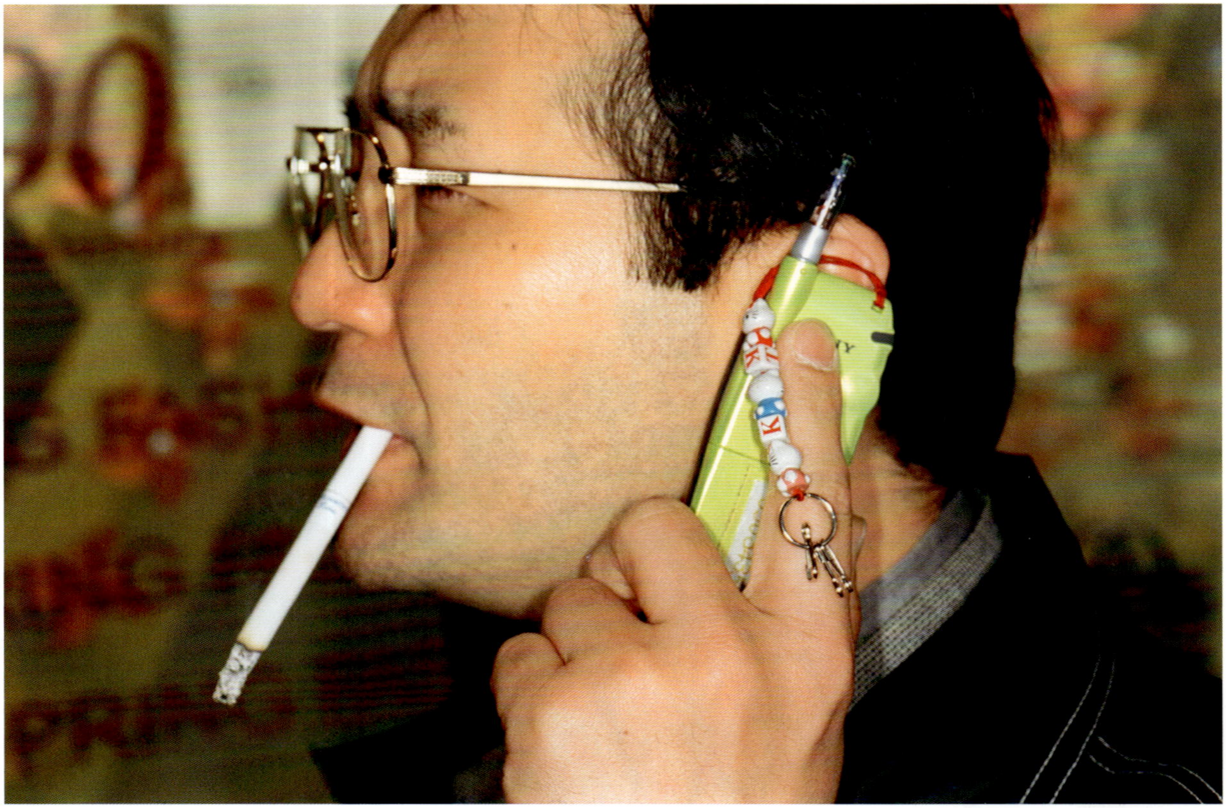

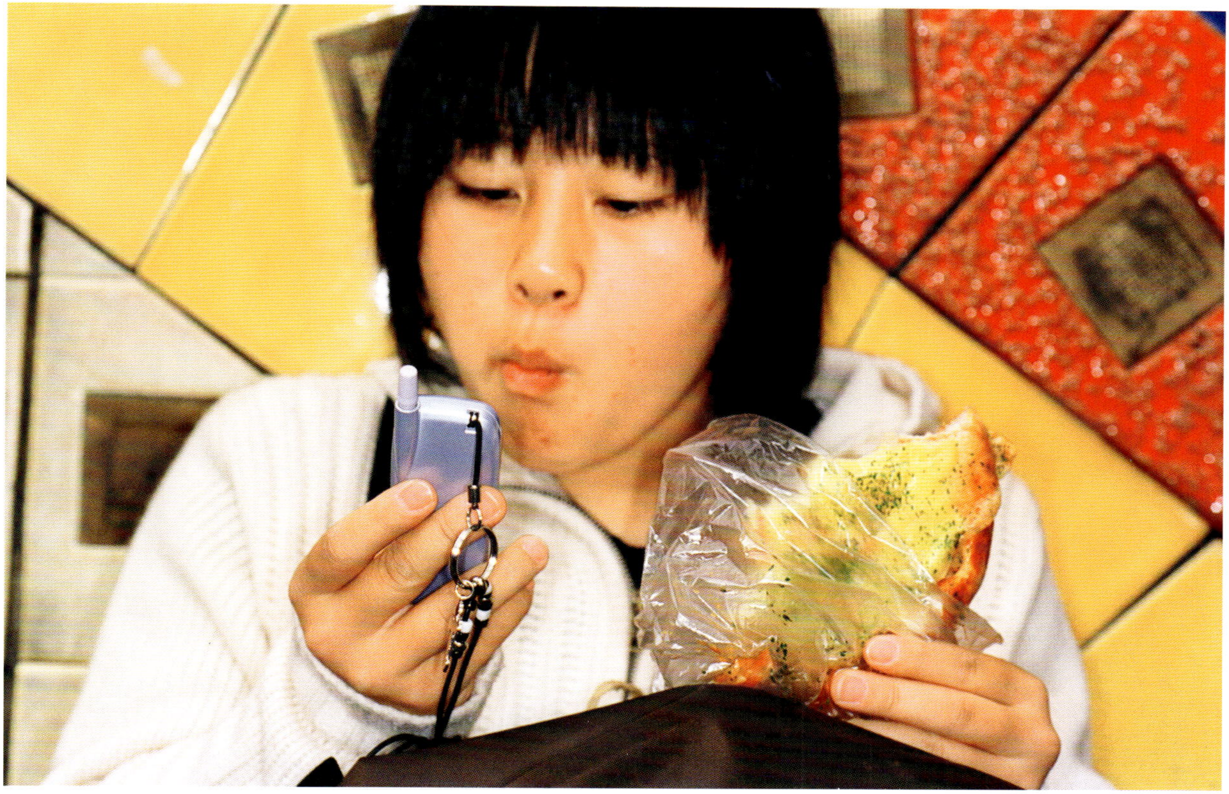

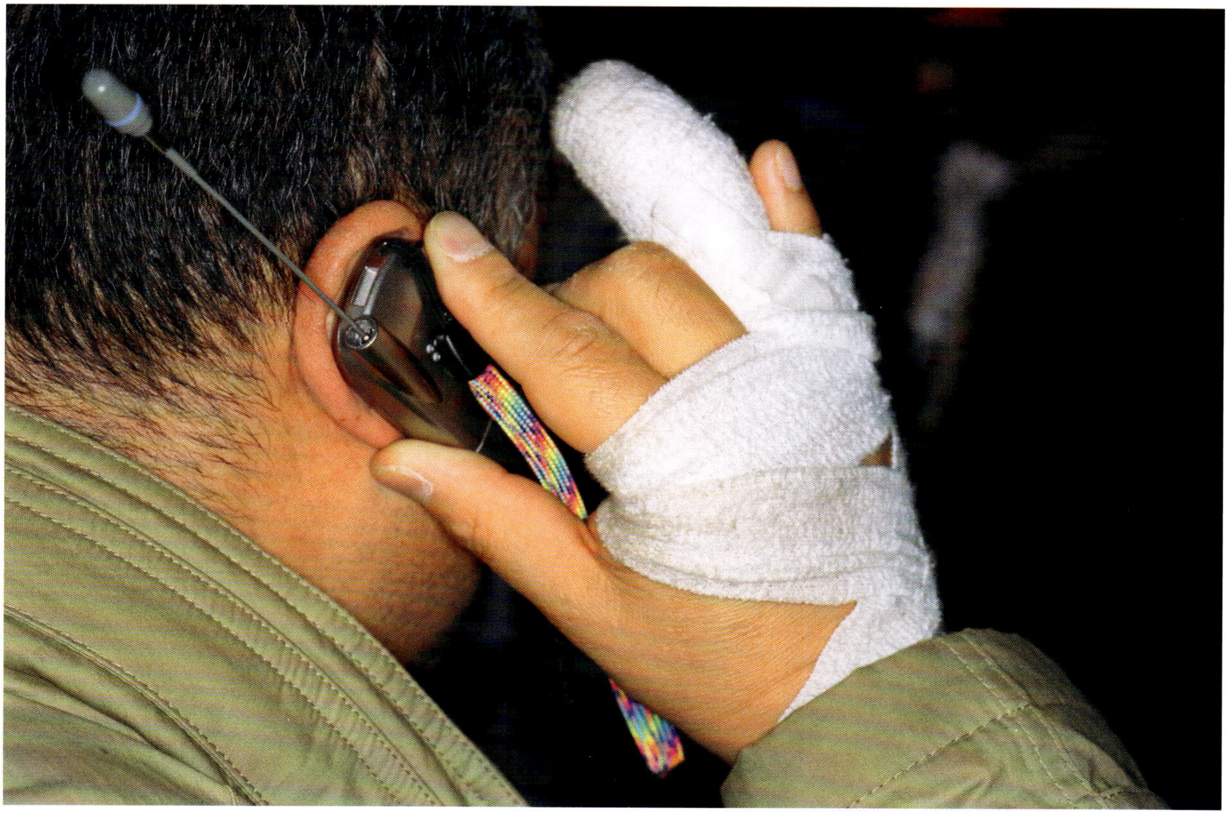

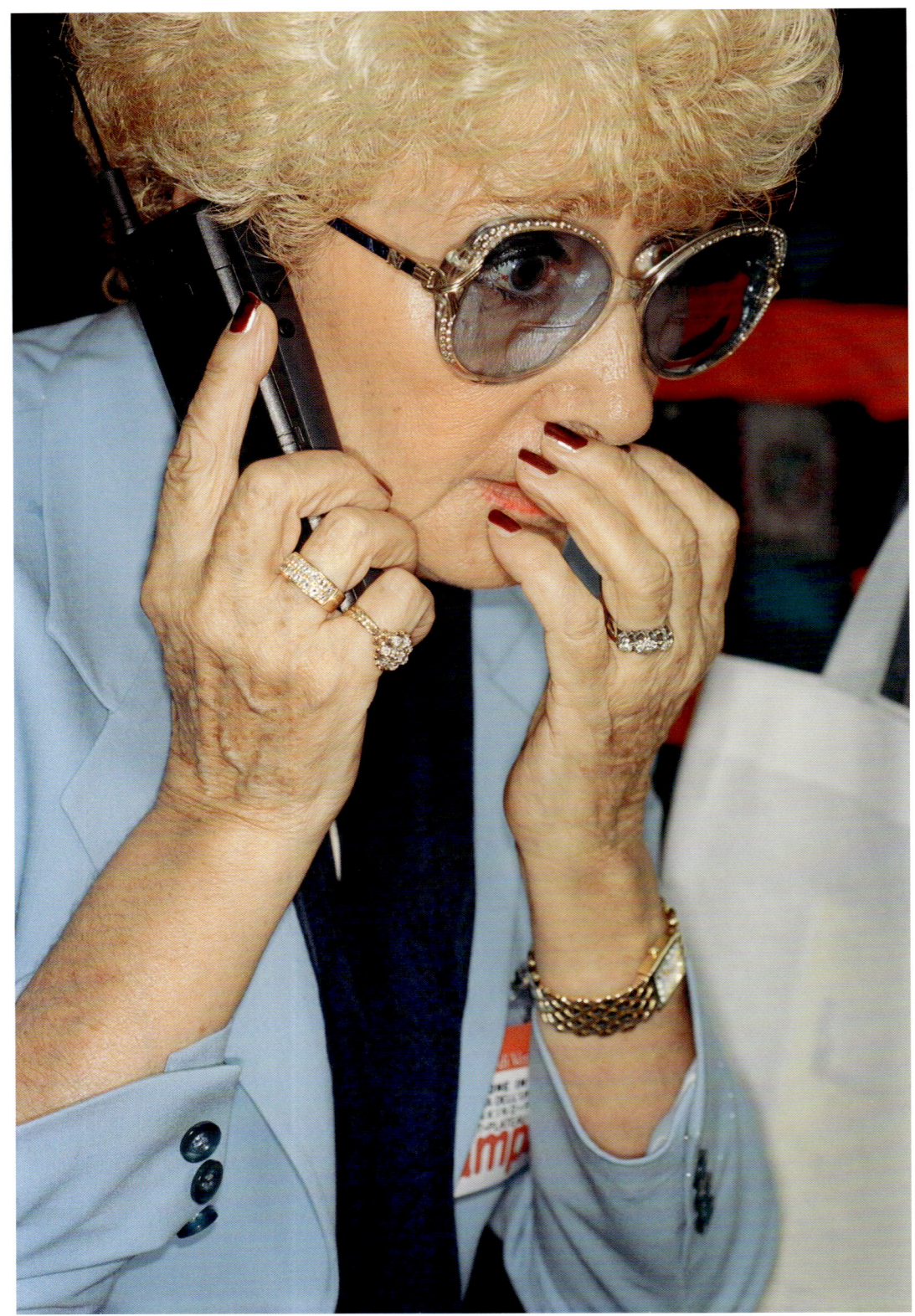

Venice, Italy, 2001

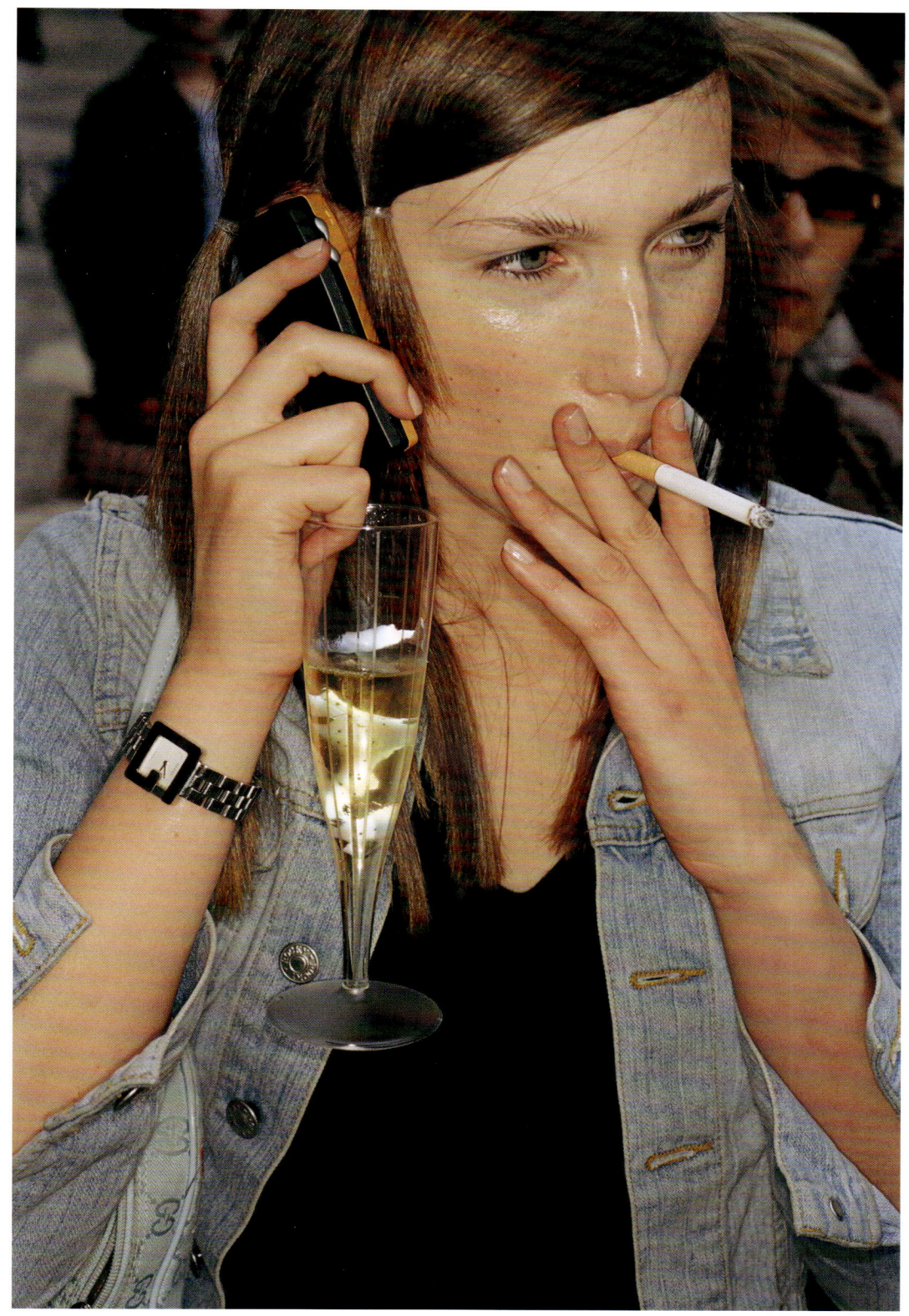

Paris, France, 2001

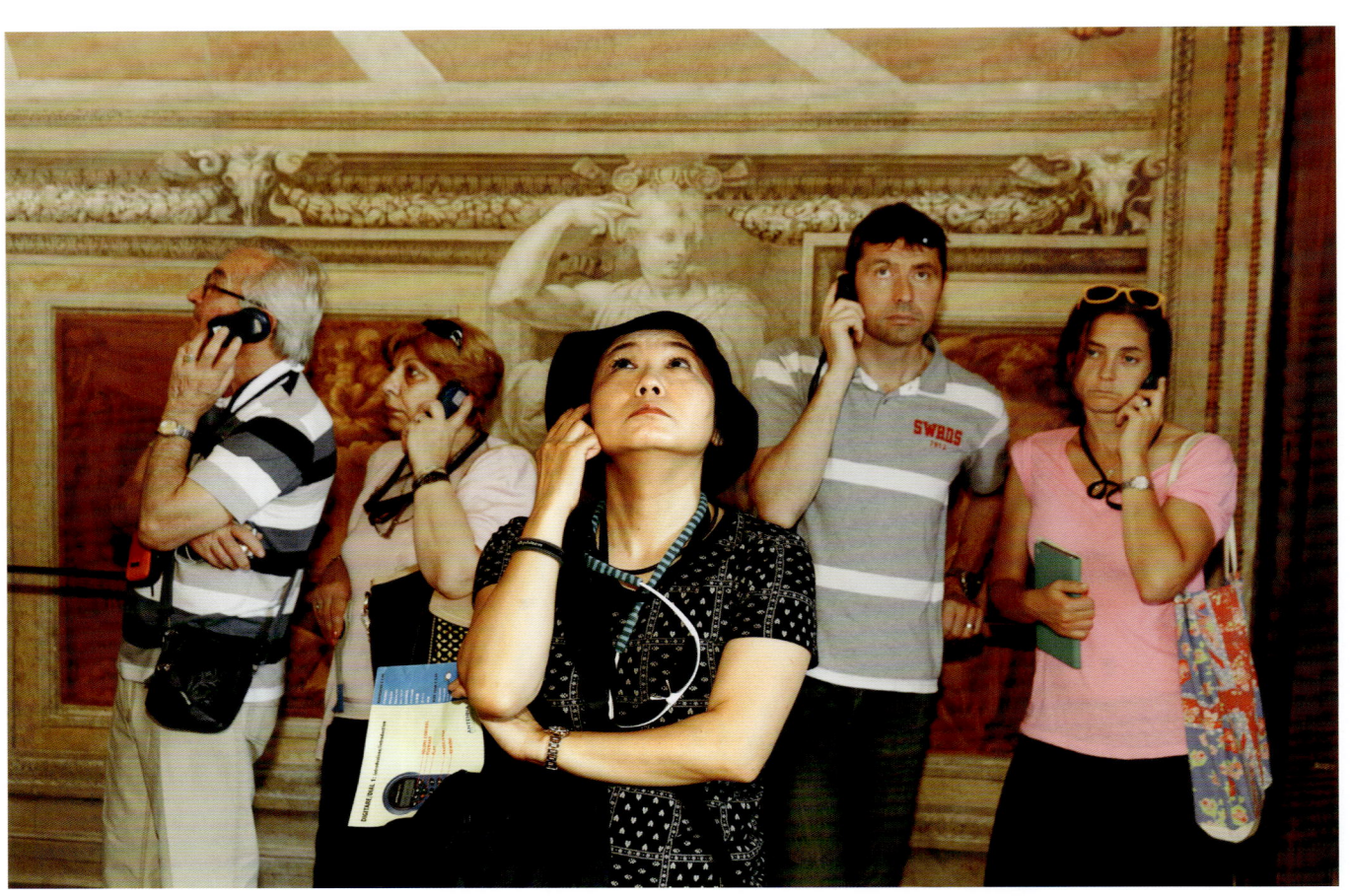

Vatican Museum, Vatican City, 2014

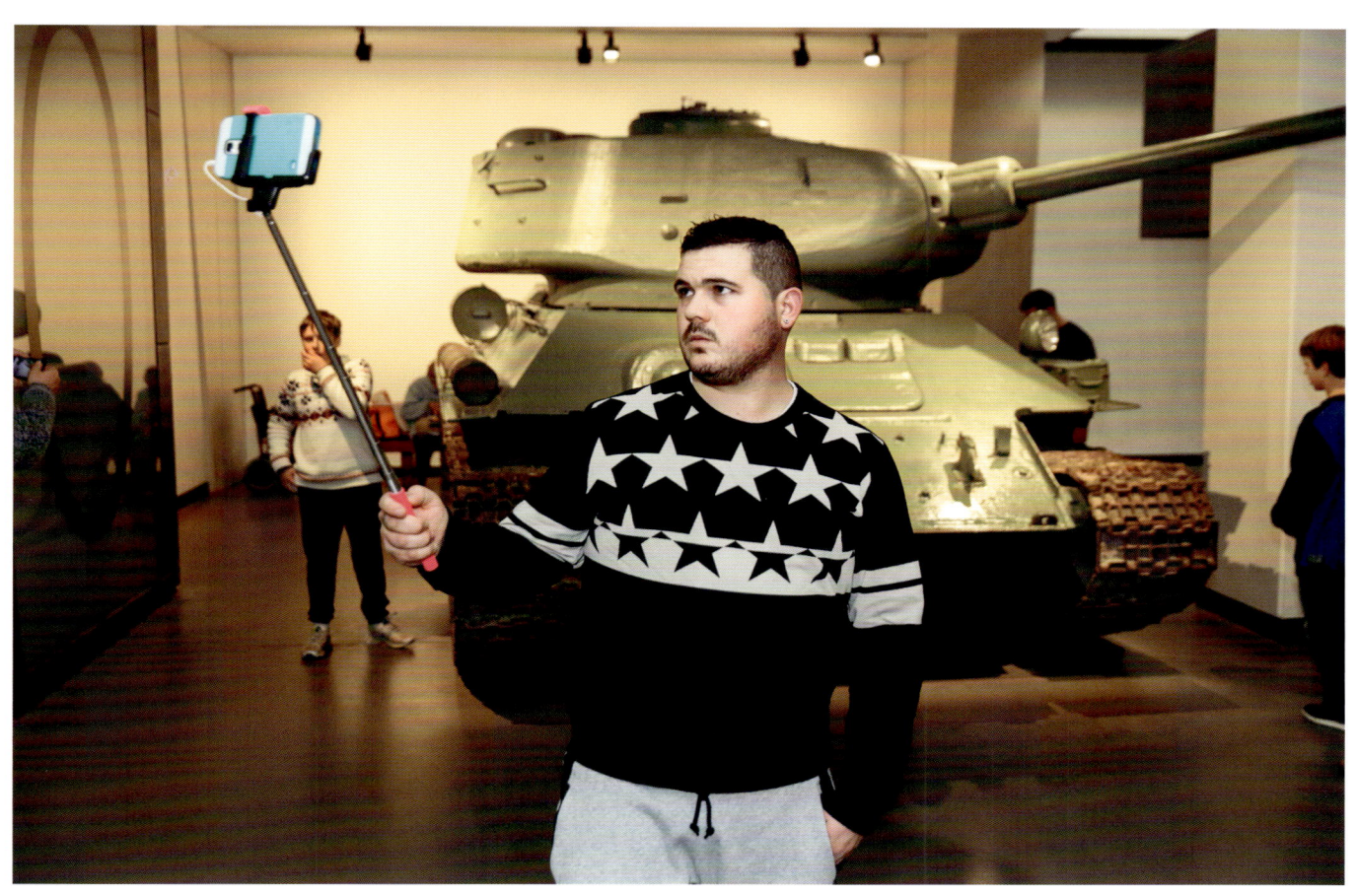

Imperial War Museum, London, England, 2015

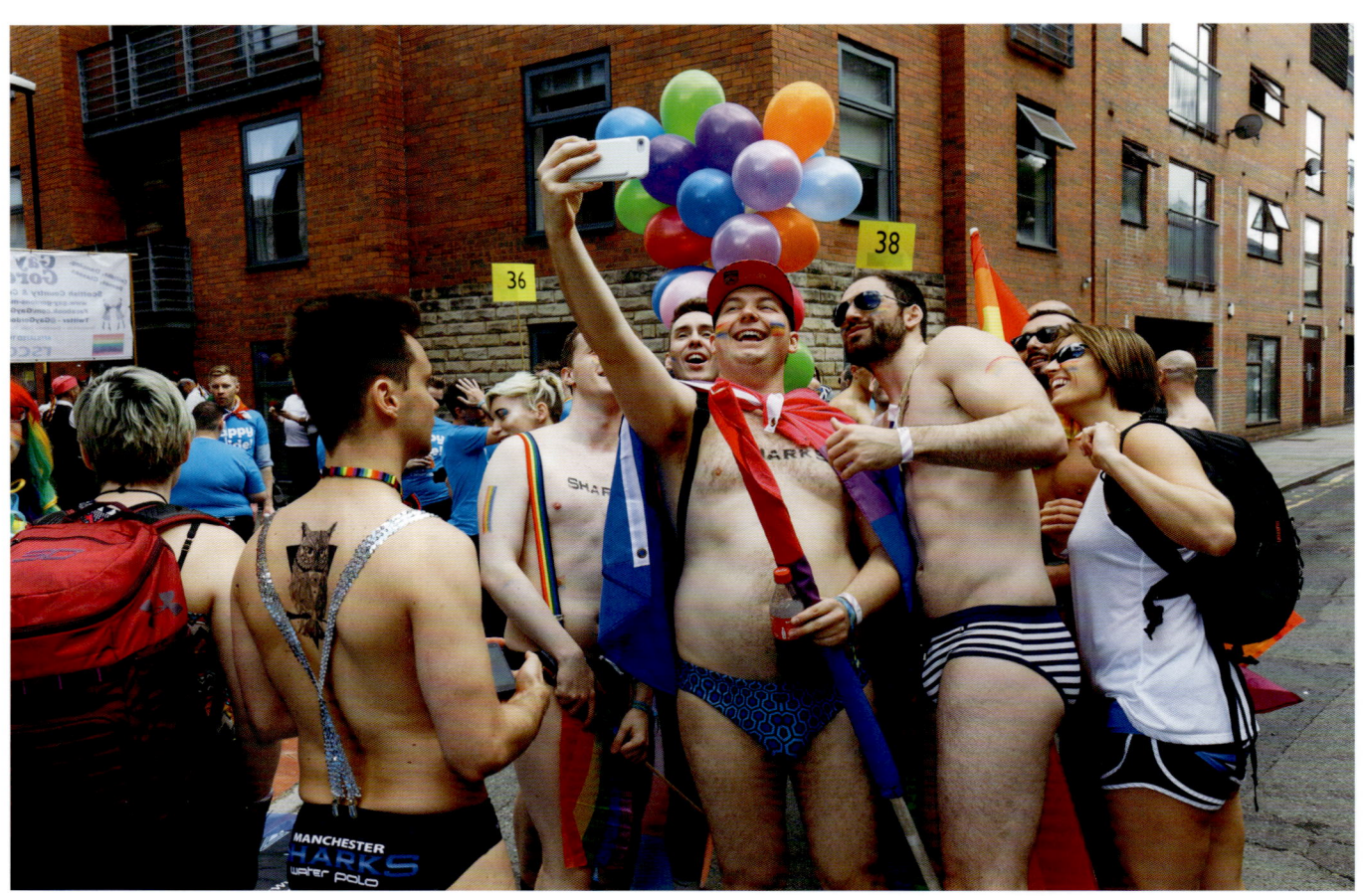

Manchester, England, 2018

À LA RECHERCHE DU TEMPS MORT, OR: THE NETWORKED ORGAN'S TALE

BY

ADAM GREENFIELD

If we're being honest, and I hope we are, I'm inclined to think there's not much one can say about an image that the image itself isn't already saying. OK, sure: those who are knowledgeable about such matters can discuss the technical details of focal plane, lighting and composition. They can explore how and why specific choices made in the image's production generate the effects (and affects) they do for the viewer, and that kind of deconstruction can often be interesting.

What I tend to resist, though, is the idea that an essay like this can shed much light on the 'meaning' of an image. The invitation to write such an essay seems like licence to overinterpret, to embroider, above all to project. This is still more so in the case of Martin Parr, notoriously a photographer whose lens is consecrated to the aggressive depiction of the ordinary. To subject a Parr to a close textual reading feels like tying oneself in knots in the attempt to extract a meaning that is already radiantly plain on the image's surface.

What I think I'm going to do, then, is write *around* the images I've been asked to comment upon. The most interesting thing about these pictures, for me, is not what's in them but what's implied by them: the arrival, and then passage into history, of a decisive moment in the evolution of our shared lifeworld. This was the moment in which developments in materials science and fabrication, antenna design, logistics and supply-chain management, interoperability standards, global tariff and trade policy and the bureaucratics of spectrum allocation all came together to place in each of our hands a device capable of connecting us with everyone else who had one – which is to say, very nearly everyone on the planet. What Parr depicts here is the remarkably compressed period during which the mobile phone became first unexceptional, then ordinary, and finally ubiquitous.

The images in this collection, taken together, form not so much a document as a topology of that moment – a diagram of where and how the pocket device came to intersect our everyday needs, habits and rituals. They have the curiously static quality of an old-fashioned relief map. There is no movement in them. People are suspended mid-conversation, mid-glance, mid-gesture. It's as though someone's hit the pause button on the world for the space of a long, slow exhale, and in that sighing hiatus made a record of what it is that we've become.

If the mobile phone is in some sense a prosthetic organ – an 'extension of man', in Marshall McLuhan's dated but nevertheless useful terms, that wires our nervous system directly into the global network – in Parr's hands it stands revealed as a remarkably democratic, even dowdy one. On present evidence, anyway, the sensations that pass through its circuits get encoded into ones and zeroes and are thereafter committed to the air seem to involve appointments with the dentist, petty fights with old friends or reminders to pick up the dry cleaning. So too the images shot during the curiously brief hegemony of the selfie stick, which evoke nothing so much as package vacations on discount carriers, and the churn and jostle of overtouristed sites that one can no longer imagine without their complement of half-bored, box-ticking visitors.

All of this, it must be said, is in blessed opposition to the breathless wonder conveyed by phone commercials, where from the very beginning the device has invariably been presented as the sovereign key to the invisible city, and all the glamorous life waiting for us there. Where that advertising has always been charged with the eros and vitality of youth, extending to the buyer the promise of infinite unfoldings across all the hours of night, Parr shows us what life with the phone is *really* like. As it turns out, there was nothing transcendent about our embrace of the networked personal device. Whatever openings it may have produced, they were neither liberating nor erotic, nor in the end even particularly connective; wherever it took us, we found ourselves already waiting there. What these images seem to suggest, then, is a very different proposition: that perhaps the flattening gravitational pull of the ordinary is so overwhelming it can bring crashing to Earth even this thing that literally traffics in streams from the aether.

This is not the utopia of the unboxing video, the promo reel's ecstatic choreography of becoming mobile. Here is the sober and sobering inverse of all of that, a flat ontology of use, wear and habituation. I think of American artist Edward Hopper, actually: a Hopper where the light source is no longer the falling sun of a century struggling to be born, but a slab of hardened aluminosilicate glass, assembled by anonymously bunny-suited workers somewhere in the Pearl River Delta. What is revealed in that diode glow but the true terminal condition of all the intimacies we were promised at point of sale?

The images presented in this collection span a few successive generations of mobile-telephony technology, from the fledgling DoCoMo *keitai denwa* of Japan, *c.*2000 – probably the last moment in which Tokyo might still plausibly claim to be capital of the future – to the generic Android handsets that now constitute something like a baseline planetary universal or digital *Existenzminimum*. In itself this makes the collection a valuable contribution to the historiography of the mobile device, but in inadvertently capturing the rapid obsolescence of objects once so suggestive of futurity, it also registers a fact that the industry generally prefers to keep at bay along with the rest of us: at no point does time cease ticking, bearing all tomorrow's parties ceaselessly into the past.

We most often see depictions of phones in the form of a 'hero image' of the type associated with advertising, where they're neutrally positioned, evenly lit and abstracted from the background. The timelessness of such imagery suspends the device in the moment just before purchase, when it remains an item in inventory and has yet to be inserted into any one individual life and the trajectory that life describes across time. But what's far more interesting is to see them in their full state of being, at close range, grimy with the patina of constant use.

This, of course, is Parr's bailiwick. His consistent practice, across the years he has been active, is to overweight or even make a fetish of everyday phenomena, raising for our consideration the abject textures of the ordinary, and all the humiliations that attend them. If this has, over the years, become something of a mannerism, it is also unquestionably

his greatest achievement as a photographer. What he offers us is a sustained sensory study, carried out through the grain and intense colour of documentary photography. And it's the same here: the touch of the thing sings from the frame, whether that involves glass against skin (see p.201), thumb against edge (see pp.198–9) or a palm curled around the cheap TPE knurling of a selfie-stick handle (see pp.203, 209).

Even the qualities that so often take Parr's work to the very verge of kitsch, the oversaturation and hard-lit collapse of depth, make of it a curiously appropriate corrective to the sterile hero photography favoured by the industry. Surely no manufacturer would ever tolerate product photography that documents the erosion, the slow and steadily accumulating violence of touch: a surface treatment stripped by thumb oil, a lens fogged by constant abrasion from the pocket-lip. Surely no marketer would ever sign off on an image detailing the way thin-film interference lacquer wears off injection-moulded polycarbonate-ABS with continued use – or the undermining effect that has, in turn, on the angle-dependent pearlescence intended by the designer. No: everything you take in here gives the lie to the implicit late-capitalist promise that the thing on which you've just dropped a decent fraction of a month's salary will remain box fresh in perpetuity. That is its redemption and its delight.

Before we go further, I need to confess my complicity. For a few years, at the very dawn of the smartphone era, I worked at Nokia's headquarters outside Helsinki, Finland, nominally heading up 'design direction for service and user-interface design' (whatever that might mean). Throughout my tenure there, our corporate slogan was 'Connecting People', and that there was meaning and value and truth in this premise was something I think the overwhelming majority of the people I worked with took seriously. I certainly did. Which is why what I see in these images now feels so personal: a reckoning with a promise those of us working on the design of these devices made in good faith and have long since failed to keep.

For the most part the people in Parr's images feel *disconnected*, in a way that isn't simply the consequence of tight cropping – if the defining photographic urbanite of the century past is Garry Winogrand's *The Man in the Crowd* (1999), the default condition of the contemporary city-dweller is technologically buffered solitude, and that's just what you see here. But these people are alone together. They're surrounded by others, each in their own similar pose; where there are groups depicted, though the tolerances between bodies are tight, in only one of the images does there appear to be anything in the way of actual we-feeling (see p.202).

There's a quiet grief to the isolation of Parr's subjects, one of the few actual emotions that can be discerned in the work, and it consists in the fact that, in the presence of the phone, any sense of being present here and now is deferred in favour of the networked elsewhere and when. The pleasures and promises of adjacency, whatever they might be, yield to the prerogatives of an imagined interlocutor outside the scene; actual experiences recede in importance when stacked up against the virtual any-future-whatever in which the images being captured will be perused as memory. In these qualities of deferral and refusal, in fact, the networked object is curiously anti-Parrlike, which may be one reason why the initial appearance of the device in his oeuvre rings such a discordant note.

You could certainly choose to tell a cruel and disdainful story about this. You could invoke the reactionary mode, never more than half a step away: 'Look at these idiots, so comprehensively head-fucked by modernity that they're forgetting to live their one and only life, even when it's right in front of them'. But that's not what I think these pictures are doing, or at least it's not how I choose to read them. Because – remember, we're being honest – I recognize the vacant, duck-billed, somewhat gormless look on these faces. I recognize all the ways in which people have by now learned to compose themselves for networked consumption, and so do you. We recognize these looks and postures because we've worn them. The vanity. The insecurity. The hunger to be seen (as an individual; as someone who has friends; as someone who goes to these places and does these things and can afford to). This is what it looks like when we try to hold our own in a world that floods us with signals and robs us of ground.

That is the real thing about these photos, I think. They're not about phones. They're about *loss* – the early ones are even about the very moment of that loss, though that probably wasn't evident at the time, either to the photographer or to his subjects (see p.198–9). They're about the evaporation, over the space of just a few years, of a world in which the social fabric had weight and materiality and some degree of tensile strength, and its wholesale replacement by a world in which that fabric is woven of nothing more than digits flickering unendingly in the dark. And they're about the half-conscious improvisations we've all been forced to make since then, in order to keep going.

I don't think it's a stretch to assert that the topic here is the asymmetry of the relationship between the network and the body, in which only one of those parties holds any sway. The great American writer William Gibson once commented that '[s]ome very considerable part of the gestural language of public places that had once belonged to cigarettes now belonged to phones'.[1]

Gibson, rarely anything less than acute in his observation of human behaviour, was never more perceptive than he was right here. Our embrace of the phone structures everything. At the microscale, every angle of shoulder, every hunch of neck; at the macro, though arguably less often now than in the first epoch depicted here, the way we will hunt for a cellular signal or an open Wi-Fi node. What Parr in his turn is reminding us is that this language is not neutral. Its grammar is shaped by the object, and by what that object offers us. The device lives inside a network, the gesture forms to the device, and the self reshapes to accommodate the gesture.

All of this does odd things to space. Even when the phone is not being touched – even when it lies on the table, or half-juts from a back pocket – it retains a kind of negative presence, as though something else is always about to happen, just slightly offstage. A call, the haptic itch of a 'notification', a breaking news alert. The device may well be here, but the happening world is always somewhere else.

When, suddenly, with the lamination into the slab of a second, forward-facing camera, we enter the selfie era, the signature gestures and expressions change yet again (see p.204). Each image of someone taking a selfie now seems like a confession of a particular kind of insecurity on their part – an iffy sense of object permanence, perhaps, such that those arrangements of the world that go undocumented have effectively ceased to exist for them. Or, more to the point, in a very real sense *never were*.

Gibson's invocation of the phone as successor to the cigarette is on point in one other way, as well. If a cigarette manifestly gives shape to the rituals of short-range sociality – you can see it now, can't you? – someone standing in a doorway, cadging a smoke from another completely unknown to them a second before, stooping with cupped hand as they proffer a light – so too is it a way of organizing time, of filling those moments in which we might otherwise be compelled to think about all the topics we prefer to keep at arm's length. And this is still truer of the phone. If the phone changed the way we move in space, its effects on the bodily perception of elapsed time are if anything more total.

Because what we can see across the period depicted in this collection, from the early 1980s to the present day, is nothing less than the disappearance of a particular state of being that has always been an enduring concern of Parr's specifically and used to be a defining feature of urban life more broadly. This is what we used to call 'dead time': the wait for the coffee to brew, the wait for the rain to stop, the wait for the bus to arrive. Once the colonization of everyday life by networked information technology was accomplished – and it was, I'd wager, for most of us in the developed world no later than 2015 or so – *dead time ceased to exist*. In the presence of the universal signifying engine in every pocket, purse or palm, everything that can be productive, communicative, entertaining or distracting will be. As a direct consequence, most of us don't 'wait' anymore, not truly – at least, not so long as our battery holds out. We scroll. We refresh. We flick through carousels of ostensibly alternative possibilities. We turn our face toward the glow. And so, the phone becomes our bulwark against an emptiness that is otherwise implacable.

All adults understand that the emptiness still exists. It just gets filled with junk-perception – content we've half absorbed, and forgotten almost before it's left the screen, thoughts we've half committed to. We haven't eliminated dead time so much as crammed it full of 'nontent'. And in so doing, we've for the most part robbed ourselves of the clarity that sometimes comes when the noise falls away and leaves us the opportunity to perceive nothing but signal. The particularly unsettling aspect of this, for those of us who've lived through the transition, is that soon, very soon, there won't be anyone left on Earth who remembers what boredom felt like.

So, who better to guide us through this moment but Martin Parr? A phone in a Parr photograph is like the sideburned assassin sitting across the train compartment from Michael Caine in the opening scene of *Get Carter*: the descent of a last end, glimpsed in the very beginning.

In the end, of course, it turned out that Audre Lorde was right, and those of us who thought we could change the world for the better by putting a networked device in every hand were wrong: you cannot, after all, dismantle the master's house with something so strongly resembling the master's tools. But the world did change, and we right along with it. The mobile prosthesis, that network-organ, has become so much a part of us that it conditions us even in its formal absence.

So let me close with the image not of a phone in use, but of something a trifle more enigmatic that Parr has captured. It's a detail from his photograph of a group of people standing up to their ankles in the surf of Mumbai's Chowpatty Beach in 2018 (see p.211). The five adults in the image are all facing different directions, with their bodies contorted in the signature geometries of people making images with mobile devices. And such devices are indeed visible in the grasp of those whose hands are enclosed by the frame – all of them, anyway, except one. Close to the centre of the image stands a woman with her arm held at full extension, performing what looks suspiciously like the familiar pinch-and-zoom gesture on the horizon itself. She is doing so empty-handed.

For all I know, the appearance of this gesture is nothing more than an accident of the moment. The woman may be shielding her eyes from the glare or explaining the relationship between apparent size and distance to the child at her feet. It could be anything, really. It is nevertheless striking that her posture is indiscernible from what it would be in a worldline right next door to ours, in which she does have a phone in her hand and *is* taking a self-portrait with it. It's as though what we do in all those moments when we don't happen to have our hands on such a device is overdetermined by those in which we do.

I will again observe, somewhat pigheadedly, that I just don't think any textual elaboration is in any way an enhancement or an improvement on the image itself. I've come to believe something that the veteran New York City-based street photographer Reuben Radding has tried to instil in me more than once over the years we've known one another: that there's no 'story' in the image, no larger narrative that can be recovered from it. Any such thing is mere speculation beyond the evidence, the kind of testimony that any judge worth their robes knows to disallow.

So, I won't assert to you that any of the thoughts about mobile devices I've shared here are somehow 'in' Martin Parr's pictures. But there is a story to tell about them, nonetheless. It's this: we didn't choose this. We didn't design the conditions that made it necessary to acquire and rely upon one or several devices to mediate our identity to the world. We didn't invent the demand to market ourselves (as employable, beddable, tolerable), or the precariousness that attends that marketing effort. We didn't invent the inanity of 'notifications' or the porosity of every moment we spend in the presence of a networked device to the world's ambient violence. Everyone in these images is, just as we are, surviving inside a system not of our making. Trying to stay connected to one another, and to ourselves. Trying to remember what it feels like and what it means to look at something, or especially some*one*, not through the intercession of a screen but directly. Trying to be present, in a world that's slipping from our grasp at a steady rate of one second per second.

Martin Parr does not shame his subjects for this, at least, but then shame has never really been the game he's playing. At worst – and at best – what he chooses to place in the frame is what it looks like when all the impossible weight of the network descends on a body held in space and time, through the aperture of a slab a few centimetres across. Whatever we feel about that depiction is surely what we bring to it, but the invitation to reflect on just what it is we're bringing is its own, rare kind of gift.

1   Gibson, William. *Zero History*.
    Penguin, 2010, p. 95.

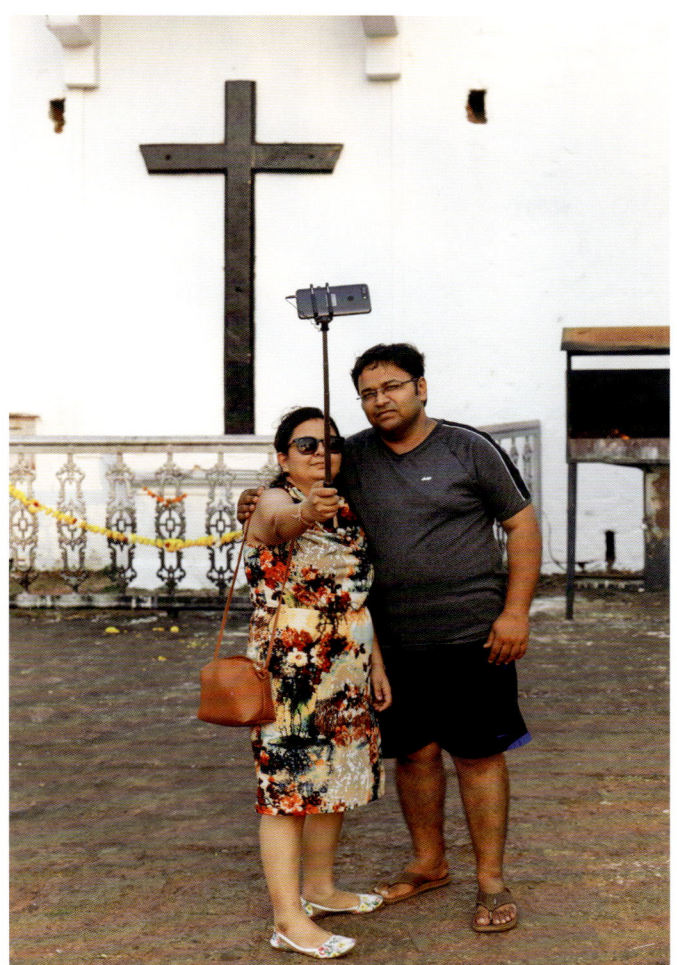

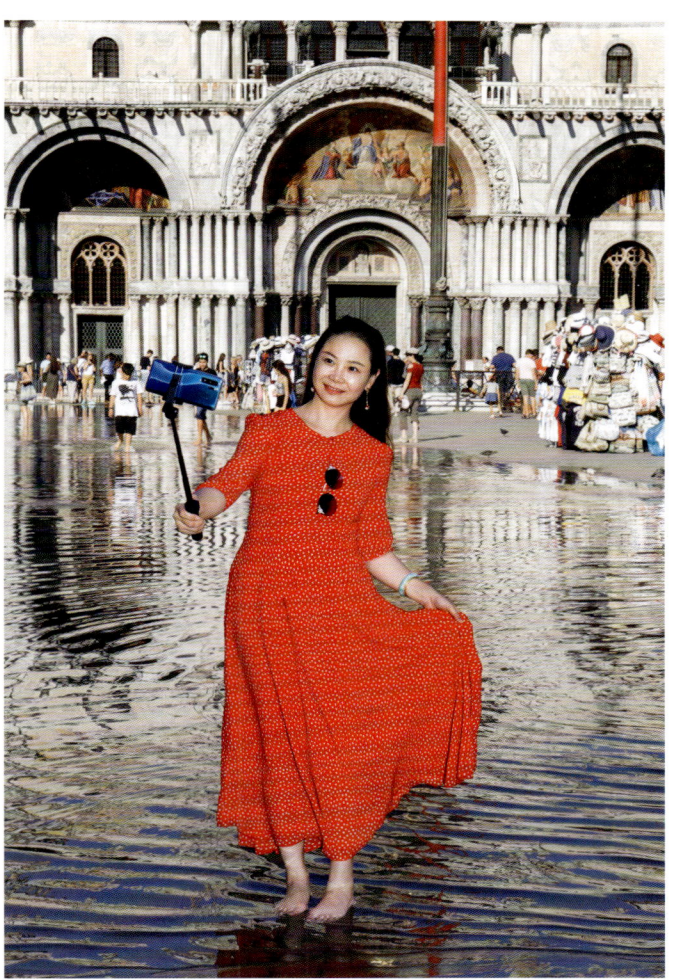

Goa, India, 2018

Venice, Italy, 2019

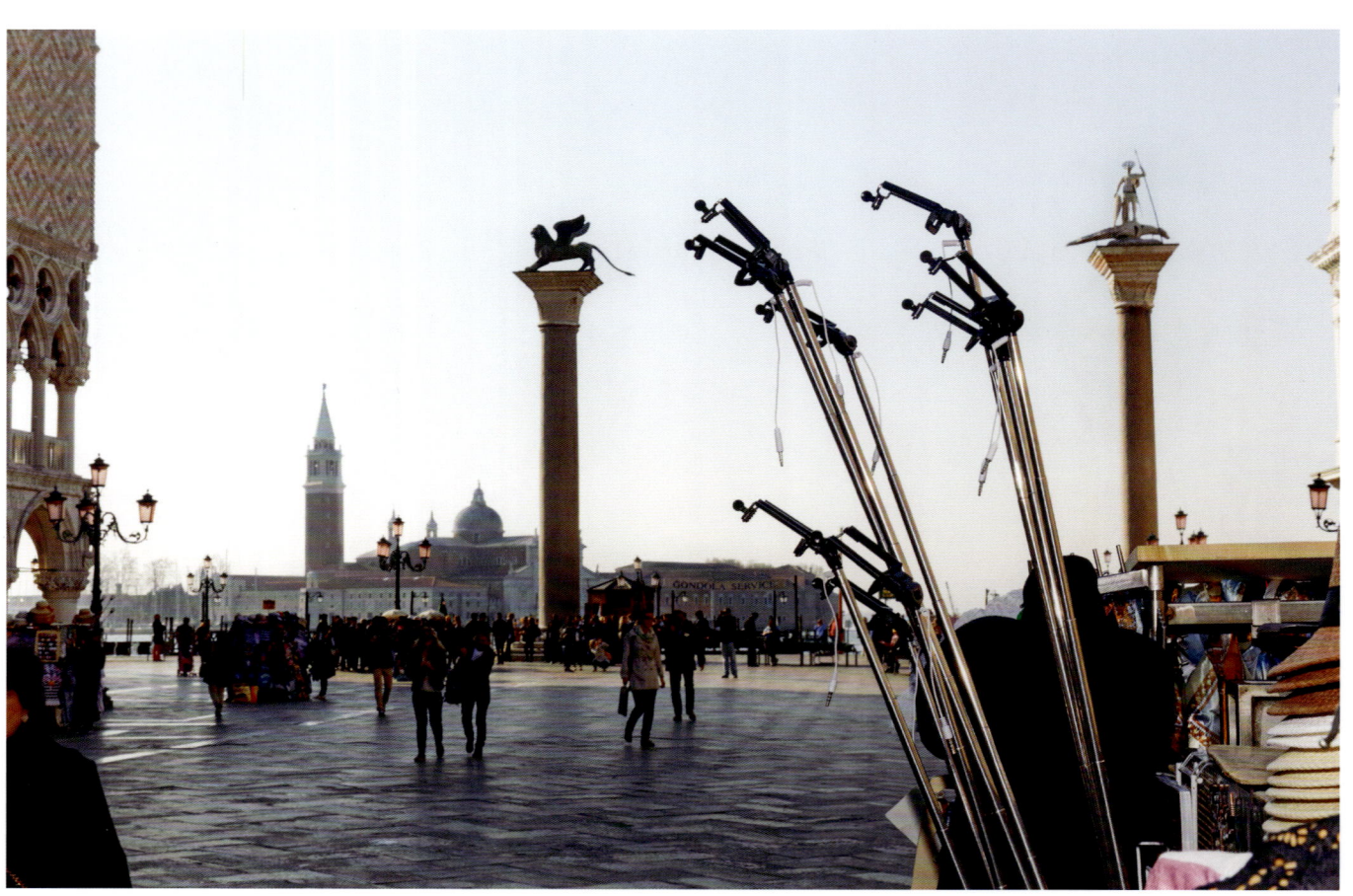

Venice, Italy, 2015

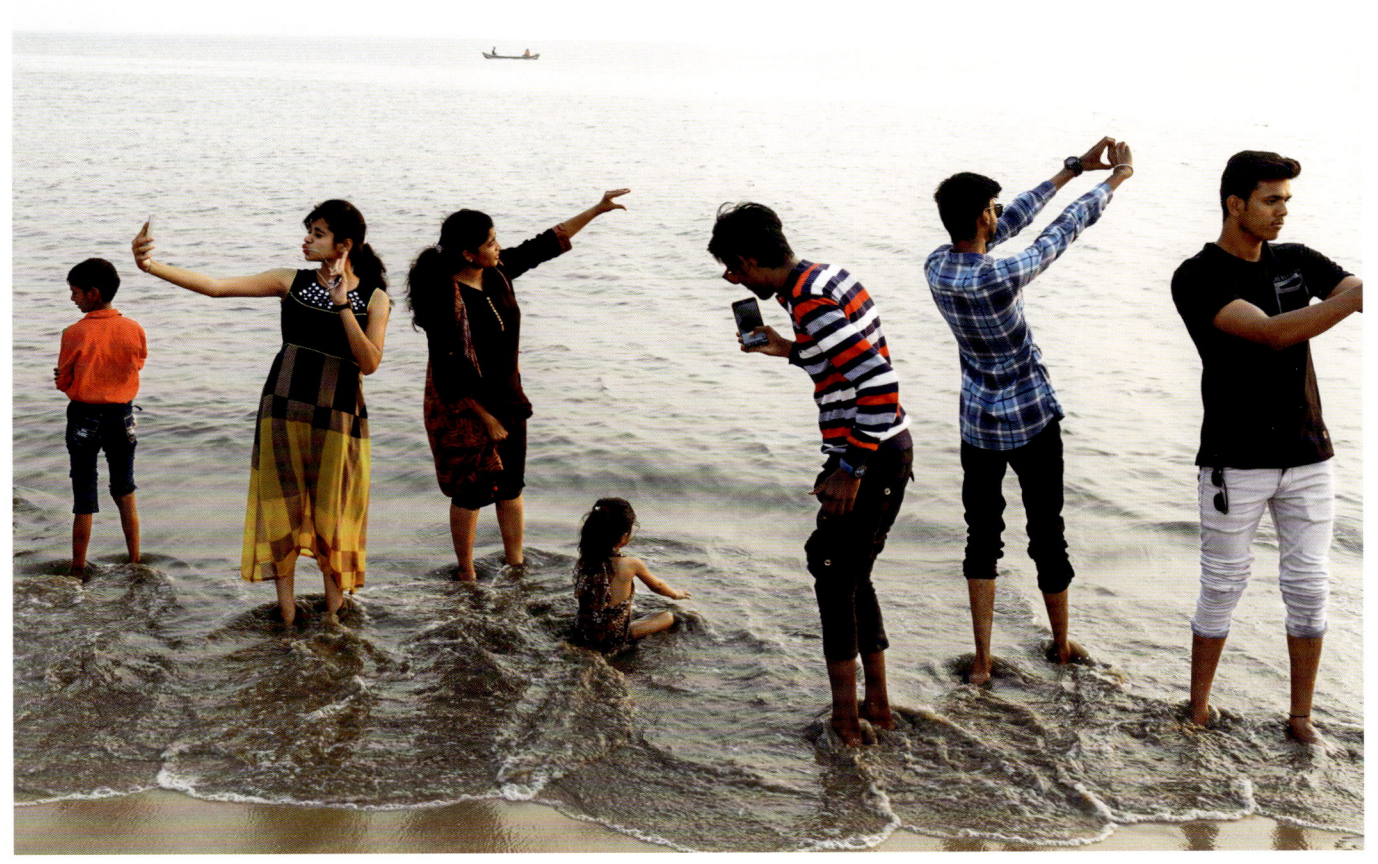

Mumbai, India, 2018

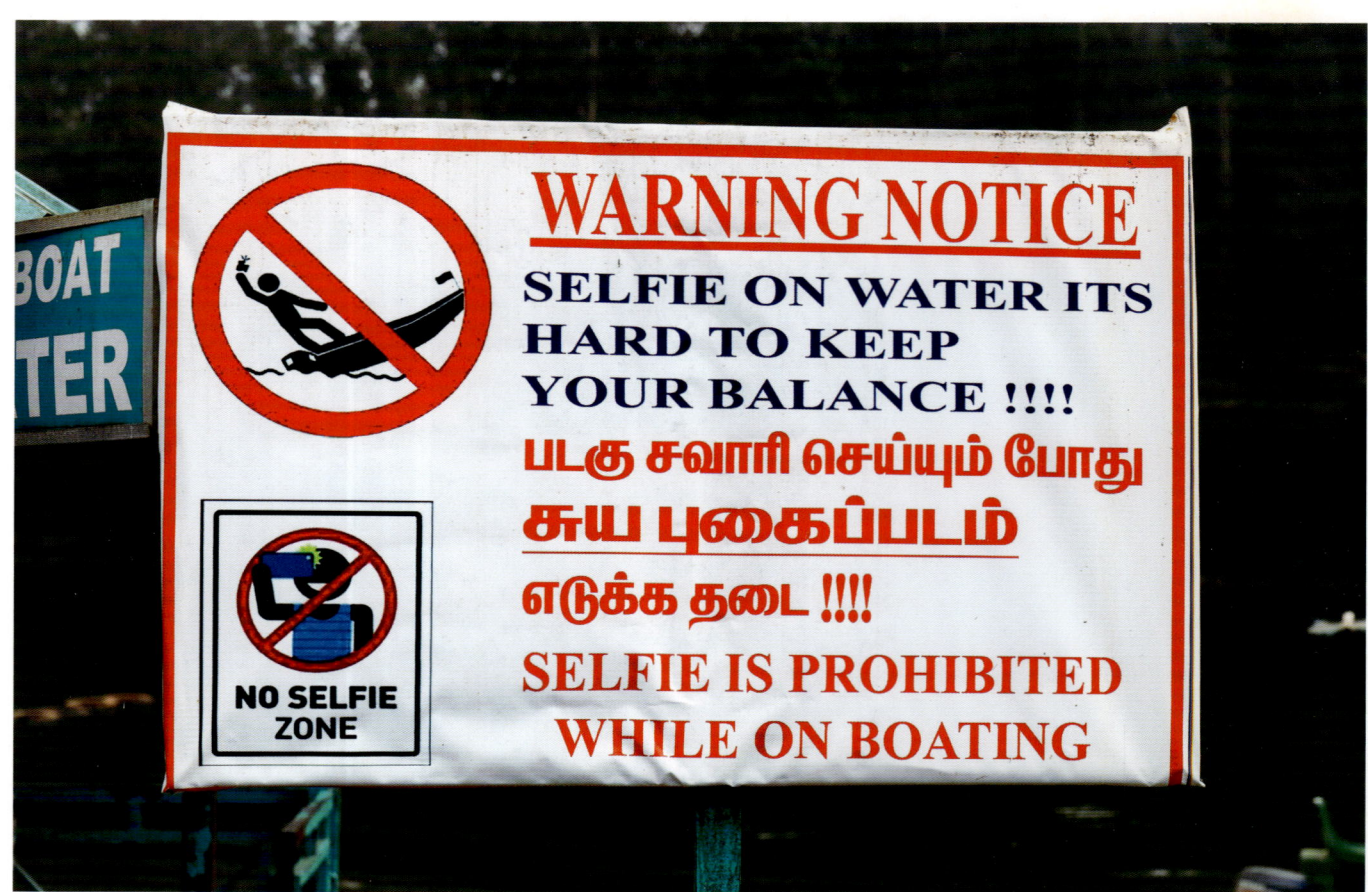

Ooty, India, 2018